Accounting

Made Simple

The Made Simple series
has been created
especially for self-education
but can equally well
be used as
an aid to group study.
However complex the subject,
the reader is taken
step by step,
clearly and methodically,
through the course. Each volume
has been prepared by experts,
taking account of
modern educational requirements,
to ensure the most
effective way of
acquiring knowledge.

In the same series

Accounting
Acting and Stagecraft
Administration in Business
Advertising
Basic
Biology
Book-keeping
British Constitution
Business Calculations
Business Communication
Business Law
Calculus
Chemistry
Child Development
Commerce
Computer Electronics
Computer Programming
Computer Programming Languages in
   Practice
Computer Typing
Cost and Management Accounting
Data Processing
Economic and Social Geography
Economics
Education
Electricity
Electronics
Elements of Banking
English
First Aid
French
German
Graphic Communication

Italian
Journalism
Latin
Law
Management
Marketing
Marketing Analysis and Forecasting
Mathematics
Modelling and Beauty Care
Modern European History
Money and Banking
MSX
Music
Office Practice
Personnel Management
Philosophy
Photography
Physical Geography
Physics
Politics
Practical Typewriting
Psychology
Russian
Salesmanship
Secretarial Practice
Social Services
Sociology
Spanish
Statistics
Systems Analysis
Teeline Shorthand
Typing

Accounting

Made Simple

Wilfred Hingley BSc(Econ), FCMA

Third edition

MADE SIMPLE
B O O K S

Made Simple Books
An imprint of Heinemann Professional Publishing Ltd
Halley Court, Jordan Hill, Oxford OX2 8EJ

OXFORD   LONDON   MELBOURNE   AUCKLAND   SINGAPORE
IBADAN   NAIROBI   GABORONE   KINGSTON

First published 1969
Reprinted 1972
Reprinted 1974
Reprinted 1975
Reprinted 1977
Reprinted 1978
Reprinted 1980
Reprinted 1981
Reprinted 1982
Second edition 1984
Reprinted 1986
Reprinted 1987
Third edition 1989

British Library Cataloguing in Publication Data
Hingley, Wilfred
  Accounting made simple.—3rd ed.
  1. Accounting
  I. Title   II. Simini, Joseph Peter
  III. Series
  657

  ISBN 0 434 98613 5

Made and printed in Great Britain
by Richard Clay Ltd, Bungay, Suffolk

Contents

Preface to third edition

As stated in the foreword to previous editions *Accounting Made Simple* is intended for two kinds of students or readers; those having some knowledge of book-keeping or elementary accounting and those having no knowledge at all, but needing an appreciation of accounting as part of business or professional training and courses. The book has been through two editions and nine reprints since originally published and so it seems reasonable to assume that those for whom it is intended, and others such as the more general reader who wishes to become familiar with the basic principles and techniques of accounting, have found the style and content appropriate. The emphasis throughout is on accounting statements, formats and procedures; their preparation, uses and interpretation. This edition is considerably enlarged and updated reflecting the changing legislation and environment since the text was previously revised. Although reviews of previous editions were favourable, sections on inflation accounting, decision making and accounting standards have been included in response to suggestions.

The book is divided into six parts. Part One is devoted primarily to financial accounting and reporting. Emphasis is upon basic financial statements – their preparation and interpretation for all types of business entity. Part Two is an exposition of growth and failure. Part Three gives examples of special forms of accounts, while Part Four contains a detailed section on management accounting. Part Five is a brief survey of current areas of interest or controversy.

The exercises in Part Six are given in two series, in the format which has proved popular in previous editions. In the first series the questions are generally shorter and designed to test the reader's understanding of the subject matter. Fully worked answers are provided for these. The questions in the second series are wider in scope and mainly from examinations of various bodies. Lack of space precludes inclusion of detailed answers to these but key figures are provided to facilitate self checking.

Reference to law and practice, except where otherwise stated, is to English law and practice. There is a continuous and expanding updating of company legislation and recommended practices such as those contained in standards referred to in the text. Emphasis is, therefore, on how and why accounts are prepared rather than details of the precise legal requirements at a particular time and place.

Accounting Made Simple is suggested as appropriate reading for students on BTEC diploma and certificate courses, business studies and accounting

degrees and A level courses and those working on the foundation and intermediate stages of professional accounting bodies and others including:

- Institute of Chartered Accountants (ICA)
- Chartered Association of Certified Accountants (CACA)
- Chartered Institute of Management Accountants (CIMA)
- Association of Accounting Technicians (AAT)
- Society of Company and Commercial Accountants (SCCA)
- London Chamber of Commerce and Industry (LCCI)
- Chartered Institute of Transport (CIT)
- Institute of Industrial Management (IIM)
- Institute of Management Services (IMS)

It is also suitable for the non-specialist or general reader requiring an
appreciation of the accounting function.

Wilfred Hingley

Acknowledgements

Thanks for their generosity and assistance are recorded as follows:

- To the Senate of the University of London, London Chamber of Commerce and Industry (LCCI), Chartered Institute of Management Accountants (CIMA), Chartered Association of Certified Accountants (CACA), Association of Accounting Technicians (AAT), Society of Company and Commercial Accountants (SCCA).
- To the Transport Development Group PLC for permission to reproduce substantial parts of their published report and accounts.
- To Guinness PLC for permission to reproduce the diagram on page 279.
- To Mrs J. Parkes for efficiently transcribing text and tabulations into presentable form.

The following books in the Made Simple series may be found useful for further reading and development of the main divisions and levels of the subject covered in this book.

Book-keeping for more detailed study of recording processes.
Cost and Management Accounting for development of management accounting.
Financial Management for more advanced treatment of company financial control and decision making.

Part One
FINANCIAL ACCOUNTING AND REPORTING

1
The business and financial environment

Most people today are confronted at some time with statements showing the financial performance of an enterprise – large or small – and the need to understand them. Such statements may be fairly basic – the report of the local angling or amateur theatrical society or they may be the published results of a large enterprise such as British Gas in which the individual has become a recent shareholder. Charities, local and central government, industrial and commercial undertakings all have to give account at various intervals of their performance to their owners. Accountancy has been called a language of business because it expresses that performance in one homogeneous i.e. common unit of performance familiar to all – money. Any economic unit that has a separate identity is regarded as an entity – an individual unit whose performance can be assessed. That unit may be small as with an individual trader or large as with a public limited company or government department.

The performance of all entities has to be assessed from time to time. A shop owner wants to know if he is better off working for himself or for others; a partner wishes to see if rewards are being shared fairly; an investor needs to confirm if the company of his shareholding is performing to expectations. In order for this assessment to be carried out a common basis for comparison is required and the accounting framework endeavours to provide this. Thus the first part of this book is concerned with introducing the common forms of financial statements and the main types of business units which operate to provide goods and services. Accounting for governments, charities and individuals is mentioned briefly but the widest scope of the accounting function is applicable to a profit-making enterprise.

1.1 The role of accounting

Accounting is the classification, recording and analysis of business transactions either to prepare periodic statements of performance or to provide information for management and decision making. Accounts obtained from records entirely related to past performance are termed **historic accounts** and are prepared primarily for stewardship purposes i.e. to satisfy the owners, government, creditors and other interested parties that the business has been conducted honestly and effectively over the period to which the accounts relate. This particular division of the accounting function is usually termed **financial accounting**. It embraces, but does not consist entirely of, **book-keeping**. Book-keeping is concerned with the recording of transactions only whereas accounting is concerned with classification analysis and interpretation. The classification may be rigidly standardized as for example to comply with legal requirements of company law or the Inland Revenue. Alternatively the classification may be specifically designed to provide for the management needs of the particular business entity, large or small. All the accounting duties may be performed by one individual in a small entity whereas larger units will see the inevitable rise of specialization. The major areas of specialization are financial accounting, external auditing, internal auditing, taxation, central and local government, management accounting and financial management. There are various associations of professional accountants catering for the needs of these areas and providing personnel qualified in all, or some, of the areas concerned. A specimen list of the main UK bodies is given on page 570.

Fortunately, for both national and international requirements, there has been a large degree of consensus about what information should be required, the format in which it should be reported and the basic principles of recording from which it should be derived. That is not to say that all information is comparable between units nationally and internationally but at least areas of difference can be identified. Representatives of the various UK organizations work jointly and from time to time issue instructions to their members about how common problems are to be treated. These are the so-termed **Statements of Standard Accounting Practice (SSAPs)**. Similarly there is representation at international level to achieve common practice across country boundaries through the International Accounting Standards Committee (IAS) and European Economic Community (EEC).

The financial results for a particular period are usually summarized into two main statements – the **balance sheet** showing the financial position at a particular date and the **profit and loss account** showing the financial results for a stated period of time. These are usually referred to as the **final accounts**, a misnomer really as the balance sheet is not an account but a statement of balances existing in the accounts on the date concerned. Recent developments have seen the inclusion, usually in the accounts of large companies, of additional statements dealing with funds flow and value added. Although these represent the end result rather than the beginning of the accountant's efforts it is necessary to understand their format and function before going further behind the scenes. Indeed for the non-specialist these are the most important documents and are introduced individually in the following sections.

1.2   The balance sheet

A balance sheet is a statement of the financial position of any economic unit as at a stated point in time. Most people attempt to assess their personal financial position from time to time. They contrast the worth of what they own – house, car etc. with amounts that may still be owing by them. If what they owe exceeds what they own then a net liability exists to some other person or institution. This is true for any form of economic unit whether business, government, charity or others. Accounting is primarily concerned in this text in relation to business activities but similar principles apply when balance sheets are prepared for other economic units. Note that:

1 The balance sheet is not an account but a statement showing a list of what the business owns (**assets**) contrasted with what the business owes (**liabilities**).
2 The balance sheet always balances – what it owns equals what it owes either to its creditor or its owners.
3 The balance sheet shows the position at a stated date. It is a static statement and the situation represented may change drastically in a short period.
4 All the items recorded have a monetary value attributed to them. Items which may help to make the business prosper such as the efficiency of the management or the loyalty of the labour force are not directly represented on the balance sheet.

The fact that the balance sheet balances does not in itself necessarily reflect a satisfactory situation. The business may have made losses which may be represented as a 'fictitious' asset or deducted from a previously surplus ownership interest.

The fundamental equation is:

assets = liabilities

A long list of unassorted assets balanced by an equally uninformative list of liabilities is not of much use. There are therefore generally accepted divisions of the two sides, of which the most important is

assets = liabilities to outsiders + liability to owners

or **assets = external liabilities + owners' interest (capital)**

Confusion is sometimes created by the appearance of ownership interests as liabilities. This is fundamental however to the notion that businesses are separate entities from their owners. It may be apparent that Glaxo PLC is not the same thing as its shareholders, but it is not so apparent that R. Jones, Carpenter is treated separately from R. Jones as a person. Such separation is essential for a variety of financial, legal and other reasons discussed later under the differing headings of proprietorship. Even at this stage however it should be appreciated that it would be impractical to assess the performance and financial position of a particular business activity if people's personal assets and liabilities were confused with those belonging to, or owed by, the business.

If the balance sheet showed only one total of assets and liabilities intelligent analysis would be frustrated. In order to facilitate meaningful measures and comparison, certain subgroups are used and generally accepted or legally required. With limited companies the format has largely been determined in the UK by successive Companies Acts up to 1985 influenced by EEC requirements. The London Stock Exchange exercises further influence by making additional requirements for a company seeking a stock exchange quotation for its shares. In the United States and countries following their practice the order of items is different. This should be borne in mind when comparing figures or texts since this volume is based on British practice.

Assets

Assets are any possessions having a monetary value. They may be **tangible** (physical objects such as land, plant, machinery) or **intangible** (possessing right to monetary value – trademarks, goodwill etc.). They are divided into **fixed assets, current assets** and **other assets**.

Fixed assets
Tangible fixed assets are those held for the purpose of producing goods or providing services. Such assets are not resold in the course of trading. Examples are freehold land and buildings, plant, machinery and furniture. They are usually relatively expensive and in use over a number of accounting periods. This characteristic requires that their initial cost be spread over an appropriate number of accounting periods rather than being charged in full against the period in which they were purchased. This process of writing off gradually is termed **depreciation** (see Section 2.2). Generally assets appear in a balance sheet at **historic cost** i.e. the price paid less depreciation to the date of the balance sheet. Exceptionally if an item has appreciated – increased in value as opposed to decreased – it may be revalued upwards. The most likely example of the latter is land but other circumstances are considered in the section on inflation accounting (see page 401).

Current assets
Assets are described as current assets if they are held for a relatively short period (say less than a year) and kept for conversion into cash at relatively short notice. Cash refers to sums of notes and coins held by the company plus bank balances. If the amount of cash on hand is considerable it may be put into an interest-yielding short-term investment. To qualify for inclusion as a current asset such an investment must be convertible into cash on demand and not held on a long-term basis or for trading purposes as described separately. The other most likely asset to be turned into cash during the next period is the **debtors** – persons or entities owing the company money. The total debtors should preferably be separated into **trade debtors** representing amounts due for trading transactions and others representing special items. The reason for this is that a large sum may be outstanding from the sale of a fixed asset such as land. To include this when making a comparison over past periods would render such a comparison meaningless. The debtor may be in the form of a **bill of exchange receivable** and as these have varying degrees of negotiability may have a separate classification. An alternative term for debtors is **accounts receivable**.

Another major group of current assets are **stocks** (or in American terminology **inventories**). In the case of a trading concern this is shown as one figure as it represents finished goods purchased for resale. In a manufacturing company the stocks may be shown under separate headings of **raw materials; work in progress** and **finished goods**. Finally we have

prepaid expenses which are items such as rent and rates which have been paid for during the current period but part of the benefit extends into following periods.

Other assets

In addition to the items described above there is an intermediate group which are usually classified separately. These might be regarded as medium-term assets and are usually in the form of **investments** in other corporate bodies or entities. **Quoted investments** are those quoted on a recognized stock exchange. **Unquoted investments** are those not so quoted and whose value is therefore much more difficult to assess. Another form is shares in, and amounts owed by, **subsidiary companies**. Subsidiary companies are those in which the company has a controlling interest as defined in the Companies Act. In the UK a company with one or more subsidiaries is normally also required to prepare a **consolidated balance sheet** (see page 156).

Liabilities

Liabilities are the financial obligations of a business and imply legal responsibilities to other parties. They comprise **external liabilities** e.g. to suppliers for goods supplied, or to a bank for providing a loan and **internal liabilities** which are liabilities to owners of the business whether proprietor, partner or shareholder. As with assets they are also classified by time.

Long-term liabilities

These are liabilities not due for repayment within one year. Businesses are frequently financed by long-term credit obtained from sources other than the owners. Such credit is usually in the form of **loans** or **debentures** from banks or subscribers. They are frequently secured by **mortgages** on the company's assets. Each item or class of debentures are shown separately with repayment dates (if applicable) and relevant rate of interest.

Current liabilities

These are liabilities which are due for repayment within a short period – usually one year – of the balance sheet date. Examples are trade and other creditors, dividends, taxation payable and bills payable. Also included are items known to have accrued such as rent due but unpaid, salaries and wages earned, but not yet paid.

Proprietors' interest

The third section of the liabilities states what the business owes to its owners (proprietors). There are three basic types of business structure and the make-up of the section will depend upon the type as shown below.

1 **Sole traders:**   An unincorporated business owned by one person.
2 **Partnership:**   An unincorporated business owned by two or more persons.
3 **Limited company:**   A business having separate legal entity from its owners whose liability for the company's debt is limited to the amount – if any – unpaid on the shares taken up by them.

Table 1.1

Business	Proprietors' interest
Sole trader	Capital account (including current account balance)
Partnership	Capital accounts (including current account balance)
Limited company	Paid up share capital plus reserves (termed net worth)

Specimen balance sheet

Historically balance sheets were shown as a listing of liabilities and assets on opposite sides corresponding to the notion of a pair of scales. The following is representative of the balance sheet of a sole trader.

John Smith
Balance sheet as at 31 December 19xx

	£	£		£	£
Capital		11,480	Fixed assets		
			Land and buildings	3,000	
Creditors			Vehicles	3,420	
Due after one year			Fixtures and fittings	1,120	
Loan		2,500		——	7,540
Creditors			Current assets		
Due within one year					
Trade	5,200		Stocks	6,300	
Accruals	1,300		Debtors	6,400	
	——	6,500	Bank	240	
				——	12,940
		——			——
		20,480			20,480

Figure 1.1   *Specimen of two-sided balance sheet*

Points to note
1 The balance sheet must be headed with the name of the business.
2 It must be dated.
3 Items must be classified in groups and in order of liquidity i.e. the difficulty or ease of conversion into cash. In British practice fixed assets are placed first, working down to cash balances. In other countries the order may be reversed but must be consistent. Similarly assets may be shown on the left hand side and capital plus liabilities on the right. In recent years preference has emerged – particularly in the case of public companies having legal requirement to publish accounts – for an alternative vertical layout.
4 When the vertical layout is adopted the short-term creditors are usually deducted from short-term assets to indicate the **net current assets** (or **net current liabilities** if the liabilities side is the greater). This net figure is alternatively referred to as **working capital** although this is a description of the items in, rather than the, net figure. In the above example the net current assets are £12,940 − £6,500 = £6,440.

Alternative format

The vertical presentation of J. Smith's balance sheet is shown in Figure 1.2. The reduced total of £13,980 compared with £20,480 does not mean the business is worth less. The presentation emphasizes that Smith has short-term assets £6,440 greater than short-term liabilities and this is a measure of the strength of the company's financial position as discussed in the ratios section below. Less importance is attached in practice to the particular method of presentation adopted for sole traders and partnerships. Balance sheets for publication have to conform to legal requirements and from the point of view of good practice the greater the degree of standardization the better. At this point reference should be made to the example of a published balance sheet shown on pages 125 and 426.

John Smith
Balance sheet as at 31 December 19xx

	£	£	£
Fixed assets			
Land and buildings		3,000	
Vehicles		3,420	
Fixtures and fittings		1,120	
			7,540
Current assets			
Stocks		6,300	
Debtors		6,400	
Bank		240	
		12,940	
Creditors: Amounts falling due within one year			
Trade	5,200		
Accruals	1,300		
		6,500	
Net current assets			6,440
Total assets *less* **current liabilities**			13,980
Represented by:			
Creditors: Amounts falling due after more than one year			
Loan		2,500	
John Smith: Capital		11,480	
Capital employed			13,980

Figure 1.2   *Specimen of vertical balance sheet*

Analysis of financial statements

The assessment of performance is a primary need of all users of accounting statements. Managers, owners, investors, creditors, bankers and employees all consult the figures produced. The essence of a useful monitor of performance is comparison. If we were told that Company A made profits of £10,000 per annum and Company B made profits of £100,000 per annum the only deduction we could make would be that Company B's profits were ten times greater than those of Company A. Is Company B more than ten times larger and if so in what sense? How much larger is Company B in terms of sales turnover, number of employees, assets used and so on. One means of comparing performance more satisfactorily is by means of ratios. A ratio is a means of demonstrating the relationship between two factors. If I travel a distance of 300 miles by car and the car consumes eight gallons of petrol these are two isolated facts but if they are expressed as a ratio of 300:8 then this can be simplified to 37.5:1 which is a ratio of petrol consumption i.e. the car is performing 37.5 miles to the gallon. This can then be compared with the car's performance (past) on previous occasions or the manufacturer's claimed figures (target/budget) to provide a basis for control.

Financial ratios can be divided into groups:

1 Ratios assessing solvency and liquidity – the ability to meet current obligations.
2 Ratios assessing working capital control.
3 Ratios appraising profitability.

Until at least one other financial statement – the revenue or profit and loss account – is available treatment is restricted to ratios assessing solvency and liquidity.

Ratios assessing solvency and liquidity
There are two important ratios – the **current ratio** and the **acid test ratio**.

1 *Current ratio:* This is a ratio of current assets to current liabilities.

$$\text{current ratio} = \frac{\text{current assets}}{\text{current liabilities}}$$

This ratio tells us how many times current liabilities are covered by current assets. It is a measure of the risk that a business may not be able to meet its liabilities promptly in the near future. The current ratio for John Smith is:

$$\frac{\text{current assets}}{\text{current liabilities}} = \frac{12,940}{6,500} = 1.99$$

A general guide for a satisfactory position is 2:1 but this must be treated with caution. For example, it is usual for bank overdrafts to be included in the current liabilities on the grounds that this is short-term finance that can be called in on the whim of the bank. Overdrafts are, however, quite justifiable sources of finance in seasonal and secured situations. The current ratio must be judged with others forming overall appraisal.

2   *Acid test ratio (or quick asset ratio or liquidity ratio):* A quick asset is one
that can be converted into cash within a very short period. They will
normally be current assets excluding stocks and including, for example,
cash in hand and in the bank, marketable securities and debtors. The
acid test ratio is quick assets to current liabilities.

$$\text{acid test ratio} = \frac{\text{quick assets}}{\text{current liabilities}}$$

The acid test ratio for John Smith is:

$$\frac{\text{quick assets}}{\text{current liabilities}} = \frac{\text{debtors + bank}}{\text{current liabilities}} = \frac{6{,}400 + 240}{6{,}500} = 1.02:1$$

A general guide is 1:1. A ratio less than this would suggest difficulty in
meeting immediate commitments.

Ratios which are high are not necessarily good for the business. The current
ratio reflects the overall working capital position whereas the acid test
emphasizes liquidity. A high current and acid test ratio means that the
company is strong in the short term but may be using current assets
ineffectively e.g. stocks are too high, debtors are taking extended credit or
cash which could be earning is lying idle in the bank. Expansion of the
analysis would require additional figures or access to the trading and profit
and loss accounts. These are now introduced.

1.3   Revenue accounts

Determinants of profit

It is doubtful if there is any single word capable of more alternative
interpretations or emotive reaction from sections of the community than
profit. It is extremely important therefore that the shade of meaning
attributed to it be accepted – for a particular purpose or user group – by the
parties concerned. The notion of profit in the fundamental accounting
approach is a simple one. With notable exceptions businesses are run for
profit and **profit arises when goods or services are sold at prices higher than
those paid to purchase or manufacture them**. A single item purchased for
£10 and resold for £12 results in a profit of £2. Therefore:

$$\textbf{profit} = \textbf{sales} - \textbf{costs}$$

In accounts profit is normally assessed, not on each transaction, but on all
transactions which have occurred in the specified **accounting period** i.e.
month, year etc. Thus time as a variable is introduced. Second, from the
basic '**matching**' premise no profit can have arisen on items not sold within
the accounting period therefore the word **cost** (as it usually does!) needs to
be qualified as the **cost of goods sold**.

Cost

The word **cost** can be defined as 'the amount of expenditure (actual or notional) incurred on, or attributable to, a given thing'* – but what are the relevant costs incurred in achieving the sales within a given or stated period? Certainly it is at least the purchase price of the goods sold but even the smallest business unit incurs costs additional to those in the course of trading. These are so called **indirect** or **overhead** costs.

The simplest case for illustration is a sole trader purchasing and retailing a single product, selling at a single price. He owns a shop and employs an assistant. He pays rates and incurs charges for heating, transport and other items in addition to the purchase of the items he sells. The 'matching' concept states that these costs should be apportioned relative to the period and/or quantity sold.

The concept of **prudence** (see page 33) may require that recognition of a revenue or receipt be deferred. It may therefore be ideally impractical to completely match certain treatments i.e. either the matching concept or the prudence concept will predominate. In the examples which follow in this chapter profit is derived on the **historical cost** concept. Only later in the text (Chapters 11 and 13) will the alternatives be applied. Difficult as it is however, some of the other interpretations and approaches must be considered briefly here to emphasize that the historic cost is not infallible and that accountants and users of accounts must realize the relationship to, and heritage from, other disciplines – notably economics.

What is profit?

According to a definition by the economist J. R. Hicks which is widely accepted, profit is what you could afford to spend and still leave yourself as well off at the end of the period as at the beginning, or as he put it 'the purpose of income calculations in practical affairs is to give people an indication of the amount they can consume without impoverishing themselves.' The term **income** in this sense is roughly equatable with our accounting notion of profit so here is yet another word which has a different meaning in a different context. Income or revenue could mean total receipts from sales but when used in relation to profit they mean **net income** or **net revenue** even though that vital adjective **net** is usually omitted. The measure suggested by Hicks and that put forward by accountants generally i.e. profit is what remains of trading sales after meeting all costs incurred in those sales would be equitable but for several factors which require a subjective i.e. arbitrary assessment and affect the validity of the measuring unit – money! The difficulties of the **historic cost approach** to the computation of profit are therefore:

1 Distinguishing clearly between capital and revenue items.
2 Assessing the partial cost of long-term assets used up in the accounting period to be charged against revenue in that period.
3 Deciding on the most appropriate length of period for reporting to managers, workers, analysts, government etc.
4 Ensuring that the profit computed is the most accurate and acceptable for the varying requirements of the user groups.

* CIMA

5   Endeavouring to produce a minimum series of statements which will be acceptable to, and useful for, all purposes.

The **deficiencies** of the historic cost approach to the computation of profit are:

1   *The measure used is not constant in value:* £100 at the end of 1988 would purchase less than £100 at the beginning of 1988 due to inflation. If inflation was at 20 per cent per annum and a business had made a 'profit' of £10 on an investment of £100 then the criteria of profit would not be satisfied in Hicks' sense even though they would be in the historic cost approach. Thus goods purchased for £100 at the beginning of the year had been sold for £110.

   (historically) profit = sales − cost of sales
                         = £110 − £100
                         = £10

   However, to be as well off at the end of the period as at the beginning we would need $(£100 \times \frac{120}{100}) = £120$ to purchase the same goods. Not only is there no profit in real terms, there is a loss of $(120 − 110) = £10$! This is developed further in Chapter 13.

2   *There is an implication that the environment – economic, political etc. – has no effect on profit:* The idea that the risk the business is operating under is unchanged from one accounting period to the next is manifestly untrue, as witness the effect of strikes, volatile raw material prices, unpredictable government action and so on.

Division of revenue accounts

Revenue accounts are prepared to show the results of activities over a defined period of time. The period may not necessarily be a year although this is usual for published accounts. For management purposes they may be prepared much more frequently. There are three subgroups of business types namely: the service industry, the trading activity and the manufacturing companies. Because of the complexities of the manufacturing situation we first consider the simple format for a trader. In this case the revenue accounts comprise two main sections – the **trading account** and the **profit and loss account**.

The trading account
The objective of the trading account is to show the **gross profit** for a particular period. This can be derived from the sales less cost of goods sold for the period. It therefore excludes any amounts in respect of selling, distribution, managerial or other expenses. The cost of goods sold in the period will not usually correspond to the purchases – we may have reduced or increased the stocks held. Gross profit will be equal to sales less the value of [opening stock plus purchases less closing stock]. In the two-sided (T) account style of presentation it would appear thus:

John Smith
Trading account for year ended 19xx

	£		£
Opening stock	7,740	Sales	32,000
Purchases	18,330	Closing stock	6,300
Gross profit	12,230		
	38,300		38,300

These book-keeping entries can be rearranged to present the information more meaningfully:

John Smith
Trading account for year ended 31 December 19xx

	£		£
Opening stock	7,740	Sales	32,000
Add: Purchases	18,330		
	26,070		
Less: Closing stock	6,300		
Cost of goods sold	19,770		
Gross profit	12,230		
	32,000		32,000

The gross profit figure is the same as previously but the important cost of goods sold figure has been emphasized.

The profit and loss account

This is the account to which all balances of income or expenses are transferred to finalize the results of a period. It is summarized in the form of an account or income statement commencing with the gross profit derived from the trading account:

John Smith
Profit and loss account for year ended 31 December 19xx

	£		£
Operating expenses		Gross profit	12,230
Selling	3,805		
Distribution	2,905		
Administration	2,520		
Net profit	3,000		
	12,230		12,230

The profit figure derived here is subject to any financial charges such as interest on loans, taxation on individual or company income and the profit after tax is the net increase (or decrease in the case of a loss) in the net worth figure from a previous period. Such an increase may be retained by the individual(s) or company or distributed in the form of **drawings** (sole traders and partners) or **dividends** (shareholders). Both the trading and profit and loss accounts are discussed in more detail in Chapter 6. The objective now is to show how the additional information can be linked with, and combined with, the balance sheet figures to complete our introduction to analysis of accounts.

Ratios assessing working capital control

1 *Stock (or inventory) turnover ratio:*   This ratio indicates the speed at which materials are moved through the business. It will vary with the nature of trading or manufacturing operations and with managerial control. It is expressed normally as the number of times the investment in stocks is replaced during a stated period – most simply on an annual basis.

$$\text{stock turnover ratio} = \frac{\text{cost of sales}}{\text{average stock held in period}}$$

The average stock is half the sum of opening and closing stocks. (In cases where a single figure only – usually the closing stock – is known then this must be used on its own as the divisor.) The cost of sales should be used on the top line since stocks should be valued at cost and this means both items are on the same basis. An approximation can be obtained by using the sales figure but we are then dividing a figure exclusive of profit into one which includes the profit mark up. The stock turnover ratio for John Smith is:

$$\frac{\text{cost of sales}}{\tfrac{1}{2}\,(\text{opening stock} + \text{closing stock})} = \frac{19{,}770}{\tfrac{1}{2}\,(7{,}740 + 6{,}300)} = \frac{19{,}770}{7{,}020} = 2.82$$

This ratio may be reasonable or otherwise as every organization has different norms depending upon type of goods, size of organization, stockholding policies and so on. In manufacturing organizations the ratios may be expressed in terms of days, months or other period held. This involves a process of conversion. In the above form it means the stocks are 'turned over' 2.82 times per year. Alternatively stated it means that stock is held on average for $\frac{12}{2.82} = 4.26$ months or $\frac{365}{2.82} = $ 129 days.

2 *Debtors turnover ratio:*   This ratio measures the speed at which debtors and other accounts receivable are transformed into cash.

$$\text{debtors turnover ratio} = \frac{\text{sales}}{\text{debtors}}$$

The debtors turnover ratio for John Smith is:

$$\frac{\text{sales}}{\text{debtors}} = \frac{32{,}000}{6{,}400} = 5:1$$

This ratio can also be expressed as the debtors collection period on a time basis:

$$\frac{12}{5} \text{ months } = 2.4 \text{ months}$$

$$\text{or } \frac{365}{5} \text{ days } = 72 \text{ days}$$

which is the average period taken by debtors to pay.

3 *Creditors turnover ratio:*   This ratio measures the speed with which creditors are paid. It should be related to the purchases in a period which will include trading and non-trading items. In trading concerns a measure can be obtained by relating the creditors to cost of sales

$$\text{creditors turnover ratio} = \frac{\text{cost of sales}}{\text{creditors}}$$

The creditors turnover for John Smith is:

$$\frac{\text{cost of sales}}{\text{creditors}} = \frac{19,770}{6,500} = 3.04$$

The ratio can be expressed as the creditors payment period on a time basis:

$$\frac{12 \text{ months}}{3.04} = 4 \text{ months}$$

$$\text{or} \quad \frac{365}{3.04} = 120 \text{ days}$$

4 *Working capital turnover ratio:*   Working capital is equal to the excess of current assets over current liabilities. A further measure of liquidity is the frequency with which this is turned over in the sales.

$$\text{working capital turnover ratio} = \frac{\text{sales}}{\text{net working capital}}$$

The working capital turnover ratio for John Smith is:

$$\frac{\text{sales}}{\text{net working capital}} = \frac{32,000}{12,940 - 6,500} = \frac{32,000}{6,440} = 5:1$$

or the working capital is turned over five times per year.

5 *Capital turnover ratio:*   Capital in this sense is the proprietorship interest or net worth. Other capital bases are used for more detailed management ratios. A high ratio would indicate low risk whereas low ratios would reflect intensive capital utilization. Comparison should be between entities or firms in the same industries because if different types of entities are compared the length of manufacturing or sales cycle will influence figures.

$$\text{capital turnover ratio} = \frac{\text{sales}}{\text{capital employed}}$$

The capital turnover ratio for John Smith is:

$$\frac{\text{sales}}{\text{capital employed}} = \frac{32,000}{13,980} = 2.29$$

The capital employed represents total assets less current liabilities employed in the business. Sometimes the ratio is used to reflect asset utilization rather than financial performance. The two common ratios used here are the asset turnover ratio and the fixed asset turnover ratio.

6 *Asset turnover ratio:*   This ratio measures the number of times the total assets are turned over by the sales for a period.

$$\text{asset turnover ratio} = \frac{\text{sales}}{\text{total assets}}$$

The asset turnover for John Smith is:

$$\frac{\text{sales}}{\text{total assets}} = \frac{\text{sales}}{\text{fixed assets} + \text{current assets}} = \frac{32,000}{7,540 + 12,940} = \frac{32,000}{20,480} = 1.56$$

This ratio assesses the efficiency with which a company is using its assets to produce sales. Since sales are the ultimate source of cash it can be considered a liquidity indicator in addition to operating performance. Accounting policies in respect of depreciation would affect validity of comparison between period or firms.

7   *Fixed asset turnover ratio:*   This ratio measures the number of times the fixed assets are turned over by the sales for a period.

$$\text{fixed asset turnover ratio} = \frac{\text{sales}}{\text{fixed assets}}$$

The fixed asset turnover for John Smith is:

$$\frac{\text{sales}}{\text{fixed assets}} = \frac{32,000}{7,540} = 4.25 \text{ times}$$

This indicates the use of fixed capacity of the business. If this ratio is close to the asset turnover then the highest proportion of total assets will be fixed. If it is considerably larger then the company is not using (relatively) large investment in fixed assets. Compare a railway company with a retail market.

Ratios appraising profitability

The primary ratio in respect of profitability of business performance is **profit : capital employed**. When comparisons are made outside the business care is needed. Two factors contribute to the primary ratio – the profit margins on/and the volume of sales; and the amount of capital used to generate those sales. Secondary ratios are used to assess these performances namely – profit to sales and sales to capital employed. The three main ratios are thus interelated:

$$\frac{\text{profit}}{\text{capital employed}} = \frac{\text{profit}}{\text{sales}} \times \frac{\text{sales}}{\text{capital employed}}$$

It can be seen that the sales figures would cancel out leaving the primary ratio.

All the terms in a particular situation need to be defined with reference to the circumstances. There are alternative levels of profit – **gross trading**, **net trading**, **profit before interest and tax** and so on. Again it depends upon the objective. The most usual basis for financial performance assessment is:

$$\frac{\text{profit before interest and tax}}{\text{share capital plus reserves}}$$

In the case of sole traders and partnership the bottom line would correspond to the owners' capital employed.

1   The profit to capital employed ratio for John Smith is:

$$\frac{\text{profit}}{\text{capital employed}} = \frac{3,000}{13,980} \times 100 = 21.5\%$$

2   The profit to sales ratio for John Smith is:

$$\frac{\text{net profit}}{\text{sales}} = \frac{3,000}{32,000} = 9.4\%$$

3   The sales to capital employed ratio for John Smith is:

$$\frac{\text{sales}}{\text{capital employed}} = \frac{32,000}{13,980} = 2.29 \text{ times}$$

Check $2.29 \times 9.4\% = 21.5\%$

It can be seen from this that a small profit to sales mark up can be offset by quick turnover of capital. This is illustrative of the point that a particular ratio should not be considered in isolation from others. In the case of large limited companies or traders with substantial loan capital the effect of **gearing** should be taken into consideration i.e. the ratio of fixed interest capital sources to equity or alternatively total capital.

For managerial purposes detailed ratios of operating expenses and efficiency performance in terms other than money are computed. Examples would be: output per direct labour hour; percentage of capacity employed. These are illustrated in appropriate sections later in the text.

See Section 1.7, page 35 for detailed worked example on ratios.

1.4   The funds flow statement

The generation of cash is fundamental to the survival and growth of any form of business. If surplus cash is not generated from trading operations the capital originally subscribed by the owners will be eroded paying for current commitments and the business will cease. All businesses have a cash flow cycle. Goods or services are sold, services or contracts paid for – money flows in financing new business and the cycle begins again. The cycle can be short as with retailing goods or long as in the case of shipbuilding or civil engineering. We have seen that the balance sheet emphasizes a particular point in time – the cash position may completely change in the course of the next day. The profit and loss accounts show the profit made over a period – but such profit may not be reflected in a cash surplus. The owner may have had excessive drawings; purchased highly costly fixed assets or repaid a long-term loan. A **funds flow statement** shows the amount and source of the inflow of funds into the business entity, the uses to which it has been predominantly put, and what has been done with any surplus or how a deficiency has been met.

There are a number of ways in which a funds flow statement may be presented and they are alternatively termed:

● The change in working capital.
● Cash flow statement.
● Source and application of funds.

The change in working capital

Working capital has been previously defined as the difference between current assets and current liabilities. If the difference between these figures is negative i.e. current assets are less than current liabilities such a situation could only be practical for a short term. Indeed we saw that a suggested figure for the ratio was 2:1. When the situation exists where the surplus is negative the difference is being made up from long-term sources and the ultimate penalty for this is failure.

The main sources and uses of working capital can be seen contrasted in Table 1.2. In this form of statement emphasis is focused on how the elements of the working capital have moved over the period i.e. stocks, debtors, cash and creditors.

Table 1.2

Sources	Uses
Excess from trading operations	Purchase of fixed assets
Sales of fixed assets	Repayments of loans or capital
Long-term borrowing	Dividend payments
New capital injections	Tax payments

Cash flow statement

This statement emphasizes receipts and payments of cash. To this extent it may not correspond to a fully detailed funds statement. In the accounting sense funds can exist in the form of non-cash items. For example, part payment for a business acquired may be in the form of shares issued by the purchaser – this is an exchange transaction not involving cash. Similarly a partner retiring may agree to leave part of the amount due to him in the form of a loan. Such statements are frequently prepared in advance of the period concerned to provide the basis of cash control.

Funds flow statement

This statement shows the source and application of all funds – cash or non-cash; operating or capital. It provides a link between an opening balance sheet, profit and loss account and closing balance sheet. For sole traders and partnerships the layout may be prepared to suit the particular – and usually not very complex – requirements. In the case of published accounts of public companies the funds flow statement forms part of the audited accounts. Since these are invariably prepared by members of the appropriate professional accounting body they comply with the layouts prescribed by the appropriate statement of Standard Accounting Practice Number 10.

A particular reference to **depreciation** must be made here as it relates to funds flow although this item is not dealt with in detail until Section 2.2. Profit is usually expressed after depreciation – which is a writing down of the recorded value of an asset on some recognized basis. The asset will possibly have been purchased and paid for a considerable number of periods previously and this is when the cash outflow (application of funds) occurred. Depreciation does not result in a further cash outflow so although as an expense for the period it has the effect of reducing profit, as far as cash/funds flow is concerned it must be added back. Any other non-cash inflow/outflow must be similarly recorded and the results from operations (trading) distinguished from capital transactions:

	£
Sources (a)	
Profit (after depreciation) as per accounts	
Add Depreciation	
Total from operations	——
Add Other sources (new capital, sale of plant etc.)	——
	═══

Applications (b)	
Purchase of fixed assets	
Dividends paid	
Tax paid	
Increase or decrease in working capital	——
	═══

a = b

Movements between the elements of working capital may take place without effecting a change in the total (net) figure as, for example, when a debtor pays his account – the debtors balance is reduced and cash/bank account increased without changing the balance of working capital. A suggested procedure is to identify the amount by which the working capital has changed, compute the changes in sources of long-term capital or creditors and assets other than current, and prepare an appropriate statement.

Exercise 1.1
The following represent (in abbreviated form) the balance sheets of Jingles and Co. on 31 March 19x8 and 31 March 19x9.

	19x8	£000s	19x9	£000s
Mr Jingles				
Capital account		104		128
Current account		56		82
		160		210
Long-term loan		50		40
Long-term capital employed		210		250
		═══		═══
Fixed assets				
Land and buildings at cost		90		95
Plant and machinery at cost	60		70	
Accumulated depreciation	15	45	20	50

	1978 £000s		1979 £000s	
Motor vehicles at cost	25		30	
Accumulated depreciation	10	15	13	17
		150		162
Trade investment at cost		40		38
Current assets				
Stock	80		50	
Debtors	60		65	
	140		115	
Less: Current liabilities				
Creditors	60		50	
Tax payable	20		15	
Bank overdraft	40	120	20	—	65	50
		210		250

For simplicity income tax on Mr Jingles' profits is paid through the firm's bank account. No sales of fixed assets took place during the year. Drawings by Mr Jingles were £10,000 in 19x8 and £12,000 in 19x9.

You are required to:
1 Prepare a funds flow statement for the year ended 31 March 19x9.
2 How could the statement you have produced be of use to Mr Jingles?

Source: AAT

Workings
Changes in balance sheets for 19x8 and 19x9

	19x8 £000 £000	19x9 £000 £000	Changes in Working capital £000	Changes in Other assets and liabilities £000	Note
Mr Jingles					
Capital account	104	128		+24	(1)
Current account	56	82		+26	(2)
	160	210		+50	
Long-term loan	50	40		−10	(3)
Long-term capital employed	210	250		+40	

Continued over.

	19x8 £000	19x8 £000	19x9 £000	19x9 £000	Changes in Working capital £000	Changes in Other assets and liabilities £000	Note
Fixed assets							
Land and buildings at cost		90		95		+5	(4)
Plant and machinery at cost	60		70			+10	
Accumulated depreciation	15		20			(5)	
		45		50		+5	(5)
Motor vehicles at cost	25		30			+5	
Accumulated depreciation	10		13			(3)	
		15		17		+2	(6)
		150		162		+12	(7)
Trade investment at cost		40		38		−2	(8)
Current assets							
Stock	80		50		−30		
Debtors	60		65		+5		
	140		115		−25		
Less: Current liabilities							
Creditors	60		50		+10		
Tax payable	20		15		+5		
Bank overdraft	40		–		+40		
	120		65		+55		
Working capital	20		50			+30	(9)
Change in assets						40	

Notes to workings and statement
1   As this is a change in fixed capital account this must represent a **new** injection of capital of £24,000.
2   This represents changes due to increases from **current** sources such as profit. Taxation does not normally appear in sole traders' accounts since the owner may have several businesses or other sources of income or allowance. It is not really part of the working capital as it represents **drawings** i.e. money withdrawn for a private purpose. The current account can be reconstructed on this basis to find the **profit** for the year.

Jingles and Co. – Current account

		£000			£000
31 March 19x9	Drawings	12	1 April 19x8	Balance	56
	Tax payable	15	31 March 19x9	Profit and Loss	53*
	Balance c/f	82			
		109			109

* Deduced as the balancing figure between (12 + 15 + 82) less 56
Depreciation is added back to this figure in the funds statement as it does not cause cash outflow.

3   As the balance on the loan account is reduced by £10,000 this amount must have been repaid.

4   Land and buildings have increased by £5,000 therefore this must represent additional purchases of land.

5   Plant and machinery (at cost) have increased by £10,000 therefore this is the **cost** of machinery purchased. The depreciation figure has increased by £5,000 thereby increasing the total book value of the plant by a '**net** figure' of £5,000 only.

6   Motor vehicles (at cost) have increased by £5,000 therefore this is the **cost** of additional vehicles purchased. The depreciation figure has increased by £3,000 thereby increasing the total book value of the motor cycles by a **net** figure of £2,000 only.

7   Total fixed assets (excluding investments) have therefore changed by (5 + 5 + 2) thousand = £12,000.

8   Trade investments (at cost) have been reduced by £2,000 indicating a sale.

9   The individual changes in the items comparing working capital are listed and the net effect is a change of £25,000 increase. The item in respect of tax payable is not strictly working capital. The true movement can therefore be ascertained as £30,000 − £5,000 in respect of the tax payable. This movement has been dealt with by adding the £15,000 due for year ended 31 March 19x9 to the debit side of the current account (Note 2) thereby **increasing** the profit and showing the £20,000 which was tax payable at the 31 March 19x8 as a use of funds since it must have been paid during the year in respect of the **previous** year's profits.

Solution

Jingles and Co.
Source and application of funds for year ended 31 March 19x9

Source

	£000	£000	£000	Workings note
Profit from trading		53		2
Depreciation		8		
			61	2
Additional capital			24	1
Sale of investment			2	8
			87	

Continued over.

	£000	£000	£000	Workings note
Uses of working capital				
Payment of taxation		20		
Drawings		12		
Purchase of fixed asset				
Land	5			4
Plant and machinery	10			5
Motor cycles	5			6
	—	20		
Repayment of loan		10		3
		—	62	
Increase in working capital			25	

Represented by:	31 March 19x8 £000	31 March 19x9 £000	Increase/ (decrease) in working capital
Current assets			
Stock	80	50	(30)
Debtors	60	65	5
Current liabilities			
Creditors	60	50	10
Bank overdraft	40	–	40
Increase in working capital			25

The statement should be useful to Mr Jingles as it shows where the working capital is coming from and how it is being used. More important, particularly under conditions of inflation, it shows the change in cash. This funds flow statement is historical and Mr Jingles would **already** be aware that there had been new capital supplied of £24,000. The funds statement is of more use in **forecasting** and budgeting. In this case projected figures can be used to ascertain whether sufficient money is forthcoming to achieve the planned objectives of the business. Should it not be the necessary requirement for new capital can be determined in order that sources may be determined or the plans revised. The statement is very desirable as an explanatory link between the two basic reports of revenue statement (profit and loss account) and balance sheet.

Published accounts – funds flow statements

The statement which shows the source of funds flowing into a business, the way in which they have been utilized and the net surplus or deficiency arising has been recognized as a vital addition to the other main statements. It both supplements the balance sheet and profit and loss account and provides an essential link between them. In the UK it forms part of the audited accounts of a public company and is the subject of Statement of Standard Accounting Practice (SSAP) Number 10. This has a suggested format to which most companies adhere.

An example is given below for a company without subsidiaries to illustrate the derivation and format. Figures are derived as shown in the workings from the profit and loss account and balance sheets.

X Ltd
Profit and loss account (for year ended 31 December 19x7)

	£000	£000
Sales		900
Depreciation	100	
Loss on sale of fixed assets	50	
Sundry expenses	600	
		750
Net profit		150
Taxation	40	
Proposed dividends	50	
		90
Retained profit		60
Balance brought forward		35
Balance carried forward		95

X Ltd
Balance sheets at year end

	31 December 19x6 £000	31 December 19x7 £000
Fixed assets		
Cost	500	400
Depreciation	200	280
	300	120
Current assets		
Stocks	400	700
Debtors	140	250
Cash	20	135
	860	1,205
Share capital	600	800
Profit and loss account	35	95
	635	895
Long-term loan	100	150
Taxation	30	40
Creditors	60	70
Proposed dividend	35	50
	860	1,205

Notes:
1 No fixed assets were purchased during the year.
2 Fixed assets sold originally cost £100,000 and had a written down value of £80,000.

Solution

X Ltd
Source and application of funds statement for year ended 31 December 19x7

	£000
Source of funds	
Adjusted net profit (see below)	300
Issue of shares	200
Increase in loan	50
Increase in creditors	10
Sale of fixed assets	30
Total source of funds	590
Application of funds	
Payment of taxation	30
Payment of dividend	35
Increase in stocks	300
Increase in debtors	110
Increase in cash	115
Total application of funds	£590

Workings

1   Calculation of net profit for source and application of funds statement:

	£000	
Net profit and loss account	150	before provision for tax and dividend
Add: Depreciation	100	
Loss on sale of fixed assets	50*	derived from 2 below
	300	

2   Changes in fixed assets:

	£000 Cost	£000 Dep.	£000 NBV
Balance 31 December 19x6	500	200	300
Less Disposal of assets	100	20* (bal. fig.)	80
Position after disposal	400	180	220
Depreciation for year		100	
Balance 31 December 19x7	400	280	120

Calculation of loss on disposal	£000
NBV of asset sold	80
Loss on sale	50
∴ sales value	30*

3   Other items:

	19x6 £000	19x7 £000	S & A Statement £000
Fixed assets	300	120	See 2 above
Current assets			
Stocks	400	700	−300
Debtors	140	250	−110
Cash	20	135	−115
Share capital	600	800	+200
Profit and loss account	35	95	See 1 above
Long-term loan	100	150	+50
Taxation	30	40	−30 (a)
Creditors	60	70	10
Proposed dividend	35	50	−35 (a)

Notes:
(a)   The previous year taxation and proposed dividends are applications of funds this year.
(b)   + = source of funds.
     − = application of funds.

Alternative presentation of source and application of funds statements

SSAP 10 does not make any special form of presentation obligatory. However, it does suggest that a distinction be drawn when presenting the statement between:

1   Funds generated from operations.
2   Funds obtained from other sources.
3   Funds absorbed/released by changes in working capital.
4   Funds applied in areas other than working capital.
5   Funds absorbed/released by changes in liquid funds. Consequently, the answer above could be redrafted as follows:

X Ltd
Sources and application of funds statement

	£000	£000
Net profit	150	
Plus/minus items not involving movement in funds:		
Depreciation	100	
Loss on sale of fixed assets	50	
Total generated from operations		300
Funds from other sources:		
Issue of shares for cash	200	
Increase in loan	50	
Sale of fixed assets	30	280
Total funds generated		580

Continued over.

	£000	£000	£000
Application of funds:			
Payment of taxation	30		
Payment of dividends	35		
	——	65	
Movement in working capital			
Increase in stocks	300		
Increase in debtors	110		
Increase in creditors	(10)		
	——	400	
		——	465
			——
			115
Changes in liquid funds			
Opening cash		20	
Closing cash		135	
		——	115

An example of the format used when dealing with the accounts of a group is shown below and in the published accounts of Transport Development Group PLC on page 428.

Sources and use of funds

	£000	£000	£000
Net overdrawn position at 1 January 19x8			2,647
Source of funds:			
Net cash assets arising on acquisition of Smalltown Co. Ltd	520		
Sale of part of investment in a subsidiary	615		
Cash flow (retained profits, depreciation, etc.)	4,983		
	——	6,118	
Use of funds:			
Capital expenditure (net)	2,743		
Net increase in working capital (other than cash)	1,830		
	——	4,573	1,545
			——
Net overdrawn position at 31 December 19x8			£1,102

Another possible form in which the statement might be prepared is as follows:

Group cash generation and disposition of funds

	£000
Cash generation:	
Retained earnings	429
Depreciation	511
Sale of assets	243
	——
	£1,183

	£000
Disposition of funds:	
Cost of acquiring new interests	462
Other expenditure by group companies on fixed assets	897
Additional working capital	220
	£1,579

The difference was financed by:

Debenture proceeds, *less* short-term investments	234
Increased borrowings	162
	£396

In this case also the form of statement is appropriate for a group of companies. The method of preparation is the same as for an individual company, except that the **consolidated balance sheets** are used and any changes resulting from the acquisition or disposal of interests in subsidiary or associated companies are segregated and shown as a separate item for instance, sale of part of investment in a subsidiary in the first example and cost of acquiring new interests in the second example.

Uses of sources and application of funds statements

External use
As stated earlier SSAP 10 requires that a source and application of funds statement be included in a company's annual report and accounts. This enables users of company accounts: shareholders, prospective investors, creditors, trade unions, etc., to identify clearly the sources from which a company has generated funds during the year, and the ways in which the funds have been applied.

Much of the information shown in the funds flow statement could be obtained from the profit and loss account, balance sheet and relevant notes to the accounts. But this would be a tedious task and extremely difficult for users with little accounting knowledge. Consequently, the sources and applications of funds statement is included to show clearly and concisely the inflows and outflows of funds during an accounting period.

Internal use
Source and application statements are frequently used by company management as part of the company's budgeting and planning system. Forecast statements are prepared, on a monthly, quarterly or annual basis, and statements showing actual results are later prepared thereby allowing the extraction of variances between actual or budget. Appropriate action is then taken by management to deal with the variances that have arisen.

1.5   Value added statements

These statements are a recent innovation in external reporting of company performance. The assessment of productivity as distinct from production has always created problems. If output per direct labour hour increases there has been an increase in labour productivity i.e. output efficiency but if this has taken place at the cost of installing expensive plant there has been a reduction of productivity per pound of capital. The introduction of **value added** as a basis for collecting taxation gave impetus to the use of this concept for reporting efficiency, although the bases used are not strictly comparable. Briefly, added value is sales less the cost of all outside purchases of materials, other goods and services. From the added value all payments to employees, government (taxation), providers of capital (dividends) and depreciation is deducted to arrive at the retained profit. A simplified statement would appear as follows:

Value added statement for year ended 31 December 19xx

	£	£
Sales		
Less Cost of materials and services purchases		———
Value added		═══
Applied as follows:		
Employees (wages/salaries)		
Investors: Interest		
Dividends		
Government (corporation tax)		
Reinvested: Depreciation		
Profit retained		———
		═══

The actual Statement for Transport Development Group PLC is reproduced below to illustrate the published format.

Transport Development Group PLC
Statement of value added

	1982 £000	1983 £000	1984 £000	1985 £000	1986 £000
Turnover	347,786	367,653	434,651	481,462	543,164
Deduct:					
Cost of services and materials purchased	185,210	192,052	230,897	258,696	284,526
Value added	162,576	175,601	203,754	222,766	258,638
Applied as follows:					
Employees	117,721	126,705	146,973	156,373	178,635
Governments (corporate tax)	7,338	7,211	9,075	11,218	14,304
Providers of capital:					
Net interest payable	5,239	5,371	7,474	8,568	8,865
Minority and preference shareholders	539	319	252	674	359

	1982 £000	1983 £000	1984 £000	1985 £000	1986 £000
Ordinary shareholders	5,914	6,651	7,874	8,921	10,811
Reinvestment in the business:					
Depreciation	21,287	22,545	25,247	28,159	31,776
Profit retained (excluding extraordinary items)	4,538	6,799	6,859	8,852	13,888
	162,576	175,601	203,754	222,766	258,638

The above figures showing the application of value added may be expressed in percentage terms as follows:

	%	%	%	%	%
Employees	72.4	72.2	72.1	70.2	69.1
Governments	4.5	4.1	4.5	5.0	5.5
Providers of capital	7.2	7.0	7.7	8.2	7.7
Reinvestment in the business	15.9	16.7	15.7	16.6	17.7
	100.0	100.0	100.0	100.0	100.0

The main effect is a shift of emphasis away from reporting merely shareholders' profits to accounting for the performance of all contributors to the organization – workers, executives and investors. By deducting all outside purchases we are assessing in monetary terms the proportion of total sales value including profit mark up contributed by the firm concerned – not the efforts of others.

Other applications of added value

Although the notion of added value has been introduced into published accounts comparatively recently it has an older history in management reporting. It was the foundation of several wage incentive schemes such as the Rucker plan. Employers realized that if employees could be pursuaded to be careful in their use of materials and resources such as power consumption then, for a given volume of sales, total costs would reduce and profit would increase. Targets were set for the added value proportion and if this was increased while costs other than labour stayed the same or increased less than in existing proportions, employees received a bonus out of the higher profit figure. Ratios were, and are, also used to assist management in assessing efficiency between periods or after production method changes. Common among these are

- Direct labout to added value
- Other wages to added value
- Depreciation to added value
- Total remuneration to added value
- Operating expenses to added value
- Added value per pound of capital employed
- Added value per employee

1.6   Concepts and conventions

In order to understand and utilize the statements discussed and the wider uses of such data it is essential that readers are aware of the assumptions and logic behind their preparation and construction. Some areas of accounting are still subject to debate and controversy in respect of the best way to present or reflect certain situations. Reference is often made to the theory of accounting but accounting itself is like medicine – a very practical art. The theory is in a sense derived from practice and attempts are then made to obtain general acceptance of a particular framework of rules. Fortunately there is much agreement nationally and internationally on what the foundations of good accounting should be. There are many words used to describe such rules, notably concepts, postulates, principles, doctrines to describe but a few. Statement of Standard Accounting Practice Number 2 suggests the term **fundamental accounting concepts** and this will be used in the following section.

Accounting concepts

A concept is defined as a general notion and in respect of the accounting function are the general assumptions which are taken for granted in the preparation of periodic financial accounts. SSAP 2 suggests that the first four listed below are fundamental but the remainder are important and relative to complete familiarity with the basis on which accounts are presented.

Going concern
The assumption that the enterprise will continue in operational existence for the foreseeable future (SSAP 2).

The monetary values attached to the items in the accounts are those reflecting the continuing of the firm's activities not those, for example, that would be realized if the business ceased tomorrow. In that event some items might be worth more than present recorded values e.g. land may have appreciated in value and be worth more than the amount shown. On the other hand stocks of goods and materials would be worth less in the event of a quick sale.

Accruals
Revenues and costs are accrued (that is recognized as they are earned or incurred, not as money is received or paid) matched with one another as far as their relationship can be established or justifiably assumed and dealt with in the profit and loss account of the period to which they relate (SSAP 2).

This is a timing of the recognition of gains or losses in respect of a particular period, when determining profit for that period. If we bought a machine for £10,000 which we expected to last ten years intuitively it would appear unfair to charge all the £10,000 against income for one year. One alternative would be to charge for the use of the machine on a time basis one-tenth of £10,000 for each year. In this case the expense for the period is £1,000 and is an attempt to match the part of total cost which has expired in the relevant period. Items such as rent and rates relate to, and must be matched to, periods hence the adjustments which take place at the end of periods to amend amounts actually paid to those relevant. Similarly the point of recognition of a sale is when the goods are invoiced not – if sold on credit – when cash is received. The notion of matching is sometimes defined separately but is really integral with the accruals concept.

Consistency

'There is consistency of treatment of like items within each accounting period and from one period to the next' (SAAP 2).

There are alternative ways in which some transactions may be treated, all of which are acceptable practice: depreciation may be on a straight line or reducing balance basis; goods may be priced out on a **first in first out** or **last in first out** basics. These distinctions are explained later but the point is they would result in differing profit figures in the same circumstances between differing companies or the same company if it changed the basis between periods. Sometimes the management may change its accounting bases if it considers it desirable but for consistency such change must be pointed out to users. In the case of public companies it would be disclosed, justified and – hopefully – endorsed with approval by the auditors. Occasionally the auditors may not approve but the change may not result in anything illegal. They would draw attention in the auditors' report to the difference of opinion and past figures would be adjusted in order that periods could be compared on a consistent basis. In the absence of this it would be quite easy, by following an inconsistent treatment, to 'improve' profit figures in the short term with serious consequences.

Prudence

'Revenue and profits are not anticipated, but are recognized by inclusion in the profit and loss account only when realized in the form of cash or of other assets the ultimate cash realization of which can be assessed with reasonable certainty. Provision is made for all known liabilities (expenses and losses) whether the amount of these is known with certainty or is a best estimate in the light of the information available' (SSAP 2).

Alternatively referred to as the concept of conservatism this implies taking what might be considered a pessimistic attitude. The application of this concept possibly assists in endorsing the general impression of accountants as staid, unadventurous personalities when compared with, say, sales managers. Thus while any known or anticipated losses are to be provided for, any gain is not included until realized. The application is particularly relevant to determining profits on long-term contracts where the actual profit achieved may not be known with certainty for a number of future accounting periods.

In addition to the four concepts described in the standard certain additional ones justify their inclusion even in such a basic list as this.

Entity

A business entity is an economic unit which has a separate identity as for instance sole traders, partnerships, limited companies, charities, clubs and so on. This concept states that accounts are prepared in respect of business entities. A sole trader is a separate entity for accounting purposes to the owner himself. He is not, however, a separate legal entity – if the business entity gets into financial difficulties he is personally liable for the consequences. By contrast a public limited company is both an economic and a legal entity. It has a separate legal existence from its owners.

Monetary

Accounting statements relate only to those activities which can be expressed in monetary terms. There are many attributes of a successful business which are not reflected in monetary values in a balance sheet – the skills of its employees, the quality of management, the loyalty of its customers and so on. These may contribute as much, or more, than the physical assets represented in the accounts. The major virtue of accounting is that all items are reflected in a single measure of value i.e. money. It is this that makes it possible to add stocks to debtors etc, which would otherwise be impractical. If the value of a monetary unit remained stable the technique would be admirable but it does not. A pound today purchases considerably less than it did one, three or ten years ago. On the balance sheet items purchased years previously are added to current bank and cash balances. This is the historic cost basis and is preserved as it is historically accurate. A physical measure such as a kilometre or litre remains the same but the price of goods changes over time, mostly rising. This implied assumption of price stability in conventional accounting statements has occasioned the most severest criticism, particularly in latter years of high inflation. To adjust the accounts in respect of inflation requires arbitrary adjustments which some accountants regard as destroying the objectivity of the statements. Conversely users of the information – investors, creditors and governments maintain that statements that do not reflect changing price levels are unrealistic. For a further discussion on this important subject see page 401. For the present at any rate it seems that accounts for non-managerial purposes will be firmly linked to the concept of historic cost i.e. that the basis of recording is the amount actually paid at the time of purchase.

Objectivity

An objective measure is one which is unbiased and capable of being verified. If two people are requested to add two plus two all would answer four. The opposite to objectivity is subjectivity in which an item is the result of a personal opinion. This explains, to a degree, the preference of accountants for historic cost as noted above. The figures are products of definitive past transactions unadjusted by any subjective allowance for price changes.

Materiality and disclosure

Financial statements should disclose separately all items which significantly affect the results contained therein. This is sometimes termed **disclosure** as the two aspects are linked. If an item is material (significant) it should be brought to the user's attention (disclosed). What is significant is a matter of judgement. In a turnover of £1,000,000 a bad debt of £1,000 would be insignificant but on a turnover of £10,000 such a debt would be a catastrophe. The concept is illustrated in the published accounts (see pages 417–47) where the figures are expressed in thousands of pounds having been approximated from the absolute amounts in the records.

Accounting bases

Accounting bases are the methods used by an entity to apply the accounting concepts to its financial transactions particularly for determining profit and constructing balance sheets. Thus, where a concept states what objective is required the base is a suggested method of arriving at it. There are a number of bases acceptable for treatment of main items appearing in final accounts. Among these are:

- Depreciation of fixed assets.
- Treatment of intangible assets.
- Valuation of stocks and work in progress.
- Treatment of hire purchase, leasing and rental of assets.
- Taxation.

The alternative bases available are discussed under the relevant items in the text. Depending upon the base chosen the ultimate profit or balance sheet item may be affected by a material amount when contrasted with the use of an alternative base.

Accounting policies

These are the specific accounting bases selected and followed by an entity in preparing its financial statements. The chosen policy should be stated in a report to the accounts and particularly if a base has been changed this should be indicated together with the reason. Management should consider with care which policies they adopt and be prepared to justify any subsequent change to the satisfaction of users or auditors of the figures. Some managements have endeavoured to use a change of accounting policy as a means of detracting from adverse performance by themselves or economic factors. This is to be deplored and any deviation from a consistent approach should therefore be carefully vetted.

1.7 Analysis of accounts

The following exercise is used to demonstrate the type of analysis and use of ratios discussed in the previous sections.

Exercise 1.2
Song Ltd has operated for many years and the financial statements for 19x1 and 19x2 were as follows:

Balance sheet as at March 31

	19x1 M$000		19x2 M$000	
Share capital and reserves				
Ordinary shares	1,200		1,200	
Retained earnings	720		726	
	1,920		1,926	
Long-term loan			600	
	M$000		*M$000*	
Current liabilities				
Creditors	420		468	
Proposed dividend	60		6	
Bank	——	480	600	1,074
		2,400		3,600
Fixed assets				
Cost		3,600		4,320
Less Depreciation		1,800		2,082
		1,800		2,238
Current assets				
Stock	150		462	
Debtors	300		900	
Bank	150	600	—	1,362
		2,400		3,600

Revenue account year to March 31

	19x1 M$000		19x2 M$000	
Sales (all on credit)	1,200		1,800	
Less Cost of goods sold	900		1,386	
Gross profit	300		414	
	M$000		*M$000*	
Less Administration expenses	60		108	
Selling expenses	120		216	
Bank interest	—		18	
Loan interest	—	180	60	402
Net profit		120		12
Less Proposed dividend		60		6
Addition to retained earnings		60		6

You are required to:
1 Using appropriate ratios, compare the profitability and liquidity of Song Ltd for the years ended 31 March 19x1 and 31 March 19x2. You should calculate at least *eight* ratios in respect of each year.
2 Discuss the limitations of comparing one year with another when assessing a company's performance and suggest any alternative standards of comparison with which you are familiar.

Source: LCC1

Key points
1 There is a requirement to assess profitability and liquidity therefore attention should be directed to both aspects.
2 The question asks for ratios and this could be interpreted literally or as a percentage – which is a ratio to a common base of 100. Sometimes answers to this type of question are expressed as a fraction which is undesirable. For example:

Net profit (before interest) : Total assets
19x1 (£000)
120 : 2,400 which should be cancelled to as small a figure as possible. In this case dividing both sides by 120 produces the preferred answer of 1 : 20

As a percentage it would be $\frac{120}{2,400} \times 100 = 5\%$

As a fraction it would be $\frac{120}{2,400} = \frac{1}{20}$

19X2 (£000)
$(414 - 108 - 216) : 3,600 = 90 : 3,600 = 1 : 40$ or 2.5% or $\frac{1}{40}$

Note that interest is excluded to indicate more clearly the relative trading performance. The overall profitability will be affected by the effective or excessive use of borrowed funds i.e. the gearing ratio, thus net profit : total assets
19x1   120 : 2,400   1 : 20 or 5%
19x2   12 : 3,600   1 : 30 or 3.3%

This would suggest that 19x2 performance had deteriorated by only 1.7% as compared with 2.5% in the first ratio, i.e. the decline in trading performance has been partially offset by the use of borrowed funds.
3 A selection of ratios in each category are given below in alternative acceptable forms.

Solution

Ratios assessing profitability	*19x1*			*19x2*		
	£000	*Ratio*	*%*	*£000*	*Ratio*	*%*
Net profit : total assets	$\frac{120}{2,400}$	1 : 20	5.0	$\frac{12}{3,600}$	1 : 30	3.3
Net profit before interest : total assets	$\frac{120}{2,400}$	1 : 20	5.0	$\frac{90}{3,600}$	1 : 40	2.5
Net profit : share capital and reserves	$\frac{120}{1,920}$	1 : 16	6.25	$\frac{12}{1,926}$	1 : 16.0	0.62

Ratios assessing profitability

	19x1			19x2		
	£000	Ratio	%	£000	Ratio	%
Gross profit : sales	$\frac{300}{1,200}$	1 : 4	25.0	$\frac{414}{1,800}$	1 : 4.35	23
Net profit : sales	$\frac{120}{1,200}$	1 : 10	10.0	$\frac{12}{1,800}$	1 : 15	0.67
Net profit before interest : sales	$\frac{120}{1,200}$	1 : 10	10.0	$\frac{90}{1,800}$	1 : 20	5.0
Selling expenses : sales	$\frac{120}{1,200}$	1 : 10	10.0	$\frac{216}{1,800}$	1 : 8.3	12
Administrative expenses : sales	$\frac{60}{1,200}$	1 : 20	5.0	$\frac{108}{1,800}$	1 : 16.7	6
Sales : total assets	$\frac{1,200}{2,400}$	1 : 2	50	$\frac{1,800}{3,600}$	1 : 2	50

Ratios assessing liquidity:

Current assets : current liabilities	$\frac{600}{480}$	1.25 : 1	–	$\frac{1,362}{1,074}$	1.27 : 1	–
Quick assets : current liabilities	$\frac{450}{480}$	.94 : 1	–	$\frac{900}{1,074}$	.84 : 1	–
Sales : debtors	$\frac{1,200}{300}$	4 times p.a.		$\frac{1,800}{900}$	2 times p.a.	
or debtors : sales	or $\frac{300}{1,200} \times 12$	3 months		or $\frac{900}{1,800} \times 12$	6 months	
Cost of sales : stock	$\frac{900}{150}$	6 times p.a.		$\frac{1,386}{462}$	3 times p.a.	
or stock : cost of sales	or $\frac{150}{900} \times 12$	2 months		or $\frac{462}{1,386} \times 12$	4 months	
Net profit before interest : interest	Not applicable			$\frac{90}{1,860}$	1.15 times	

Comments

The immediate impression is that performance for the year 19x2 has deteriorated considerably from that of 19x1, although turnover has increased by 50 per cent (£120,000 to £180,000). The cost of goods sold as a proportion of sales and hence the gross profit ratio has remained fairly constant. The net profit ratio has been reduced by an increase in the ratio of selling costs to sales of 2 per cent and an increase in the ratio of administrative costs to sales of 1 per cent.

If the selling expenses had been maintained at 10 per cent of sales for 19x2 they would have been 10 per cent × 1,800 (000s) = 180 – a reduction of 36.

Similarly maintaining administrative expenses at 5 per cent of sales would have produced 5 per cent × 1,800 = 90 – a reduction of 18.

Had this been achieved net profit (before interest) would have been 90 + 36 + 18 = 144 and the appropriate ratio $\frac{144}{1800} \times 100 = 8$ per cent compared with 10 per cent in 19x1. If the figures are further adjusted to take account of the newly incurred interest costs then adding back these costs would produce the following figures $\frac{144 + 18 + 60}{1,800} = \frac{222}{1,800} = 12.33$ per cent.

Main sources of the decline in performance are disproportionately increased selling and administration costs combined with financial charges for the new long-term loan which was presumably utilized to purchase the increased fixed assets.

Liquidity
The current ratio appears reasonably stable and similarly the quick asset ratio in spite of the substantial overdraft. The latter has apparently been used to keep the creditors down in relation to the higher purchases required for the increased turnover. The debtors turnover has deteriorated sharply and requires action as does investigation of the stock levels. Maintaining these ratios at the level achieved in 19x1 would substantially reduce the overdraft level.

The limitations of comparing one year with another include:

(a)   One of the periods may have had exceptionally good or bad performances due to freak circumstances such as a large one-off order (good) or loss due to fire (bad).
(b)   The economic climate may have changed affecting all companies in the industry.
(c)   There may have been a significant change in accounting practices.
(d)   A change of ownership may have produced better or poorer management.

Alternative standards instead of one year with another would include:

(a)   Use of budget or target ratios.
(b)   Published ratios from commercial or economic sources.
(c)   Interfirm comparisons produced by trade associations, chambers of commerce and others.
(d)   If a group of companies – comparison of achievement within the group.
(e)   Detailed subanalysis of major items in the accounts if available such as the make up of cost of goods sold in terms of material, labour and overhead. This would enable attention to be focused on the unfavourable aspects of performance thus saving management time and effort.

Common errors
(a)   Submitting ratios devoted exclusively to one section or not specifically relevant to profitability and liquidity.

(b)   Not indicating clearly the basis of computation. For example (a), (b) and (c) are accepted ratios expressing return on capital employed (ROCE) but it is better to make clear the basis of the figures and the object, if necessary, of its computation.

(c)   Careless arithmetic – the answer should be inspected to assess if the figure seems 'reasonable'. A moment's though might indicate a profit of 3000 per cent to be unlikely even in a theoretical example.

(d)   Ignoring parts of the problem particularly those requiring comment or interpretation such as 2 in this question. In examinations the ability to interpret results is of paramount importance and would carry a substantial weighting of marks. In practice it is the main thrust of the accounting function.

Key words
● Profitability
● Liquidity
● Current ratio
● Acid test
● Return on capital employed (ROCE)

2
More on balance sheet items

This chapter contains a brief introduction to the items included in the balance sheets of most entities. The simplest form for a sole trader illustrated on page 8 should be contrasted with that for a large public company on page 426. The difference is really one of size only – the same principles apply. The balance sheet must balance and items must be grouped into logical divisions of assets and liabilities. As can be seen from the accounts of the Transport Development Group PLC the main balance sheet is a summary – an explanation of the detailed make-up of any particular item is given in a separate note. This is merely to avoid overloading one statement with details. Under current assets for example stocks are shown (page 426) as one item worth £14,280,000 but the make-up of this figure is given separately in Note 11 (page 438) and shows the different types of stock making up the total thus:

Stocks	*£000*
Raw materials	5,783
Work in progress	2,811
Finished goods	2,138
Consumable supplies	5,476
	16,208
Deduct receipts on account of work in progress	1,928
	14,280

In the following sections each major group of asset or liability is dealt with in more detail.

2.1 Fixed assets: Types of asset

In order to begin manufacturing or trading any business entity – sole trader, partnership or company – must acquire certain facilities. These facilities are grouped into a variety of classifications for accounting purposes but a major classification is into **fixed** and **current** assets. The nature of the item does not decide the initial category of fixed or otherwise. A motor vehicle purchased by a business for use by its staff is a fixed asset whereas motor vehicles purchased for resale are current assets. Thus the cost of a typewriter purchased by a garage would appear as part of the fixed assets, possibly under a general heading of office machinery and equipment whereas the value of the stock of cars kept for resale may exceed the value of the typewriter many times. Fixed assets are therefore those assets having a long life – certainly in excess of one year – used by the business in providing goods or services and not held for resale in the ordinary course of trading. A second categorization of fixed assets is into **intangilble assets, tangible assets** and **investments** (see page 214).

Intangible fixed assets

These are fixed assets having no physical identity. The categories are:

1 *Development costs:*   These are only to be treated as a fixed asset if the conditions described later in the section on research and development costs are complied with.
2 *Patents, copyrights, trademarks:*   These have the common characteristic of being evidenced by contract and having a time span decided by agreement or statute.
3 *Goodwill:*   Usually the amount created by the payment for a business of a price in excess of the book value of the net assets. It must be written off over a period not exceeding its useful life.

Tangible fixed assets

The word tangible is used to denote assets having a physical existence. They can therefore be seen and if necessary physically measured, counted and valued. Under historic cost accounting all tangible assets are recorded initially in the accounts at the monetary cost of purchase. The distinction between purchase of fixed assets and items purchased for the purpose of trading is in the subsequent accounting treatment. Tangible fixed assets are usually subdivided for balance sheet presentation into several classifications dependent upon the size and nature of the business i.e. whether the business is manufacturing, distributive or service. In the case of public limited companies there are specific classes laid down in the Companies Act. In this case the classifications with examples are:

1 *Land and buildings:*   Although usually classified together land has the unique characteristic of not wearing out or being destroyed. It should be separated into freehold and/or leasehold. Buildings on the other hand do wear out and this creates a different problem in valuation as discussed later.
2 *Plant and machinery:*   This includes items such as machine tools, assembly lines, presses, material handling conveyors and so on.
3 *Fixtures, fittings, tools and equipment:*   These are items usually smaller in individual valuations than the previous category. They include jigs and fixtures specially made for production processes. Office and shop fittings would also be included.

Valuation of fixed assets

Fixed assets are assets held for a time span in excess of the accounting period and primarily for production or to achieve whatever else is the major objective of the business.

Land

Land is a particular form of fixed asset in that it can neither be created (if we exempt certain forms of reclamation schemes such as draining ditches and swamps) or destroyed. The amount in existence is limited and therefore it tends to increase in value due to scarcity irrespective of use. In times of inflation its value may be well in excess of original cost but the accounts prepared on historic cost would not reflect this.

Buildings

The value attributable to buildings is much more subjective since:

1 They deteriorate or wear out and it is difficult to determine the rate at which they will wear out or depreciate.
2 When the cost concept is combined with the **going concern** concept it is assumed that the buildings will continue to be required for the initial purpose for which they were purchased. If sold at a particular time the proceeds may be greater or less than the figure based on cost. The value may be higher due to a general rise in property value or it may be lower as the building is so specialized that it is of little use for other purposes than those for which it was originally constructed.

Plant and machinery

This is likely to be even more specialized than buildings. There are certain categories of engineering equipment which are general purpose – lathes, grinding machines, drills – which would command a reasonable *second-hand* i.e. resale market. On the other hand machinery constructed – and certainly jigs, moulds, dies, or patterns – for an end product such as a particular model of car would be of little use to a competitor and even less – except for scrap – to other sectors of the business community.

The difficulty of valuing long-term or fixed assets has for years been a major problem in reporting of accounts. Historic cost less cost-based depreciation had, until recent years, been accepted with known reservations. It was recognized that technological innovation resulted in better machines and that design changes in the end product rendered certain production methods obsolete before the end of the life expectancy computed when purchased. These inconsistencies were, however, rendered relatively minor in effect compared with the effect in more recent years of a rapid rate of inflation. Debate over the last ten years had intensified over the dubious nature of profit figures computed on historic cost when the real value of economic cost of replacing the resources used up, has had to be measured in monetary currency depreciating in value at a rapid rate. For the present, however, historical cost is still the accepted basis for compliance with legal requirements and preferred reporting practice. The remaining sections of this chapter are concerned with methods of computing value to the business when the depreciation expense is based on the original price paid for the asset. Methods used when endeavouring to assess worth of assets to the business on a basis other than historic cost are discussed in Sections 3.5 and Chapter 13.

Depreciation

'Depreciation is a measure of the wearing out, consumption, or other loss of value of a fixed asset whether arising from use, effluxion of time or obsolescence through technology or market changes' (SSAP 12). If the asset is a **natural asset** (or wasting asset) such as a coal mine which loses value as the coal is extracted the process can be termed **depletion**, but the principles of treatment remain the same. A provision for depreciation is an attempt to assess in a regular and standard form the amount to be charged in the accounting period for use of the asset during the period. There are four variables to be determined in ascertaining the amount which will be charged.

1   *The cost of fixed assets:*   All costs incurred in putting the asset into a revenue earning condition must be included in the initial cost. Thus, the **capital cost** of a machine should include any additional carriage charges, cost of digging foundations and constructing a concrete base and other installation charges. Whether these tasks are performed by outside contract or the business's own labour the relevant amounts should be capitalized.

2   *The scrap value of the asset:*   This refers to the expected disposal value of the asset at the end of its useful life. Sometimes termed the **salvage value**, in effect it will reduce the total cost which the business incurs in respect of the use of the asset.

3   *Depreciable cost:*   This is the difference between 1 and 2 and is the amount which must be recovered by means of period debits (charges) in the accounting period.

4   *Useful life:*   This refers to the estimated time span over which the depreciable cost is to be written off. In some instances, particularly in the case of leases, it is referred to as the **amortization period**. Problems arise in some instances where a particular basis of depreciation is not expressed in time but in units of output. This may involve some process of reconciliation. For example, the life of a car may be stated in years but its life is more a function of miles travelled. Depreciation might therefore be related to expected output in *miles* rather than years. Similarly machine tools such as presses will wear out more quickly when used intensively than when used infrequently. In this case we may have alternative bases being used – one treating depreciation as a function of time – the other treating depreciation as a function of use.

2.2   Fixed assets: Methods of estimating depreciation expense

Exercise 2.1

The Volley Manufacturing Co., has recently purchased a machine for $81,000 and expects to use it for three years at the end of which period it will be sold as scrap. The following estimates have been agreed concerning its operation and year end valuation:

	Running hours	Market Value $
Year 1	9,600	39,000
Year 2	12,300	18,000
Year 3	9,300	3,000 = Scrap value

You are also informed that the company could invest funds temporarily outside the firm during the three year period to yield 10 per cent interest. In order to accumulate sufficient funds for replacement the company would therefore have to set aside $23,565 at the end of each of the three years.

Required:
1 Calculate for each of the three years the annual depreciation charge, using each of the following methods:

(a) Straight line method
(b) Reducing balance (reducing instalment) method (66⅔%)
(c) Usage (units of service) method
(d) Revaluation method
(e) Sinking fund method (including interest on the sinking fund)

2 Briefly discuss the arguments normally put forward *in favour* of the use of each of the above methods.

Source: LCCI

Solution
(a) Straight line method
Under this method an equal portion of the depreciable cost is charged according to some measure of the asset's life. In general usage it is an equal period of time normally corresponding to the accounting period.

Let P = original cost of machine with accessories and cost of fixing

Let R = residual (scrap or salvage) value at end of n years

Let n = number of useful years life

Let D = depreciation cost charged per year

$$\text{the } \dot{D} = \frac{P - R}{n} \ \$ \text{ per annum}$$

$$\text{Annual depreciation charge} = \frac{\$81,000 - 3,000}{3}$$

$$= \$26,000 \text{ per annum}$$

(b) Reducing balance method
Some accountants hold the view that as the life of an asset increases so the charge for repairs and maintenance increases. A combination of straight line depreciation provision and the repair cost would lead to an increasing

total cost as the asset got older. They therefore claim that a more equitable basis is to have a higher depreciation cost in the early years when the machine is new and – presumably – more reliable and lower depreciation costs as the cost of maintenance and repairs increase, thus equating the combined costs. The reducing balance method therefore charges to each accounting period a **fixed percentage of the value of the asset after deducting the amounts previously provided**:

				$
Initial cost	=	(P)	=	81,000
Scrap value	=	(R)	=	3,000
Depreciable cost		= (P − R)		78,000

Annual depreciation charge:

	$
Year 1 66⅔% × $78,000 =	54,000
Year 2 66⅔% × $(78,000 − 54,000)	16,000
Year 3 66⅔% × $(78,000 − 54,000 − 16,000)	8,000
Total provided at end of Year 3	78,000

As a general guide the reducing balance rate would be one and a half to double the percentage used on a straight line basis i.e., the straight line percentage above is $\frac{D}{3} \times 100 = 33\frac{1}{3}$ per cent and the reducing balance method is twice this amount. The percentage can be computed on a more mathematical basis by using the following formula:

Let r = Reducing balance percentage required
Let P = Initial cost
Let R = Scrap value
Let n = number of years useful life

It can be proved mathematically that $r = 1 - \sqrt[n]{\dfrac{R}{P}}$

i.e. above example $r = 1 - \sqrt[3]{\dfrac{3}{81}}$

$= 1 - \sqrt[3]{0.03703}$

$= 1 - 0.333$

$= 0.666$ as a fraction

or 66⅔%

Note that if the residual or scrap value (R) is *nil* then a nominal value of $1(or other unit) must be assumed otherwise the answer would always be zero.

(c)   Usage (units of service) method
This method is alternatively termed the **production unit method**. A rate per unit of production is obtained by dividing the depreciable cost by the number of units it is estimated the asset will produce in its working life. Alternatively the usage can be expressed in terms of depreciation cost per production hour instead of units. In any event this makes the total

depreciation charge in any period dependent upon the actual quantity produced or time utilized in that particular period and therefore makes the depreciation cost a function of units produced or operating time. For example, if a car is estimated to last five years and costs £5,000 with a scrap value of £1,000 the annual depreciation charge on the straight line method would be:

$$\frac{£5,000 - £1,000}{5} = £800 \text{ per annum}$$

in **any** of the four years

If the production unit was defined as per 100 miles however and the car was estimated to be capable of 80,000 miles during its life then the depreciation cost per 1000 miles would be $\frac{£5,000 - £1,000}{80} = £50$.

If in Year 1 the car travelled 15,000 miles the depreciation charge would be $15 \times 50 = £750$. If in Year 2 the car travelled 25,000 miles the depreciation charge would be $25 \times 50 = £1,250$.

The depreciation charge applicable to a particular accounting period, therefore, is dependent upon the use made of the asset in that period and does not depend solely upon either time or a fixed percentage. In the exercise:

$$\text{Initial cost (P)} = \$81,000$$
$$\text{Scrap value (R)} = \$3,000$$

Estimated total production over
$$\text{life of asset (H)} = 9,600 + 12,300 + 9,300$$
$$= 31,200 \text{ running hours}$$
$$\text{Depreciation rate} = D = \frac{P - R}{H} = \frac{£81,000 - £3,000}{31,200} = \$2.50 \text{ per hour}$$

$$\$$$

Depreciation charge Year 1 = $\quad 9,600 \times 2.5 = 24,000$
Depreciation charge Year 2 = $12,300 \times 2.5 = 30,750$
Depreciation charge Year 3 = $\quad 9,300 \times 2.5 = 23,250$

Depreciable cost $\qquad = 78,000$

(d) Revaluation method
Strictly this could be defined as a method of providing for depreciation by means of periodic charges, each of which is equivalent to the difference in value between the values assigned to the asset at the beginning and the end of an accounting period. The problem here, however, is that if applied to some assets in periods of quickly rising prices then the result may be an **appreciation** in value rather than a depreciation. Land, for example, could increase in value or the cost of an asset may so escalate due to inflation that the second-hand value at the end of the period may be in excess of the original cost. To accept this value into the accounts may offend the concept of prudence and certainly disturb the concept we have maintained so far i.e., the concept of historical cost, as the basis for our accounts. The only time, therefore, that the revaluation method could justifiably be utilized *under an historical cost basis* is for small items of tools and plant. These are

things such as drills, taps, dies and so on which are estimated to have a value according to the degree of wear sustained in the period.

It is important that the term **revaluation** be limited in this context under historical cost. If we attempt to use the word in its widest sense then we enter into a controversy not yet settled. This centres upon the usefulness and reality of a balance sheet or any accounting document prepared exclusively on the basis of historical cost. Use of data other than historical cost does, however, change the objective nature of the 'model' i.e., the approach used and a wider discussion of these conflicts is reserved for Chapter 13.

From the data in this exercise the following computation would result:

	Cost/value b/f $	*Market value* $	*Depreciation* $
Year 1	81,000	39,000	42,000
Year 2	39,000	18,000	21,000
Year 3	18,000	3,000	15,000
			78,000
	(a)	(b)	(c) = (a − b)

The depreciable cost in this instance is still equal to the cost ($81,000) less residual value ($3,000). The historic cost concept has been maintained relevant to the life of the asset, it is merely that the allocation in a particular year has varied considerably.

Sinking fund method
Strictly this is both a method of providing for depreciation by means of fixed periodic charges and ensuring similar cash amounts are invested which – aggregated with compound interest – over the life of the asset equal the cost of the asset. It is implicit that a sum of money equal to this amount would be invested in fixed interest securities which would accumulate at compound interest **to provide at the end of the life of the asset a sum equivalent to its cost**. This is the only method so far then which involves investment of cash simultaneously with the charge for depreciation.

		$
Initial cost	P = 81,000	
Scrap value	R = 3,000	

Years of useful life n =   3
Interest rate   r =   0.10   (10% decimalised)
Depreciation contribution per year = $23,565

Amount set aside at
        end of Year 1 =

$$
\begin{aligned}
&\text{end of Year 1} = && 23{,}565 \\
&\text{Year 2} = 23{,}565 + 0.10\,(23{,}565) && = 25{,}921.5 \\
&\text{Year 3} = 23{,}565 + 0.10\,(23{,}565 + 25{,}921.5) && = 28{,}513.55 \\
\end{aligned}
$$

$$78{,}000.05$$

More challengingly, how was the amount of $23,565 determined so that it balanced with our required figure of $78,000? If we use the depreciation fund by putting money into a deposit account or other revenue earning securities we shall receive interest and if the interest is compounded i.e., reinvested at the end of each period we have:

At end of Year 1: Depreciation fund	$= D$
At end of Year 2: Depreciation fund	$= D + r(D) + D = 2D + rD$
At end of Year 3: Depreciation fund	$= r(2D + rD) + (2D + rD) + D$
	$= 2rD + r^2D + 2D + rD + D$
	$= r^2D + 3rD + 3D$

At end of Year n this can be simplified to $\quad = \dfrac{D}{r}(1 + r^n) - 1$

This must equal the depreciable cost $P - R$

$$\text{i.e. } P - R = \frac{D}{r}(1 + r)^n - 1$$

$$\therefore D = \frac{r(P - R)}{(1 + r)^n - 1}$$

$$\text{i.e. } D = \frac{0.10(81,000 - 3,000)}{(1 + 10)^3 - 1}$$

$$= \frac{0.10 \times 78,000}{(1.10)^3 - 1}$$

$$= \frac{7,800}{0.331}$$

$$= 23,565$$

It is not necessary, fortunately to work this out every time as tables have been worked out which give us the value at the end of 'n' years for £1 invested p.a. at a given interest rate i.e., the value of $\dfrac{(1 + r)^n - 1}{r}$ in the expression above. After three years £1 p.a. invested at 10% at the end of each year would produce a total of £3.31. Therefore if we require £78,000 at the end of three years we simply divide 78,000 by 3.31 to get £23,565.

(f)   *Sum of the digits method*
A common method not requested in the problem but added here is the sum of the digits method:

Let n = Estimated life of asset
of the digits $= 1 + 2 + 3 \ldots n$

Periodic charge for first period $= \dfrac{n}{1 + 2 + 3 \ldots n} \times$ depreciable cost

Periodic charge for second period $= \dfrac{n - 1}{1 + 2 + 3 \ldots n} \times$ depreciable cost

Periodic charge for third period $= \dfrac{n - 2}{1 + 2 + 3 \ldots n} \times$ depreciable cost
and so on

Using the figures from the exercise:

			$
Initial cost	P	=	81,000
Scrap value	R	=	3,000
Depreciable cost	P – R		78,000

Annual depreciation charge:

$$\text{Year 1} = \frac{3}{1+2+3} \times 78{,}000 = \tfrac{1}{2} \times 78{,}000 = \quad 39{,}000$$

$$\text{Year 2} = \frac{2}{1+2+3} \times 78{,}000 = \tfrac{1}{3} \times 78{,}000 = \quad 26{,}000$$

$$\text{Year 3} = \frac{1}{1+2+3} \times 78{,}000 = \tfrac{1}{6} \times 78{,}000 = \quad 13{,}000$$

$$= \text{depreciable cost } 78{,}000$$

Obsolescence through technology or market changes

At the time of purchase an asset may be considered to have a forseeable life of, say, ten useful years. Within a short time, however, new technology may result in equipment being available which is so vastly superior that it may be cheaper overall to buy the new equipment and replace the old, long before it would be necessary to, in the purely technical sense. The original plant is not worn out – it has been rendered **obsolete** by technological development. It is recommended in this case that the difference between the value obtained for the old asset as scrap (if any) and the existing written down value be charged immediately to the profit and loss account. This is an application of the **prudence concept** i.e. providing for known losses as soon as practicable. Obsolescence may not always arise through technological development of the asset. The product concerned may be rendered obsolete as, for example, the development of disposable razors reducing considerably the demand for old-style safety razors and blades, the introduction of ballpoint pens reducing the demand for conventional fountain pens.

If the estimate of the useful life is revised then the amount not yet written off should be charged over the revised remaining useful life.

Sometimes an allowance in respect of possible obsolescence is built into the system. Engineers may assess the potential normal life of a machine tool as twelve years before wearing out but may deliberately reduce this period to 8 years in anticipation of it being superseded by more efficient equipment. Similarly if it is anticipated that a piece of special purpose plant will last fifteen years but the product it produces will not be required after ten years, then it is the latter figure which should be used in any method used for providing for depreciation.

The Statement of Standard Accounting Practice concludes that it is: 'Not appropriate to omit charging depreciation because market value is greater than net book value. If account is taken of such increased value by writing up the net book value of a fixed asset an increased charge for depreciation will become necessary.' This point of view is by no means generally accepted, particularly in relation to an asset such as land. It is a departure from the historic cost concept and can be claimed to be confusing if combined with it.

2.3   Current assets: Stocks and stock control

The problem of dealing with stocks arises in the smallest business unit. In order to assess the profit for a period the **cost of goods sold** in that period has to be determined. It is necessary, therefore, to ignore items purchased in the period, but not yet sold and similarly it is necessary to account for items which were in stock at the beginning of the accounting period and sold during its duration. The physical computation is quite simple. Suppose John Brown Trader sells a single type of good of one quality and the following represents transactions in the period of one month ending 31 March 19x1:

1 March	Stock	100 units
8 March	Sold	25 units
10 March	Purchased	100 units
12 March	Sold	80 units
25 March	Sold	30 units

The **physical stock** (i.e. number of items) remaining must – subject to no pilferage, returns or breakages be:

$$100 - 25 + 100 - 80 - 30 = 65 \text{ units}$$

This is an objective measure i.e. there is no opinion in it. Similarly if all the items both in stock and purchased cost £5 each and were sold for £8 the cost of goods sold could be computed objectively by a straight multiple:

	£
Sales 135 at £8	1,080
Less Cost of goods sold 135 at £5	675
Profit	405

The profit can be checked on a unit basis:

Total profit = quantity sold × profit per unit = $135 \times (8 - 5) = £405$

Even under historical cost concept, however, prices are subject to change so consider the position when goods are purchased and resold at a variety of prices. Assume the same quantities as above but with the following additional information:

1 March	Stock	100 units at £5 each
8 March	Sold	25 units at £8 each
10 March	Purchased	100 units at £5.50 each
12 March	Sold	80 units at £8 each
25 March	Sold	30 units at £8 each

The physical stock is still sixty-five units, the selling price is the same but what is the value of the stock at 31 March?

There are a variety of methods available, all of which are acceptable accounting bases so the accountant must choose the most appropriate or practical for the particular situation.

First in first out method (FIFO)

This method is based on the assumption that the first items received are the first items issued for sale. In the above example therefore:

8 March	Units sold	25 at £5 each leaving 75 at £5 each
10 March	Units purchased	100 at £5.50
12 March	Units sold	80 of which 75 cost £5.00 each and 5 cost £5.50 each leaving 75 cost £5.50
25 March	Units sold	30 cost £5.50 each leaving 65 cost £5.50

The cost of goods is therefore
$$(25 \times 5) + (75 \times 5) + (5 \times 5.50) + (30 \times 5.50) = £692.5$$

Profit = Sales − Cost of goods sold = $1,080 - 692.5 = 387.5$

A conventional profit and loss account would appear thus:

	£	£
Sales		1,080
Stock at beginning (100 × 5)	500	
Add Purchases (100 × 5.50)	550	
	1,050	
Less Stock at end (65 at 5.50)	375.5	
Cost of goods sold		692.5
Profit		387.5

Last in first out method (LIFO)

This method is based on the assumption that the latest items received are the first items issued for sale. Using the data from the above example therefore:

8 March	Units sold	25 at £5 each leaving 75 at £5 each
10 March	Units purchased	100 at £5.50
12 March	Units sold	80 at £5.50 leaving 20 at £5.50 and 75 at £5.00 each
25 March	Units sold	20 at £5.50 and 10 at £5.00 leaving 65 at £5.00 each

The cost of goods sold is therefore
$$(25 \times 5) + (80 \times 5.50) + (20 \times 5.50) + (10 \times 5.0) = £725$$

Profit = Sales − Cost of goods sold = $1,080 - 725 = £355$

A conventional profit and loss account would appear:

	£	£
Sales		1,080
Stock at beginning (100 × 5)	500	
Add Purchases 100 × £5.50	550	
	1,050	
Less Stock at end 65 at £5	325	
		725
		355

There is a difference in profit £387.5 − £355 = 32.5 − a considerable amount and yet either answer could be correct on a historical cost basis. There are alternative methods to the two described above but LIFO and FIFO illustrate both the more common errors and assumptions in approaching stock valuation and the fundamental deficiency of these methods in determining profit.

It was emphasized in the definitions that LIFO and FIFO are based on assumptions about the actual physical movement of the goods. If a firm is using small washers, all identical in quality and appearance, then as new goods are delivered they may well be unloaded on top of the old stock and sold or used first. The pricing system may well be on the basis of FIFO and the goods sold or used will be charged to the cost of sales irrespective of which actual items were used. Similarly in the case of perishable goods the latest items received may well be utilized first to avoid wastage but they could still be priced or valued on a FIFO basis. They are methods of pricing issues and *not* methods of issuing goods. This may be an obvious statement but it is very frequently confused. The pricing system is determined by the accountant − the rotation of issues is determined by the storekeeper and nature of the goods.

Average price

To avoid the extremes of FIFO and LIFO methods recourse is frequently made to averaging. There are two methods: **simple average price** and **weighted average price**.

Simple average price
Under this method a price is calculated by dividing the total of the prices of the goods in stock from which the goods could be issued or sold by the number of prices used in that total.

In the example on page 51 there were only two prices in the period concerned and these were £5 and £5.50.

$$\text{Simple average price} = \frac{£5 + £5.50}{2} = £5.25$$

Cost of goods sold	= (25 + 80 + 30) × £5.25 = £708.75
Value of stock	= 65 × 5.25 = £341.25
Profit	= £1,080 − £708.75 = £371.25

This method is simple to use as it takes no account of quantities purchased at a particular price. For this very reason however – particularly where deliveries vary in quantity and/or price changes are frequent it is not a very acceptable method. A far more satisfying answer statistically can be obtained if the alternative average which uses the weighting principle is applied.

Weighted average price

Under this method a price is computed by dividing the total cost of the goods from which these goods could be drawn by the total quantity in that stock. In most examples it is assumed that the average is recomputed every time a transaction – receipt or issue – takes place.

Using the data from page 57 a formalized stock record would appear as follows:

Component No. Bin No.							Max stock Min. stock		
	Receipts			Issues			Balance		
Units	*Unit cost*	*Total*	*Units*	*Unit cost*	*Total*	*Units*	*Unit cost*	*Balance*
	(£)	(£)		(£)	£			£	
1 March							100	5.00	500.00
8 March				25	5.00	125	75	5.00	375.00
10 March	100	5.50	550				175	5.286	925.00*
12 March				80	5.286	422.8	95	5.286	502.2*
25 March				30	5.286	158.6	65	5.286	343.6*
a	b	c	d	e	f	g	h	j	k

*   To nearest decimal place

The data has been arranged in a simplified revision of stock recording which is termed **perpetual inventory**, that is the balance is recorded and recalculated manually or electronically after each transaction – similar to the familiar bank statement. When the purchase is recorded on the 10th the new price in Column j is computed by adding the value of the purchases (Column d) to the previous value in stock (Column k) and dividing the total by the new total quantity available (Column b + Column h) $= \dfrac{£550 + 375}{100 + 75} = \dfrac{925}{175} = 5.286$

Note that the term perpetual inventory relates exclusively to the recording process and does not imply physical stock checking. This price will remain constant until there is a price change or goods at a previous price are returned to store (in which case the return is treated in the same way as a purchase).

Under this method:

Cost of goods sold = 125 + 422.8 + 158.6 = 706.4
Value of stock   =   343.6
Profit equals £1,080 − £706.4 = 373.6

A summary of the methods described briefly above and the conflicting computations of profit and stock valuation are given below:

	Profit (£)	Stock valuation (£)
FIFO method	387.5	357.5
LIFO method	355	325
Simple average	371.25	341.25
Weighted average	373.6	343.6

It is important to recapitulate what has been discussed:

1 The historic cost concept is applied consistently in all methods as the information which is used is derived directly from historic cost records.
2 The basis of valuation has been changed to illustrate the effect of alternative bases. A business would, however, be expected to apply the same basis between consecutive accounting periods unless there were sound published reason for change.
3 In accounting literature LIFO, FIFO and average costs are frequently referred to as methods of valuing stocks. Strictly speaking they are not – they are methods of pricing issues of goods for use or sale and the value of the stock is the net monetary balance remaining. It is doubtful if this anomaly in terminology, will be removed.
4 There are other methods of stock valuations using both historic and non-historic cost figures but these are discussed in Chapter 11 in the more relevant section on Control of cost.
5 Reference is frequently made to stock being valued on the **lower of cost or market value**. This begs the question of *which* cost as it has been demonstrated above that at least three 'cost' figures could exist at the end of an accounting period. In the case of profits computed on the historic cost convention it is really intended to be an application of the rule of prudence, primarily applicable when items in stock are not in effective demand or have been scrapped for some particular purpose and would not fetch their original historic cost if they were sold.
6 **Stocktaking** is a systematic count of items in stock at the end of an accounting period and the subsequent evaluation in monetary terms of the value of the count by applying prices derived under a system described above or in Chapter 11. A physical stocktaking is sometimes used in order that the cost of goods sold can be deduced or as a check on stock valuations already available from the perpetual inventory or similar stock records.
7 The list of activities given refer to passive aspects of stock evaluation. The question of stock control and the minimization of capital tied up in stocks is a wider issue referred to in Chapter 11.

Gross profit method of estimating stock value

Methods of stock valuation referred to above imply that appropriate records of all items sold and purchased are kept so that the number of items theoretically in stock is always available and in the case of perpetual inventory records their value also. This recorded figure may or may not agree with the actual stock position due to pilferages, scrap, returns, over or under counting on issues or receipts and so on. All businesses have physical checks on these figures at regular or – preferably – irregular periods to **audit** the stock and ensure some degree of reliability in the valuation produced.

The gross profit method is used to **estimate** the value of stock at the end of an interim – shorter – trading period when the expense of a physical check is not desirable or alternatively to confirm as far as practicable the actual stock valuation determined by physical check. It is based on the assumption that the **rate of gross profit** is static from period to period. This would only occur if a single good had been sold at a fixed **mark up** or the sales mix and margin percentages of a number of products had remained constant i.e. the **weighting** was unchanged.

Example

		£
1 January 19x1	Opening stock at cost	6,000
	Purchases during year	78,000
	Sales during year	120,000
	Mark up	40% on sales

In order to compute the value of the stock on the gross profit basis we can construct the statement

		£
Opening stock 1 January 19x1		6,000
Add Purchases		78,000
		84,000
Less Cost of goods sold at selling price	120,000	
Deduct profit	48,000	
		72,000
Stock at 31 December		12,000

Check: The above computation can be checked by reconstructing the revenue account in the more familiar manner:

Profit and loss account for year ended 31 December 19x1

	£	£
Sales		120,000
Stock 1 January 19x1	6,000	
Add Purchases	78,000	
	84,000	
Less Stock 31 December 19x1	12,000	
Cost of goods sold		72,000
Gross profit		48,000

$$\text{Gross profit } (\%) = \frac{48,000}{120,000} \times 100 = 40\%$$

This method is restricted in use by the conditions stated but can be useful in estimating profits, even in a situation where a large product mix exists due to the statistical phenomena of the law of inertia in large-scale numbers. It is not a substitute for physical cost counting however, and strict audit procedure must be followed at intervals if error and/or fraud are to be avoided.

Accounting for stocks

The **closing stock** valuation must be brought into the accounts. The figure for stock normally existing in any trial balance will be that in respect of the **opening stock** for the period but both opening and closing stock are required to compute the **cost of goods sold** in the period. Because the closing stock does not exist as an account it should be brought into the ledger via a journal entry and as an asset it must be a debit balance. The corresponding credit will be to the profit and loss account, thus adding to the value of sales or alternatively reducing the values of goods sold. For example:

			£	p	£	p
31 December	Stock account	Dr	12,000	–		
	Trading account				12,000	–

being value of stocks at end of year transferred

This creates a debit balance on the stock account from 1 January in the following period which is the opening stock in respect of the following accounting period.

2.4   Current assets: Debtors and debtors control

Goods sold on credit result in the creation of **debtors** to the business. To the extent that they are expected to pay these debts within the normal accounting period they are a current asset – **more liquid** than stocks since the goods have been sold – **less liquid** than bank and cash balances as they have not yet been transferred into cash. The purchaser is made aware of the terms of payment at the point of sale, a typical example is:

'5% monthly account otherwise strictly net'

This means that provided the amount is paid within thirty days of the month following that in which goods are invoiced 5 per cent can be deducted from the payment due, otherwise the full amount is payable. Net means that either no cash discount is allowed, or the period in which the debt must be settled to merit such discount has been exceeded. **Cash discount** should not be confused with **trade discount** which is merely a deduction from a recommended selling price granted by a supplier to a wholesaler or a wholesaler to a customer and is an artificial reduction of a nominal price. Because cash discounts are given for prompt payment by debtors they are distinguished from normal trading losses. The full amount is due in respect of goods and is therefore credited as sales and debited to purchaser. The entry recording the discount allowed is made at the time the account is settled. In order to balance the account the total of cash received and discount allowed is posted to the customers' account. The corresponding entry is in the discount allowed column in the cash book where it is accumulated and periodically transferred to the debit of the discount allowed account. The double entry therefore consists of individual entries in the customers' account and the total entry in the discount allowed account. In practice multiple entries are avoided by the use of **control accounts** particularly where data is machine or computer posted. Sometimes **discounts allowed** and **discounts received** (see Creditors) are confused but this is only the case where basic concepts are not fully appreciated. *The business is a separate entity from the owner* whether it be sole trader, partnership or company and the accounts are prepared from the standpoint of the business. If the business suffers a reduction in its income by offering inducements for early payment the business is 'allowing' the discount and it is a loss. It is discount allowed *by* the business.

Example

John Brown Trader sells goods to William Smith valued at £1,000 on 13 March, terms being 5 per cent monthly account and William Smith pays on 28 April by means of a cheque for £950.
The entries are:

Sales Account (1)

Date	Details	F	£	Date	Details	F	£
				13 Mar	W Smith	2	1,000

William Smith (2)

Date	Details	F	£	Date	Details	F	£
13 Mar	Goods	1	1,000	28 Apr	Bank	3	950
				28 Apr	Discount		50
			1,000				1,000

Cash book (3)

Date	Details	F	Discount Allowed	Cash	Bank	Date	Details	F	Discount Received	Cash	Bank
28 Apr	W Smith	2	50		950						

The discount allowed column shown in the cash book is a convenient method of accumulating the discount allowed over the period. When accounts are **closed** at the end of an accounting period this total is posted to the debit of the discounts allowed account. The discount allowed to an individual customer would not, therefore, ordinarily appear in the discount account itself.

When accounts are prepared at the end of a period it will be known approximately what proportion of the total debtors will be likely to take advantage in the period immediately following. A **provision** will therefore be made for the amount of discount likely to be allowed, the appropriate entries being to debit the profit and loss account and credit the provision for discount allowed account. This figure will be shown as a reduction of the total debtors figure on the balance sheet thus indicating as accurately as possible the potential cash flow due from debtors.

Bad debts

If an amount receivable from a debtor is considered to be irrecoverable for any reason then it is no longer a current asset and the amount must be **written off**. The term implies what is to be done. As it is likely that more than one debt will accumulate in the period a bad debts account is opened to which all such amounts are debited. The balance on the customers account is thereby eliminated.

Example
Suppose after repeated efforts by the **credit controller** to obtain payment for the goods supplied to John Brown Trader for £1,000 it was decided to write it off at 31 December the entries would be:

William Smith (2)

Date	Details	F	£	Date	Details	F	£
13 Mar	Goods	1	1,000	31 Dec	Bad Debts	4	1,000

Bad debts account (4)

31 Dec		2	1,000

Ultimately the total of the bad debts account will be closed by posting to the debit of the profit and loss account.

Periodically an amount which has, on the basis of **prudence**, been written off will be recovered, that is a debtor will eventually honour his debts either wholly or in part. The entries will therefore be the reverse of the above. Assuming all the above debt is recovered the journal entries would be

William Smith	Dr	£1,000	
Bad debts			£1,000
Cash	Dr	£1,000	
William Smith			£1,000

This method is known as the **direct write off method**. Frequently because it is not known at the end of an accounting period which debts, if any, are likely to be bad a reserve or more specifically a **Provision for bad debts account** is created. This is an arbitrary figure based on past experience which is reduced from the debtors in the balance sheet. The figure is usually computed as a percentage of credit sales, total sales or debtors outstanding at the end of the period. Any actual trade debts incurred are written off against the provision for bad debts account. At the end of the period the balance is recomputed and the difference transferred to the profit and loss account.

Credit control is the process of ensuring, as far as practicable, that every debtor will pay within the contracted period. It is effected by keeping every account under surveillance initiating pressures for payment up to litigation stages if necessary. The extreme of such litigation would be the taking of steps to initiate a liquidation. Separation of the balances into age groups is useful. This is termed an **ageing schedule** and is the basis for pressure procedures – other subdivisions will come from separate ledgers for areas, market sectors, wholesalers distinct from retailers and so on. It is essential to formalize the knowledge of each customer's history of credit worthiness to ensure that they do not build up debts beyond their ability or willingness to pay. The risk of bad debts must always be assessed against the extra volume and profits from expanded sales. Pressure from the marketing function to continually ease credit procedures to boost sales should be resisted.

The extension of credit to most business customers is on the basis of ratings provided by credit reference organizations such as Dun & Bradstreet Ltd. The rating is related to the size of the company in terms of tangible net worth and a composite credit appraisal. For smaller businesses or individuals, the granting of credit may be on the basis of a report from a credit rating bureau or on such factors as a potential customer's earnings, past credit record, marital status and bank reference.

Factoring

There are times when a company may require cash quicker than it is available from the normal **debtors cycle** or it may decide that it prefers others to take on the onus of debt collection and credit control. A **factor** advances sums of money to a business against the specific security of its debtors. Frequently this service is offered by subsidiaries of banks or special factoring companies. The advance may typically be 80–90 per cent of selected debtors, for which an interest charge is made for the period. The business assigns the indebtedness to the factor who sometimes intervenes to collect the debt direct or, if it is wished that their participation be kept confidential, then the business collects and transfers the receipts back to the factor.

Additional and optional services are offered by the factors to control administratively the debtors of the business. This will involve the sales ledger accounting, order approvals and payments control. A service fee is charged for this. This form of financial servicing has grown tremendously from a small foundation and is now a popular form of using trade debtors as a source of finance.

Credit cards

These are basically of two kinds: **bankers credit cards** and **in-house credit cards**.

Bankers credit cards
Some banks and other financial institutions have established credit card

systems. The credit application is made by the individual to the institution that approves a credit limit and issues the card. The business pays a fee to become part of the system. When the sale is made, a credit sales slip is prepared and the business turns this slip over to the institution for cash, receiving the amount of the sale less a predetermined charge. Typical examples are American Express, Barclaycard, Visa and Access.' The payment is guaranteed if the checking procedure is followed at the point of sale so risk of bad debts is transferred to the financial institution.

In-house credit cards

Many larger stores have instituted their own credit card schemes. Under this method credit to a predetermined limit is granted to the customer who repays at an agreed rate. This enables the stores to boost sales and also receive interest for the financing operations. The rate is usually higher than the bank card and the risk of bad debts lies with the store itself. Familiar names are Burton, Marks and Spencer etc.

Debtors control accounts

In the records each customer will have their own account. The number of such accounts would probably be extremely high and it would be difficult and time consuming to ascertain the total value at a particular time. The total balance can be obtained however if the totals of the various transactions for a period are posted to one account. In the case of debtors this is termed the **debtors control account**. A control (or total) account is one which shows in total, information which is available in detail in other accounts. It is used for items other than debtors – in particular in the costing system to ensure reconciliation of detailed figures. A second advantage of the control account system is that if the total derived from the control account does not agree with the sum of the individual balances there must be an error in one of the subsidiary accounts or the control account itself. Dividing the control accounts into sales areas, groups of customers, groups of products means work and responsibilities can be shared and errors more quickly located.

The data required for the construction of debtors control account is shown in the pro forma ruling below.

Debtors control account

	£		£
Balance of previous period		Cash received from	
Total sales		customers	
Cheques dishonoured		Total returns from	
		customers	
		Total discount allowed	
		Total bad debts	
		Balance carried forward	

Example

From the details given below show how the debtors control account would appear at the end of January 19x1:

19x1		£
1 January	Balance brought forward	2,300
31 Janary	Total sales	3,670
	Sales returns	76
	Discounts allowed	63
	Cash received from debtors	3,430
	Bad debts incurred	27

Debtors control account

January		£	January		£
1	Balance b/fwd	2,300	31	Total cash received	3,430
31	Total sales	3,670		Total returns	76
				Total discounts allowed	63
				Total bad debts written off	27
				Balance c/fwd	2,774
		6,370			6,370
Feb	Balance b/fwd	2,774			

The total of £2,774 should agree with the total of individual accounts in the sales debtors ledger.

Balance sheet debtors

Various classes of debtors should be distinguished on the balance sheet. The minimum requirement for compliance with the Companies Act for published accounts is inclusion of the following:

● Trade debtors
● Amounts owed by group companies
● Amounts owed by related companies
● Other debtors
● Called up share capital not paid
● Prepayments and accrued income

Called up share capital not paid may alternatively be shown separately as the first item of assets. Prepayments and accrued income may be shown here or separately as the final separate class of current assets.

For sole traders and partnerships it is usual to show gross trade debtors less any provision for **doubtful debts**. Distinguishing between trade and other debtors would be recommended. The items in respect of group transactions would not be relevant. Special cases of **hire purchase** and **long-term contracts** are dealt with in the appropriate sections.

2.5   Current assets: Cash and cash control

Cash, as a balance sheet item, may appear as a favourable balance – current asset – or an unfavourable balance – current liability. If an asset, the term is frequently used to cover both literally coins and notes in hand and current or deposit account balances at banks. An unfavourable balance in the form of an overdraft or short-term loan would be a current liability. If the loan was repayable after a period greater than one year it would be shown separately. Control of **cash flow** is the most important element of business success. Some businessmen equate increase in profit with increase in cash but as the flow of funds statement, illustrated in Section 1.4, is designed to illustrate, this is not likely to be the case. The business may invest heavily in stocks, allow debtors too much time to pay, repay loans, withdraw excessive amounts for private purposes or dividends or purchase additional fixed assets. A great deal of trouble can be avoided by negotiating, in advance, bank facilities for seasonal or periodic excessive payments. In order to illustrate the procedure it is necessary to anticipate some of the concepts dealt with more extensively in Sections 11.3 and 11.4.

Cash budgets

The objectives of the **cash flow budgets** are to forecast the balance which will be in hand, or the deficit anticipated, over future time periods and to providing a measure of control between such forecasts and actual achievement. Whereas some readers may have problems appreciating other aspects of business management most people are familiar with the situation of wanting to do more things in a given space of time than money available will permit. Businesses have the same problem and effective budgeting and monitoring are essential elements in ensuring smooth operations and avoiding situations which ultimately end in bankruptcy or liquidation.

There are two ways in which cash forecasts may be prepared: the **receipts and payments method** or **funds flow method**. The latter was introduced on pages 18–29 as one of the requirements for good financial reporting of the past situation but it is, as shown below, adaptable for control purposes.

Receipt and payments basis

This is, in effect, a forecast cash account but usually in a modified columnar format. The interval between balances may be monthly, quarterly, six monthly or whatever period is desirable for the firm concerned. Information is required as below:

Item	Source
Receipts	Sales debtors, interest received, rent, sale of assets, dividends received

Continued over.

Item	Source	
Payments:		
Materials, wages and salaries	Purchases – direct and indirect	All adjusted for credit period granted or given and cash discounts allowed or received
Expenses – power, light etc.	Payroll plus deductions accounts	
	Invoices received	
	Contracted payments	
Non-trading	Interest paid, dividends	

Most manufacturing and wholesale sale of goods is on credit. Even retailers are having to grant more facilities for delayed payment by means of cheques, credit cards, in-house budget cards and so on. A typical time schedule for receipts might be 20 per cent paid in cash, 30 per cent in the month following sale, 30 per cent after two months and the remainder in the following month. The sales budget will have been converted to the debtors budget and it is the latter that provides the input for cash received. Addition must be made for non-trading receipts such as investment income, sale of assets, rent received or additional share or loan capital.

For all payments the figures in the cash budget must be inserted in the period when they are to be paid not when liabilities are incurred. Rent may be payable half yearly in advance, material purchases on one month credit, wages weekly in arrears, salaries at the end of the current month and so on.

The total cash payments made are subtracted from those received in the same period. A positive figure would show a surplus for the period and a negative one would show a deficit. To this must be added (or deducted) any opening balance, the final figure representing the balance at the end of the period. It is at this stage that the benefit of period by period budgeting becomes apparent. Payment of a large annual tax bill may produce a large negative (overdraft) balance. This may be wholly or partly offset by some unusual income in the following period. Being able to demonstrate to a bank manager or other grantor of credit the sequence of timing between being granted and repaying a loan is much more likely to result in sympathetic consideration. If obtaining an overdraft is not feasible or desirable then, depending upon the size of the deficit, recourse may have to be made to other methods such as:

● Extra long-term finance from shareholders.
● Debentures or similar medium-term finance from specialist bankers.
● Government assistance where possible.
● Sale of surplus assets or sale and lease back.
● Shortening credit period extended to debtors.
● Extending credit taken from suppliers.
● Considering taking or giving cash discounts.

Preparation of cash budget (receipts and payments format)

The data described in the sources above are worked out for the period concerned on a cash flow worksheet. The computations and presentation can be prepared on inexpensive small computers and print-outs obtained from standard commercial programmes and discs. The ease with which the data can be corrected or updated makes the tasks ideal for computer application.

Exercise 2.2

The Stoke Manufacturing Company are to manufacture a new product. This will be launched on the market on 1 January 19x5. The company has set aside £35,000 in cash as working capital. Using the information available prepare a cash budget for the four months December 19x4, January, February and March 19x5. Production will start in December 19x4 so that stock will be available to meet the immediate demand in January. The estimated sales for the first four months are:

19x5	Units	Sales value
January	6,000	£48,000
February	8,000	£64,000
March	9,000	£76,000
April	10,000	£84,000

The factory variable cost per unit is budgeted as follows:

Direct material	£3.00
Direct labour	2.00
Variable overhead	1.00
Factory variable cost	£6.00

Fixed overhead, estimated at £30,000 per annum, is incurred in equal amounts each month from 1 December 19x4. Twenty per cent of the fixed overhead is depreciation.

It is estimated that 80 per cent of each month's sales will be produced in the current month while the remaining 20 per cent will be produced in the previous month.

Forty per cent of the direct materials required for the production will be purchased in the month prior to production. Direct materials will be paid for in the month following purchase.

Direct wages for the month will be paid for in the same month.

Variable and fixed overhead will be paid for in the month following usage.

Twenty-five per cent of the sales are expected to be cash transactions; 50 per cent of the sales are expected to be paid for in the month following sale and 20 per cent in the third month. It is possible that at least half of the remainder will not be recovered.

Source: LCCI

Workings

	Dec	Jan	Feb	March	April
Sales (units)	–	6,000	8,000	9,000	10,000
		£	£	£	£
Value of sales		48,000	64,000	76,000	84,000
Receipts					
Cash sales 25%		12,000	16,000	1900	
Previous month 50%			24,000	32,000	
Previous two months 20%				9,600	
Materials					
Production					
Jan Sales	1,200	4,800			
Feb sales		1,600	6,400		
Mar sales			1,800	7,200	
Apr sales				2,000	8,000
	1,200	6,400	8,200	9,200	8,000
	£	£	£	£	£
Material used at £3.00 per unit	3,600	19,200	24,600	27,600	24,000
Previous month (50%)		9,600	12,300	13,800	12,000
Current month (50%)		1,800	9,600	12,300	13,800
		11,400	21,900	26,100	25,800
Payment (following month)			11,400	21,900	26,100
Direct wages		2,400	12,800	16,400	18,400
Variable overhead			1,200	6,400	8,200
Fixed overhead			2,000	2,000	2,000

Fixed overhead total	= £30,000
Less depreciation (non cash)	= 6,000
Cash costs per annum	= 24,000
Cash costs per month	= $\dfrac{24,000}{12}$ = 2,000

First production is in December so first payment is in January.

Stoke Manufacturing Company
cash budget for four months 1 December 19x4 to 31 March 19x5

	Dec (£)	Jan (£)	Feb (£)	March (£)
Receipts				
Cash sales 25%		12,000	16,000	19,000
Previous month 50%			24,000	32,000
Previous two months 20%				9,600
Three months or more 5%				
Total from debtors		12,000	40,000	60,600
Investment income				
Others				
Total		12,000	40,000	60,600
Payments				
Materials		11,400	21,900	26,100
Wages	2,400	12,800	16,400	18,400
Variable overhead		1,200	6,400	8,200
Fixed overhead		2,000	2,000	2,000
Interest charges				
Loan repayments				
Purchase of assets				
Others				
Total	2,400	27,400	46,700	54,700
Net cash gain/(loss)[1]	(2,400)	(15,400)	(6,700)	5,900
Opening balance[2]	35,000	32,600	17,200	10,500
Indicated cash balance[3]	32,600	17,200	10,500	16,400
Cash required[4]				
Closing balance c/f[5]	32,600	17,200	10,500	16,400

Notes

Items other than those included in this particular exercise have been included to illustrate the suggested standard format.

Line 1 represents the net cash gain or loss for the month or other particular period concerned. Line 2 is the opening balance and was given for the first month. Subsequent months are derived from the closing balance (line 3) computed for the previous month since the closing balance for one period must be the opening balance for subsequent ones.

Line 3 is the sum of 1 + 2 and indicates what the closing balance will be if no action is to be taken to change the figure. When computed it may be unacceptable e.g. above an agreed overdraft limit.

If the figure in Line 3 is not acceptable the amount and source of any finance necessary to adjust line 5 will be inserted in Line 4. In that event the required (budgeted) figure would be the first inserted in Line 5 and 4 would equal 5 − 3. It is not required in the circumstances of the question.

Line 5 is either the same as Line 3 or, where a specified balance is required, equal to the difference between Line 3 and Line 5.

Control statements

Strictly speaking a budget prepared as above is a projected cash flow statement for several periods. Each period would require comparison – monitoring – with the actual situation to ensure the position was satisfactory and to prompt action if it was not. In the example it is stated that half of the final balance of debtors (half of 5 per cent) is anticipated bad debts. The actual variance would have to be checked and credit control improvement investigated. The budget would be repeated on a period basis with adequate columns for showing actuals, variances and reasons as illustrated in Section 11.4.

2.6 Liabilities: Short and long term

A **liability** is the legal obligation of a business to other entities or persons in respect of monies owing for goods or services already received. The entities or persons to whom the sums are owed are classified into two main groups.

1 *Current liabilities:* Sums falling due for payment within a short period of time – usually one year. In respect of sole traders, partnerships and small companies they would comprise trade creditors, bills payable and accruals. For public limited companies additional subgroups are required particularly in respect of group accounts (see Section 4.2).
2 *Long-term liabilities:* Sums falling due for payment after one year from the balance sheet date. In respect of sole traders, partnerships and small companies examples would be loans from proprietor or partners, loans from third parties such as banks and debentures raised by the owners or through subscription in the case of a public limited company. Any items of bank loans or overdrafts, trade creditors or taxation not falling due for more than one year would also be included in this section.

Current liabilities

Trade creditors
Goods and services purchased on credit result in the creation of current liabilities – in the form of creditors – by the business entity. We saw with trade debtors that a normal period of credit granted was thirty days. Similarly with a purchase we shall be granted a period before payment is expected. We may be offered a cash discount as an inducement to prompt payment. In this event a discount will be received. The accounting entries recording this will be similar in principle to those shown for debtors but, of course, the entries will be reversed.

Example
James Black Trader purchases goods from Samuel Jones valued at £2,000 on 20 March the payment terms being 5 per cent net monthly account and James Black pays on 28 April, in full settlement with a cheque for £1,900. The accounts and entries concerned are:

Samuel Jones (1)

Date	Details	F	£	Date	Details	F	£
28 Apr	Bank	3	1,900	20 Mar	Goods	2	2,000
	Discounts received		100				
			2,000				2,000

Purchases (2)

Date	Details	F	£	Date	Details	F	£
20 Mar	Samuel Jones	1	2,000				

Cash book (3)

Date	Details	F	Discount allowed	Cash	Bank	Date	Details	F	Discount received	Cash	Bank
						28 Apr	Samuel Jones	1	100		1,900

The discount received column is a convenient method of accumulating the discount received over the period. When the accounts are closed at the end of an accounting period the total is posted to the credit of the discounts received account. The discount received from an individual supplier would not, therefore, ordinarily appear in the discount account itself. The credit period taken is in excess of thirty days but as in the case of debtors payment is normally allowable up to the end of the month following that in which the invoice(s) were received.

Control of creditors
Once orders have been placed with suppliers and goods delivered a legal obligation to pay has been incurred. Effective control must therefore

commence with the **purchasing** routine. The authority to issue purchase orders must be restricted and all orders should only be initiated by a **purchase requisition**. This is a request to the purchasing function to procure the goods concerned, so authority for the initiation of the purchase – whether day-to-day materials or expensive fixed assets – has been established. The responsibility of the accounting department in respect of valuation and recording of issues, stocks levels and usage is dealt with in Part Four on management accounting. The accounting routine for payment should include the following stages.

- Confirm that the invoice has been approved by the purchasing department in that material received, price and terms agree with the purchase order.
- Check with materials received note that all the items were satisfactory. If not procedure should have started for the amount invoiced to be adjusted by means of a credit note from the supplier. All calculations and extensions verified.
- Enter into accounting records through purchase journal.
- Record for payment at the appropriate time and with discount adjustment noted if applicable.

The opportunities for fraud at various stages in the purchasing and payment routine render it essential that all standard procedures for its avoidance should be taken. Advice should be sought if necessary from the firm's auditors on suitable internal control steps.

Non-trade creditors

There are special requirements in respect of disclosure of other creditors falling due within one year indicated in the limited companies section. In other entities it would be preferable to disclose:

- Debenture loans – due for repayment.
- Bank loans and overdrafts – if short term.
- Payments received on account.
- Bills of exchange payable.
- Other creditors including taxation.

Accruals

An **accrued liability** is an amount in respect of wages, salaries or other expenses such as rates which have to be recognized although not paid. Such a procedure is necessary to satisfy the **matching concept**. In most circumstances the amounts will be construed proportionately on a time basis but if other bases are more relevant to the particular expense e.g. commission payable on sales then the appropriate basis should be used.

Long-term liabilities

These are the sums in respect of amounts falling due after more than one year. The most prominent group is **debentures** and other forms of **loan capital**, but there are others including any item with a similar heading to those in the previous section that are not due for payment within one year.

Debentures

Long-term loans can be utilized as a source of finance for a business entity provided the lender is reasonably sure that the loan is secure and the interest – the cost of providing the loan – will be met. In the case of small traders and partnerships such loans are likely to be from banks, other individuals or financial institutions. The bank will take security for the advance on both the business and the individual partners' private assets. This may be evidenced by a **floating charge** on all the business assets plus specific **mortgages** on property or other assets. A large public entity will need greater sums and will have the facility to appeal to the public to subscribe loan capital in the same way as it does for shares. Such investments appeal to individuals and institutions who desire greater security of capital and income than might be the case of shareholders. The alternative appeals to the business owners as the cost of financing (interest) is allowed as a deduction against taxable profits so that the real cost to the company is lower than the nominal rate. It also leaves managers free to direct the activities of the business since, providing the interest is paid and conditions of security met, the loan or debenture holder has no say in the management of the company. The example and discussion which follow, although for a debenture security, would apply in principle to all loans of a long-term nature having the characteristics described. A debenture is a loan to a company, usually under its seal, and with a trust deed setting forth the conditions affecting the payment of interest, repayment of principal and nature of security over the company's assets. A simple, unsecured or naked debenture is one for which no security has been given. **Mortgage debentures** are those secured by specific charges on specified fixed assets whereas **floating debentures** are secured on all assets of the company other than mortgage until such time as the company ceases trading in which event the charge becomes fixed. In contrast to a shareholder a debenture holder is a creditor not a proprietor; receives interest not dividends; and is entitled to repayment of loan at expiry of term unless the debentures issued are classed as irredeemable. The terminology in relation to fixed interest securities should be referred to when contrasting alternatives particularly the situation in respect of **quoted debentures** i.e. those capable of being dealt with on the stock exchange:

- **Nominal value (or par value)** – face value of the security.
- **Interest (or coupon) rate** – the fixed percentage of the nominal value payable per annum as a reward for lending.
- **Market value** – the price at which the securities are currently being exchanged on the stock market.
- **Yield** – the actual rate of return on the security as a ratio of interest received to purchase (or current market) price.

Example

A debenture is issued with £100 nominal (par) value and a coupon (or contract) rate of interest of 12 per cent. The present market price is £91. What is the yield on the debenture?

Solution

When prices of fixed interest investments are quoted in the press the '£' sign is frequently omitted but it is the price per £100 of the stock concerned. For £91 we are buying an income of (12 per cent of £100) £12 per year. Since we paid less than £100 for this the yield will be higher than the rate.

$$\text{Yield} = \frac{\text{interest received}}{\text{market price}} \times 100$$

$$= \frac{12}{91} \times 100 - 13.19\%$$

This is termed the **gross yield** as it is before income tax on the holder's investment. The after tax yield is the **net yield** and is the figure after taxation at the standard rate has been allowed for. A further complication arises as most debentures have a redemption date and the amount payable on redemption is usually the nominal value. If the debentures in the above example were due for redemption in four years time the holder would receive £100 for the £91 paid – a capital gain of (gross before tax) £9. If a company was trying to raise money by debentures then – ignoring other factors – it would have to offer a rate above 13.19 per cent or offer other inducements. One such inducement would be to offer the debentures at a discount. In this case the company would receive £91 only for every £100 nominal. The liability is for £100 and £12 per annum interest and the discount would be £9 in respect of each £100 raised. If market conditions had changed in favour of the company the reverse situation would apply and the company would be able to issue the debentures at a premium. We are more concerned here with the accounting entries than aspects of financial management and the following exercise is illustrative of the treatment. The debenture subscriber may be asked to pay in full on application or, as a further inducement, be given the opportunity to pay in instalments (or calls).

Exercise 2.3

Able PLC wants to raise £250,000 in secured debentures with an interest rate payable of 12 per cent. Assuming the issue was fully subscribed and paid up show the accounting entries under the following circumstances.

1 (a)   Issued at par payable in full on application.
    (b)   Issued at par payable 20 per cent on application, 30 per cent on first call and the balance on final call.
2 Issued at £91 payable in full on application.
3 Issued at £110 payable in full on application.

Solution

1(a)   **12% Debenture holders**

	£		£
12% Debentures	250,000	Bank	250,000
		Bank	
	£		
12% Debenture holders			
	250,000		

12% Debenture account

			£
		12% Debenture holders	250,000

1(b)   **Application and allotment account**

	£		£
12% Debentures	125,000	Bank	50,000
		Bank	75,000
	125,000		125,000

12% Debentures account

	£		£
Balance c/d	250,000	Application and allotment	125,000
		First and final call	125,000
	250,000		250,000
		Balance b/d	250,000

Bank account

	£		£
Application and allotment	50,000		
Application and allotment	75,000		
First and final call	125,000		

First and final call account

	£		£
12% Debentures	125,000	Bank	125,000

2   **12% Debentures account**

	£		£
Balance c/d	250,000	Bank	227,500
		Discount on debentures	22,500
	250,000		250,000
		Balance b/d	250,000

Discount on debentures

	£		£
12% Debentures account	22,500	Balance c/d	22,500
Balance b/d	22,500		

Bank account

	£		
12% Debentures account	227,500		

The balance on the discount on debentures account must be written off against reserves such as a share premium account. Failing this it is deductible in the balance sheet from the total of shareholders' interests. The full nominal value of the debentures must be maintained in the debenture account.

3   **12% Debentures account**

	£		£
Balance c/d	250,000	Bank	250,000

Premium on debentures

	£		£
Balance c/d	25,000	Bank	25,000

Bank account

	£		
12% Debentures	250,000		
Premium on debentures	25,000		

The premium on debentures can be used to create a reserve account which can be used for restricted purposes such as writing off intangible assets as indicated in the section on limited companies.

Capital employed
The financial obligations of the business remaining when all external liabilities have been characterized as above is to the owners and is equivalent to the **capital employed**. These interests will be those of proprietorship in the case of sole traders and partners and shareholders of all classes in the case of limited companies. Since the objective of most businesses is to increase profits which can be used to increase capital employed or distributed to these providers of capital the effect of movements in capital employed is discussed in Chapter 3.

3
Types of business organization and their accounts

We have seen that accounts can be prepared for any form of entity – any economic unit being separately identifiable, be it an individual, church or local angling club. A business entity is usually one existing with a view to profit and this may be the stated objective. Sometimes the natural progression of the business entity, if it prospers, is through the stages of individual ownership, partnership and finally limited company private or public. Each form of enterprise has problems peculiar to its structure caused by the economic and legal framework in which it operates. The basic accounting rules and documents are the same but distribution of profits, maintenance and increase of capital, taxation and treatment in event of failure are among items that are treated differently in each form. If the business entity is owned exclusively by one person it is termed a sole trader, if by two or more persons associated for the purpose of trade it is a partnership. The desire for limited company status further influences the data, accounts and format required. The particular requirements for each of these types of business organizations is dealt with in the following sections.

3.1 Double entry and basic records

There are two aspects to every business transaction. For every seller there must be a buyer, for every borrower there must be a lender, for every purchase there must be a sale.

The foundation of **double entry** lies then in the double-sided nature of each transaction. Recognition and recording of this produces a self-balancing check on the book-keeping records. Consider what happens when John Brown Trader sells goods for £300 to William Smith Merchant for which he does not immediately receive payment. It is obvious that William Smith is receiving goods and that John Brown is giving up the goods – not giving them away of course but nonetheless John Brown is relieved of their value and a debt to him is thereby created. The double-sided aspect of these transactions was formally and even now to some extent recognized by the use of **'T' accounts** i.e. a double-sided format thus:

The intention of the 'T' account was to assist recognition of the **receiving** and **giving** aspects of each transaction.

The person or account receiving value is said to be in **debit** (Dr) while the person or account giving up value is said to be in **credit** (Cr). To illustrate the transaction above, therefore required two accounts in the books of John Brown:

Dr	Sales account		Cr
	William Smith		300

Dr	William Smith		Cr
Sales account – Goods	300		

If we were concerned with the books of William Smith there would be dual recording but the nature of the transaction would alter. To William Smith it was a purchase (receiving) of goods and creation of a liability so the books would appear as follows:

Dr	Purchases account		Cr
John Brown – Goods	300		

Dr	John Brown		Cr
	Purchases		300

It is suggested that the reader attempts to show the accounts after William Smith has paid for the goods. In practice the dates of the transactions would be entered.

As we have seen from the balance sheet all transactions result in acquisition or disposal of assets and acquisition or disposal of liabilities. Those assets and liabilities which are acquired and disposed of in the **normal** course of the individual unit or company's trading or other operations are termed **revenue items** while those affecting assets or liabilities not **ordinarily** acquired or disposed of in the normal course of business are termed **capital items**. This distinction is important and must constantly be borne in mind by the reader as progression is made through more advanced sections.

Balancing accounts and extraction of trial balance

The practice of double entry enables accounts to be balanced frequently in order to establish the position of the accounts individually and in total either at the end of a specified accounting period or at any point in between.

Exercise 3.1

Suppose that transactions had taken place between John Brown and William Smith as follows:

10 January	William Smith	Purchased goods	£300
15 January	William Smith	Returned goods	£50
28 January	William Smith	Purchased goods	£400
30 January	William Smith	Paid cheque	£250

Show the account of William Smith in the books of John Brown at 31 January and bring down the balances.

Solution

William Smith   L4

19xx		F	£ p	19xx		F	£ p
10 Jan	Sales	L2	300.00	15 Jan	Returns	L3	50.00
28 Jan	Sales	L2	400.00	30 Jan	Bank	L1	250.00
				31 Jan	Balance	c/f	400.00
			700.00				700.00
1 Feb	Balance	b/f	400.00				

Balances can be struck or taken out at any time and **balancing an account** is establishing on which side the surplus lies. It is necessary to insert a figure of £400 on the credit side to make both sides of the above account agree but it is a debit balance established by bringing it forward on the debit side to commence the next period of recording from 1 February. Note how this reflects the actual situation. The cheque for £250 represents *net* payment for the satisfactory goods delivered i.e. £300 or original sales less £50 worth of unsatisfactory goods returned. At 31 January there is a *debtor* of £400 representing the value of goods supplied not paid for. What of the *dual aspect* or double entry? An account must be opened which reflects each aspect of the transactions not yet dealt with; thus we need:

Bank account   L1

30 Jan	William Smith	L4	250.00				

Sales account   L2

				10 Jan	William Smith	L4	300.00
				28 Jan	William Smith	L4	400.00

Sales returns					L3
15 Jan	William Smith	L4	50.00		

It is accepted that if the above system is utilized then debit entries are recorded on the left and credit entries on the right. We shall see later that most machine or computer-produced records arrive at a similar result using a different format but this does not affect the dual aspect of the recording process. The above example is simplified as it was assumed that Smith had no previous dealings with Brown (or the account was clear) but it is unlikely that other sales had not been made or purchases and payments created. Nonetheless irrespective of the number of entries or accounts the books can be balanced periodically and a **trial balance** taken out. A trial balance is the listing of balances in a **ledger** on any given date. A ledger is a set of accounts kept in such a form as to record values received (**debit**) and values given (**credit**). The column adjacent to the monetary column should the ledger be kept in 'T' form is termed **folio** and used to cross index the source or destination of the dual aspect of the transaction (F).

Exercise 3.2

On the basis of the information given for the transactions of John Brown write up the ledger accounts for the month ended 31 January 19xx and extract a trial balance at this date.

Bank account								L1
		F					F	
30 Jan	William Smith	L4	250.00	31 Jan	Balance		c/f	250.00
1 Feb	Balance	b/f	250.00					

Sales account								L2
31 Jan	Balance	c/f	700.00	10 Jan	William Smith	L4	300.00	
				28 Jan	William Smith	L4	400.00	
			700.00				700.00	
				1 Feb	Balance	b/f	700.00	

Sales returns								L3
15 Jan	William Smith	L4	50.00		Balance		c/f	50.00
1 Feb	Balance	b/f	50.00					

William Smith account								L4
10 Jan	Sales	L2	300.00	15 Jan	Returns	L3	50.00	
28 Jan	Sales	L2	400.00	30 Jan	Bank	L1	250.00	
					Balance	c/f	400.00	
			700.00				700.00	
1 Feb	Balance	b/f	400.00					

The following is the trial balance extracted from the books of John Brown as at 31 January 19xx:

Ledger Folio		Dr £	Cr £
L1	Bank	250.00	
L2	Sales		700.00
L3	Sales returns	50.00	
L4	William Smith	400.00	
		700.00	700.00

All the entries used to illustrate the above procedures have been drawn from revenue items and the result is not fully illustrative of all transactions which would occur either in an established business or one just commencing. What is missing? No capital and no fixed assets are included. There are various ways in which the assets and liabilities of the business would be changed as the result of business transactions. These are primarily those shown in Table 3.1.

Table 3.1

	Long-term	*Short-term*
Acquiring assets	Land, buildings, machinery	
Recording expense or loss		Materials, labour and services received
Disposal of liabilities	Repayment of mortgages, Debentures, preference shares	Payment to trade creditors
Withdrawals by owners	Withdrawing capital	Withdrawing profits or dividends
Disposal or reduction of asset	Sale of plant	Depreciation, sales
Acquiring Liabilities	Raising of loans Overdrafts etc.	

Capital

For most of the items considered **source or original documents** will exist. An original document is one which provides the authority for the posting i.e. entry into the account. These documents comprise items such as invoices, statements, wage payrolls and credit notes. Some items, however, do not have source documents from outside or formal sources and these comprise such things as the original investment of capital, the determining of profits to be withdrawn, the amount to provide for depreciation and so on. A formal record for these decisions and authority for entry into the accounts can be provided by means of the **journal**. Originally all items were entered into the journal in chronological i.e date order before being posted to the **ledger**. Over time it became clear that in trading or manufacturing operations most items concerned the purchase or manufacture and sale of goods and therefore subsidiary books were introduced to enable these items to be dealt with separately.

The main subsidiary books were:

- Purchase day book – for recording purchases.
- Purchase returns book – for recording goods returned to suppliers.
- Sales day book – for recording sales.
- Sales returns book – for recording goods returned by customers.

This enabled transactions involving the above to be posted at convenient intervals. The **cash book** became an anomaly since it remained a journal (recording all cash and bank items in chronological order) and an account. In spite of restricted practical use the journal is frequently used as a shorter means of testing an examinee's ability to sort out the destination of entries into a variety of accounts, so for theoretical and practical purposes it is necessary to appreciate its ruling and objective.

Date	Particulars of account and narration	Ledger folio	Dr	Cr
1	2	3	4	5

1 The date is an essential element of the journal since the items are in chronological order.
2 This space is for the names of account(s) affected and also a brief explanation of the entry.
3 This column records the folio or page reference which identifies the appropriate page in the ledger.
4 This column records the amount(s) of the accounts which are to be debited.
5 This column records the amount(s) of the accounts which are to be credited.

Example

John Brown Trader finds that William Smith owes £200 which is deemed irrecoverable due to the likely bankruptcy of Smith and wishes to remove this account from the books. It is an **abnormal** event; Brown does not exist to sell to defaulters but it is not a unique event since other customers may not pay. He decides to **write the debt off** to the bad debts account as a loss. He cannot use either of the books of original entry as described and therefore utilizes the journal. The entry will appear as follows:

				Dr	Cr
31 Jan	Bad debts account	Dr	7*	200	
	To William Smith		10*		200
	Being bad debt				
	written off				
	*assumed				

Note that the abbreviation Dr appears adjacent to the folio column, the word 'To' is inset and the narration commences with a traditional word

'Being' – although these are nowadays frequently omitted. The narrative should be brief and entries can, on occasion, be consolidated e.g. suppose we had an additional bad debt in respect of Samuel Jones for £90 this could be journalized at the same time as shown below:

				Dr	Cr
31 Jan	Bad debts account	Dr	7	290	
	William Smith				200
	Samuel Jones				90

Notes:

1 Here the 'To' has been omitted in accordance with modern practice.
2 This does not mean that the bad debts account will be debited with **one** figure. The individual entries in respect of Smith and Jones will still be made.
3 Ultimately the bad debts account' will be **written off** to the profit and loss account i.e. closed by transfer to the profit and loss account (see page 59).

Many students and readers spend too much time trying to assess the exact title and form which best practice or the examiner would like to see. Although in this respect it is highly satisfactory to agree completely with either of these requirements they very often come with experience. The motto should be – **when in doubt open an account**. It is more important to ensure that the ultimate destination of each transaction is correct and provided the debits and credits are correctly done then some accountants may utilize several steps to achieve what others do in one! Obviously if consolidated entries were requested in the answer then marks would be lost for treating each entry separately. However, there are usually other parts to these problems and it is probably more important to get these correct; e.g. the accounts themselves.

Adjustment and final accounts

Proprietors' capital

It must be emphasized again that it is standard accounting practice to regard the assets and liabilities of a business, be it sole trader partnership or public limited company, as being entirely separate from those of its owner(s). Thus if a business prospers *its* assets increase and to the extent that the increase is not required to satisfy claims of creditors the balance will be an increase in capital and this is a **liability of the business to its owners**. The original investment by the proprietors in whatever form of business unit will have to be recorded via a journal entry as described above. In the simplest case a sole proprietor may decide to 'put £10,000 into the business'. If he is John Brown then the very first **dual aspect** should now be easily identifiable. The business has received cash of £10,000 and John Brown has supplied it – it has therefore acquired a liability to John Brown of £10,000. The books of the business can be opened and the very first balance sheet constructed.

Journal					J1
1 Jan	Bank account Dr	1	£10,000		
	Capital account of John Brown	2		£10,000	
	Cash investment at 1 Jan, 19xx				

Ledger
Capital account   L1

	1 Jan Bank		2 £10,000

Bank account   2

1 Jan Capital	L1 £10,000		

John Brown
Balance sheet as at 31 Jan 19xx

Liabilities	£	Assets	£
Capital	10,000	Cash at bank	10,000

At the end of the **accounting period** it may be desired to determine how the business has progressed over the period and what its position is at that particular date. This normally involves adjustments in addition to those already mentioned, in respect of the matching principle, two of the most notable, in the case of a trading concern, being:

1   The depreciation of fixed assets.
2   The value of stocks unused or unsold.

Difficulties of evaluating the amounts for these are considered in Section 6.1 but their treatment, once determined, can be considered. Depreciation is considered an expense since it is a reduction in the value of an asset. Stock must be reduced from total purchases since in attempting to evaluate profit on cost basis goods which have not been sold cannot have contributed profit. Accepting this for the present it should be possible to work through the consolidating exercise.

Exercise 3.3
J. Smith commenced business on 1 January 19xx with a capital of £4,000 in cash. On 3 January he occupied an office and warehouse for which he agreed to pay a quarterly rent of £200. The rent was payable half yearly on 31 March and 30 June. On 8 January he purchased a van for £2,600 cash. The following transactions subsequently took place.

10 Jan	Purchased goods on credit from J. Brown £700.
17 Jan	Paid wages (cash) £40.
21 Jan	Purchased goods for cash £360.
23 Jan	Sold goods on credit to A. Perry £420.

24 Jan	Paid wages cash £48.	
31 Jan	Paid wages cash £40.	
4 Feb	Sold goods on credit to B. Harris £150.	
5 Feb	Paid J. Brown £700 less £30 cash discount.	
10 Feb	A. Perry paid £420 and was allowed £20 cash discount.	
14 Feb	Paid wages (cash) £60.	
18 Feb	Purchased goods on credit from N. White £2,200.	
25 Feb	Sold goods for cash £120.	
26 Feb	Received £120 from B. Harris.	
27 Feb	Paid wages cash £60.	
1 Mar	Returned unsatisfactory goods to N. White £180 duly credited.	
5 Mar	Sold goods on credit A. Perry £700.	
12 Mar	Paid wages £60.	
14 Mar	Received payment on account from A. Perry £400.	
16 Mar	Sold goods for cash £310.	
18 Mar	A. Perry paid £265 in full settlement of his account to date.	
19 Mar	Received loan from F. Green £1,000.	
20 Mar	Sold goods on credit to A. Perry £1,350.	
26 Mar	Paid wages cash £60.	
26 Mar	Paid N. White in full settlement £1,860.	
28 Mar	Informed that B. Harris was unable to pay remainder of debts.	
31 Mar	Paid rent £400.	

It was estimated that the value (at cost) of stock unsold at 31 March 19xx was £1,020 and depreciation on the van was estimated at £120 at that date. Assume all payments and receipts are in cash.

Required:
1 Write up the necessary journal and day book entries to record the above events (see pages 90–1).
2 Write up the appropriate ledger accounts for the three months to 31 March 19xx.
3 Prepare final accounts – revenue accounts and balance sheet at 31 March 19xx from the information you have prepared.

Solution

Capital account (01)

31 Mar	Balance c/d	4,407	1 Jan	Cash	(02)	4,000
			31 Mar	Net Profit for the quarter		407
		£4,407				£4,407
			1 Apr	Balance b/d		£4,407

Cash account (02)

1 Jan	Capital	(01)	4,000	8 Jan	Motor van	(03)	2,600
10 Feb	A. Perry	(08)	400	17 Jan	Wages	(06)	40
25 Feb	Sales	(07)	120	21 Jan	Purchases	(04)	360
26 Feb	B. Harris	(09)	120	24 Jan	Wages	(06)	48
14 Mar	A. Perry	(08)	400	31 Jan	Wages	(06)	40
16 Mar	Sales	(07)	310	5 Feb	J. Brown	(05)	670
18 Mar	A. Perry	(08)	265	14 Feb	Wages	(06)	60
19 Mar	F. Green – Loan	(15)	1,000	27 Feb	Wages	(06)	60
				12 Mar	Wages	(06)	60
				26 Mar	Wages	(06)	60
				26 Mar	N. White	(12)	1,860
				31 Mar	Rent	(16)	400
					Balance c/d	(02)	357
			£6,615				£6,615
1 Apr	Balance b/d		357				

Motor van account (03)

8 Jan	Cash	(02)	2,600	31 Mar	Balance	c/d	£2,600
1 Apr	Balance	b/d	2,600				

Purchases account (04)

10 Jan	J. Brown	(05)	700	31 Mar	Tfr Trading account		3,260
21 Jan	Cash	(02)	360				
18 Feb	N. White	(12)	2,200				
			£3,260				£3,260

J. Brown (05)

5 Feb	Cash	(02)	670	10 Jan	Purchases	(04)	700
	Discount received	(10)	30				
			£700				£700

Wages account (06)

17 Jan	Cash	(02)	40	31 Mar	Tfr Profit and loss account	368
24 Jan	Cash	(02)	48			
31 Jan	Cash	(02)	40			
14 Feb	Cash	(02)	60			
7 Feb	Cash	(02)	60			
2 Mar	Cash	(02)	60			
26 Mar	Cash	(02)	60			
			£368			£368

Sales account (07)

31 Mar	Tfr Trading A/c		3,050	23 Jan	A. Perry	(08)	420
				4 Feb	B. Harris	(09)	150
				25 Feb	Cash	(02)	120
				5 Mar	A. Perry	(08)	700
				16 Mar	Cash	(02)	310
				20 Mar	A. Perry	(08)	1,350
			£3,050				£3,050

A. Perry (08)

23 Jan	Sales	(07)	420	10 Feb	Cash	(02)	400
5 Mar	Sales	(07)	700		Discount allowed	(11)	20
20 Mar	Sales	(07)	1,350	14 Mar	Cash	(02)	400
				18 Mar	Cash	(02)	265
					Discount allowed	(11)	35
				1 Apr	Balance c/d		1,350
			£2,470				£2,470
1 Apr	Balances b/d		£1,350				

B. Harris (09)

4 Feb	Sales	(07)	150	26 Feb	Cash	(02)	120
				28 Mar	Transfer bad debts	(14)	30
			£150				£150

Discount received (10)

31 Mar	Tfr Profit and loss account		190	5 Feb	J. Brown	(05)	30
				26 Mar	N. White	(12)	160
			£190				£190

Discount allowed (11)

10 Feb	A. Perry	(08)	20	31 Mar	Tfr Profit and loss account	55
28 Mar	A. Perry	(08)	35			
			£55			£55

N. White (12)

1 Mar	Purchase returns	(13)	180	18 Feb	Purchases	(04)	2,200
26 Mar	Cash	(02)	1,860				
	Discount received	(10)	160				
			£2,200				£2,200

Purchase returns (13)

31 Mar	Tfr Trading account		£180	1 Mar	N. White	(12)	£180

Bad debts account (14)

28 Mar	B. Harris	(09)	£30	31 Mar	Tfr Profit and loss account		£30

F. Green – loan account (C15)

31 Mar	Balance	c/d	£1000	19 Mar	Cash	(02)	£1,000
				1 Apr	Balance	b/d	£1,000

Rent account (16)

31 Mar	Cash	(02)	400	31 Mar	Trf Profit and loss account		200
				31 Mar	Prepayment c/d	(16)	200
			£400				£400
1 Apr	Prepayment b/d		200				

Purchase day book

10 Jan	J. Brown	(05)	700
18 Feb	N. White	(12)	2,200

Purchase returns day book

1 Mar	N. White	(12)	180

Sales day book

23 Jan	A. Perry	(08)	420
4 Feb	B. Harris	(09)	150
5 Mar	A. Perry	(08)	700
20 Mar	A. Perry	(08)	1,350

Journal

1 Jan	Cash account	O2	4,000	
	Capital account – J. Smith	O1		4,000
	Being capital introduced at commencement of business			
28 Mar	Bad debts account	I4	30	
	B. Harris	O9		30
	Being bad debt written off			
31 Mar	Profit and loss account	I8	120	
	Depreciation of motor van account	I7		120
	Being depreciation written off the motor van for the three months to 31 March 19xx			
31 Mar	Stock	I8	1,020	
	Trading account			1,020
	Being the stock in hand at 31 March 19xx			

Trial balance as at 31 March 19xx

		Dr	Cr
J. Smith – Capital	(01)	–	4,000
Cash	(02)	357	–
Motor van	(03)	2,600	–
Purchases	(04)	3,260	–
J. Brown	(05)	–	–
Wages	(06)	368	–
Sales	(07)	–	3,050
A. Perry	(08)	1,350	–
B. Harris	(09)	–	–
Discount received	(10)	–	190
Discount allowed	(11)	55	–
N. White	(12)	–	–
Purchase returns	(13)	–	180
Bad debts	(14)	30	–
F. Green – loan	(15)	–	1,000
Rent	(16)	400	–
		£8,420	£8,420

Depreciation of motor van account (17)

31 Mar	Balance	c/d	£120	31 Mar	Tfr Profit and loss account		£120
				1 Apr	Balance	b/d	£120

Stock account (18)

31 Mar	Tfr Trading account	£1,020		

Trading and profit and loss account for the three months ended 31 March 19xx

Purchases	3,260		Sales	3,050
Less Returns	180			
	———			
Net Purchases		3,080		
Less Closing stock		1,020		
		———		
Cost of sales		2,060		
Gross profit carried down		990		
		———		———
		£3,050		£3,050
		=====		=====
Wages		368	Gross profit brought down	990
Discount allowed		55	Discount received	190
Bad debts written off		30		
Rent		200		
Depreciation of motor van		120		
Net profit		407		
		———		———
		£1,180		£1,180
		=====		=====

Balance sheet as at 31 March 19xx

Liabilities			*Assets*			
Capital Account – J. Smith			Motor van at cost		2,600	
Capital introduced	4,000		*Less* Depreciation		120	
					———	2,480
Add Net Profit for the						
three months	407					
	———		*Current Assets*			
	4,407		Due from A. Perry		1,350	
Loan account – F. Green	1,000		Payment in advance (rent)		200	
			Stock in hand		1,020	
			Cash in hand		357	2,927
	———		Cash in hand		———	
	£5,407					£5,407
	=====					=====

3.2   The sole trader

In the previous section the accounts of a sole trader were illustrated from the commencement of the business to the preparation of accounts and balance sheet at the end of the first quarter year. Accounts prepared for this purpose are termed **final accounts** and will normally be produced at least once a year. **Interim accounts** may be prepared more frequently for managerial purposes. They are prepared to show the state of the business and particularly the changes, and source of changes, in the proprietors' interests whether sole traders, partners or shareholders. The format of the main statements has been discussed and illustrated. The particular treatment of each is now taken in turn.

If a business prospers the result will be an increase in the proprietors' interests but the owners may withdraw such surplus from time to time. Consider the position at the end of the period in respect of John Smith.

J. Smith – Capital account

		£			£
31 Mar	Balance c/d	4,407	1 Jan Cash		4,000
			31 Mar Profit and loss		407
		4,407			4,407
			1 Apr Balance		4,407

The balance sheet repeated this information in a vertical form

	£
Capital introduced	4,000
Add Profit for period	407
Capital employed*	4,407

* Or **proprietorship** or **net worth**.

If J. Smith had withdrawn £200 for living expenses in the three months concerned then these would be classified as **drawings**. The account could then be shown as follows:

J. Smith – Capital account

		£			£
31 Mar	Cash	200	1 Jan Cash		4,000
	Balance c/d	4,207	31 Mar Profit and loss		407
		4,407			4,407
			1 Apr Balance		4,207

This would be repeated on the balance sheet as follows:

	£
Capital introduced at 1 Jan	4,000
Add Profit for period to 31 Mar	407
	4,407
Less Drawings	200
	4,207

If Smith had withdrawn £600 this would be in excess of the profit for the period and would reduce the original investment. Prudence suggests that drawings should be less than the profits as in the original case. The increase in capital is thus represented by the **retained profits** i.e. £407 less £200 equals £207. In order to clearly emphasize the change from the original capital the two parts may be separated using a current account. This records items such as profits, salary of owner, interest on any loan on the one hand and withdrawals in cash or kind on the other. Although all the profits of a sole trader belong to the owner he may pay himself a salary to assess whether he is better or worse off than working for someone else but it is still part of the profit. Similarly he may put additional money into the business as a loan rather than capital. Interest will be transferred on the debt again to see if the earnings are in excess of what could be obtained elsewhere. These items are more important in partnerships where different skills and capitals are contributed (see page 93). The current account for J. Smith above would appear as follows:

Current account

		£			£
31 Mar	Cash	200	31 Mar	Profit and loss	407
	Balance c/d	207			
		407			407
			1 Apr	Balance b/d	207

This would be repeated on the balance sheet as follows:

	£	£
Capital		4,000
Current Account		
Profit for period	407	
Less Drawings	200	
		207
		4,207

The total capital employed is the same as previously £4,207. If the current account is in debt it will normally be shown as a (fictitious) asset rather than being deducted from the original capital. Such a situation may be temporary and revert in the following period. The advantage of a current account is that it facilitates immediate comparison between the profit earned and amounts withdrawn with which the business was started. The following exercise shows in more detail how the data would be collected and presented.

Exercise 3.4

On 1 January 19x1 Jackett started in business as a small trader, opening a bank account with his initial capital of £3,000. He has kept no proper records of his business transactions and in April 19x3 he received a large, estimated tax demand. This has made him seek help in preparing some accounts, and he has now produced the following information:

	19x1	19x2
	£	£
Cash sales, all banked	14,630	16,970
Cheque payments, analysed:		
Stock purchases	7,292	8,896
Sundry expenses	2,649	2,982
Drawings	3,000	3,500
Fixtures and fittings	1,000	300
Stock at 31 December	3,790	5,740
Stock taken for private use	520	780
Trade creditors at 31 December	1,980	2,100

Required:
1 Trading and profit and loss accounts for 19x1 and 19x2.
2 Balance sheets as at 31 December 19x1 and 19x2.
Ignore depreciation. Show all calculations.

Source: SCCA

Key points
Stock taken for private use must be reintroduced into books of account.

Workings

	19x1 £	19x2 £
Purchases		
Creditors at *end* of the year	1,980	2,100
Add Cheque payments	7,292	8,896
	9,272	10,996
Less Creditors at the beginning of year	–	1,980
Credit purchases for year	9,272	9,016
Sales	14,630	16,970
Bank		
Opening balance	3,000	3,689
Add Deposits	14,630	16,970
	17,630	20,659
Payments		
Stocks + Expenses + Drawings + Fixtures	13,941	15,678
Closing balance	3,689	4,981

Note: See reconstructed bank account below as alternative means of establishing this figure.

	19x1	19x2
Drawings	3000	3,500
Stock withdrawn for private use	520	780
	3,520	4,280

Bank account

	£	£		£	£
Capital	3,000		Purchases	7,292	8,896
Sales	14,630	16,970	Sundry expenses	2,649	2,982
Balance b/f		3,689	Drawings	3,000	3,500
			Fixtures and fittings	1,000	300
			Balance c/d	3,689*	4,981*
	17,630	20,659		17,630	20,659
Balance b/d	3,689*	4,981*	* balancing figures		

Solution
Part 1

Jackett
Trading and profit and loss accounts for year ended

	19x1		19x2	
	£	£	£	£
Sales		14,630		16,970
Less Cost of sales				
Stock at 1 January	–		3,790	
Add Purchases	9,272		9,016	
	9,272		12,806	
Less Stock for private use	520		780	
	8,752		12,026	
Less Stock at 31 December	3,790		5,740	
		4,962		6,286
Gross profit		9,668		10,684
Sundry expenses		2,649		2,982
Net profit transferred to capital account		7,019		7,702

Part 2

Balance sheet for year ended 31 December

	19x1		19x2	
	£	£	£	£
Fixed assets				
Fixtures and fittings		1,000		1,300
Current assets				
Stock	3,790		5,740	
Bank	3,689		4,981	
	7,479		10,721	
Less Liabilities				
Trade creditors	1,980		2,100	
		5,499		8,621
		6,499		9,921
Capital				
Introduced at 1 January		3,000		6,499
Profit for year		7,019		7,702
		10,019		14,201
Less drawings		3,520		4,280
		6,499		9,921

Alternative with current account

Current account

		£			£
19x1	Drawings bank	3,000	19x1	Profit and loss	7,019
	Drawings stock	520			
	Balance c/d	3,499			
		7,019			7,019
19x2	Drawings bank	3,500	19x2	Balance b/d	3,499
	Drawings stock	780		Profit and loss	7,702
	Balance c/d	6,921			
		11,201			11,201
			1983	Balance b/d	6,921

Balance sheets

	19x1		19x2	
	£	£	£	£
Capital		3,000		3,000
Current account				
Balance at start	–		3,499	
Add Profit	7,019		7,702	
	7,019		11,201	
Less Drawings	3,520		4,280	
		3,499		6,921
Proprietors' funds		6,499		9,921

The total capital employed is still the same but the segregation emphasizes that Smith has left a substantial sum in the business.

3.3 Partnerships

A business may be inaugurated by one person or from the beginning two or more people may pool their financial and other resources. Alternatively a sole trader may prosper and may seek a partner(s) for the following reasons:

1 Special expertise is required – for example managerial or marketing skills that the sole trader does not possess and can only be acquired by offering a share in the business to another person.
2 Additional capital is needed and the sole trader would prefer it to be in a permanent form rather than a loan.
3 A desire to merge two existing businesses for mutual benefit.

4   Desire by the proprietor for continuity of the business past his retirement.

The Partnership Act of 1890 defines a partnership as: 'The relationship which subsists between two or more persons carrying on a business with a view to profit.' The minimum number of partners is two and the maximum twenty – with the exception of certain professional businesses. The disadvantages of a partnership are predominantly:

1   Each partner is liable for all the debts of the firm to the full extent of their personal possessions.
2   The liability is joint – that is if one partner cannot provide his share of any deficiency the remainder may be called upon to make good the shortfall.
3   In the normal course of trade any partner commits the firm by any agreement he makes. There are exceptions but the other party to the contract must be aware of such limitations.

There are exceptions to 1 above in that there may be **limited partners** who take no part in the management of the business and are registered under the Limited Partnership Act of 1907 but there must be at least one partner with unlimited liability. These are unusual in that if such limitation is preferred the advantages of forming a limited liability company outweigh the benefits of partnership. Finally, a **sleeping partner** is one who takes no active participation in the business but who has a capital investment. They are usually people who were in the business originally and have retired or financial speculators.

The partnership agreement

It is preferable that an agreement be drawn up in writing rather than reliance being placed upon recollection of some oral statements. This avoids possible litigation later and clarifies relations with people outside the partnership. A typical agreement would include some, or all, of the following:

1   The name under which the firm is to trade.
2   The capital and loans to be introduced by the partners and if interest is to be paid on them.
3   The proportion and method of division of profits or losses.
4   If salaries are payable to individual partners.
5   The drawing of funds from the business by the partners and if any interest is to be charged on such funds.
6   The method of introducing new partners.
7   The method of valuation of goodwill.
8   The keeping of proper books of account and their audit.
9   Provision for continuation of the partnership in the event of death or withdrawal of the partner.
10   Procedure on dissolving the partnership.
11   The means of arbitration to be used to finalize matters which cannot be mutually agreed upon.

In the event of no agreement or if a dispute occurs on a matter not covered by an agreement it will be decided in accordance with rules incorporated in the Partnership Act of 1890. The main applications of this Act which affect the accounts and financial matters are as follows:

1 Profits and losses will be shared equally whether in respect of capital or revenue.
2 No undisclosed profit shall be made by a partner out of the firm.
3 Interest at the rate of 5 per cent will be paid on all *loans* by the partners to the partnership.
4 No interest is payable on the capital of the partners.
5 No partner shall be entitled to a salary.
6 Every partner (other than a limited one) shall be entitled to partake in management of the firm.
7 The firm's books should be kept at the principal place of business with all partners having access to them.

It must be reiterated that the Act only applies in the absence of any agreement to the contrary.

Partnership accounts

Since the business will be seriously affected if a partner withdraws his original capital it is even more desirable that the original capital account will be separated in the case of partnerships than in the case of sole traders – the reasons remaining the same. For this reason the agreement may specify that the capital account be fixed or maintained at the original amount invested. Separate current accounts are opened for each partner and also an account for drawings, the balance of which is transferred at intervals to the current account. The following pro forma indicates the items likely to be found in the account:

Current account

Drawings: Cash or goods	Salaries where payable
Interest on drawings (if charged)	Interest on capital if allowed
	Interest on loans from partners
	Net profit from profit and loss account

If a loss is incurred the share of loss would be debited to the current account. There is, therefore, a capital account, current account and drawings account usually created for each partner. The profit and loss account is prepared in the same way as for the sole trader but once the net profit or loss has been established for the firm it is transferred to a second part of the account referred to as the **profit and loss appropriation account**. This shows the details of how the net profit has been apportioned between the partners including amounts in respect of salaries, interest received or charged on capital and drawings respectively. Interest on a loan is chargeable before net profit has been established as it is a financial cost of lending.

Example

Smith and Jones set up in partnership on 1 January 19x1 estimating the funds required to be £50,000. It was agreed that each partner would subscribe £15,000 as capital and Smith would provide the remaining £20,000 in the form of a loan carrying interest at 10 per cent per annum.

Profits were to be shared equally and at the end of Year 1 the profit amounted to £12,000 before charging loan interest. Below are the balance sheet at the start of the business, the accounts in respect of distribution of profit and the closing balance sheet to the extent that the figures allow.

Balance sheet of Smith and Jones as at 1 January 19x1

	£		£
Capital accounts		Bank	50,000
Smith	15,000		
Jones	15,000		
	30,000		
Loan			
Smith	20,000		
	50,000		50,000

Smith and Jones
Profit and loss account for year ended 31 December 19x1

	£		£
Loan interest (Smith)	2,000	Profit (before interest)	12,000
Net profit c/d	10,000		
	12,000		12,000

Appropriation account for year ended 31 December 19x1

	£		£
Current account		Net profit b/d	10,000
Smith share of profit	5,000		
Jones share of profit	5,000		
	10,000		10,000

Balance sheet of Smith and Jones as at 31 December 19x1

	£		£
Capital accounts		Sundry assets	62,000
Smith	15,000		
Jones	15,000		
Current accounts			
Smith loan interest	2,000		
Smith share of profit	5,000		
	7,000		
Jones share of profit	5,000		
Loan account			
Smith	20,000		
	62,000		62,000

The balance sheet may be presented as above or vertically or (frequently requested in examinations) in a columnar format with partners side by side. The following example shows a more detailed application of current accounts.

The trial balance of Able and Willing at 31 December 19x2 was as follows:

	£	£
Capital accounts		
Able		12,000
Willing		12,000
Loan account: Willing		30,000
Current account at 1 Jan 19x2		
Able	2,000	
Willing		5,000
Net profit for year to 31 Dec 19x2		25,000
Drawings account		
Able	4,000	
Willing	5,000	
Plant and machinery (written down value)	15,000	
Fixtures and fittings (written down value)	4,000	
Stocks	3,000	
Debtors	14,000	
Creditors		3,000
Freehold premises (cost)	26,000	
Cash in hand and at bank	14,000	
	87,000	87,000

The net profit is before charging salary of £5,000 for Able. Provision must be made for interest on drawings, Able £100 and Willing £200, and also interest on loan at 10 per cent. Profit is to be shared equally between the partners.

Solution

Current account

	Able £	Willing £		Able £	Willing £
Opening balance	2,000		Opening balance		5,000
Drawings	4,000	5,000	Interest on loan		3,000
Interest on drawings	100	200	Salary	5,000	
Balance c/d	7,550	11,450	Profit (see below)	8,650	8,650
	13,650	16,650		13,650	16,650

Profit and loss account for year to 31 December 19x2

	£		£
Loan interest – Willing	3,000	Net profit 1 b/d	25,000
Balance c/d	22,000		
	25,000		25,000
Salary – Able	5,000	Balance b/d	22,000
Share of profit		Interest on drawings	
Able	8,650	Able	100
Willing	8,650	Willing	200
	22,300		22,300

Note: It is not necessary to designate the appropriation section as such provided it is clearly separated and shows only the items concerned.

Able and Willing
Balance sheet as at 31 December 19x2

	£	£		£	£
Capital accounts			Fixed assets		
Able	12,000		Freehold premises		
Willing	12,000		(at cost)	26,000	
		24,000	Plant and machinery		
			(net)	15,000	
			Fixtures and fittings		
			(net)	4,000	
					45,000
Current accounts			Current assets		
Able	7,550		Stocks	3,000	
Willing	11,450		Debtors	14,000	
		19,000	Cash and bank	14,000	
Loan – Willing		30,000			31,000
Creditors		3,000			
		76,000			76,000

Admission of new partners

A person buying a successful business will have to pay for **goodwill**. This, briefly, is the advantage of buying an established business as compared with building it up from the very start. It was formally defined by a judge as 'the benefit arising from connection and reputation' or 'the benefit coming from the fact that old customers will resort to business with the old firm'. It comes from the production of good products or quality of services provided. Because it is an intangible asset then convention and prudence dictate that it is not shown in the partnership accounts unless:

1 It has been purchased.
2 It has been created upon:
   (a) The admission of a partner.
   (b) The withdrawal of a partner.
   (c) The death of a partner.
   (d) The conversion of the partnership into a limited company.

Valuation of goodwill

The real value of a business as distinct from that recorded in the accounts, is what someone is prepared to pay for it at a particular point in time. The purchaser may wish to buy the business for aspects other than its profits – it may be on a prime building site; it may be next door and he wants to expand; he may wish to eliminate competition and so on. There will still be a difference between purchase price and book value. i.e. the recorded value of the assets in the accounts. Even if these had been brought up to agreed values an amount would still be asked for goodwill. There are various conventional ways in which this is computed.

Number of years purchase of the average profits
The amount paid for goodwill is agreed as – usually – between two and four

times the average profits for the latest years. If there are any **abnormal** gains or losses in the years concerned they must be removed to **normalize** the profit. A typical example of such abnormality would be a one-off profit on the sale of land. If the profits of the previous four years were £8,000, £8,000, £9,000 and £11,000 respectively and (n) the number of years purchase was three then goodwill would be :

$$3 \times \frac{8,000 + 8,000 + 9,000 + 11,000}{4} = £27,000$$

Because of the significance of later years sometimes the goodwill computation is a weighted average with greater weight being given to later years.

Year	£		Weight		£
1	8,000	×	1	=	8,000
2	8,000	×	2	=	16,000
3	9,000	×	3	=	27,000
4	11,000	×	4	=	44,000
			10		95,000

$$\text{Weighted average} = \frac{95,000}{10} = 9,500$$

3 years purchase $= 3 \times 9,500 = £28,500$

Super profit

In assessing a viable price a prospective purchaser usually has at least one alternative risk-free investment into which he can put his money. Unless the business concerned can offer a premium above this rate compatible with the element of risk involved then there is little point in taking such risk. Assume average annual profits to be £66,000 per annum and an agreed current value of net assets as £250,000. It is then necessary to calculate the normal return from such an investment taking into account both the pure (risk-free) interest and the risk element usual for that class of business. Any excess above this combined average is **super profit** which is then capitalized. Assume that the current interest rate is 12 per cent and the risk premium for this particular type of business is 10 per cent then:

		£	£
Average profits per annum			66,000
Less Risk free return required	= 12% × 200,000 = 24,000		
Less Risk premium return required	= 10% × 200,000 = 20,000		
	22% × 200,000		= 44,000
Super profits			22,000

The capital sum which would yield £22,000 at 22 per cent interest is:

$$£22,000 \times \frac{100}{22} = £100,000 \text{ Value of goodwill}$$

There are additional ways such as the present value of the stream of profits expected at an appropriate rate for the industry. Alternatively it can be computed on a sinking fund basis.

There are a number of variations which can be used both for computation of goodwill and for its treatment in the books of account. The accounting treatment will now be considered. For other computations see Section 3.5

Payment of premium on admission

If the partners do not wish to raise a goodwill account they must still be compensated for their past efforts in building up the business. The new partner may introduce capital into the business but in addition he pays each partner privately an agreed premium in respect of goodwill on admission. The two ways of dealing with this are as follows:

1   The new partner may pay the agreed amount privately to the existing partners in their profit sharing ratios. In this event neither the premium or its division is recorded.
2   The premium is paid into the firm but is shown in the bank account as having been received from the existing partners. The capital accounts are credited with the amount agreed. The advantages are that the transaction is recorded in the books and the money is available for use in the business until withdrawn by the partner.

Example

A and B are in partnership sharing profits 3/5 and 2/5 respectively. The capital account balances are A, £50,000 and B, £20,000. C is to be admitted as a partner on payment of £10,000 for capital and £6,000 premium in respect of goodwill. No account is to be raised in the books for goodwill but cash is to be paid into the firm's account.

Capital account A

		£			£
Balance	c/d	53,600	Balance	b/d	50,000
			Bank account (3/5 × 6,000)		3,600
		53,600			53,600
			Balance	b/d	53,600

Capital account B

		£			£
Balance	c/d	22,400	Balance	b/d	20,000
			Bank account (2/5 × 6,000)		2,400
		22,400			22,400
			Balance	b/d	22,400

Capital account C

		£
	Bank – Capital introduced	10,000

Bank account

	£		
C – Capital introduced	10,000		
Premium on goodwill			
Transfer from A	3,600		
Transfer from B	2,400		

New partner – no capital introduced

Frequently partners are brought in because of their expertise and may not have funds to invest in the business. In this case goodwill is valued according to the partnership agreement and credited to the existing partners' capital accounts in the ratio in which they shared profits before the new partner was admitted. This creates an asset in the form of goodwill which is matched in the liabilities by a total increase of a similar amount in the existing partners' capital accounts. This assumes no account exists at present in the books in respect of goodwill. If it did then the total would be adjusted.

Example

A and B are in partnership sharing profits ⅗ and ⅖ respectively. The capital account balances are A, £50,000 and B, £20,000 respectively. C is to be admitted without payment of capital and subsequent profits are to be shared: A ⁴⁄₁₀, B ³⁄₁₀ and C ³⁄₁₀. Goodwill is valued at £20,000.

Goodwill account

		£			£
Created on admission of C			Balance	c/d	20,000
Transfer to A		12,000			
Transfer to B		8,000			
		20,000			20,000
Balance	b/d	20,000			

Capital account A

		£			£
Balance	c/d	62,000	Balance	b/d	50,000
			Goodwill account		12,000
		62,000			62,000
			Balance	b/d	62,000

Capital account B

		£			£
Balance	c/d	28,000	Balance	b/d	20,000
			Goodwill account		8,000
		28,000			28,000
			Balance	b/d	28,000

Capital account C

	Capital introduced		nil

Goodwill entered into books

Having paid a premium it may be that the value attributed to goodwill is to be brought into the books and the new partner is to be credited with his share. In this case goodwill is created and shared in the new profit sharing ratio.

Example

A and B are in partnership sharing profits $\frac{3}{5}$ and $\frac{2}{5}$ respectively. The capital account balances are A, £50,000 and B, £20,000. C is to be admitted as a partner on payment of £10,000 for capital and £6,000 premium to be credited in old ratio to A and B. In addition a goodwill account is to be raised for the sum of £20,000 and apportioned to the three partners' capital accounts in the new profit sharing ratio of A $\frac{4}{10}$, B $\frac{3}{10}$ and C $\frac{3}{10}$.

Goodwill account

	£			£
Goodwill on introduction of C		Balance	c/d	20,000
Transfer to A capital	8,000			
Transfer to B capital	6,000			
Transfer to C capital	6,000			
	20,000			20,000
Balance b/d	20,000			

Capital account A

		£			£
Balance	c/d	61,600	Balance	b/d	50,000
			Bank – Premium from C		3,600
			Goodwill		8,000
		61,600			61,600
			Balance	b/d	61,600

Capital account B

	£			£
Balance	28,400	Balance	b/d	20,000
		Bank Premium from C		2,400
		Goodwill		6,000
	28,400			28,400
		Balance	b/d	28,400

Capital account C

	£			£
Balance	16,000	Bank Capital introduced		10,000
		Goodwill		6,000
	16,000			16,000
		Balance	b/d	16,000

Balance sheet of A, B and C as at 19xx

	£		£
Capital Account		Goodwill	20,000
A	61,600	Total other assets –	
B	28,400	liabilities i/c £16,000	
C	16,000	additional cash	86,000
	106,000		106,000

Retirement of a partner

Reconsideration of the value of the business has to take place on retirement or death of a partner. A partner retiring may, with agreement of existing partners, dispose of his interest directly to another person. In this event the only entry necessary is to change the name in the books. Similarly the remaining partners may agree to purchase the retiring partner's interest out of their private resources. The only entry in the books of the partnership will be a transfer of the retiring partner's capital to those remaining, in the agreed ratio. It is more likely, however, that a **revaluation** of all assets plus the valuation of goodwill may be required before agreeing what is due to the outgoing partner. How the sum due is to be settled may be in the partnership deed. The remaining partners may be hard pressed to find the cash necessary and so the partner may leave some or all of his interest in the firm as a loan.

Example

X, Y and Z are in partnership sharing profits and losses equally. At 31 December 19x9 the balance sheet appears as follows:

XYZ
Balance sheet at 31 December 19x9

	£		£
X Capital	13,200	Freehold property	11,000
Y Capital	12,900	Stock	8,500
Z Capital	11,700	Sundry debtors	10,600
Creditors	5,700	Cash and bank	13,400
	43,500		43,500

Z is to retire from this date but it is agreed that some assets are to be revalued: property £12,500, stock £8,200 and debtors £10,060. It is also agreed that up to £10,000 will be paid to Z in settlement out of the partnership bank account and any balance will be left in as a loan to the new partnership. Goodwill has been valued at £9,000 and is to be shown in the books.

Revaluation account

	£		£
Stocks	300	Goodwill	9,000
Sundry debtors	540	Property	1,500
Capital X	3,220		
Capital Y	3,220		
Capital Z	3,220		
	10,500		10,500

Note that all increases in assets are credited and decreases debited. This adjusts the old values in the books to the revised figure. The specific debtors in this case would be identified and written off. The surplus is divided in profit sharing proportions and transferred to the capital accounts thus closing the revaluation account. If there is a loss on revaluation the entries are reversed. The capital account for Z and the balance sheet after the retirement would appear as follows:

Capital account Z

	£			£
Bank	10,000	Balance	b/d	11,700
Transfer to loan account	4,920	Revaluation		3,220
	14,920			14,920

Balance sheet of X, Y as at 1 January 19x0

	£			£
X Capital	13,200		Goodwill	9,000
	3,200	16,420		
Y Capital	12,900		Property	12,500
	3,220			
		16,120		

Z Loan account	4,920	Stock	8,200
Creditors	5,700	Debtors	10,060
		Bank (£13,400 −	
		£10,000)	3,400
	43,160		43,160

Dissolution

A partnership may be **dissolved** on the death or retirement of a partner and subsequent failure to find a replacement or the inability of existing partners to finance the paying out of the outgoing partner. It may be dissolved when a new partner is admitted but not necessarily discontinued. If the business continues with new persons the firm itself will continue. **Liquidation** occurs when a partnership is dissolved permanently and proceeds shared. Such a process may be voluntary as when all partners agree to a sale of the business or it may be brought about as a result of poor results due to inefficiency, economic circumstances or personal problems of one or more partners. If the business can meet all its obligations there is no problem but sometimes a debit balance may be created on one (or more) of the partner's capital account. In this event the partner(s) concerned are required to bring in money from their own resources. If a partner is unable to pay off all or part of his debts then the other partners are required to make up the deficit. This creates complications because a ruling established early in the century in the case of Garner *v* Murray states that in the absence of agreement to the contrary the debit balance on the insolvent partner's capital account must be borne by the solvent partners in the proportions of last agreed capitals not in profit sharing ratio.

In order for the Garner *v* Murray rule to apply there must be no agreement to the contrary and the insolvent partner must be unable to contribute anything to the partnership. If fixed unalterable capitals are laid down in the agreement those are the last agreed capitals. Failing any evidence to the contrary if fixed capitals are not specified the last agreed capitals are those set out in the latest balance sheet signed by the partners. In the accounting process the loss on realization must first be ascertained and divided between all the partners. If one partner is unable, then, to make good any deficit in his capital account the rule is applied.

Example
The following is the latest balance sheet of X, Y and Z who are in partnership sharing profits and losses X one half, Y on third, and Z one sixth.

Balance sheet of X Y and Z as at 31 December 19x9

	£		£
Capital account X	6,000	Freehold property	7,300
Capital account Y	4,000	Stocks	9,900
		Debtors	5,700
Creditors	15,900	Bank	1,800
		Z Capital account	1,200
	25,900		25,900

Z is unable to meet any of his capital deficiency and has been declared bankrupt. The partners have decided to dissolve the partnership with effect from the balance sheet date subject to the following revaluations. Property £5,600, Stock £7,600, Debtors £5,500. Expenses of dissolution are expected to amount to £300. There is no clause in the partnership agreement anticipating this situation. The realization account, bank account and (in columnar form) the capital accounts of the partners to record this, assuming assets were realized for cash are shown below:

Note: **Columnar accounts** are frequently used to avoid repeating the same narrations and to save time.

Realization account

	£			£
Property	7,300	Bank: Property		5,600
Stock	9,900	Stock		7,600
Debtors	5,700	Debtors		5,500
Bank: Expenses	300	Loss on realization		
		X ½	2,250	
		Y ⅓	1,500	
		Z ⅙	750	4,500
	23,200			23,200

The asset accounts and expenses account are closed by debit to the realization account. The amount received for the assets is credited to the realization and debited to bank. The difference represents a loss on realization which must first be apportioned in profit sharing ratio. If the debits were less than the credits there would be a profit on realization and capital entries would be reversed.

Capital accounts

		X £	Y £	Z £			X £	Y £	Z £
Balance	b/f			1,200	Balance	b/f	6,000	4,000	
Loss on realization		2,250	1,500	750	X Capital				1,170
Z Capital		1,170	780		Y Capital				780
Bank		2,580	1,720						
		6,000	4,000	1,950			6,000	4,000	1,950

Z's deficiency of (1,200 + 750) 1,950 is shared between X and Y in ratio of:

$$6,000 : 4,000 \text{ i.e. } \frac{6}{10} \times 1,950 = 1,170 \text{ to X and } \frac{4}{10} \times 1,950 = 780 \text{ to Y}$$

The cash due to X and Y is the balancing figure credited to the bank account.

Bank account

		£		£
Balance	b/d	1,800	Expenses	300
Property		5,600	Creditors	15,900
Stock		7,600	Capital account X	2,580
Debtors		5,500	Capital account Y	1,720
		20,500		20,500

Conversion or sale to a limited company

The advantages of **limited companies** compared to partnership are considerable (see Section 3.4) and frequently when a partnership prospers the firm is converted to a limited company. Alternatively its success comes to the attention of an established company and they are incorporated by takeover. The purchase consideration is frequently, in the latter case, settled in shares as an alternative to cash. The accounting treatment is similar to that described previously except that frequently current liabilities as well as assets are taken over.

Exercise 3.5

Winter and Fenton are partners sharing all profits in the ratio 2:1. Their balance sheet at May 31 19xx ran as follows:

	£		£
Creditors	1,373	Cash	58
Capital: Winter	2,300	Debtors	705
Fenton	2,590	Premises	4,500
	5,263		5,263

Business has been poor, and the partners accept an offer from Buckingham Stores Ltd, to take over all their assets (save cash) and the creditors, on 1 June. The price is £3,700 (£1,400 in cash plus 2,000 new £1 ordinary shares issued by Buckingham Stores and valued at £1.15).

Closing expenses are £33, borne by the partnership and paid in cash. On 10 June, the price is paid, the partners each take 1,000 shares, and the partnership is wound up.

Required:

1 The accounts in the partners' ledger to show the dissolution.
2 Journal entry in the company's books to record the purchase (the old book values being retained, except that the premises are revalued at £4,390).

Key points
Although the cash is not being taken over the realization expenses are to be borne by the partnership and therefore will be debited to the realization account to ascertain profit or loss on realization.

Workings

		£
1	Net assets acquired by Buckingham Stores Ltd	
	= £4,500 + £705 − £1,373 =	3,832
	Consideration from Buckingham	3,700
	Loss	132
	Add Expenses on realization	33
	Total loss	165

Winter ⅔ × £165 = £110 Fenton ⅓ × £165 = 55
2   Consideration is £3,700 of which £2,300 (2,000 × £1.15) is in shares and share premium, therefore, cash balance must be £1,400. Since the shares are apportioned equally each partner will receive £1,150.
3   The cash balance after receipt from Buckingham Ltd plus the opening balance less the realization expenses is (£58 + £1,400 − £33) = £1,425. This is distributed to the partners according to balance due on the capital accounts – £1,040 (Winter) and £385 (Fenton) respectively.

Solution

1

Realization account

		£			£
1 June	Premises	4,500	1 June	Creditors	1,373
	Debtors	705		Buckingham Stores Ltd	3,700
	Cash-realization				
	expense	33		Loss on realization	
				Winter ⅔	110
				Fenton ⅓	55
		5,238			5,238

Premises account

			£			£
1 June	Balance	b/f	4,500	1 June	Realization account	4,500

Debtors account

			£			£
1 June	Balance	b/f	705	1 June	Realization account	705

Creditors account

		£				£
1 June	Realization account	1,373	1 June	Balance	b/f	1,373

Capital account – Winter

	£			£
1 June Realization account –		1 June Winter	b/f	2,300
loss	110			
Shares in Buckingham				
Ltd	1,150			
Cash	1,040			
	2,300			2,300

Capital account – Fenton

	£		£
1 June Realization account –		1 June Balance	1,590
loss	55		
Shares in Buckingham			
Ltd	1,150		
Cash	385		
	1,590		1,590

Buckingham Stores Ltd

	£		£
1 June Realization account	3,700	1 June Shares in Buckingham	
		Ltd	2,300
		Cash	1,400
	3,700		3,700

Shares in Buckingham Stores Ltd

	£		£
1 June Buckingham Stores Ltd	2,300	1 June Winter Capital account	1,150
		Fenton Capital Account	1,150
	2,300		2,300

Cash account

		£		£
1 June Balance	b/f	58	1 June Realization account	33
Buckingham Stores Ltd		1,400	Winter Capital account	1,040
			Fenton Capital account	385
		1,458		1,458

2   **Buckingham Stores – Journal**

			Dr	Cr
1 June	Sundry assets			
	Premises	Dr	4,390	
	Debtors		705	
	To creditors			1,373
	Winter and Fenton			3,700
	Capital reserve			22
			5,095	5,095
	Being assets and liabilities taken over at agreed purchase price and balance *transferred* to capital reserve			
1 June	Winter and Fenton	Dr	3,700	
	To Cash			1,400
	Ordinary share capital			2,000
	Share premium			300
			3,700	3,700
	Being satisfaction of purchase consideration on acquiring Winter and Fenton by issue of 2000 £1 ordinary shares at agreed price of £1.15 and balance in cash.			

3.4   The limited company

The logical step in business expansion is from sole trader to partnership but because it has so many advantages the **limited company** is the dominant form of business entity. Small companies are frequently formed instead of partnerships or grow out of partnerships so that although the number of sole traders and partnerships is greater limited companies control a far greater volume of business.

A limited company is a business which is a **separate legal entity** from its owners whose rights and obligations are determined by the shares they hold. There are three types of companies – **unlimited, limited by guarantee** and **limited by shares**. Unlimited companies are the same as large partnerships and are rare. Companies limited by guarantee are usually those formed for non-profit making purposes such as professional bodies and charities. In the event of financial difficulties the members have guaranteed to meet the company's liabilities up to a limit per member. The most important class is the company limited by shares. Any shareholder agrees to take up a number of shares of a specified price and when he has paid the full amount for the shares he cannot be called on further in respect of any debts the company incurs. There are two types of company limited by shares.

1   *Private limited companies:*   These are indicated by the word **limited** or abbreviation **Ltd** after the name of the company. These companies are usually (but not always) small and like partnerships the members normally take active part in management. Being limited does protect

the members from having to risk their personal wealth other than the amount of shareholding. It also enables easier continuity of the business and wider facilities for raising finance. Such companies may not raise money directly from the public.

2   *Public limited companies:*   These are indicated by the words Public Limited Company or more frequently the abbreviation PLC after the name of the company. These companies have to meet special requirements which include not less than two directors and a minimum issued share capital of £50,000.

Formation of a limited company

All limited companies are required to conform to the legislation contained in the various Companies Acts issued between 1948 and 1985. The company is formed by the promoters who submit two major documents, the **memorandum of association** and the **articles of association**. The memorandum of association must contain five items:

1   The name of the company.
2   The part of the United Kingdom in which the registered office is to be situated.
3   The objects of the company – which must be stated in detail and will be strictly adhered to.
4   A statement to the effect that the liability of its members is to be limited.
5   Details of the share capital with which the company is to be registered and the division of it into shares of a fixed amount.

The memorandum of association is the document which determines and regulates the company's dealings with the outside world. There are a number of features which are common to all commercial and industrial companies which may be listed as follows:

1   The capital required may be subscribed by any number of shareholders (maximum 2) in differing amounts as convenient, and is not normally returnable to shareholders.
2   Liability of shareholders is limited as previously stated.
3   Shares may be transferred from one person to another without affecting the existence or the management of the company.
4   The company is treated as a legal entity in its own right, distinct from the shareholders comprising it at any one time, with regard to its dealings with its shareholders and the world at large.

The internal dealings of a company are controlled by the articles of association. The Companies Act 1985 contains a model set of 'Articles' known as Table A. A company may adopt all or part of Table A, or it may draft its own articles, which normally deal with the following:

1   Powers and duties of directors and officers.
2   The issue of share capital, its transfer and foreiture etc.
3   The keeping of books of account.
4   The appointment of auditors.
5   The holding of shareholders' meetings, voting.

This broad guide to the methods of working of limited companies is not intended to cover Company Law in detail, and students must make their own detailed studies in that area as required. The law relating to accountancy matters will, however, be dealt with in more detail in the appropriate places.

In the accounts of a sole trader, the capital introduced to start the business is debited to the bank or cash account and credited to the traders' capital account. In the case of a partnership the capital introduced by each partner is credited to his individual capital account. The same system is operated in the case of a limited company, though, since there are likely to be many shareholders, it would not be reasonable to maintain a capital account for each, so a total **share capital account** is kept, with a **share register**, which is not part of the double entry system, to record the holding of each individual shareholder.

Capital

Dealing with the capital of a limited company differs from dealing with the capital of a sole trader or partnership as:

1   There may be a very large number of shareholders.
2   There may be more than one class of share.
3   The rights and obligations of the shareholders are closely defined by law.
4   Capital is repaid to shareholders only in exceptional circumstances and then is subject to conditions laid down by law.

Shares may be of different classes:

1   *Preference shares:*   A class of shares having a priority claim on any profits for the dividend specified and usually upon the assets in event of liquidation or winding up. They may be cumulative in which case all arrears of dividends are payable out of future profits or non-cumulative.
2   *Ordinary shares:*   A class of shares entitling the holder to participate in the balance of distributable profits after the prior claims have been met. These shares also normally carry voting rights which means the holders ultimately control the company, although some strong companies have issued non-voting ordinary shares. Occasionally by reason of large sums paid to them on purchase the original founders may take ordinary shares in the consideration (purchase price) which have deferred rights – that is they do not participate in profits until all other shareholders have received a return.

Issuing of shares

The accountant is primarily concerned with recording the transactions involved and compliance with the legal requirements where necessary when a **share issue** is made. Shares may be issued at any time up to the level of **authorized capital** stated in the company's memorandum. Separate accounts must be opened for each class of share capital. Entries into the accounts are made by means of a journal entry which states:

●   How many shares were issued.
●   What class they were.
●   What their nominal value was.
●   How much was payable at the time.
●   The authority e.g. directors' resolution for the issue.

Shares may be issued:

1   At *par value:*   This means that a share of nominal value of £1.00 is issued to a new or existing shareholder at a price of £1.00.

2   At *a premium:*   This means that a share is sold for a price higher than its nominal value. It is only practicable if the offer for sale is a popular one. The premium i.e. profit on the sale of the shares has to be treated differently to normal trading profits. If a share with a nominal value of £1.00 is sold for £1.25 this represents a premium of 25p over the par value of £1.00 for each share issued.

3   Section 100 of the Companies Act 1985 prohibits the issue of shares at a discount.

Shares may be:

1   Payable in full on issue, in cash.

2   Payable by instalments in cash.

3   Payable in full or in part in some other consideration other than cash – as when the seller agrees to accept shares in a company in payment for his business.

4   Issued as bonus shares – payable from undistributed profits or reserves.

Most shares are issued requiring payment in instalments. This makes the offer more attractive as the investor does not have to find all the money at one time. The stages in dealing result in accounts being opened corresponding to each stage:

1   *Application account:*   This records monies received from all prospective shareholders. It is, in effect, a control account of all the individual applicants. It is unlikely that the number of shares applied for will equate with those on offer. If the issue is **oversubscribed** i.e. the number of shares applied for is greater than the quantity offered, the surplus money is returned to unsuccessful applicants or transferred on their behalf to successive stages. If shares applied for are less than on offer the issue is **undersubscribed** and the deficiency taken up by underwriters – if previously agreed.

2   *Allotment account:*   If an application is successful a second instalment is usually due when the shares are allotted to the holder. If he has not had any surplus application money transferred then this payment must be made in a stated period of receiving notice of the allotment. For convenience these two stages are usually combined into one application and allotment account. This avoids unnecessary transfers between them.

3   *Call account:*   A **call** takes place every time an instalment of the full price of the share is requested from the shareholder. A typical sequence for a £1.00 share might be payment of 25p on application, 25p on allotment, 20p on first and second call and 10p on the final call. Accounts for these are opened on the appropriate dates and when completed the shares are **fully paid up** and the shareholder cannot be called on for any further payment.

Calls in arrear

If a shareholder fails to pay the money due on allotment or subsequent call the amount must be credited to the appropriate call account and debited to a **calls in arrear** account. If the amount due is not subsequently forthcoming the shares may be forfeited. In this event the money received is not returnable and the shares may be reissued for an amount to cover the balance or up to the total original price – thus making a profit.

Exercise 3.6

On 1 April 19x2 the directors of Blissett PLC issued 60,000 £1 ordinary shares at £1.25 a share, 50p payable upon application (including the premium) 30p on allotment, 20p on 1 November 19x2 and the balance on 1 January 19x3.

By 9 April 19x2, when the lists were closed, applications for 90,000 shares had been received. It was decided to reject completely the applications for 10,000 shares, and to allot the shares to the other applicants in proportion to their application. On 15 April cash was returned to the rejected applicants, but the other oversubscription money was carried forward to be set off against the allotment. The shares were issued.

The balance due on allotment was received in full on 28 April.

All shareholders, with the exception of the holder of 1,000 shares, paid the first call. The unpaid shares were declared forfeit in December 19x2, but had not been reissued by the time of the balance sheet date, 31 December.

Required:
1 Prepare journal entries including those for cash to record these transactions.
2 Show the relevant entries in the company's balance sheet as at 31 December 19x2.

Source: SCCA
The accounts have also been included in the solution below to complete illustration of treatment.

Key points
The 50p payable on application includes the premium which is £1.25 less £1.00 (nominal value) = 25p share hence only the balance of 25p is in respect of the capital. It is essential to follow the transactions in date sequence. The treatment on forfeiture must be noted and all adjustments made accordingly. There is no refund of money paid by the company to the original subscriber.

Workings

Number of shares applied for	= 90,000
∴ Application money received	= 90,000 × 50p = £45,000
Application rejected	= 10,000
∴ Refund of application money	= 10,000 × 50p = £5,000
Balance of shares applied for	= 80,000
Number of shares allotted	= 60,000
∴ Oversubscription money	= 20,000 × 50p = £10,000
Money due on allotment	= £60,000 × 30p = £18,000
∴ Balance due on allotment	= £18,000 − £10,000 = £8,000

(a)	(b) £	(c)	(d)	(e) £	(f)
10,000	5,000	Nil	Nil	5,000	
80,000	40,000	60,000	48,000	–	8,000
90,000	45,000	60,000	48,000	5,000	8,000

(a)   Number of shares applied for.
(b)   Application money received – Column (a) × 50p.
(c)   Number of shares allotted.
(d)   Money due for application and allotment – Column (a) × 60p.
(e)   Refund due Column (a) × 50p (for application rejected).
(f)   Balance due on allotment Column (c) × 30p – £10,000.

Common errors
Miscalculation of, and failure to balance, money and share entries at every stage. Incorrect dates for transactions. Reversing entries in the journal.

Key words
● Application   ● Forfeit
● Premium   ● Oversubscribed
● Allotment

Solution

1   **Blisset PLC**
                                        Journal

1982			£	£
9 Apr	Bank	Dr	45,000	
	To application and allotment account			45,000
	Application monies received for 90,000 shares at 50p each			
15 Apr	Application and allotment account		5,000	
	To bank			5,000
	Monies returned at 50p per share on 10,000 applications rejected			
15 Apr	Application and allotment account		48,000	
	To share premium account			15,000
	Ordinary share capital account			33,000
	Share premium at 25p per share on 60,000 shares and balance at 55p* credited to capital account			
28 Apr	Bank		8,000	
	To application and allotment account			8,000
	Balance due on allotment of 60,000 shares			
1 Nov	First call account		12,000	
	To ordinary share capital account			12,000
	Total money due on 60,000 shares at 20p per share			
1 Nov	Bank		11,800	
	To first call account			11,800
	Being call money of 20p per share received on 59,000 shares			
Dec	Ordinary share capital account		750	
	Share premium account		250	
	To first call account			200
	Forfeited shares account			800
	Monies received to date on 1,000 shares forfeited for non-payment of call			

* 55p = 25p + 30p

2

Blisset PLC
Balance sheet as at 31 December 19x2

	£
Assets employed	
Current assets	
Cash at Bank	59,800
Financed by:	
Ordinary share capital – Authorized issue	
59,000 ordinary shares of £1	
75p per share called up	44,250
Reserves and surplus	
Share premium	14,750
	59,000
Forfeited shares	800
	59,800

Ordinary share capital account

		£			£
Dec	Forfeited shares	750	15 Apr	Application and allotment	33,000
	Balance	44,250	1 Nov	First call	12,000
		45,000			45,000
				Balance	44,250

Application and allotment account

		£			£
15 Apr	Share premium	15,000	9 Apr	Bank	45,000
15 Apr	Ordinary share capital	33,000	28 Apr	Bank	8,000
15 Apr	Bank	5,000			
		53,000			53,000

First call account

		£			£
1 Nov	Ordinary share capital	12,000	1 Nov	Bank	11,800
				Forfeited shares	200
		12,000			12,000

Share premium account

		£			£
Dec	Forfeited shares	250	15 Apr	Application and	15,000
	Balance	c/d 14,750		allotment	
		15,000			15,000
				Balance	14,750

Forfeited shares account

		£			£
Dec	First call	200	Dec	Ordinary share capital	750
	Balance	c/d 800		Share premium	250
		1,000			1,000
				Balance	800

The accounts in respect of debentures are kept on a similar basis to the above. If the amounts are payable in full on application then the entries are as follows:

Debit	Sundry shareholders
Credit	Capital account
	with full value of shares
Debit Bank	
Credit	Sundry shareholders
	with money received

Summary of terms used in reference to share capital

- *Authorized:* The capital that is specified in the memorandum of association. The type, class number and amount must be stated. It must also be stated on the balance sheet. Alternative terms are **registered** or **nominal**.
- *Issued or subscribed:* All the shares so far issued either for cash or in consideration for acquisitions.
- *Called up:* That part of the issued capital which has been called up by the company.
- *Paid up:* That part of the called up capital which has been paid or issued for consideration on acquisition.
- *Uncalled:* The part of the share price which has still not been called up.

Share issues not providing additional funds

A company may, on occasion, issue shares which do not raise additional finance. Alternative terms used for these issues are **bonus issues**, capitalization issues or **scrip issues**. The term preferred is scrip issue since the word bonus implies the giving of something extra when this is not so. A scrip issue may be made to bring the nominal share capital more into line with market values. This may be desirable because reserves have accumulated over the years and the market price per share is high inhibiting dealings on the stock exchange. Alternatively the company may have made good profits but have no cash to pay out dividends. In this case the receiving shareholder may sell the shares received if he prefers the money.

Example

Balance sheet of AB Ltd as at 30 September

	£
Issued share capital	
50,000 ordinary shares of £1	50,000
Revenue reserves	25,000
	75,000
Represented by	
Net tangible assets	75,000
Market value per share	£2.00

It is proposed to make a scrip issue of one £1 nominal value ordinary share for every two now held. The effect of the proposals on the balance sheet of AB Ltd after the scrip issue are shown below and the position of the holder of 100 shares, before and after the issue is indicated.

On a balance sheet basis each share is worth $\frac{£75,000}{50,000} = £1.50$ before the issue. After the issue the balance sheet will appear as follows:

	£
Issued share capital	
75,000 ordinary shares of £1	75,000
Represented by	
Net tangible assets	75,000

On a balance sheet basis each share is now worth $\frac{£75,000}{75,000} = £1.00$.

Before the issue the shareholder had $100 \times £1.50 = £150$ equity interest. After the issue the shareholder has $150 \times £1.00 = £150$ equity interest, i.e. his position is unaltered.

Market values

Total market value before scrip issue $= 50,000 \times £2.00 = £100,000$
Total market value after scrip issue $= £100,000$

But since there are now 75,000 shares each share is worth $\frac{£100,000}{75,000} = £1.33$.

Market value of 100 shares before scrip issue $= 100 \times £2 = £200$
Market value of 150 shares after scrip issue $= 150 \times £1.33 = £200$

The above figures demonstrate how *theoretically* the financial position of the shareholder is unaffected in terms of total valuation. In *practice*, his total value will probably be affected since the market may take the view that the dividend rate (in the absence of legal restraint) may be maintained at the same level on the new nominal holding. Thus if a rate of 10 per cent was being paid before the issue, the dividend due on a holding of 100 £1 shares would be £10, but after the issue the entitlement with a *maintained* rate of 10 per cent on a holding of 150 shares would be £15. In view of this increased distribution the share price may move upward. Conversely, if existing and potential investors take a pessimistic view of the company's potential then the share price will move downard.

For similar reasons a company may decide to split its shares, i.e. to reduce their nominal value. If each £1 nominal value share is converted to two 50p shares then the market value of each original share will be halved. The distinction between this and the operation described in the previous paragraph is that there would be no movement out of reserves to nominal capital on the balance sheets. The total nominal share capital would remain unaltered and only the quantity and par value of the shares would be affected; a maintained dividend of 10 per cent would provide only the same sum in dividends as previously.

'No-par-value' shares

Although it is illegal in the United Kingdom, some countries permit the issue of shares of **no par value**. In the first instance such shares are issued at a price determined by the company and the proceeds are credited to a no-par-value share capital account. If further no-par-value shares are issued at a later date, they are issued at a price as close to the market price as possible and the proceeds are credited to the no-par-value share capital account. Consequently, the total amount received from the issue of shares accumulates in this account, and there is no question of any share premium arising. The use of no-par-value shares is advocated on the grounds that after a company has been successful for a considerable period and has ploughed back profits, the par value of the shares gives no guide to the value of the assets representing the shareholder's interest in the company.

No complications arise since each no-par-value share is entitled to the same voting rights and the same amount of dividend at each distribution of profit. There is no par value to mislead anyone trying to work out the asset value of the shares.

Redemption or purchase of shares

A major change confirmed by the Companies Act 1985 was the granting of permission for a company to purchase its own shares – a practice which had been legal for some time in many EEC countries and the USA. There are limitations – primarily that some of the remaining shares *must* be irredeemable, the dealing must be permitted by the articles of association, shareholders' approval must be obtained and disclosure of the dealings must be made. Prior to this the only shares which could be redeemed were preference shares specifically indicated to be redeemable at the time of original issue. So that the position of creditors shall not be unfavourably affected by the redemption, the funds required for the purpose may only come out of profits which would be available for distribution or out of the proceeds of a further issue of shares or share premium.

When such shares are redeemed out of profits it is necessary to open a capital redemption reserve, crediting this account with the amount paid in redemption of the shares and debiting the account or accounts where the undistributed profits are recorded (usually the revenue reserve account or the profit and loss appropriation account). For example, had the only entries been in the cash account and the redeemable preference share capital account, the revenue reserves would remain on the balance sheet and there would be nothing to prevent the company distributing them later by way of dividend. If this were done, the cash for the repayment of the shares would have come from other resources of the company, thus reducing the amount which creditors could expect to be available to meet the company's debts.

If we assume that Central Provision Store PLC had raised the additional capital by an issue of 50,000 6 per cent redeemable preference shares repayable ten years later, the balance sheet would have appeared as follows:

Central Provision Store PLC
Balance sheet as at 1 January 1979

	£	£
Total assets		253,600
Total external liabilities		99,000
Capital and reserves		
Called up share capital		
100,200 ordinary shares of £1.00 each	100,200	
50,000 6% redeemable preference shares of £1 each	50,000	
		150,200
Revenue reserves		
Balance of profit and loss account		4,400
		253,600

Let us now look into the future and assume that in ten years £60,000 profits have been ploughed back into the company and that by a happy coincidence these profits are reflected by an increase in cash of £60,000 while all other items remained unchanged. The company is going to repay the redeemable preference shares in cash on 1 January 1989.

The balance sheet at 31 December 1988 will differ from the one at 1 January 1979, only in the following respects:

	1979	1988
	£	£
Total assets	253,600	313,600
General reserve and balance of		
Profit and loss account	4,400	64,400

The entries on redeeming the shares would be:

6% Redeemable preference share capital account

	£		£
Cash	50,000	Balance	b/f 50,000

Cash account

	£		£
Balance	?	Redeemable preference share capital	50,000

General reserve

	£		£
Capital redemption reserve	50,000	Balance	b/f 60,000
Balance	c/f 10,000		
	60,000		60,000
		Balance	b/f 10,000

Capital redemption reserve account

		£
	General reserve	50,000

On 1 January 1989, after the shares have been redeemed, the balance sheet would appear as follows:

Central Provision Store PLC
Balance sheet as at 1 January 1989

	£	£
Total assets (£313,600 *less* £50,000)		263,600
Total external liabilities		99,000
Capital and reserves		
Called up share capital		
100,200 ordinary shares of £1	100,200	
Reserves		
Capital redemption reserve	50,000	
General reserve	10,000	
Balance of profit and loss account	4,400	
		164,600
		263,600

The capital redemption reserve may be used for the issue of **bonus shares** as described on page 118. Over a number of years a company may plough back part of its profits, or after a number of years of rising prices a company may revalue its assets. The result will be an increase in reserves and will normally cause a rise in the market price of the company's shares. Companies may not like the market price of their shares to be much above the par value. They are not in a position to distribute their reserves by way of dividend because the resources involved are invested in the business; the cash is not available. The alternative is the issue of **bonus shares** to the existing shareholders, the company paying for them in full out of the reserves. Thus, a company whose capital is £100,000 and which has £50,000 in the form of reserves (share premium, capital redemption reserve and/or balance of the profit and loss account), may issue 50,000 bonus shares of £1.00 each. This will raise the issued capital to £150,000 and reduce the reserves by £50,000. Such an action is usually contemplated when the company is in a position to continue paying the same rate of dividend on the enlarged capital. In the example given, it would mean increasing the amount of profits distributed by 50 per cent.

The final accounts of limited companies

The main distinction between the unlimited liability business entities – sole traders and partnerships – and limited liability entities is that frequently ownership is separated from control. If the sole traders or partners are incompetent then they will suffer a major financial loss. If the directors of a public limited company act incompetently the losses fall on the shareholders. Obviously the larger the individual shareholding the greater would be the proportionate share of the losses and in the case of private limited companies the owners are probably majority shareholders. With large public companies history has shown that the investors need protection from the activities of careless, criminal and unscrupulous promoters and directors of companies. Legislation in the form of Companies Acts has been introduced and successively modified by various Acts between 1892 and 1985. Major legislation was created in 1948, 1967, 1976, 1980 and 1981 and the latest act is a codifying one of 1985 confirming and amending previous legislation still applicable. All limited companies have to comply with the requirements of the Act and this includes a requirement to deliver audited accounts to the registrar. The majority of companies are small in size and until the Act of 1967 were classified as exempt private companies and a private company was excused from filing accounts with the registrar of companies. This concession was abolished in the Companies Act 1967. The legislature recognized, however, that there was a preponderance of smaller companies and in the 1981 Act introduced definitions of small and medium-sized companies with less stringent requirements. The Companies Act covers all aspects of legislation in respect of limited liability – the following sections are concerned only with the accounting requirements particularly in respect of published accounts.

The main accounting requirements are set out in Schedule 4 to the Companies Act 1985. This covers companies other than those engaged in banking, insurance and shipping which have modifications. A major impetus for revision was to bring UK practice into line with the requirements of the European Economic Community. Important provisions are that every balance sheet and profit and loss account shall show a **true and fair view**. A major change introduced is that the accounts have to be presented in one of the standard formats contained in the Act. The order of items is laid down and if items are combined details must be shown in notes. Items must comply with four accounting principles enshrined in the Act and they are:

● The company's business shall be assumed to be a going concern.
● Accounting policies shall be consistently applied.
● Amounts should be decided on a prudent basis.
● The matching concept shall be followed i.e. all accrued income and charges shall be accounted for.

If accounts are prepared on any basis other than the above a note must be appended to the accounts. There are two alternative forms of balance sheet and four alternative forms of profit and loss account.

Balance sheets

Every balance sheet must show the items listed in either of the two formats permitted. Once adopted the directors must continue to use the same format unless there are special reasons for the change. The most popular format for published accounts is Format 1 – **vertical presentation** – (see page 125). The alternative Format 2 (see page 128) is the older dual sided version. As discussed in Section 1.2 although Format 2 is a logical one since a balance sheet is a list of final balances, Format 1 is becoming increasingly standard for all forms of final accounts including sole traders and partnerships. The format shown in Figure 3.1 is taken from the pro forma included in the Companies Act 1981 but specimen figures have been included in order to show the relationship between the two alternatives in practice. The letters identifying the various subgroups e.g. 'E' in the case of amounts falling due within one year may be omitted in practice and a particular section or item may be omitted if there is no amount for the current or preceding year. Any item may be shown in greater detail than required by the format if it is considered desirable but the following items may no longer be treated as assets in the balance sheet

1 Preliminary expenses.
2 Expenses of, or commission on, any issue of shares or debentures.
3 Costs of research.

Comparative figures for the previous years must be shown.
The following are important points to note:

● Called up share capital not paid can appear in either position indicated.
● Concessions, patents, licences, trade marks and similar rights and assets are only to be included if acquired for valuable consideration and not shown under goodwill or if they have been created by the company itself.

- Goodwill is only to be included to the extent that it was acquired for valuable consideration.
- Nominal value of own shares held should be shown separately.
- The amounts falling due after more than one year should be noted in respect of each class of debtors.
- Prepayments and accrued income may be shown in the alternative positions indicated.
- The amount of any convertible loans should be shown separately.
- Payments received on account should be shown separately if not shown as deductions from stocks.
- The amount of creditors in respect of taxation and social security should be shown separately from other creditors.
- Accruals and deferred income may be shown in alternative positions.
- Net current assets must take account of prepayments and accrued income whenever shown.
- Called up share capital which has been paid up must be distinguished from allotted share capital.
- For creditors, amounts falling due within one year must be aggregated and shown separately from those due after one year in respect of each item.

Figure 3.1   *Balance sheet Format 1*

			£000
A	**Called up share capital not paid**		4
B	**Fixed assets**		
I	Intangible assets		
	1 Development costs	180	
	2 Concessions, patents, licences,		
	trademarks and similar rights and assets	200	
	3 Goodwill	320	
	4 Payments on account	10	
			710
II	Tangible assets		
	1 Land and buildings	1,300	
	2 Plant and machinery	1,800	
	3 Fixtures, fittings, tools and equipment	450	
	4 Payments on account and assets in course		
	of construction	140	
			3,690
III	Investments		
	1 Shares in group companies	600	
	2 Loans to group companies	50	
	3 Shares in related companies	120	
	4 Loans to related companies	20	
	5 Other investments other than loans	25	
	6 Other loans	10	
	7 Own shares	15	
			840
			5,240
C	**Current assets**		
I	Stocks		
	1 Raw materials and consumables	1,215	
	2 Work in progress	1,325	
	3 Finished goods and goods for resale	2,465	
	4 Payments on account	12	
			5,017
II	Debtors		
	1 Trade debtors	635	
	2 Amounts owed by group companies	27	
	3 Amounts owed by related companies	13	
	4 Other debtors	12	
	5 Called up share capital not paid	–	
	6 Prepayments and accrued income	16	
			703

Continued over.

III	Investments			
	1	Shares in group companies	13	
	2	Own shares	6	
	3	Other investments	24	
				43
IV	Cash at bank and in hand		117	
D	**Prepayments and accrued Income**		–	
				5,880

E	**Creditors: amounts falling due within one year**			
	1	Debenture loans	12	
	2	Bank loans and overdrafts	8	
	3	Payments received on account	13	
	4	Trade creditors	516	
	5	Bills of exchange payable	43	
	6	Amounts owed to group companies	19	
	7	Amounts owed to related companies	3	
	8	Other creditors including taxation and social security	186	
	9	Accruals and deferred income	13	
				(813)

F	**Net current assets/liabilities**		5,067
G	**Total assets *less* current liabilities**		10,311

H	**Creditors: amounts falling due after one year**			
	1	Debenture loans	800	
	2	Bank loans and overdrafts	35	
	3	Payments received on account	10	
	4	Trade creditors	14	
	5	Bills of exchange payable	12	
	6	Amounts owed to group companies	25	
	7	Amounts owed to related companies	17	
	8	Other creditors including taxation and social security	135	
	9	Accruals and deferred income	16	
				1,064
I	**Provisions for liabilities and charges**			
	1	Pensions and similar obligations	38	
	2	Taxation including deferred taxation	1,720	
	3	Other provisions	63	
				1,821
J	**Accruals and deferred income**		–	
				(2,885)
				7,426

K		**Capital and reserves**		
	I	Called up share capital		5,500
	II	Share premium account		80
	III	Revaluation reserve		210
	IV	Other reserves		
		1 Capital redemption reserve	180	
		2 Reserve for own shares	55	
		3 Reserve provided for by articles of association	30	
		4 Other reserves	45	
				310
	V	Profit and loss account		1,326
				7,426

Notes: Prepayments and accrued income may be shown in position CII6 *or* as a separate item D. Accruals and deferred income may be shown in position E9, H9 or as separate item J. Comparative figures must be included. The items described as group or related companies will only be met in consolidated accounts of groups of companies.

Figure 3.2   *Balance sheet – Format 2*   *£000*

A		**Called up share capital not paid**			4
B		**Fixed assets**			
	I	Intangible assets			
		1 Development costs	180		
		2 Concessions, patents, licences trademarks and similar rights and assets	200		
		3 Goodwill	320		
		4 Payments on accounts	10		
				710	
	II	Tangible assets			
		1 Land and buildings	1,300		
		2 Plant and machinery	1,800		
		3 Fixtures fittings, tools and equipment	450		
		4 Payments on account and assets in course of construction	140		
				3,690	
	III	Investments			
		1 Shares in group companies	600		
		2 Loans to group companies	50		
		3 Shares in related companies	120		
		4 Loans to related companies	20		
		5 Other investments other than loans	25		
		6 Other loans	10		
		7 Own shares	15		
				840	
					5,240
C		**Current assets**			
	I	Stocks			
		1 Raw materials and consumables	1,215		
		2 Work in progress	1,325		
		3 Finished goods and goods for resale	2,465		
		4 Payments on account	12		
				5,017	
	II	Debtors			
		1 Trade debtors	635		
		2 Amounts owed by group companies	27		
		3 Amounts owed by related companies	13		
		4 Other debtors	12		
		5 Called up share capital not paid	–		
		6 Prepayments and accrued income	16		
				703	
	III	Investments			
		1 Shares in group companies	13		
		2 Own shares	6		
		3 Other investments	24		
				43	
	IV	Cash at bank and in hand		117	
D		**Prepayments and accrued income**		–	
					5,880
					11,124

			£000	
A		**Capital and reserves**		
	I	Called up share capital	5,500	
	II	Share premium account	80	
	III	Revaluation reserve	210	
	IV	Other reserves		

		£000	£000
1	Capital redemption reserve	180	
2	Reserve for own shares	55	
3	Reserve provided for by articles of association	30	
4	Other reserves	45	
			310

			£000	£000
	V	Profit and loss account	1,326	
				7,426
B		**Provisions for liabilities and charges**		
	1	Pensions and similar obligations	38	
	2	Taxation including deferred taxation	1,720	
	3	Other provisions	63	
				1,821
C		**Creditors**		
	1	Debenture loans (800 + 12)	812	
	2	Bank loans and overdrafts (35 + 8)	43	
	3	Payments received on account (10 + 13)	23	
	4	Trade creditors (14 + 516)	530	
	5	Bills of exchange payable (12 + 43)	55	
	6	Amounts owed to group companies (25 + 19)	44	
	7	Amounts owed to related companies (17 + 3)	20	
	8	Other creditors including taxation, and social security (135 + 186)	321	
	9	Accruals and deferred income (16 + 13)	29	
				1,877
				11,124

Profit and loss accounts

The Companies Act offers the choice of four formats for presenting the profit and loss. Guidance as to layout is again given in Schedule 1, Part 1 of the 1981 Act. Formats 1 and 2 are vertical representations and Formats 3 and 4 are horizontal or twin-sided formats.

Figure 3.3   Profit and loss account – Format 1

		£000	£000	£000
1	Turnover		5,600	
2	Cost of sales		(4,120)	
3	Gross profit or loss		1,480	
4	Distribution costs		(105)	
5	Administrative expenses		(453)	
6	Other operating income		32	
7	Income from shares in group companies		76	
8	Income from shares in related companies		16	
9	Income from other fixed asset investments		19	
10	Other interest receivable and similar income		7	
11	Amounts written off investments		(15)	
12	Interest payable and similar charges		(135)	
13	Tax on profit or loss on ordinary activities		(260)	
14	Profit or loss on ordinary activities after taxation		662	
15	Extraordinary income	42		
16	Extraordinary charges	(23)		
17	Extraordinary profit or loss	19		
18	Tax on extraordinary profit or loss	(7)		
			12	
19	Other taxes not shown under above items		(9)	
20	Profit or loss for the financial year		665	

Figure 3.4   Profit and loss account – Format 2

		£000	£000
1	Turnover		5,600
2	Change in stocks of finished goods and in work in progress		25
3	Own work capitalized		60
4	Other operating income		32
5	(a) Raw materials and consumables	(1,123)	
	(b) Other external charges	(937)	(2,060)
6	Staff costs:		
	(a) Wages and salaries	(1,980)	
	(b) Social security costs	(230)	
	(c) Other pension costs	(106)	(2,316)
7	(a) Depreciation and other amounts written off tangible and intangible fixed assets	(358)	
	(b) Exceptional amounts written off current assets	(13)	(371)
8	Other operating charges		(16)
9	Income from shares in group companies		76
10	Income from shares in related companies		16
11	Income from other fixed asset investments		19
12	Other interest receivable and similar income		7
13	Amounts written off investments		(15)
14	Interest payable and similar charges		(135)
15	Tax on profit or loss on ordinary activities		(260)
16	Profit or loss on ordinary activities after taxation		662
17	Extraordinary income	42	
18	Extraordinary charges	(23)	
19	Extraordinary profit or loss	19	
20	Tax on extraordinary profit or loss	(7)	
			12
21	Other taxes not shown under the above items		(9)
22	Profit and loss for the financial year		665

Figure 3.5   Profit and loss account – Format 3

A		Charges	£000	B		Income	£000
	1	Cost of sales	4,120		1	Turnover	5,600
		Gross profit/loss	1,480				
			5,600				5,600
						Gross profit	1,480
	2	Distribution costs	105		2	Other operating income	32
	3	Administrative costs	453		3	Income from shares in group companies	76
	4	Amounts w/o investments	15		4	Income from shares in related companies	16
	5	Interest payable	135		5	Income from other fixed asset and investment	19
	6	Tax on profit/loss on ordinary activities	260		6	Other interest receivable and similar income	7
	7	Profit (loss) on ordinary activities	662				
			1,630				1,630
					7	Profit on ordinary activities after taxation	662
	8	Extraordinary charges	23		8	Extraordinary income	42
	9	Tax on extraordinary profit/loss	7				
	10	Other taxes not shown under above items	9				
	11	Profit/loss for financial year	665				
			704				704

Figure 3.6   Profit and loss account – Format 4

A	Charges	£000	B	Income	£000
1 Reduction in stocks of finished goods or work in progress			1 Turnover		5,600
			2 Increase in stock of finished goods or work in progress		25
2 (a) Raw materials and consumables	1,123		3 Own work capitalized		60
(b) Other external charges	937		4 Other operating income		32
		2,060	5 Income from shares in group companies		76
3 Staff costs			6 Income from shares in related companies		16
(a) Wages and salaries	1,980		7 Income from other fixed assets and investments		19
(b) Social security costs	230				
(c) Other pension	106		8 Other interest receivable and similar income		7
		2,316			
4 (a) Depreciation and other amounts w/o tangible and intangible fixed assets	358				
(b) Exceptional amounts w/o current assets	13				
		371			
5 Other operating charges		16			
6 Amounts w/o investment		15			
7 Interest payable and similar charges		135			
8 Tax on profit/loss on ordinary activities		260			
9 Profit on ordinary activities after taxation		662			
		5,835			5,835

Continued over.

A	Charges	£000	B	Income	£000
			9 Profit on ordinary activities after taxation		662
10 Extraordinary charges		23	10 Extraordinary income		42
11 Tax on extraordinary profit/loss		7			
12 Other tax not shown under above items		9			
13 Profit/loss for financial year		665			
		704			704

The distinction between Format 1 and Format 2 is that Format 1 is analysed on a functional basis whereas Format 2 is on an expense basis. The choice is likely to be influenced by the nature of the business and the desires for disclosure by the board. Format 1 emphasizes the cost of sales and gross profit and is suited to trading organizations whereas Format 2 details the types of costs and information presented in traditional manufacturing accounts. In either case much more disclosure is now required than previously and the choice, once made, has to be maintained. Note that items 17–22 in Format 2 correspond to items 15–20 in Format 1. Profit or loss on ordinary activities after taxation is the same and must be disclosed. No details are given of balances brought forward or appropriations in the formats so these items will be additional in actual layouts.

Formats 3 and 4 are dual sided (horizontal) versions of Formats 1 and 2. They are unlikely to be found a great deal in published accounts and as these are the ones most people have access to, emphasis throughout this book is on vertical layouts. Additionally most published accounts are in respect of groups of companies so that reference to group and related companies is included here although the accounts of such companies are not fully described until Chapter 4. An example of Formats 3 and 4 using the same illustrative data as for Formats 1 and 2 is shown on pages 132–4.

Historic cost basis

The Companies Act lays down in Section B of Part II Schedule 4 the rules to be followed if using the **historic cost basis**. Section C contains the so-called **alternative accounting** rules. The latter apply in the unusual situations where accounts are prepared at current costs. The following rules apply to balance sheet items where their value is determined under historical cost rules.

Fixed assets

The amount to be included is the purchase price or production cost less any provision made for depreciation.

Current assets

These must be included at purchase price or production cost except where net realizable value is less than these. Production cost comprises direct costs plus reasonable overhead and interest. Distribution costs may not be included. The purchase price or production cost of items of stock or fungible assets including investments may be determined by one of the following methods. A fungible asset is one which is interchangeable in function or value and for practical purposes indistinguishable from another e.g. debtors and short-term investments. The method chosen must be one which appears appropriate to the directors.

Permitted methods are:

1 FIFO (first in first out).
2 LIFO (last in first out).
3 Weighted average price.
4 Any other similar method.

Some of these methods, particularly LIFO, are not advocated by SSAP 9 but are, nonetheless legal.

Notes to the accounts

Schedule 4 also gives details of notes which may be appended to the accounts to supply additional information or comply with disclosure requirements. Paragraph 36 states that the accounting policies adopted by the company in determining the amounts to be included in respect of the items shown in the balance sheet and determining the profit or loss of the company shall be stated including those concerned with depreciation. Some paragraphs are devoted to information supplementing the balance sheet and to information supplementing the profit and loss account. This information is summarized below.

Information supplementing the balance sheet

● Share capital and debentures, the authorized share capital and, where shares have been allotted, the number and aggregate nominal value of each class, the redemption dates, alternative options and any premium on redeemable shares must be stated.
● If any allotment of shares has been made during the financial year, the reason for the allotment, the class of share and the number, aggregate value and consideration received.
● With respect to contingent right to the allotment of shares the number, description and amount of the shares to which the right is exercisable, the period during which it is exercisable and the price to be paid.
● If any debentures have been issued and if so the reason for issue, class amount and consideration for each issue.
● Particulars of any redeemed debentures which the company has power to reissue.

1 *Fixed assets:*　The appropriate amounts in respect of each item at the beginning of the year and at the balance sheet date. The effect on any item of any acquisition, transfer or disposal during the year. Assets to be recorded at purchase price or production cost as previously defined

unless under alternative (current cost) basis. The cumulative amounts of provisions for depreciation at the beginning and end of the year with adjustments in respect of any acquisition transfer or disposal. Land and buildings to be split between freehold and leasehold and leaseholds to be distinguished between long lease and short lease (fifty years or less).

2 *Investments:*Listed investments must be segregated into those listed on recognized stock exchanges and those of other listings. Whether fixed or current assets the aggregate market values must be shown. If the market value included in the accounts is higher than the stock exchange value then this too must be shown.

3 *Reserves and provisions:*   The amounts at the date of beginning of the year and at the balance sheet date must be shown together with any amounts transferred to or from the reserves or provisions and the source and application of any amount so transferred.

4 *Provision for taxation:*   Amount of any provision other than deferred taxation is to be stated.

5 *Indebtedness:*   Under creditors the amounts payable must be stated otherwise than by instalments due more than five years from the first day following the end of the financial year (usually the balance sheet date). Second, the amounts repayable by instalments due more than five years from the end of the financial year and the aggregate amount of instalments falling due after the end of the period should be disclosed for each item. The terms of repayment and interest date payable on each debt must be disclosed, except that directors are permitted to give a general indication of terms of debt and interest if a list of all amounts should prove to be excessive. If security has been given for any debt the amount and nature of the securities given must be stated. The amounts falling due for creditors within one year and after more than one year other than those described previously must be separately disclosed. Finally, if any fixed cumulative dividends are in arrears the amount and the period of arrears for each class must be disclosed.

6 *Guarantees and financial commitments:*   Particulars shall be given of:

- Any charge on assets of the company including the amount, if possible, to secure the liabilities of any other person.
- Contingent liabilities in respect of the amount, its legal nature and any security provided.
- Aggregate or estimates of contracts for capital expenditure if not provided for and the same details of capital expenditure authorized by directors but not contracted for.
- Pension commitments which have been provided for and any commitment for which no provision has been made. If they are in respect of payments to past directors they must be separately disclosed. The aggregate amount of recommended dividend must be stated.

Information supplementing the profit and loss account
The Act sets out information to be provided in, or supplementary to, the profit and loss account. The most significant of these are:

- The amount of interest in respect of loans separated as to first, those repayable otherwise than by instalments and falling due for repayment before the end of five years beginning with the day following the end of the financial year, second, those repayable by instalments the last of which falls due before the end of that period i.e. within five years and third, loans of any other kind made to the company.
- The amounts set aside for redemption of share capital and loans.
- Income from listed investments.
- Rents from land (net) if forming substantial part of income.
- Sums payable in respect of hire of plant or machinery.
- Remuneration of auditors including expenses.

1 *Taxation:*　The basis on which the charge for UK corporation tax and UK income tax is computed shall be stated. The amounts are to be stated separately in respect of:
- (a) Charge for UK corporation tax.
- (b) If that amount would have been greater but for double taxation relief the amount of that relief.
- (c) Charge for UK income tax.
- (d) Charge for taxation imposed outside UK.

2 *Turnover:*
- (a) The turnover (excluding VAT) for each substantially different class of business.
- (b) The profit or loss attributable to each class.
- (c) The classification is decided by the directors.
- (d) The turnover attributable to each substantial geographical area.
- (e) If the directors decide that such segregation of the turnover would aid competitors then they can omit it, but the fact that omission must be commented upon by them.

3 *Staff:*　The following must be disclosed:
- (a) The average number of persons employed by the company in the financial year.
- (b) The average number of persons employed in the different categories of business as decided by the directors.
- (c) The aggregate amounts of: wages and salaries paid for the year, social security costs incurred and other pension costs in respect of each category of employees so decided.

4 *Miscellaneous:*　The effect on profits of any of the following must be stated:
- (a) Amounts included in any item from the previous year.
- (b) Any extraordinary income or charges arising in the financial year.
- (c) Any transaction which although in ordinary line of business is exceptional by virtue of size.

5 *General:*　Figures for the previous year must be included adjusted to comparable bases where necessary. If items were originally in foreign currencies the basis of conversion to sterling (£) must be indicated.

Presentation of accounts

Small or medium-sized companies may be permitted under the Act to file modified accounts. To obtain this concession such companies must satisfy two of the following criteria:

	Small company	Medium company
Turnover not exceeding	£1,400,000	£5,750,000
Balance sheet total (gross assets)	£700,000	£2,800,000
Average number of employees not exceeding	50	250

The concessions do not apply to public companies, companies in banking, insurance or ineligible groups similar to these.

A small company:

● Need not file a profit and loss account with the registrar.
● Is permitted to submit a modified balance sheet.
● Need not file a directors' report.
● Need only cover accounting policies, share capital, particulars of debt, particulars of share allotments, basis of translation of foreign currency, loans to directors and officers and comparative figures for previous years in the notes to its accounts.

A medium-sized company:

● May submit a modified profit and loss account but must submit a complete balance sheet, directors' report and other information. The exemptions must be claimed in a statement by the directors and auditors must certify that the requirements for exemption are complied with.

Directors' reports

The accounts other than those of a small company must be accompanied by a **directors' report** giving a fair review of the development of the business over the period under review. Items to which reference should be made includes events which have taken place since the last accounting date, likely future developments, any research and development activities and particulars of any acquisition by a company of its own shares under the provisions of the Companies Act 1985.

Other reports

Supplementary statements are frequently produced by companies in simplified formats for the information of employees, unions and general publicity. These are referred to in the Act as abridged accounts and do not have to comply with the detailed rules above but a statement has to be published with them as to the extent to which they are full accounts and whether the auditor has reported on and/or qualified the full accounts. These reports are discussed further in Part Five.

The report and accounts for the Transport Development Group for 1986 has been reproduced on pages 417–47. It is not possible in a book of this nature to do justice to the quality and colour of the original report. Such brochures include photographs of activities and achievements as part of the public relations exercise which most companies combine with their financial reporting. These photographs have not been reproduced but other items in the report have been included to give an indication of the number of companies and activities, nationally and internationally, that large groups can be engaged in and the complexity of accounting problems that could therefore arise. Most accounts available to investors, students and general readers other than those of their own companies are likely to be group accounts. This does not seriously inhibit their usefulness for illustrating general legal requirements but any terms and practices specifically relating to group and consolidated accounts are covered more fully in Chapter 4.

3.5   Valuation of a business and goodwill

It is difficult to define the concept of **value** because it is a subjective measure i.e. it is a matter of opinion and circumstances. Quite frequently the term value is automatically equated with cost or monetary equivalent. This is incorrect as there are at least four types of value: **use value**, **exchange value**, **esteem value** and **cost value**. Water in the UK has a low cost value but its use value is extremely high. In times of shortage or drought the exchange value and the cost value increase rapidly. As water became more scarce a higher price or cost would be quoted. Here is the difference between cost and value. We can easily increase the cost of an item without adding one penny to its usefulness.

Similar difficulties exist in creating *one* basis by which a business may be valued. The purpose for which the valuation is being made, the status of the parties concerned and the particular time are a few of the circumstances affecting the figures arrived at. Business and share valuations are carried out primarily for one or more of the following purposes:

1   For taxation and estate duty settlements.
2   Determining a selling price as a going concern.
3   For benefit of creditors in event of liquidation.
4   To assess realism or otherwise of figures in recorded accounts.
5   Determining the price at which shares in a company might be issued.
6   By one business of the value of another with a view to an investment or takeover.
7   On creation, introduction or expansion of partnerships.

As with all answers to subjective problems the solution will vary with the technique and method adopted but any answer is merely a guide. The ultimate price paid by a buyer may be influenced by completely illogical attitudes e.g. determination *at any price* to crush or outbid a competitor.

In all cases of valuation the approach is by reference to one of two different bases:

1   What the business owns i.e. its assets.
2   What the business can create i.e. its earnings.

The two methods may produce results which are very different from each other. The earnings potential of a company may be based on factors uninfluenced directly by the value of its productive resources as for example reputation of a brand name or technical innovation in being first in the market with a desirable product. Even within the methods the particular base will depend upon the objective as specified above.

Valuation on assets basis

Fixed assets are recorded in conventional accounts at purchase price and reduced generally by a depreciation charge based on that cost over the life of the asset. Current assets are recorded at current costs subject to the rule of cost or net realizable value for stocks and adjustment for bad debts in the case of debtors.

Example

Balance sheet of XY Ltd as at 31 December 19xx

	£000		£000	£000
Share capital		Fixed assets		
Authorized, issued and		Land and buildings		
fully paid up		(at cost)		1,280
Ordinary shares of £1	2,000	Plant and machinery		
Reserve i/c profit and		(cost)	6,500	
loss	2,800	*Less* Depreciation	3,000	
	———			3,500
	4,800	Fixtures and fittings		
		(cost)	120	
		Less Depreciation	40	
Loan capital				80
10% debentures	1,400			———
Current liabilities				4,860
Taxation	230	Trade investments (cost)		100
Creditors	680			
	——— 910			
		Current assets		
		Stocks	850	
		Debtors	920	
		Cash and short-term		
		deposits	380	
				2,150
	7,110			7,110

Book value

The first step is to compute the net worth of the business to the shareholders. Total assets are £7,110,000 but some of this is committed to outside interests. £230,000 is owed for taxation, £680,000 to creditors and £1,400,000 to debenture holders all of whom would have to be compensated before distributing the balance to shareholders.

Computation

	£000	£000
Book value of total assets		7,110
Less Amounts due to:		
Taxation	230	
Creditors	680	
Debentures	1,400	
	———	2,310
		4,800

Number of ordinary shares $\dfrac{£2,000,000}{£1}$ = 2,000 thousand

Value per share = £2.40

Note that the same answer is obtained if the total of share capital and reserves is used since this represents the net worth.

Going concern

If the business is thriving it may be sold as a **going concern** and prospective purchasers would need to satisfy themselvs as to both the value of the assets and the earnings potential. A revaluation would therefore be required. Factors affecting the amounts attributed to the various assets would be as follows:

1   *Land and buildings:*   It is comparatively easy to establish a figure for land but buildings would require separate valuation. They may be overvalued due to poor maintenance and age or undervalued due to applying depreciation when prices are in fact rising.
2   *Plant and machinery:*   This is particularly difficult in practice since:
   (a)   Quite frequently a machine when worn out is not replaced with an identical or even similar model. Methods and design improvements, automation and technological advances prevent this.
   (b)   There may not be a reliable plant register or items may be very numerous. In this event plant and machinery items are frequently grouped into categories and evaluated by indices representing price movements from date of purchase.

   An example of machine groupings would be
   ● Heavy plant – slow speed e.g. presses.
   ● Medium duty – capstan lathes drillers.
   ● Precision – high speed e.g. precision grinders.
3   *Trade investments:*   The general practice is to show these in historical accounts at cost or market price whichever is lower. Opinion may differ as to value in the immediate future as the owners may have insider knowledge of good or bad prospects. Similarly the purchaser may not be interested in acquiring the investment forcing a sale at current market price.
4   *Current assets:*   Stocks may contain redundant items. Although possibly based on convention of cost or market price whichever is lower revaluation may mean substantial changes since the last balance sheet date. Similarly debtors represent the best estimate of the actual

realizable cash figure. The bank and cash balances are not of course subject to any amendment.

5   *Current liabilities:*   These are not normally adjusted since in the case of creditors they represent known sums due for trade creditors, taxation dividends and similar items. Any contingent liabilities would have to be carefully vetted as to the likelihood of materialization into definite commitments.

6   *Loan capital:*   It is possible that these are repayable at some future date at amounts differing from the nominal value. The effect on the valuation will depend upon the amount of the difference and the time span. There may also be special terms in the event of change of ownership for transference of the loan.

7   *Preference shares:*   The remarks applicable to loan capital may apply even more so in the case of preference shares as they may be eligible to participate in any changes when ownership is amended. This is more likely in event of break up as discussed below.

Example

XY Ltd (above) has been approached by CD Ltd with a view to purchase by the latter. The management of XY Ltd has therefore commissioned revaluation and audit to ascertain current worth with the following results. Land and buildings together are deemed to be worth £1,500,000; plant and machinery £3,600,000 and fixtures/fittings £50,000. The present realizable value of the investments is £120,000. Included in the stock are items valued at £85,000 which are now expected to realize only £35,000 due to fashion changes. Debtors include debts now considered bad £20,000 and of the balance remaining 5 per cent are doubtful.

Computation

		Book value £000	Assets basis Going concern £000	adjustment £000
Fixed assets				
Land and buildings		1,280	1,500	220 +
Plant and machinery		3,500	3,600	100 +
Fixtures and fittings		80	50	30 −
		4,860	5,150	290
Investments		100	120	20 +
Current assets				
Stocks		850	800	50 −
Debtors		920	855	65 −
Cash		380	380	−
		7,110	7,305	195 +
Less Amount due to				
Taxation	230			
Creditors	680			
Debentures	1,400			
		2,310	2,310	−
		4,800	4,995	195

Number of Shares = 2,000,000
Value per share = £2.5

The actual value works out at £2.4975 (for practical purposes £2.50) or 10p per share greater than the book value. Note the movements in opposite directions e.g. land increase, stocks decrease tend to have a compensating effect.

If the business is to be discontinued the circumstances will again determine value. It may be that the firm occupies a prime site which a developer desperately needs to complete a project. In this event minor losses on forced sale of stocks would be insignificant by virtue of the high price commanded for the land. On the other hand the company may be located in a depressed area where even property prices have lost momentum. The sale may be forced by virtue of lease closure, death of major shareholder or partnership disagreement. Potential buyers will adjust their offers accordingly.

Example

XY Ltd (above) is ceasing to trade and the liquidation values are determined as follows: land and buildings £1,300,000; plant and machinery £2,700,000; fixtures and fittings £30,000. Investments are still expected to realize £120,000 but due to quick sale stocks are expected to realize only £600,000. Debtors £855,000 as in previous example.

Computation

		Book value *£000*	*Assets basis* *Adjustment* *£000*	*Break up* *£000*
Fixed assets				
Land and buildings		1,280	1,300	20 +
Plant and machinery		3,500	2,700	800 −
Fixtures and fittings		80	30	50 −
		4,860	4,030	830
Investments		100	120	20 +
Current assets				
Stock		850	600	250 −
Debtors		920	855	65 −
Cash		380	380	−
		7,110	5,985	1,125 −
Less Amount due				
Taxation	230			
Creditors	680			
Debentures	1,400			
		2,310	2,310	
		4,800	3,675	1,125

Number of shares 2,000,000

Value per share £1.84

The actual value works out at £1.8375 for practical purposes £1.84 or 36p less than the book value.

Earnings basis

The assets bases ignore the ability of those assets directly to generate profits which is really what business activity is about. The alternative approach, therefore, is to pay a price for the future earnings – profits – of the business. Some methods require the maintaining of a stated percentage return on the price paid while others are founded on a **number of years purchase** of profits or more strictly **average maintainable earnings**. Quite simply this latter phrase means that in computing profits exceptional gains or losses for a particular period should be excluded. The number of years purchase method tends to be used for small businesses and professional practices whereas **return on capital employed** (ROCE) methods are used for companies. In any event one base can be converted to the other by means of ratios. The price that is paid for these capitalized earnings is termed goodwill. This has been defined as

● The benefit arising from connection and reputation – the probability that customers who have been used to dealing with a particular business will continue to do so.

or

● The difference between the value of a business as a whole and the aggregate of fair values of its separable assets (SSAP 22).

There is no real difference between these terms but the first implies valuation on some basis of the worth of the goodwill – creation of an intangible asset. The total value of the business will be determined by adding the amount thus determined to the agreed valuation of tangible fixed and current assets. The price is usually a number of years purchase of profits – simple or weighted – or computation of super profits on a method described below. In the second case a price is determined for the business as a whole and goodwill becomes the balancing figure. This is more usual in the case of companies – particularly quoted companies – where the **price earnings ratio** determines the overall value attributed to the company by market forces.

Simple average method

The most recent three year profits of AB Ltd are as follows:
Year 7 – £12,300, Year 8 – £14,000, Year 9 – £16,000. Y Ltd has agreed to buy the business for five years purchase of the average of the last three years. The price to be paid for goodwill is as follows:

$$\text{Average profits} = \frac{12,300 + 14,000 + 16,000}{3} = £14,100$$

Value of goodwill = 5 × 14,100 = £70,500

Weighted average

Profits of AB Ltd are as previous but the price is agreed as five years purchase of the average of the last three years but the average weighted in favour of the most recent performance. The weighting factors may be stated but if not are assumed to be the reverse order of the years concerned. Thus in the above example the period for computation of the average is three years so we have Year 7 weighting 1, Year 8 weighting 2 and Year 9 weighting 3.

£

Year 7   £12,300 × 1 = 12,300
Year 8   £14,000 × 2 = 28,000
Year 9   £16,000 × 3 = 48,000

_____   _____
6   88,300
_____   _____

Weighted average = $\dfrac{£88,300}{6}$ = £14,716

Value of goodwill = 5 × 14,716 = £73,580

It is claimed that this method produces better results particularly if earnings are rising and prospects good, as it emphasizes performance of the latter years.

Super profits

In assessing an acceptable rate of return a prospective business purchaser has at least one alternative in that he can put his capital into a comparatively risk-free investment. The difference between this rate and the return he gets from investing in a particular business is the **risk premium**. In this approach only the return above the risk-free rate is considered goodwill.

Exercise 3.7

The balance sheet of AB Ltd as at 31 December 19x4 is as follows:

	£	£
Fixed assets		
Land and buildings (cost £20,000)	20,000	
Plant and machinery (cost £25,000)	12,500	
		32,500
Quoted investments		15,000
Current assets		
Stocks	19,000	
Debtors	21,850	
Bank	22,000	
	62,850	
Less Current liabilities		
Creditors	15,450	
Net current assets		47,400
Total asset *less* Current liabilities		94,900
Represented by:		
Creditors due after more than one year		
10% Debentures		10,000
Capital and reserves		
5,000 8% Preference Shares of £1	5,000	
25,000 Ordinary shares of £1	25,000	
Profit and loss account	54,900	
		84,900
		94,900

Profits for the latest three years have been: 19x2 – £14,500, 19x3 – £18,750 and 19x4 – £15,500 respectively. The following conditions apply to a prospective sale of the business.

1   The market value of the quoted investments is currently £18,000.
2   The profit for 19x4 included £1,740 profit on sale of machinery.
3   Provision for bad debts of 5 per cent of debtors for 19x4 is deemed excessive and not likely to be required.
4   The property has been revalued and has a market value of £24,000.
5   Depreciation on plant and machinery has been excessive and second-hand (i.e. disposable) value is expected to be £25,000.
6   The amount for debtors for 19x4 is after providing a reserve of 5 per cent for bad debts which is not now deemed to be required.
7   Remaining values attributed in the books to current asset and liabilities is deemed realistic.
8   In the event of liquidation preference shares and debenture holders are repayable at par.
9   In the event of sale as a going concern notes (1) to (7) above will apply but the preference shares will be sold by the vendor to another purchaser for 70p per share and the purchasing company will acquire the debentures for cancellation at a discount of 25 per cent.

Required:
Value the company on the following alternative bases:

Assets basis
(a)   Book value.
(b)   Break-up value subject to adjustments indicated above.
(c)   Going concern subject to adjustments indicated above.

Earnings basis
(d)   An amount equivalent to (c) plus four years purchase of the simple average of profits for the last three years for goodwill.
(e)   An amount equivalent to (c) plus four years purchase of the weighted average of the last three years.
(f)   An amount whereby the purchaser will pay a price calculated such that he will obtain a return of 10 per cent on the net physical assets attributable to the ordinary shares plus – for goodwill – four times the average super profits (i.e. profits over 10 per cent) of the previous three years as adjusted.
(g)   It is agreed that the price be determined by reference to the price earnings ratio for the appropriate industrial group as published in the financial press at the balance sheet date. This was ascertained to be 8.0. Ignore box.

(a)   Book value

		£
Total assets *less* current liabilities		94,900
Less		
Amount due to preference shareholders	5,000	
Amount due to debenture holders	10,000	
		15,000
		79,900

Number of Shares (£1) = 25,000

Value of one share = $\dfrac{79,900}{25,000}$ = £3.20

(b) Break-up value (liquidation)

Property		24,000
Plant		25,000
		49,000
Quoted investment		18,000
Net current assets		
Stocks	19,000	
Debtors $(21,850 \times \frac{100}{95})$	23,000	
Bank	22,000	
	64,000	
Less Creditors	15,450	
		48,550
Total assets *less* current liabilities		115,550
Less attributable to preference shareholders	5,000	
debentures	10,000	
		15,000
Net physical assets attributable to ordinary stockholders		100,550

Value of one share = $\dfrac{100,550}{25,000}$ = £4.02

(c) Assets only – going concern

The preference shares have been sold to another purchaser for £3,500 and this goes to the vendor. The debentures have been purchased from the *holder* for £7,500 but the losses (difference between nominal value and price paid) are borne by the holders of these securities. If the debentures are redeemed interest will no longer be payable and therefore an additional source of profit. Liability for dividend on the preference shares will still exist as will the ultimate liability for repayment of £10,000 to new preference shareholders.

	£
Total assets *less* current liabilities adjusted as (b) above	94,900
Less attributable to preference shares	10,000
Net physical assets attributable to ordinary shareholders	84,900

Value of one share = $\dfrac{£84,900}{25,000}$ = £3.40

(d)   Average profits

	£
Profits for 3 years to 31 December 19x4	
14,500 + 18,750 + 15,500	48,750
Add	
Debenture interest not required if redeemed	
3 years × 10% × £10,000	3,000
Provision for bad debts (19x4) not required	
$21,850 \times \dfrac{5}{95}$	1,150
	52,900
Less Non-recurring income	
Sale of plant 19x4	1,740
3 years total adjusted profit	51,160
Average annual profit $\dfrac{50,160}{3}$	17,053
Less annual preference dividend	400
	16,653
Average earnings = £16,320	
Goodwill – 4 years purchase = 4 × 16,320 =	66,612
Plus net physical assets as in (c)	84,900
	151,512

Value of one share $= \dfrac{151,512}{25,000} = £6.06$

(e)

Profit for 19x2 = £14,500 + debenture interest − preference dividend
$\qquad = £14,500 + 1,000 - 400 = £15,100$
Profit for 19x3 = £18,750 + 1,000 − 400 = £19,350
Profit for 19x4 = £15,500 + 1,000 − 400 = £16,100

Less profit on sale of plant	(1,740)
Plus bad debt reserve not required	1,150
	15,510

Weighted average		
Year 19X2 15,100 × 1	=	15,100
Year 19X3 19,350 × 2	=	38,700
Year 19X4 15,510 × 3	=	46,530
		100,330

Weighted average $= \dfrac{100,330}{6}$	=	16,722
Goodwill = 4 years purchase = 4 × 16,722		66,888
Plus net physical assets as in (c)		84,900
		151,788

Value of one share $= \dfrac{151,788}{25,000} = £6.07$

(f)

Profits required for 10% annual return on net physical assets as at (c) above		
$= 10\% \times £84,900$	$=$	8,490
Annual profit as anticipated (d)		16,320
$\therefore$ Annual super profits	$=$	7,830
Goodwill $= 4$ years at 7,830	$=$	31,320
Net physical assets		84,900
Total value		116,220

Value of one share $= \dfrac{116,220}{25,000} = £4.65$

(g)

Average annual maintainable earnings for 19xx is £16,320 per annum as computed in (d)

The p/e ratio is 8

Total market value of AB Ltd $= 8 \times 16,320 = £130,560$

In this case if assets are valued on the going concern basis as computed for part (c) the goodwill becomes the difference between £130,560 and £84,900 = £45,660

Value of one share $= \dfrac{£130,560}{25,000} = £5.22$

Yield bases

Limited companies – particularly quoted companies – have valuations derived on similar bases to those described above except that they are primarily expressed in one of two forms of ratios.

Price/earnings ratio

This is defined as the market value of a share related to earnings per share after company taxation. It represents the number of years required at that rate for the original investment to be repaid. If the market value (MV) of one share is £2.00 and the earnings per share (EPS) is 16p then:

$$\text{P/E (price/earnings) ratio} = \frac{\text{market value of share (MV)}}{\text{earnings per share (EPS)}}$$

$$= \frac{£2.00}{£0.16} = 12.5$$

Another way of expressing this is to use the earnings yield.

$$\text{Earnings yield} = \frac{\text{EPS}}{\text{MV}} \times 100 = \frac{£0.16}{£2.00} \times 100 = 8\%$$

In most cases **earnings** for companies are net of corporation tax but specific examples should be examined to confirm this. Money which is actually paid out as dividends is usually subject further to income tax and although dividends are also used to compute ratios they need to be confirmed as gross or net of tax to a standard ratepayer. In the UK it is important to remember that dividend **rates** as opposed to yields are expressed relative to the nominal value of the share as follows:

Suppose that the share above had a nominal value of 50p and the company had declared a dividend of 20 per cent.

Dividend per share = 20% × 50p = 10p

$$\text{Gross dividend yield} = \frac{\text{dividend}}{\text{market value}} \times 100 = \frac{£0.10}{£2.00} \times 100 = 5\%$$

At present the actual amount distributed by UK companies is subject to income tax at standard rate before distribution. Assuming an income tax rate of 30 per cent the net dividend would be 10p less 30 per cent = 7p per share and therefore:

$$\text{net dividend yield} = \frac{\text{net dividend}}{\text{market value}} \times 100 = \frac{£0.07}{£2.00} \times 100 = 3.5\%$$

Dividend cover is the earnings per share divided by the net dividend per share and represents the number of times the profits available to the equity shareholders cover the actual net dividends payable for the period. In the above example:

$$\text{Dividend cover} = \frac{\text{earnings per share}}{\text{net dividend per share}} = \frac{16p}{7p} = 2.29 \text{ times}$$

As valuation guides dividend yields are not as useful as earnings yields. Companies' distribution policies vary – some firms regularly distributing most of their income, others retaining profits for capital growth. The tax position of individual shareholders will affect their preference and in turn the price of the company share. Some theoretical examples are sometimes used in examination papers as a matter of convenience for testing but it is earnings that predominate in practice.

Part Two
Growth and Failure

We saw in Section 1.3 how the various types of business entity tend to reflect the scope and size of the form of organization. Sole traders take in partners and in turn form limited companies – in the first instance private ones. The first major growth status is acceptance for, and formation of, a public limited company with its shares quoted on the Stock Exchange. Entrepreneurs still pursuing further growth may do so because of pressure of national and international competition; an aggressive management team or the usual economic objective of vertical or horizontal integration.

In this text we are predominantly concerned with the accounting requirements of such business combinations. Frequently the gains forecast when such mergers and takeovers are being touted by their advocates in no way compare with subsequent achievements. Certainly the accounts other than in computable redundancy costs do not reflect the social and other upheavals caused to districts and employees when 'unprofitable' parts of a group are axed. There are social, political, economic and other consequences of uncontrolled expansion, but only to the extent that the effects can be reflected in monetary terms by traditional accounts, are they considered in the following section.

Similarly with business failure. With the protection of limited liability it is far easier for a company to pass the consequences of its lack of success on to its creditors than is the case with sole traders and partners. An outline of the methods used is given in Chapter 5.

4
Expansion

We are concerned here with the expansion and growth of companies and the appropriate accounting treatment. The major means by which such growth is achieved are as follows:

1 *Absorption*. In this case one company completely takes over the other, the purchase being effected by cash or shares. The name of the company absorbed usually disappears.
2 *Amalgamation*. Here two or more companies combine to form a new company. The name may be completely new or incorporate those of the amalgamating companies e.g. Smith PLC and Jones PLC may amalgamate to become Smith-Jones PLC.
3 *Holding companies*. It is not necessary, to form a company, to absorb or amalgamate entirely with another company to gain control and the main benefits of ownership. A holding of 51 per cent of the voting shares will be sufficient for complete control but in practice, because of the scattered nature of small holdings, effective control can be obtained with a much smaller percentage. This is termed **administrative control** because the management manipulates the use of the structure. Accounting for each situation is now considered in turn.

4.1   Amalgamation and absorption of two or more companies

A company may be formed to take over and combine two or more existing companies, by taking over the assets and liabilities of the companies being amalgamated, and issuing shares in proportion to the previous holding.

The valuation of all individual assets and liabilities in the separate companies must be undertaken and agreed before the amalgamation can take place and the entitlement of shares in the new company calculated to everyone's satisfaction.

Example
Assuming that companies A Ltd and B Ltd are to be amalgamated into a new company C Ltd, assets and liabilities have been independently revalued and agreed as follows:

Balance sheets

	A Ltd £	B Ltd £		A Ltd £	B Ltd £
Capital–Shares of £1 each	180,000	150,000	Freehold buildings	160,000	–
Capital reserve	50,000	20,000	Plant and machinery	80,000	100,000
Profit and loss account	130,000	30,000	Sundry debtors	120,000	50,000
			Stock	35,000	40,000
Sundry creditors	42,000	18,000			
			Cash	7,000	28,000
	402,000	218,000		402,000	218,000

The first step is to calculate the net assets of each company as follows:

	A Ltd £	B Ltd £
Total assets from balance sheet	402,000	218,000
Less Sundry creditors	42,000	18,000
	360,000	200,000

The total share issue will therefore be £560,000. Shares will be issued to the shareholders in the former companies in the following ratios:

A Ltd – Two shares in the new company C Ltd for each share held in the old company.

B Ltd – Four shares in the new company C Ltd for every three shares held in the old company.

A Ltd, shareholders have 360,000 £1 shares in the new company. At present they have 180,000 £1 in A Ltd therefore they must be issued with $\frac{360,000}{180,000}$ = two shares for each one now held.

B Ltd shareholders are entitled to 200,000 shares in the new company. At present B Ltd shareholders have 150,000 £1 shares therefore they must be issued with $\frac{200,000}{150,000} = \frac{4}{3}$ = four shares for each three now held. Note that it is the ratios of the net assets which determine the ratio of shares between A and B *not* the ratio of the original capitals which was 180,000 : 150,000.

The balance sheet of the new company would now be prepared as follows:

C Ltd
Balance sheet

	£		£
Capital–Shares of £1 each fully paid	560,000	Freehold buildings	160,000
		Plant and machinery	180,000
Sundry creditors	60,000	Sundry debtors	170,000
		Stock	75,000
		Cash	35,000
	620,000		620,000

The existing shareholders of A Ltd and B Ltd could also have agreed to take part of their holding in the new company in the form of either partly paid up shares, or debentures or any combination of fully paid up shares, partly paid up shares and debentures.

Absorption of one company by another

It often happens that a successful company buys out, or absorbs, a smaller or less successful company, the smaller company going out of existence and its shareholders accepting shares, debentures or cash in the larger company in consideration for the net assets taken over.

Example

Assume that the new company C Ltd above has agreed to take over the assets and liabilities of D Ltd at balance sheet valuations as follows:

Balance sheet

	£		£
Share capital	150,000	Plant and Machinery	120,000
Debentures	100,000	Sundry debtors	50,000
		Stock	60,000
		Cash	20,000
	250,000		250,000

It is agreed that C Ltd should make an issue of shares of four shares in C Ltd for each three shares held in D Ltd and that debentures should be reissued in C Ltd in the same conditions as they were held in D Ltd.

Four shares for three shares at the existing nominal value of £1 will mean that the consideration for the net asset taken over is $\frac{4}{3} \times 150,000 =$ £200,000. The net assets being taken over are £250,000 less the amount attributable to the debenture holders of £100,000 equals £150,000. Since we are acquiring only £150,000 value of assets for £200,000 we need to insert a fictitious asset of £50,000 which must be attributed to goodwill. The share capital of C Ltd has been increased by £200,000 from £560,000 to £760,000 to finance the acquisition and the reissued debentures will now be a liability of C Ltd.

The balance sheet of C Ltd after absorption will appear as follows:

C Ltd
Balance sheet

	£		£
Capital–Shares of £1 each fully paid	760,000	Goodwill	50,000
Debentures	100,000	Freehold buildings	160,000
Sundry creditors	60,000	Plant and machinery	300,000
		Sundry debtors	220,000
		Stock	135,000
		Cash	55,000
	920,000		920,000

D Ltd would of course be wound up in the normal way, as described in the next section, this being a **voluntary liquidation**, the shareholders would appoint one or more liquidators to achieve this end.

4.2   Holding companies, group accounts and consolidated balance sheets

In the previous section the situation was that all the share capital of the company taken over was acquired by the other company. Some companies deliberately set out to acquire merely sufficient of the shares of other companies to gain effective control of their operations. Where a substantial proportion of such shares are acquired the interests of the remaining shareholders – termed the **minority interest** – may be affected. In the United Kingdom company law provides certain safeguards and requires that the company acquiring such shares – known as the **holding company** – should prepare and circulate **group accounts** consisting primarily of a **consolidated balance sheet** and a **consolidated profit and loss account**. The company whose shares are thus acquired is known as a **subsidiary company** and the Companies Acts define the circumstances in which this relationship is deemed to exist. A holding company may have more than one subsidiary company and in such cases the subsidiary companies are required to indicate on their balance sheets any amounts owing to or from fellow subsidiaries as well as to or from the holding company.

A **group** of companies consists of a **holding company** and its **subsidiary company** (or companies) SSAP. 14 on group accounts defines a subsidiary company in the following terms:

A company shall be deemed to be a subsidiary of another if, but only if:

(a)   That other either:

(i)   is a member of it and controls the composition of its board of directors; or

(ii)   holds more than half in nominal value of its equity share capital; or

(b)   the first mentioned company is a subsidiary of any company which is that other's subsidiary,

and it otherwise comes within the term of Section 736 of the Companies Act 1985.

A holding company is defined as:

A company is a holding company of another if, but only if, that other is its subsidiary as defined above.

The structure of a group and the relationships between the holding company and its subsidiaries and between the subsidiaries themselves can vary considerably.

The simplest situation is where the holding company has a single subsidiary, whether partly or wholly owned as shown in Figure 4.1.

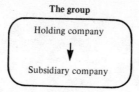

Figure 4.1

A more complex structure arises when the subsidiary company(s) itself has a subsidiary (T). In this case T is also deemed to be a subsidiary of the holding company (H) (Companies Act 1948, Section 154 (i)).

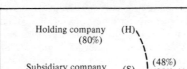

Figure 4.2

It should be noted that although the holding company in Figure 4.2 it has an indirect holding in T of only 48 per cent, the latter is still a subsidiary of the former by virtue of the provisions of Section 736 of the Companies Act 1985.

With certain exceptions Section 229 of the Companies Act 1985 requires the holding company to prepare group accounts. Such accounts should, with certain exceptions, be consolidated accounts comprising a consolidated profit and loss account and a consolidated balance sheet disclosing the profit and loss and financial position of the holding company, and its subsidiaries together.

Section 228 deals with the content of group accounts by stating that they must give a **true and fair view** of the state of affairs of the group, and that if the group accounts are consolidated accounts they must comply with the **disclosure** provisions of Schedule 4. If the group accounts take a form other than consolidated accounts, they must give the same or equivalent information as that required by Schedule 4.

Consolidated balance sheets

When a company (H) acquires an interest in another company (S), the shares acquired will appear as an investment in H's balance sheet.

Example

The following balance sheets were prepared as at 31 December 19x1. On that date H acquired the entire share capital of S at a cost of £5,000 paid in cash.

H Ltd
Balance sheet as at 31 December 19x1

	£		£
Share capital	5,000	Fixed assets	3,000
Revenue reserves	3,000	Current assets	2,000
		Cash	5,000
	8,000		
Current liabilities	2,000		
	10,000		10,000

S Ltd
Balance sheet as at 31 December 19x1

	£		£
Share capital	4,000	Fixed assets	5,000
Revenue reserves	1,000	Current assets	3,000
	5,000		
Current liabilities	3,000		
	8,000		8,000

Following acquisition the balance sheet of H will appear as follows:

H Ltd
Balance sheet as at 31 December 19x1

	£		£
Share capital	5,000	Fixed assets	3,000
Revenue reserves	3,000	Current assets	2,000
	8,000	Investment in S Ltd at cost	5,000
Current liabilities	2,000		
	10,000		10,000

Note that the 'investment in S Ltd at cost' simply replaces the equivalent cash amount in H balance sheet.

However, to prepare a consolidated balance sheet it is necessary to consolidate or aggregate the assets and liabilities of the holding and subsidiary company. But before doing this it must be clearly understood that when H acquired the shares of S it also acquired the revenue reserves, since these belong to the shareholders. Alternatively, it could be said that H acquired the net assets of S. Thus in return for the £5,000 cash H has purchased:

	£
Share capital	4,000
Reserves	1,000
	5,000

or alternatively:

Fixed assets	5,000	
Current assets	3,000	
	8,000	
Less Current liabilities	3,000	
Net assets	5,000	

Consolidated balance sheet: H Ltd and its subsidiary

	£		£
Share capital	5,000	Fixed assets (£3,000 + £5,000)	8,000
Revenue reserves	3,000	Current assets (£2,000 + £3,000)	5,000
	8,000		
Current liabilities (£2,000 + £3,000)	5,000		
	13,000		13,000

Note that only the assets and current liabilities are aggregated.

Minority interests

In the above example H acquired the entire share capital of S. When, however, the holding company does not acquire all the subsidiary's shares, those shares remaining in outside shareholders' hands comprise the **minority interest** in the subsidiary. Thus if H acquired 80 per cent of the shares of S, the minority interest would be 20 per cent. The minority shareholders' interest in the net assets of the subsidiary is shown as a separate item in the consolidated balance sheet.

Example

H acquired 80 per cent of the shares of S on 31 December 19x1. The balance sheets of the two companies immediately following acquisition are as follows:

Balance sheets as at 31 December 19x1

	H Ltd £	S Ltd £		H Ltd £	S Ltd £
Share capital (£1 shares)	300,000	100,000	Fixed assets	300,000	160,000
Reserves	130,000	50,000			
	430,000	150,000	Investment in S at cost	120,000	
Current liabilities	30,000	40,000	Current assets	40,000	30,000
	460,000	190,000		460,000	190,000

It is first necessary to identify the amount of net assets acquired by the holding company, and the amount of the minority shareholders' interest in the subsidiary. This can be carried out as follows:

	Net assets at acquisition	Holding company 80%	Minority interest 20%
	£	£	£
Share capital	100,000		
Reserves	50,000		
	150,000	120,000	30,000
Cost of acquisition		120,000	
Goodwill or capital reserve		Nil	

It should be noted carefully that in this example the amount H paid for the shares is equivalent in value to the net assets required, therefore no goodwill or capital reserve arises on acquisition. Had the purchase price *exceeded* the value of the net assets acquired, the excess would comprise *goodwill*, had the price been *less* the difference would be transferred to *capital reserve*.

The consolidated balance sheet can now be prepared:

Consolidated balance sheet H Ltd and its subsidiary

	£		£
Share capital	300,000	Fixed assets	460,000
		(£300,000 + £160,000)	
Reserves	130,000	Current assets	70,000
		(£40,000 + £30,000)	
Minority interest	30,000		
Current liabilities	70,000		
(£30,000 + £40,000)			
	530,000		530,000

Goodwill or capital reserve on acquisition

As explained above, when the purchase price of the subsidiary's shares exceeds the value of the net assets acquired, the excess represents goodwill on acquisition. Conversely if the price of the shares is less than the value of the net assets acquired, the difference is transferred to capital reserves. Goodwill arising in this way is frequently termed **cost of control**. In most cases gains or losses on acquisition will be passed through a cost of control account. If a debit balance results it will be goodwill, if a credit balance it will be a gain or profit and transferred to capital reserve.

Example

H acquired 75 per cent of the issued share capital of S on 31 December 19x1. The balance sheets immediately following acquisition are shown below.

Balance sheet as at 31 December 19x1

	H Ltd £	S Ltd £		H Ltd £	S Ltd £
Share capital	400,000	200,000	Sundry assets	260,000	280,000
Reserves	100,000	80,000	Investment in S Ltd at cost	240,000	–
	500,000	280,000		500,000	280,000

The first step is to calculate goodwill or capital reserve arising on acquisition and minority interest at acquisition date as follows:

	Net asset on acquisition £	Holding company 75% £	Minority interest 25% £
Share capital	200,000		
Reserves	80,000		
	280,000	210,000	70,000
Cost		240,000	
Goodwill arising on acquisition		30,000	

The consolidated balance sheet can now be prepared:

Consolidated balance sheet of H Ltd and its subsidiary

	£		£
Share capital	400,000	Goodwill	30,000
Reserves	100,000	Sundry assets	540,000
	500,000		
Minority interest	70,000		
	570,000		570,000

Post acquisition profit

The previous discussion and illustrations all assumed the preparation of a consolidated balance sheet immediately following acquisition. In this section we are concerned with the manner in which profits earned subsequent to acquisition are dealt with. The principles that must be borne in mind in this context are as follows:

1 Pre-acquisition profits and reserves must be divided between the holding company and the minority interest, as illustrated in the last two examples above. The holding company's share is transferred to cost of control (i.e. taken into account when computing goodwill on acquisition) and is therefore **capitalized**. The minority interest share is simply transferred to the credit of the minority interest account.

2 Post-acquisition profits are also split between the holding company and the minority interest. The latter's share is again credited to the minority interest account, but the holding company's entitlement must be transferred to consolidated reserves (i.e. treated as revenue).

These principles can be illustrated as shown in Figure 4.3.

	Holding company	**Minority interest**
Pre-acquisition profits	Capitalize by transferring to cost of control	Credit to minority interest account
Post-acquisition profits	Transfer to consolidated reserves (i.e. treated as revenue)	

Figure 4.3

Example

H Ltd acquired a 90 per cent interest in S Ltd on 31 December 19x1 when the balance on the latter's reserves was £60,000. The balance sheets of the two companies at 31 December 19x2 were as follows:

Balance sheets

	H Ltd £	S Ltd £		H Ltd £	S Ltd £
Share capital	500,000	200,000	Fixed assets	420,000	240,000
Reserves	200,000	100,000	Investment in S at cost	280,000	
	700,000	300,000	Current assets	400,000	120,000
Current liabilities	400,000	60,000			
	1,100,000	360,000		1,100,000	360,000

The first step is to calculate goodwill arising on acquisition and minority interest share of net assets at acquisition date are follows:

Net assets on acquisition		*Holding Company 90%*	*Minority Interest 10%*
	£	£	£
Share capital	200,000		
Reserves at acquisition	60,000		
	260,000	234,000	26,000
Cost		280,000	
Goodwill		46,000	

The next step is to apportion post-acquisition profits between the holding company and minority interest as follows:

		Holding company 90%	*Minority interest 10%*
	£		
S Reserves at balance sheet date: 31.12.19x2	100,000		
S Reserves at acquisition date; 31.12.19x1	60,000		
S post-acquisition retained profits	40,000	36,000	4,000

The consolidated balance sheet can now be prepared as follows:

H Ltd and its subsidiary
Consolidated balance sheet as at 31 December 19x2

	£		£
Share capital	500,000	Fixed assets	660,000
Reserves (H £200,000		Current assets	520,000
+ H share of S post-		Goodwill	46,000
acquisition profits			
£36,000)	236,000		
	736,000		
Minority interest			
(at acquisition £26,000 +	30,000		
share of S post-			
acquisition profits			
£4,000)			
Current liabilities	460,000		
	1,226,000		1,226,000

Accounting entries

The general principles relating to consolidated balance sheets have been outlined above. In this section the accounting entries relating to the consolidation process are discussed.

The application of double entry principles to the preparation of consolidated accounts involves two processes.

1 The notional transfer of figures from the accounts of the group companies to the consolidation working papers. This process does not involve double entry book-keeping, but is merely the transferring of particular items for consolidation processes.
2 The use of double entry book-keeping principles within the consolidation working papers in order to prepare the consolidated accounts.

These processes can be illustrated as shown in Figure 4.4.

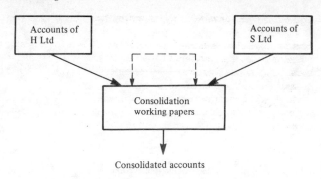

Figure 4.4

The accounts required within the consolidation working papers are as follows:

Account	Function
Cost of control account	To calculate goodwill or capital reserve arising on acquisition.
S Ltd reserves	To allow for the division between pre and post-acquisition profit.
Consolidated reserves	To disclose total distributable group profits.
Consolidated assets	To calculate group assets e.g. buildings, debtors, etc.
Consolidated liabilities	To calculate group liabilities e.g. creditors.
Minority interest	To disclose the minority shareholders' interest in the net assets of the subsidiary.

Example

The following are the balance sheets of H Ltd and S Ltd as at 31 December 19x4.

Balance sheets

	H Ltd £	S Ltd £		H Ltd £	S Ltd £
Share capital (£1 shares)	90,000	50,000	Sundry assets	90,000	76,000
Reserves	30,000	18,000	Investment in		
Current liabilities	20,000	8,000	S Ltd at cost	50,000	
	140,000	76,000		140,000	76,000

H acquired 80 per cent of S shares when the latter's reserves were £10,000.

In the accounts below, figures extracted from H Ltd's books are shown with an H alongside, those extracted from S Ltd's books are shown with an S alongside. Actual double entry adjustments within the consolidation working papers are shown with a D alongside.

The first step is concerned with the calculation of goodwill or capital reserve arising on acquisition. As in previous examples the cost of the investment is off-set against the value of the net assets acquired.

Cost of control account

	£		£	
Investment in S	50,000	S Ltd shares acquired	40,000	(S)
		S Ltd reserves – pre-acquisition profits acquired	8,000	(S)
		Goodwill c/d	2,000	
	50,000		50,000	
Goodwill b/d	2,000			

The second step is concerned with:

1 Dividing S Ltd reserves between the holding company and minority interest.
2 Dividing the holding company's share between pre and post-acquisition reserves.

S Ltd reserves account

	£		£
H Ltd Share:		S Ltd reserves	18,000 (S)
Cost of control – pre-acquisition profits (£10,000 × 80%)	8,000 (D)		
Consolidated reserves – post acquisition profits (£18,000 − £10,000) × 80%	6,400 (D)		
Minority interest share:			
Minority interest account – pre-acquisition profits (10,000 × 20%)	2,000 (D)		
Minority interest account post-acquisition profit (£18,000 × 20%)	1,600 (D)		
	18,000		18,000

The third step is concerned with aggregating the distributable profits of the group as follows:

Consolidated reserves account

	£		£
Balance c/d	36,400	H Ltd reserves	30,000 (H)
		S Ltd reserves – share of	
		post-acquisition profits	6,400 (D)
	———		———
	36,400		36,400
	———		———
		Balance b/d	36,400

The fourth step is concerned with identifying the minority shareholders' interest in the net assets of the subsidiary as follows:

Minority interest account

	£		£
Balance c/d	13,600	Shares held in S Ltd	10,000 (S)
		S Ltd reserves – share of	
		pre-acquisition profits	2,000 (D)
		S Ltd reserves – share of	
		post-acquisition profits	1,600 (D)
	———		———
	13,600		13,600
	———		———
		Balance b/d	13,600

The fifth step is concerned with aggregating the assets of the group as follows:

Consolidated assets account

	£		£
Balance c/d	166,000	H Ltd assets	90,000 (S)
		S Ltd assets	76,000 (S)
	———		———
	166,000		166,000
	———		———
		Balance b/d	166,000

The sixth step is concerned with aggregating the liabilities of the group as follows:

Consolidated liabilities account

	£		£
Balance c/d	28,000	H Ltd liabilities	20,000 (H)
		S Ltd liabilities	8,000 (S)
	———		———
	28,000		28,000
	———		———
		Balance b/d	28,000

The balances on the above accounts can now be transferred to the consolidated balance sheet:

H Ltd and its subsidiary
Consolidated balance sheet:

	£		£
Share capital	90,000	Goodwill	2,000
Reserves	36,400	Sundry assets	166,000
	126,400		
Minority interest	13,600		
Current liabilities	28,000		
	168,000		168,000

4.3 Inter-company transactions

A major principle underlying the preparation of consolidated statements is that the results of **inter-company transactions** must be eliminated prior to the preparation of the consolidated profit and loss account and the consolidated balance sheet. This is because the consolidated statements must show the performance and financial position of the group resulting from the group activities with outsiders.

Current accounts

These are usually maintained by all group companies to record inter-group transactions. Prior to the preparation of group accounts at the year end, the current accounts must be balanced.

Debentures and other loan stock

Inter-company debentures must be cancelled out at the year end. Thus, of the total debentures/loan stock issued by group companies, only that portion held outside the group will be shown as a group liability. Interest payable/receivable in respect of inter-company holdings will be recorded and disclosed in the normal way in the accounts of the individual companies concerned. But in the consolidated accounts only that portion relating to the non-group companies will be taken into account.

Bills of exchange

Just as inter-group holdings of debentures are cancelled prior to the preparation of the consolidated balance sheet, so too are bills of exchange. Thus, in the consolidated balance sheet only bills payable/receivable outside the group will appear as liabilities/assets.

Where bills have been discounted by group companies at the balance sheet date, a note of the contingent liability must be appended to the balance sheet of the individual company concerned. However, in the consolidated balance sheet, the note will relate only to non-group bills discounted, since the actual liability relating to inter-group bills will be shown.

Example
H Ltd balance sheet – bills payable £40,000 (all to S Ltd)
S Ltd balance sheet – bills receivable £22,000 (£10,000 receivable from H Ltd)

In the balance sheet of S Ltd there will be a contingent liability note of the bills discounted by S Ltd amounting to £30,000 (i.e. £40,000 − £10,000). In the consolidated balance sheet inter-group bills must be eliminated. Thus the £10,000 receivable by S Ltd from H Ltd will be cancelled against the £40,000 payable by H Ltd. Therefore, in the consolidated balance sheet, bills payable will be shown as £30,000 (£40,000 − £10,000) and bills receivable as £12,000 (£22,000 − £10,000). Since the actual liability in respect of the bills discounted is shown, there is no need to include a contingent liability note in respect of the *same* bills.

Dividends paid by subsidiary companies

Dividends from post-acquisition profits
Where dividends have been *paid* by the subsidiary they will have been debited to that company's profit and loss account. As the holding company will have received the dividends they will be credited in its profit and loss accounts. Consequently the two entries will automatically cancel out for consolidated purposes.

Where a subsidiary company has proposed a dividend which has to be paid at year end, the profit and loss account will be debited with the dividend and the balance sheet will contain a provision for the amount of the dividend. If the holding company has anticipated payment of the dividend it will have credited its profit and loss account with the dividend, and will show the dividends receivable as an asset. Thus the entries in the accounts of the holding company and the subsidiary company will cancel out. Where the holding company has *not* anticipated the dividend and has not made entries in its accounts in respect of the dividend, the proposed dividend should be added back to the subsidiary company's profit for consolidation purposes. The provision for the proposed dividend in the subsidiary company's balance sheet will naturally be eliminated from the consolidated balance sheet.

Dividends from pre-acquisition profits
Where the holding company receives dividends from a subsidiary which are paid out of pre-acquisition profits, such dividends are in the nature of a capital receipt (since the purchase price of the subsidiary's shares will reflect the dividend) and must be credited to the 'Investment in S Ltd account' in the holding company's books. Under no circumstances should dividends paid from pre-acquisition profits be credited to the holding company's profit and loss account.

Inter-company transfers of goods and services

Where transfers of goods and/or services take place between group companies; and the transfer prices include a profit element, then if at year end the goods/services have not been disposed of by the company, consolidated adjustments will be required to arrive at the correct amount of group profit and asset values.

Example
H Ltd transfers goods to S Ltd for £10,000. These goods originally cost H Ltd £6,000. All these goods were kept in stock by S Ltd at year end. In this example the profit and loss account of H Ltd will show a profit of £4,000 in respect of the goods transferred (£10,000 − £6,000). S Ltd's profit and loss account will disclose purchases of £10,000 and a closing stock of £10,000. However, the goods have not yet been sold outside the group. Therefore, for consolidation purposes the £4,000 profit in H Ltd's accounts must be eliminated, and the stock of £10,000 reduced to £6,000 (i.e. the cost to the group).

4.4   Consolidated profit and loss accounts

The basic principle involved in preparing profit and loss accounts is that the profit and loss accounts of the holding and subsidiary companies must be **aggregated**. During this process the results of transactions entered into between group companies and outsiders will be included, but the results of inter-group transactions must be excluded.

Example
The profit and loss accounts of H Ltd and S Ltd for the year ended 31 December 19x1 are as follows:

	H Ltd £	S Ltd £
Opening stock	30,000	20,000
Purchases	200,000	130,000
	230,000	150,000
Closing stock	40,000	30,000
	190,000	120,000
Sales	300,000	200,000
Gross profit	110,000	80,000
Expenses	80,000	60,000
Net profit	30,000	20,000

Included in H Ltd's sales and S Ltd's purchases are goods sold by H Ltd to S Ltd amounting to £20,000. These goods originally cost H Ltd 15,000. At year end these goods remain unsold by S Ltd.

The consolidated profit and loss account will be prepared as follows:

	H Ltd Profit and loss account £	S Ltd Profit and loss account £	Adjustments	Consolidated Profit and loss account £
Opening stock	30,000	20,000		50,000
Purchase	200,000	130,000	− 20,000 (a)	310,000
	230,000	150,000		360,000
Closing stock	40,000	30,000	− 5,000 (b)	65,000
	190,000	120,000		295,000
Sales	300,000	200,000	− 20,000 (c)	480,000
	110,000	80,000		185,000
Expenses	80,000	60,000		140,000
Net profit	30,000	20,000	− 5,000	45,000

The adjustments are made for the following purposes:

(a)   £20,000 is eliminated from the consolidated profit and loss account since the purchase by S Ltd represents an inter-group transfer.

(b)   £5,000 is deducted from the closing stocks as this represents the amount of unrealized profit in stocks.

(c)   £20,000 is eliminated from sales as this represents an inter-company transaction.

In effect group profit consists of H Ltd profit plus S Ltd profit less the inter-company unrealized profit:

	£
S Ltd	30,000
H Ltd	20,000
	50,000
Unrealized profit	5,000
Group profit	45,000

The minority shareholders of S Ltd are entitled to their share of S Ltd's profit. This is shown as a separate item on the face of the profit and loss account. Using the example above, but assuming a minority interest of 20 per cent, the appropriate part of the consolidated profit and loss account will appear as follows:

Consolidated profit and loss account (extract)

	£
Group profit	45,000
Less Minority interest	4,000
Group profit attributable to holding company	41,000

Note: the minority interest is calculated as follows:

	£
Net profit of S Ltd	20,000
Minority share thereof (20%)	4,000

Consolidated appropriation account

As discussed above, the consolidated profit and loss account is merely an aggregation (excluding inter-company transactions) of the individual group companies' profit and loss accounts. However, the **appropriation account** is prepared under different principles. These are perhaps best explained by stating the method of dealing with each item in the appropriation account balance brought forward – this consists of the holding company's balance plus the holding company's *share* of the subsidiary company's post-acquisition retained profits.

● *Taxation:* This comprises taxation of the holding company and the subsidiary company.
● *Dividends:* Holding company dividends *only* are included.
● *Transfers to reserves:* This consists of the holding company's transfers plus the holding company's share of the subsidiary company's transfers.
● *Balance carried forward:* This comprises the holding company's balance plus the holding company's *share* of the subsidiary company's post-acquisition retained profit.

Example
The appropriation accounts of H Ltd and S Ltd are shown below. H Ltd acquired an 80 per cent holding in S Ltd several years ago when the balance on the latter's profit and loss account was £10,000.

Appropriation account

	H Ltd £	S Ltd £		H Ltd £	S Ltd £
Taxation	8,000	6,000	Balance b/d	40,000	30,000
General reserves	6,000	4,000			
Dividends	5,000	3,000			
Balance c/d	21,000	17,000			
	40,000	30,000		40,000	30,000
			Balance b/d	21,000	17,000

The consolidated appropriation account can be prepared the following way:

		£
Balance b/d:	H Ltd	40,000
	S Ltd (£30,000 − £10,000) × 80%	16,000
	Consolidated appropriation account	56,000
Taxation:	H Ltd	8,000
	S Ltd	6,000
	Consolidated appropriation account	14,000
General reserves	H Ltd	6,000
	S Ltd (£4,000 × 80%)	3,200
	Consolidated appropriation account	9,200
Dividends:	H Ltd only	5,000

Consolidated appropriation account

	£		£
Taxation	14,000	Balance b/d	56,000
General reserves	9,200		
Dividends	5,000		
Balance c/d	27,800		
	56,000		56,000
		Balance b/d	27,800

Exercise 4.1

H Ltd acquired a 60 per cent interest in S Ltd several years ago when the balance on the latter's profit and loss account was £20,000. The profit and loss accounts of the two companies for the year ended 31 December 19x5 are as follows:

	H Ltd £	S Ltd £
Opening stock	60,000	40,000
Purchases	300,000	200,000
	360,000	240,000
Closing stock	30,000	20,000
	330,000	220,000
Sales	600,000	400,000
Gross profit	270,000	180,000
Expenses	150,000	110,000
Net profit	120,000	70,000
Taxation	40,000	20,000

Profit after tax	80,000	50,000
Proposed dividend	20,000	10,000
Retained profits	60,000	40,000
Balance b/d	120,000	90,000
	180,000	130,000
Transfer to general reserve	40,000	30,000
Balance c/f	140,000	100,000

Included in the closing stock of S Ltd are goods purchased from H Ltd for £6,000; these originally cost H Ltd £4,000.

Solution

	H Ltd Profit and loss account £	S Ltd Profit and loss account £	Adjustment	Consolidated Profit and loss account £
Opening stock	60,000	40,000		100,000
Purchase	300,000	200,000	− 6,000 (1)	494,000
	360,000	240,000		594,000
Closing stock	30,000	20,000	− 2,000 (2)	48,000
	330,000	220,000		546,000
Sales	600,000	400,000	− 6,000 (3)	994,000
Gross profit	270,000	180,000		448,000
Expenses	150,000	110,000		260,000
Net profit	120,000	70,000	−2,000	188,000
Taxation	40,000	20,000		60,000
Profit after tax	80,000	50,000		128,000
Less minority interest			(£50,000 × 40%)(4)	20,000
				108,000
Proposed dividends	20,000	10,000	holding company only (5)	20,000
Retained profit	60,000	40,000		88,000
Balance b/f	120,000	90,000	(6)	176,000
	180,000	130,000		264,000
Transfer to general reserve	40,000	20,000	(7)	64,000
Balance c/f	140,000	110,000		200,000

The reasons for the adjustments are outlined below:

Adjustment 1 and 3	These adjustments cancel out the inter-company transfer of £6,000.
Adjustment 2	The £2,000 unrealized profit in stock must be eliminated for consolidated purposes.
Adjustment 4	The minority interest in S Ltd profit after tax must be disclosed as a separate item in the consolidated profit and loss account.
Adjustment 5	Holding company dividends only are shown in the consolidated profit and loss accounts.
Adjustment 6	In the consolidated profit and loss account the balance brought forward comprises that of the holding company, plus its share of the subsidiary company's retained profit *since acquisition* i.e. £120,000 + (£90,000 − £20,000 × 80%) = £176,000.
Adjustment 7	This comprises the holding company's transfer plus the holding company's share of the subsidiary's transfer i.e. £40,000 + (£30,000 × 80%) = £64,000.

5
Decline and failure

Neither individuals nor companies are always prosperous in their business activities. Businesses carried on by sole traders and partnerships are separate entities from their owners but the latter are still responsible for their debts. If they cannot pay, individuals are adjudged bankrupt and all assets are realized and paid to creditors. A company is not an individual and cannot be made bankrupt. If, like an individual, it becomes **insolvent** – unable to pay its debts – it may be **liquidated**. When a company ceases to trade in its own name it is said to be **wound up**. But winding up a company does not necessarily mean the company is insolvent. As seen in the previous section it may be absorbed by another company. Alternatively it may have been formed for a specific project now completed but accomplished with success – as, for example, companies being formed to exploit special trading conditions at an Olympic Games site. If for any reason the company fails to pay its way it may be wound up voluntarily by the creditors or members or compulsorily by order of the court. The following pages deal very briefly with these alternative situations as far as companies are concerned.

5.1 Capital reduction

There are a number of reasons why a company can find itself in the situation of needing to reduce its capital. A company limited by shares may, if authorized by its articles of association, by special resolution, reduce its share capital, subject to confirmation by the Court. The Court may direct the company to add 'and reduced' to its name for a period to be determined by the Court.

Such a reduction may take the form of any of the following:

1 Reducing the number of fully paid up shares.
2 Reducing the nominal value of each fully paid up share.
3 Cancellation of part, or all, of the paid up or uncalled portion of the shares so that a £1 share of which £0.50 has been called up could become either a £0.75 share with £0.25 called up, or a £0.25 share fully paid.

Since management can usually find ways of using any surplus capital which may be available, the usual reason for capital reduction is: (a) **where share capital is not represented by available assets**. This situation is usually shown up by a net loss being carried forward on the profit and loss account, or by assets standing in the balance sheet either actually being worth less than their stated value, or by their suddenly having a nil value due to obsolescence.

Example

XY Ltd
Balance Sheet

	£		£
Ordinary shares of £3 each fully paid	150,000	Net assets	100,000
		Profit and loss account (loss balance)	50,000
	150,000		150,000

In this case it is assumed that the balance sheet asset valuation is a realistic one, and that the loss balance has been on the company's books for some years. It is not usual for a company to be able to pay a dividend while there is a loss balance on the profit and loss account, and even if profits are currently being made, it may be some years before such a loss balance can be cleared.

It would, subject to the usual procedures, be possible to reduce the company's share capital by cancelling that portion which is no longer represented by assets i.e. £50,000.

This could be achieved in either of two ways; either by reducing the value of each share from £3 to £2 or by reducing the number of shares of £3 each held by shareholders, which is done by issuing two new £3 shares for each three of the old shares held.

The balance sheet after reduction will appear as follows:

XY Ltd
Balance sheet (after reduction)

	£		£
Capital–Shares of £3 each fully paid	100,000	Net assets	100,000

The accounting entries to bring about the above situation are as follows:

1 To reduce the share capital account:

- *Debit* Share account   £50,000
- *Credit* Capital reduction account   £50,000

2 To write off the loss on the profit and loss account:

- *Debit* Capital reduction account   £50,000
- *Credit* Profit and loss account   £50,000

3 If there had been a reduction in the value of assets then:

- *Debit* Capital reduction account
- *Credit* Assets account by the amount of the reduction

4 If there had been a reduction in the value of liabilities (usually an agreed reduction as part of a large overall scheme):

- *Debit* Liability account
- *Credit* Capital reduction account with the amount of the reduction

The above example is a simple solution, in practice, however, *all* interested parties would have to be considered, and the Court has to agree to the reduction, having of course satisfied itself that all parties have been adequately considered.

When some of the company's assets are no longer required for the efficient running of the company – usually brought about by the contraction of the business where assets such as buildings or plant etc., may be sold, and the cash no longer needed in the company (a less likely situation than above) is repaid.

In such cases, subject to normal procedures, surplus cash is returned to shareholders by either of the following:

1 Reducing the number of shares held by each shareholder.
2 Reducing the nominal share value of each share held.

The accounts procedure is as follows:

● *Debit* Share capital account by the amount to be repaid
● *Credit* Sundry shareholder's accounts
● *Debit* Sundry shareholder's accounts with cash being repaid
● *Credit* Cash account

Exercise 5.1

The balance sheet of GHK Ltd at today's date is as follows:

GHK Ltd
Balance sheet

	£000		£000	£000
Authorized and issued		Goodwill		12
share capital		Freehold property		130
Ordinary shares of 50p		Machinery at cost	148	
fully paid	100	less depreciation	79	69
5% cumulative		Investments		32
preference shares of £1	50	Preliminary expenses		3
10% Debentures 1985	100	Profit and Loss Account		68
(secured on property)		Stock		37
Creditors	43	Debtors		28
Bank overdraft	81			
Accrued debenture interest	5			
	379			379

The company has suffered heavy losses in recent years, and the dividends on the preference shares are now two years in arrears. The necessary approval has just been given for the following capital reduction scheme:

1 The profit and loss account and all intangible assets are to be written off completely.
2 Debts of £3,000 and stock with a book value of £11,000 are to be written off.
3 The machinery is to be written down to £48,000.
4 The debenture holder is to take over the property at a valuation of £200,000 and pay the company the balance in cash, after deducting the amount due to him.

5   All investments are to be sold for £36,000.
6   The existing ordinary shares are to be written down to a nominal value of 20p each.
7   The nominal value of the preference shares is to be reduced to 80p per share. The holders are to receive two ordinary shares for every £1 of dividends in arrear. Future preference dividends are to be at 8 per cent per annum.
8   The authorized share capital is to be changed to 250,000 ordinary 20p shares and 100,000 8 per cent preference shares.

Required:

1   The capital reduction account in the books of GHK Ltd, giving effect to the provision of the scheme.
    Note: Journal entries are *not* required
2   (a)   What are the main objectives of a capital reduction scheme?
    (b)   Briefly discuss whether they have been achieved in this case.
    Source: LCCI

Workings

1   All the assets which are written off including the debit balance on profit and loss are transferred to the debits of the capital reduction account thus closing those accounts.
2   £3,000 must be debited to the capital reduction account thus reducing the balance to £25,000 and similarly £11,000 transferred from the stock account reducing the value of stock to £26,000.
3   To reduce the machinery to £48,000 will require an additional £21,000 depreciation to be written off the machinery account.
4   The amount due to the debenture holder is £105,000 comprising the debentures of £100,000 plus interest due of £5,000. The net effect on the reduction account is a debit and this could be shown instead of the details listed.
5   The net gain on investments is £4,000 which could be credited to the capital reduction account instead of the two separate entries.
6   The ordinary share capital is reduced by 200,000 (50p − 20p) = £60,000.
7   The preference share capital is reduced by 50,000 (£1.00 − 80p) = £10,000. The new preference share capital will be 50,000 shares of 80p per share. Ordinary share capital will have to be increased by (two years × 5 per cent × £50,000) = £5,000 × 2 = 10,000 shares. Since they are 20 p each the nominal value in total will be £2,000.
8   These figures to be incorporated onto the balance sheet.

Solution

Capital reduction account

	£000		£000
Goodwill	12	Debentures	100
Preliminary expenses	3	Debenture interest	5
Profit and loss	68	Bank (property)	95
Debtors	3	Bank (investment)	36
Stocks	11	Ordinary share capital	60
Depreciation of machinery	21	Preference share capital	10
Property	130		
Investments	32		
Ordinary share capital (P/S)	2		
Balance – Capital reserve	24		
	306		306

Balance sheet of GHK Ltd (reconstructed)

	£000	£000
Fixed assets		
Tangible assets		
Machinery (cost)	148	
Less Depreciation	100	48
Current assets		
Stocks	26	
Debtors	25	
Bank (95 + 36 − 81)	50	
	101	
Less Creditors: Amounts falling due within one year	43	
		58
		106

Represented by:		
Share capital	Authorized	Called up
	£	£
Ordinary shares of 20p	50,000	42,000
Preference shares of 80p	40,000	40,000
		82
Capital reserve		24
		106

5.2   Capital reconstruction or reorganization

The term reconstruction is usually meant to cover the situation in which a company which is short of funds, goes into voluntary liquidation selling its assets and liabilities to another company, formed for the purpose, with the same name, objects and shareholders as the original company, but such shareholders are required to provide any additional capital required. A reconstruction will usually do either of the following:

1   Effect a compromise with shareholders who will be required to provide additional capital and/or creditors who will agree to accept shares or debentures in satisfaction of their debts.
2   Widen the scope of the objects clause contained in the memorandum of association or change the domicile of the company.

The required accountancy entries are in two parts:

1   In the liquidated company the normal entries to close off the company, as explained in the next section.
2   In the new company, the normal entries for the takeover of assets and liabilities in exchange for shares which may be fully or partly paid up, as explained in Chapter 4.

Reorganization is the term used to cover a rearrangement of a company's share capital by either (a) the consolidation of shares into shares of a larger nominal value, or the subdivision of shares into a smaller nominal value, such alterations are covered under the Companies Act 1985, the only statutory requirement being notification to the Registrar of Companies in accordance therewith: or (b) by subdivision of the share capital into various classes of shares or by consolidation of various classes of shares into a lesser number of classes or different classes. Revision of preferential rights will require the authorization of the shareholders and may well require confirmation by the Court.

Example

A company with an ordinary share capital of £500,000 being 250,000 shares of £2 each fully paid, decides to reorganize its capital structure, so that for each existing ordinary share, the shareholder will receive one £1 10 per cent preference share secured on the plant and machinery of the company and one £1 ordinary share of £1 each.

This reorganization not only requires the authorization of the shareholders, but since, by securing the preference shares on the plant and machinery of the company, the situation of the creditors is affected, it will also require confirmation by the Court. The accountancy entries required would be as follows:

Debit the ordinary share capital account	£500,000
Credit the new ordinary share capital account	£250,000
Credit the new preference share capital account	£250,000

All existing share certificates would need cancelling and new ones issuing for each class of share.

Liquidation – voluntary and compulsory

A company which is to cease functioning for whatever reason is said to go into liquidation. Such liquidation may be either voluntary or compulsory depending on the circumstances which call for the closure of the company.

Voluntary liquidation
Basically a company goes into voluntary liquidation when the shareholders decide to discontinue the existence of the company, and it is able to repay all its debts to the outside world in full, excluding shareholders. In such a situation the shareholders appoint one or more liquidators to wind up the company in compliance with the Companies Act.

Compulsory liquidation
When a company has got into difficulties and is unable to repay its debts in full, the creditors on realizing this, may call for a compulsory winding up of the company to safeguard their debts. In such a situation it is usual for the official receiver to take charge of the company, until such time as a liquidator has been appointed by the company and the creditors.

The procedure as far as the accounts are concerned will be the same in each situation.

Example
Let us assume that the balance sheet of D Ltd appeared in the books as follows: It is proposed to wind up the company and accept the offer of C Ltd to purchase:

D Ltd
Balance sheet

	£		£
Share capital	150,000	Plant and machinery	140,000
Debentures	100,000	Sundry debtors	50,000
Profit and loss account	20,000	Stock	70,000
Reserves	10,000	Cash	20,000
	280,000		280,000

The purchase consideration agreed was £200,000 in shares of C Ltd and the reissue of £100,000 debentures.

In the books of D Ltd:

Realization account

	£		£
Balance sheet value of assets disposed of:		C Ltd	
		Purchase consideration	200,000
Plant and machinery	140,000		100,000
Sundry debtors	50,000		
Stock	70,000		
Cash	20,000		
Shareholders account – profit on realization	20,000		
	300,000		300,000

Share capital

	£		£
Shareholders account	150,000	Balance b/d	150,000

Debentureholders account

	£		£
C Ltd – reissure	100,000	Balance b/d	100,000

Profit and loss account

	£		£
Shareholders account	20,000	Balance b/d	20,000

Reserves account

	£		£
Shareholders account	10,000	Balance b/d	10,000

Shareholders account

	£		£
C Ltd purchase consideration:			
200,000 Shares of £1 each		Realization account	
fully paid	200,000	Profit on realization	20,000
		Share capital	150,000
		Profit and loss account	20,000
		Reserves account	10,000
	200,000		200,000

C Ltd

Realization account	300,000	Debenture account	100,000
		Shareholders	200,000
	300,000		300,000

All other items which belonged to the D Ltd shareholders, which were not taken over by C Ltd, were transferred to the shareholders account, these items included the share capital, profit and loss and reserves balances.

The transfer of the profit on realization to the shareholders account balances the books off, thereby effectively closing the books of the company.

Part Three
Analysis of Income and Costs

The sequence of events through a manufacturing organization will be to make and sell. In a trading organization it will be to buy and sell. As we have seen in Section 1.3 the cost of sales is equal to the sum of opening stock plus purchases less closing stock. A manufacturing organization is more complex because it requires computation of the cost of goods manufactured in the period. A major problem is with the valuation of work in progress (alternatively termed work in process). This is because work in progress consists of materials issued, labour expended and value added in the form of services such as power, rent, use of machines and salaries of managers and others. Additionally some work will be almost completed whereas other work will only have just commenced, and thus incurred less expenditure. The matching and accruals principles require that such costs be dealt with accordingly and the problems inherent in this are dealt with more extensively in Part Four.

The trading account has as its primary objective the ascertainment and control of gross profit. It can be analysed by products, areas, branches and other suitable control divisions. More details are given in this part of the book as to how this is achieved. Similarly attempts may be made to apportion profits or expenses in the profit and loss account and this is illustrated.

Special forms of accounts could be the subject of another extensive volume and therefore the accounts illustrated in Chapter 7 are those most likely to be encountered in theory or practice.

Taxation is introduced only to the extent that it is necessary to appreciate its inclusion in the accounts. The UK system of taxation is predominantly of interest to the residents of that country and even this is changed every fiscal year. Consequently it is better to refer to an up-to-date text on that aspect of interest should more detailed knowledge be required.

6
More on revenue account items

6.1 The manufacturing account

To reiterate, the analysis of revenue and costs comprises three stages – manufacturing, trading, and profit and loss accounts. This is also the sequence of events; we make, sell and (hopefully) achieve a profit. Manufacturing accounts are accounts prepared to show costs of production i.e. manufacturing only. A pure trading organization does not require this account, merely a trading account, but a manufacturing organization requires both. Sometimes firms are divided into divisions which correspond to producing and distributing. Such segregation enables divisionalized control of separate functions and aids management. The separation of manufacturing or production costs can be into two major groups – **prime cost** and **overheads**. Prime cost theoretically varies with quantity produced and comprises **direct material, direct wages** and **direct expenses** (see Chapter 9). Overheads are always indirect expenses, some of which remain substantially unchanged in amount irrespective of the level of production. Expenses which are entirely associated with manufacturing such as depreciation of machinery should be charged entirely to the manufacturing account. Other expenses such as rent, rates and power cost may apply to factory buildings (manufacturing) or warehouse and garage (distribution). All selling and distribution costs are charged to the profit and loss account. In simple examples so are the administration costs but in others the salaries and expenses associated with factory management and administration are separated and apportioned.

The format of a manufacturing account will be similar to the following layout.

Manufacturing account for year ended 31 December 19x1

	£	£	£
Work in progress at 1 January 19x1			30,000
Direct materials used			
Material stock at 1 January 19x1	40,000		
Add purchases *less* returns	90,000		
	130,000		
Carriage inwards	4,000		
	134,000		
Less material stock at 31 December 19x1	32,000		
Direct material consumed		102,000	
Direct wages		210,000	
Direct expenses		15,000	
Production overhead*		305,000	
Cost of production for year			632,000
			662,000
Less work in progress at 31 December 19x1			42,000
Cost of goods completed in year			620,000

* This would be detailed as indicated in the example on page 193 or would represent absorbed overhead on one of the bases described in Section 9.5.

An important point regarding the manufacturing account is that the work in progress should be valued to include the same costs as those that make up the total of the cost of production i.e. they should be on the same basis.

An alternative layout to the above segregates the prime cost items first thus:

Manufacturing account for year ended 31 December 19x1

	£	£
Direct material consumed (details as above)	102,000	
Direct wages	210,000	
Direct expenses	15,000	
Prime cost		327,000
Production overhead		305,000
Cost of production for year		632,000
Add work in progress at 1 January 19x1		30,000
		662,000
Less work in progress at 31 December 19x1		42,000
Cost of goods completed in year		620,000

In this case the basis of stock valuation may well be prime cost only. Sometimes it is necessary to show an intermediate profit figure. This is frequently the case if price of sale is determined in competition with others. The difference between selling value of production and its cost is in this event termed **manufacturing profit** or something similar. The figure so determined is carried down to the second section of the revenue accounts and treated similarly to gross profit. Assuming the sales value of the goods produced above was £800,000 the result would be as follows:

	£
Sales value of production	800,000
Less manufacturing cost for year	620,000
Manufacturing profit	180,000

To the extent that any of the goods remained unsold at the end of the period, or if there was an opening stock of finished goods in the warehouse the stock movements would have to be adjusted in the trading account, to eliminate any unrealized profit.

6.2 The trading and profit and loss account

Trading and profit and loss accounts have already been introduced in Section 1.3 and there is not much to add in respect of the layout of these. It is comparatively easy to create separate trading accounts – usually in columnar form for different geographical areas, product groups or operating divisions. The following example is a combined exercise to illustrate the principles of, and construction of, a manufacturing account and a trading account with more than one product. Detailed notes are included to show the treatment of adjustments and also a profit and loss account and balance sheet to revise the contents of Chapter 1.

Exercise 6.1
You are required for APF Limited, a company which manufactures and sells two products X and Y, to prepare in vertical and columnar form:

1 Manufacturing, trading and profit and loss accounts for products X and Y for the year ended 30 June 19x7.
2 An appropriation account for the year.
3 A balance sheet as at 30 June 19x7.

The trial balance of APF Ltd at 30 June, 19x7 was as follows:

	£	£
Ordinary shares of £1, issued and fully paid (authorized £800,000)		800,000
6% Preference shares of £1, issued and fully paid (authorized £200,000)		100,000
Share premium		150,000
Retained profits, at 1 July 19x6		441,000
Fixed assets, at cost £1,200,000	914,000	
Stocks at 1 July, 19x6		
Materials	80,000	
Work in progress:		
Product X	34,000	
Product Y	29,000	
Finished products:		
Product X	280,000	
Product Y	150,000	
Debtors and creditors	306,000	90,000
Bad debts provision at 1 July 19x6		12,500
Sales: Product X (120,000 units)		1,200,000
Product Y (180,000 units)		1,200,000
Purchases of materials	720,000	
Manufacturing wages: Product X	100,000	
Product Y	200,000	
Manufacturing expenses	208,000	
Creditor for royalties, at 1 July 19x6		62,000
Payments for royalties	391,000	
Administration expenses	139,500	
Selling and distribution expenses	214,000	
Cash at bank and in hand	290,000	
	£4,055,500	£4,055,500

The following information is given:

1 Depreciation is to be provided on fixed assets at the rate of 10 per cent per annum on cost. Additions to fixed assets during the year amounted to £100,000, purchased on 31 December 19x6. The annual depreciation charge is to be apportioned among manufacturing, administration, and selling and distribution in the proportions of 8:1:1.

2 During the year the cost of materials consumed was £300,000 for Product X and £400,000 for Product Y.

3 Work in progress for both products was constant in quantity and value at the beginning and end of the year.

4 Stocks of finished product were:

	1 July 19x6 in units	30 June 19x7 in units
Product X	40,000	20,000
Product Y	30,000	50,000

These stocks are to be valued at manufacturing cost (i.e. materials consumed, manufacturing wages, royalties, manufacturing expenses and the depreciation apportioned to manufacturing).

5   Royalties of £2 per unit for Product X and £1 per unit for Product Y are payable on the quantities of products completely manufactured.

6   Manufacturing expenses, including the apportionment of depreciation, are to be divided between the products in proportion to the number of completed articles transferred from the factory to the finished product stock. All products are transferred immediately on completion.

7   Bad debts of £6,000 are to be written off and the bad debts provision is to be made equal to £15,000. These items are a selling and distribution expense.

8   Administration expenses, including the proportion of depreciation, are to be divided between the products in proportion to the number of products sold.

9   Selling and distribution expenses, including the proportion of depreciation, bad debts written off and any increase or decrease in the bad debts provision, are to be divided between the products in proportion to sales values.

10   Prepaid and accrued expenses at 30 June 19x7 were:

	Prepaid £	Accrued £
Administration expenses	2,000	1,000
Selling and distribution expenses	1,000	7,000

11   Provision is to be made for:

	£
Corporation tax on the year's profit	135,000
Preference dividend	6,000
Ordinary dividend	120,000

12   Advance corporation tax on dividends is to be ignored.

Source: CIMA

Workings

1   £100,000 was added to the value of fixed assets at cost halfway through the year, therefore, at 10 per cent per annum only six months depreciation is chargeable. The amount applicable is therefore 10 per cent (£1,200,000 − £100,000) plus 10 per cent $\times \frac{6}{12} \times$ £100,000) = £115,000. It is split in the ratio of 8:1:1. This means 80 per cent to manufacturing, 10 per cent to administration and 10 per cent to selling and distribution i.e. £92,000, £11,500 and £11,500 respectively.

2   Closing stocks are not given so they are deduced as the balancing figure when the cost of material consumed is deducted from the sum of opening stock and purchases.

3   It is not strictly necessary to include opening and closing work in progress since they are the same amounts and will cancel each other out. They are included to show where they will appear in the more

likely event that they are different figures, and for consistency with the format shown on page 188.

4   Manufacturing cost is specified as the basis of stock valuation and we therefore need to know the quantity produced in the period for the divisor into the costs incurred:

	Product X	Product Y
Units sold	120,000	180,000
Less in stock at 1 July 19x6	40,000	30,000
	80,000	150,000
Add in stock at 30 June 19x7	20,000	50,000
Produced in period	100,000	200,000
Manufacturing costs this period	£700,000	£1,000,000
Cost per unit*	£7.00	£5.00
Value of stock at 30 June 19x7	£140,000	£250,000

*   This is the same cost per unit as in the previous period which in practice is extremely unlikely.

5   Royalties for Product X, 100,000 units produced at £2.00 each £200,000. Royalties for Product Y 200,000 units produced at £1.00 each = £200,000.

6   Manufacturing expenses £208,000 plus depreciation £92,000 is equal to exactly £300,000 and the number of units transferred is 100,000:200,000 so the allocation will be £100,000 to Product X and £200,000 to Product Y.

7   There is a bad debt of £6,000 plus an increase in the provision of £2,500 making £8,500 write off to the selling and distribution expenses.

8   The total administrative expenses are £150,000 and are shared in proportion to the number of units sold 120,000:180,000 giving Product X £60,000 and Product Y £90,000.

9   Selling and distribution costs total £240,000 and being shared in proportion to sales value of £1,200,000:£1,200,000 means that each product takes an equal share of £120,000.

10   The net effect of the prepaid and accrued expenses is £1,000 reduction in the administration expenses and £6,000 increase in the selling and distribution expenses. They are shown separately in the balance sheet as they may not be similar items.

11   The taxation amounts to 50 per cent of computed profits. Preference and ordinary dividends have to be provided for in the appropriation account. They also appear as a short-term liability in the balance sheet.

The data can also be used to illustrate the main ratios derived from revenue accounts and demonstrate why subdivision of the figures is essential for control. These figures have been added to the answer.

Solution

APF Ltd
Manufacturing, trading and profit and loss account for year ended 30 June 19x7

Note		Product X £000	Product Y £000	Total £000	
3	Work in progress 1 July 19x6	34	29		63
	Material consumed				
	Stock at 1 July 19x6			80	
	Purchases			720	
				800	
2	Stock at 30 July 19x7			100	
2	Material consumed	300	400	700	
	Manufacturing wages	100	200	300	
6 ∫	Manufacturing expenses			⎰ 208	
1 ⎱	Depreciation	100	200	⎱ 92	
	Royalties	200	200	400	
	Costs incurred in period	700	1,000		1,700
		734	1,029		1,763
3	Work in progress 30 June	34	29		63
	Cost of goods finished during year	700	1,000		1,700
	Sales	1,200	1,200		2,400
	Finished goods stock 1 July 19x6	280	150	430	
	Cost of goods finished during year	700	1,000	1,700	
		980	1,150	2,130	
	Finished goods stock 30 June 19x6	140	250	390	
	Manufacturing cost of sales	840	900		1,740
	Gross profit	360	300		660
	Selling and distribution costs			⎰ 214	
1	Depreciation			⎟ 11.5	
10	Expenses due – net			⎟ 6	
7	Bad debts w/o and provision			⎱ 8.5	
		120	120	240	240
		240	180		420
	Administration costs			139.5	
10	Prepayments – net			(1)	
1	Depreciation			11.5	
		60	90		150
	Profit before taxation	180	90		270

Continued over.

	Total £000
Profit before taxation	270
Corporation tax	135
Profit after taxation to appropriation account	135

Profit and loss appropriation account for year ended 30 June 19x7

	£000
Profit for financial year	135
Less dividends on preference shares	6
Profit attributable to ordinary shareholders	129
Dividends on ordinary shares	120
Profit retained for year	9
Balance brought forward from previous years	441
Retained profit at end of year	450

APF Ltd
Balance sheet as at 30 June 19x7

	£000	£000	£000	£000
Fixed assets				
Tangible assets				
Fixed assets at cost			1,200	
Less depreciation			401	
				799
Current assets				
Stocks: Raw materials	100			
Work in progress	63			
Finished goods	390			
		553		
Debtors	306			
Less bad debts	(6)			
Less provision for bad debts	(15)			
		285		
Prepayments		3		
Cash at bank and in hand		290		
		1,131		
Creditors: amounts falling due within one year				
Trade creditors	90			
Royalties due	71			
Accrued expenses	8			
Provision for taxation	135			
Preference dividends	6			
Ordinary dividends	120			
		430		
Net current assets			701	
Total assets *less* current liabilities			1,500	

	£000	£000	£000
Represented by:			
Capital and reserves	*Authorized*		
Issued and fully paid up capital			
6% Preference shares of £1 each	200	100	
Ordinary shares of £1 each	800	800	
	1,000	900	
Share premium account		150	
Profit and loss account		450	
Capital employed			1,500

Analysis of the revenue account (supplementary to question)

	Product X	Product Y	Total
	%	%	%
Cost of goods manufactured to sales	58	83	71
Gross profit to sales	30	25	27.5
Net profit (before tax) to sales	15	7.5	11.3
Selling and distribution expenses to sales	10	10	10
Administration expenses to sales	5	7.5	6.25

The cost of manufacture per pound of sales is much higher for Product Y implying we would be better off selling more of Product X or seeking some cost reduction in the manufacture of Product Y. The selling and administration ratios are determined partly by the basis of apportionment between the products and these should be checked to see if they are really appropriate.

6.3 Departmental accounts

Many trading concerns deal in a variety of goods as is the case with supermarkets or department stores. Although the word department is used to refer also to other separate activities such as different production activities, it is usually reserved in financial accounts to describe the format of accounts used for retailing activities. Where a large number of different items are bought and sold effective management requires analysis of purchases, sales and expenses incurred in selling each line or group of products. Some products may have a high group gross profit ratio but a low rate of turnover and heavy incidence of selling and other costs. Others may have a low gross profit but high sales volume and fast turnover. Departmental analysis means these differences can be monitored. The main requirement is for separate analyses of:

- Purchases
- Sales
- Stock accounts
- Cash and credit sales
- Petty cash and other expenses

This is most simply prepared using columnar analysis similar to that already described. In a manual system this would mean columnized ledgers and day books. In computerized systems it is a simple matter for programmes to be compiled which will collate and present the data in the required format. The exact form of sales analysis depends upon the nature of the products. In a department store divided into separate selling areas there is usually at least one cash point per department and stationery used would have a suitable code or other identification. In a supermarket or other outlet where the customer collects the goods the analysis is usually at the checkout point. This may require the cashier to enter the code of the goods from information on the labels or, alternatively and more frequently these days, modern computerized systems pick up the coded details from the package by means of a scanner. This in turn obtains the price from the data store and automatically updates the stock records for the item. When the sales have been collected for the relevant period they are classified and totalled for posting to columnar accounts or computerized presentation.

The problem of expense analysis is similar. In a department store the salaries and wages of the sales staff can be exclusively assigned to that particular department e.g. furniture. In the supermarket the assistant may be responsible for keeping all shelves – food, household, wine etc. stocked up and similarly the cashier deals with all items. Here the amount of separation possible is restricted. Similarly packaging costs can be depart-mentalized but rent and rates cannot. The general procedure would be as follows:

1   Decide upon the departments or sales centres.
2   Analyse sales to departments.
3   Analyse all expenses which relate exclusively to the departments.
4   Decide upon a relevant basis of sharing or apportioning other expenses.
5   Agree with the various levels of management the expenses which are considered controllable by them.
6   Compile operating statements (profit and loss accounts) which facilitate control e.g. actual period figures compared with past periods and budgets, £ sales per square metre of space used, salaries and expenses per £ sales.
7   Ensure an effective system of control by internal audit to ensure minimum risk of fraud in handling cash, pilfering and inaccurate recording.

If attempts are made to compile accounts and present them on this basis the manager can see the performance of his department and be better motivated to control or improve it. Such statements also help to prevent incorrect data being used for decision making as the following example illustrates. Other examples of the principles involved will be found in Section 6.2 and Part Four.

Example

The following accounts reflect the performance of XY Trading Ltd, a store with two main departments selling furniture and electrical goods.

Trading and profit and loss acount for three months ended March 31 19x8

	Furniture		Electrical		Total	
	£000	%	£000	%	£000	%
Sales	180	100	120	100	300	100
Cost of sales	93	51.7	75	62.5	168	56
Gross profit	87	48.3	45	37.5	132	44
Selling and distribution costs	45	25	30	25	75	25
Departmental profit	42	23.3	15	12.5	57	19
Administration costs	26	14.4	13	10.8	39	13
Net profit	16	8.9	2	1.7	18	6

It can be seen that the information available from the two column analysis for furniture and electrical is an improvement on that which would be available in a single conventional account as shown in the total column. But this could still be misleading. Suppose that on the strength of the percentages revealed above the general manager advocates that because of the small profit made by the electrical department it would be better to close this down and save the costs involved thus increasing the total profit.

Questions requiring answers would include:

● How much space would be released and what would be done with it?
● Could we increase the sales of furniture?
● Would ceasing to sell electrical goods affect sales of furniture?
● What are the closure costs involved e.g. redundancy payments etc?
● How much of the selling and administration costs will we really save?

The last question is particularly relevant as can be illustrated by the following data and additional information. Suppose that you ascertain that the selling and distribution costs of XY Ltd above totalling £75,000 had been apportioned between the departments on the basis of the sales of each department and the administration costs had been apportioned in the ratio of 2:1. Further investigation shows that of the £75,000, wages, salaries and expenses directly attributable to the furniture department was £25,000 and to the electrical department £20,000. In the case of administration costs £10,000 was incurred specifically in respect of the furniture department and £5,000 in respect of the electrical department. The remaining costs are considered fixed and would be incurred whatever the decision. We would then have:

XY Trading Ltd
Revised trading and profit and loss account for three months ended 31 December

	Furniture £000	Furniture %	Electrical £000	Electrical %	Total £000	Total %
Sales	180	100	120	100	300	100
Cost of sales	93	51.7	75	62.5	168	56
Gross profit	87	48.3	45	37.5	132	44
Allocated selling and distribution costs	25	13.9	20	16.6	45	15
	62	34.4	25	20.9	87	29
Allocated administration costs	10	5.5	5	4.2	15	5
Department contribution	52	28.9	20	16.7	72	24
Fixed costs						
Selling and distribution					30	10
Administration					24	8
Net profit					18	6

The nature of contribution in the accounting sense is explained further in Part Four as is the treatment of fixed and variable costs. The rate of contribution for furniture is 20.9 per cent of sales compared with 16.6 per cent for electrical. (Compare these figures with 48.3 per cent and 37.5 per cent for gross profit.) If the sales of electrical goods were discontinued the total contribution would be that of the furniture department only i.e £52,000. But we would still have to find fixed expenses of £54,000 and so the net effect would be to transfer a total present profit of £18,000 into a total loss of £2,000. Costs for decision making are frequently different to costs prepared for day-to-day control or end-of-the-year results. Nevertheless the dangers of sharing out costs on simple but misleading bases should continuously be borne in mind when preparing accounts such as above.

7
Special forms of accounts

7.1 Branch accounts: home branches

When a business operates in a number of different places financial control is obviously more difficult than when all activities take place in one location. The most common examples are retail chain stores and department stores but the problems apply equally to multiple manufacturing units. It is usual to divide the approach according to one of three situations:

1 Branches where most accounting records are kept by head office.
2 Branches where separate accounts are kept by branches.
3 Foreign branches and transactions.

Branch accounts kept at head office

Goods may be invoiced to branches at cost or selling price. The selling price method is utilized particularly when items have a separate physical existence as one unit and actual or recommended selling prices exist. Invoicing at selling price provides a check on branch honesty and efficiency since losses can be isolated into cost and importance. The branch records consist of cash receipts/payments and stock. The branch will incur certain local expenses which may be payable by the manager. These should be paid out of a separate cash 'float' and preferably as much as possible by cheque. Large bills, wages and salaries should be paid by the head office to minimize fraud. The main accounts are the **branch stock account** which records receipts and sales and the **goods sent to branch account**. Where there is a constant profit percentage mark-up on cost or sales the branch stock account may be recorded in two columns – one at selling price and one at cost price thus automatically providing the theoretical stock value. Debits on the account would be any opening stocks and goods sent to branches. Credits would be sales, whether credit or cash, any returns to head office and any recognized losses. If there were a deficiency between the balance and the value of stock taken and valued at the date of the account an investigation would be required. Where goods are sold with a variety of margins a **branch adjustment account** is used. This enables an average mark-up to be computed and also provides the means of 'adjusting' theoretical to actual profit.

Exercise 7.1

Emu has a head office and two branches. On 1 January Year 8 he decided to reduce his branch staff and to purchase all goods (for resale) through his head office. Under the new system head office purchased the goods and invoiced them to Branches E and U at their fixed selling price of cost plus 20 per cent.

The stocks at cost price on 31 December Year 7 (i.e. immediately before the introduction of the new system) were: Head office £85,000, Branch E £30,000 and Branch U £28,000.

During Year 8 the following transactions took place:

1   Head office purchases of goods for resale amounted to £1,700,000.
2   Goods invoiced by head office to branches at selling price – Branch E £480,000, Branch U £420,000.
3   Sales to customers – Head office £1,050,000, Branch E £450,000, Branch U £402,000.
4   Transfers from Branch E to Branch U of stock at selling price – £2,400.

On 31 December Year 8 stocktaking revealed shortages at head office (at cost) £2,000, at Branch E £600 (at selling price), and at Branch U £660 (at selling price).

Required:

1   Prepare for Emu in respect of Year 8 in the head office books:

(a)   Head office stock account (at cost)
(b)   Branch stock accounts for E and U (at selling price) in columnar form.
(c)   Branch stock adjustment accounts for E and U in columnar form.

2   Suggest the reasons for invoicing goods to branches at selling price.

Source: LCCI

Workings

1   The opening debit balance on the head office stock account is £85,000 Branch and this is increased by purchases of £1,700,000.
2   Selling price is cost plus 20 per cent therefore £480,000 goods to E must be worth $480,000 \times \frac{100}{120}$ at cost = £400,000 and similarly goods to U must be $420,000 \times \frac{100}{120}$ at cost = £350,000. These amounts are debited to the branch accounts.
3   The opening debit balances on the existing branch stock accounts are at cost price. They must be increased by 20 per cent to inflate to selling price the credit being to the branch stock adjustment account as this is the profit that should be realized when sold. The £480,000 and £420,000 (selling price) contain the profit element already so that the profit to be accounted for ultimately in the adjustment account is $\frac{20}{120}$ of £480,000 = £80,000 and $\frac{20}{120}$ of £420,000 = £70,000.

4 Sales to customers by head office $= \frac{100}{120} \times £1,050,000 = £875,000$ (at cost).

5 The profit on sales from branches is $\frac{20}{120} \times £450,000$ (E) and £402,000 (U) respectively. These figures of £75,000 and £67,000 are the profit achieved and are transferred from the adjustment account to credit of profit and loss.

6 Entry must also be made in respect of the profit no longer attainable on the revealed shortages $- \frac{20}{120}$ of £600 (E) and £660 (U) respectively. These debits of £100 and £110 reduce the amounts to the cost price of the losses.

7 The profit on the items transferred must be transferred between the branches with a contra entry of £400. This ensures branch profits are corrected.

8 The closing balance on the adjustment account is derived from, and should agree with, $\frac{20}{120}$ of closing stock balances on the branch stock account.

Solution

Head office stock account

		£			£
Balance	b/f	85,000	Branch stock (E)		400,000
Creditors		1,700,000	Branch stock (U)		350,000
			Cost of sales (HO)		875,000
			Profit and loss – shortage		2,000
			Balance	c/d	158,000
		1,785,000			1,785,000

Branch stock accounts

		E £	U £			E £	U £
Balance	b/f	30,000	28,000	Sales		450,000	402,000
Adjustment (to SP)		6,000	5,600	Branch U		2,400	
Head office stock and				Profit and loss –			
adjustment		480,000	420,000	shortage		600	660
				Balances	c/d	63,000	53,340
Branch E			2,400				
		516,000	456,000			516,000	456,000

Branch stock adjustment accounts

	E £	U £		E £	U £
Profit and loss	75,000	67,000	Branch stock	6,000	5,600
Branch stock	100	110	Branch stock	80,000	70,000
Branch U	400		Branch E		400
Balance c/d	10,500	8,890			
	86,000	76,000		86,000	76,000

Branches keeping their own records

This system gives far more freedom and imposes responsibility upon branch managers. Even where it is adopted some degree of centralization e.g. capital projects and large creditors may be preferred. This system may be more prevalent where price fixing and weight control is difficult as in chain butchers. A current account is created in the head office books for each branch and transactions pass through this, thus we would have Y Branch current account, Z Branch current account and so on. Each branch will have a head office current account which will show the entries in reverse. Any transactions initiated at the branch will have to be separately recorded. The following example illustrates the system.

Example
The following transactions were recorded between John Brown of London and its branch in Birmingham up to 31 December Year 5.

Goods sent by head office to branch, £60,000 of which goods to the value of £4,000 had not been received by the end of the year. A sum of £15,000 had been remitted at the opening of the branch on 1 January Year 5 to provide an imprest. Cash to the amount of £42,000 had been remitted by the branch to head office but £3,000 of this had not been received by 31 December. Goods retained during the year amounted to £2,500.

Account in the head office books

Birmingham Branch current account

Year 5		£	Year 5		£
	Cash	15,000		Returns	2,500
	Goods	60,000		Cash	39,000
				Balance c/d	33,500
		75,000			75,000
Year 6	Balance	33,500			

Account in the Birmingham Branch books

Head office current account

Year 5		£	Year 5	£
	Cash	42,000	Cash	15,000
	Returns	2,500	Goods	56,000
	Balance	c/d 26,500		
		71,000		71,000
			Year 6 Balance	26,500

When accounts are prepared at the end of a period a degree of consolidation has to take place and the balances on current accounts reconciled. The above balances differ by £7,000 because goods to the value of £4,000 had not been received by the branch and cash amounting to £3,000 had not been received by the head office. Temporary accounts may be opened to reconcile the position for year end accounts thus:

Head office books

Goods in transit account

	£	
Birmingham Branch	4,000	

Cash in transit account

	£	
Birmingham Branch	3,000	

The branch current account in the head office books can now be amended.

Birmingham Branch current account

		£		£
Balance	b/d	33,500	Goods in transit	4,000
			Cash in transit	3,000
			Balance c/d	26,500
		33,500		33,500

Exercise 7.2 shows preparation of final accounts under this system combined with the policy of invoicing goods at selling price. The closing stocks are not given so book value is deduced after all known entries have been made in the trading and profit and loss accounts. Care must be taken to ensure that where data is given at selling price it is adjusted to cost price.

Exercise 7.2

Mak, a retailer with a business in Queenstown, opened a new branch in Changi on 1 January Year 3. He continued to buy all goods at Queenstown and those he sent to the branch he invoiced at selling price, which included the consistent gross profit percentage of 20 per cent of selling price throughout his business. Separate books of account were kept at the two establishments.

At 31 December Year 3 the trial balances were:

	Queenstown £	£	Changi £	£
Capital		57,800		
Drawings	3,800			
Purchases	103,090			
Sales		78,100		50,900
Goods sent to branch		55,000		
Goods from head office			53,450	
Stock (HO) at 1 Jan Year 3	7,570			
General expenses	12,490		8,110	
Sundry fixed assets	32,000		16,000	
Bank	480		150	
Debtors	8,680		3,010	
Creditors		5,900		3,560
Branch current a/c	28,690			
Head office current a/c				26,260
	196,800	196,800	80,720	80,720

At that time no entries had been made in respect of the following matters:

1 There was a stock shortage at Changi in respect of goods with a selling price of £350. There was no stock deficiency at Queenstown.
2 Goods in transit to the branch were invoiced at £1,550, and cash in transit to Queenstown was £880.

Required:

1 Prepare trading and profit and loss accounts for head office and for the branch for the year ended 31 December Year 3, and a balance sheet for the entire business at that date. *Note:* Ignore depreciation of fixed assets.
2 Briefly explain the function of the current accounts in the trial balances.

Workings
1 Goods to branch 55,000 × ⅘ = 44,000
2 Stock in transit 1,550 × ⅘ = 1,240
3 Stock shortage 350 × ⅘ = 280
4 Profit: Queenstown 20% × 78,100 = 15,620
              Changi 20% × 50,900 = 10,180

5   Closing stock: Queenstown $82,280 - 78,100 = 4,180$

                   Changi $54,180 - (50,900 + 1,240 + 280) = 1,760$

6   The stock shortage of 280 is transferred to the debit of the profit and loss account thus writing it off.

Solution

Trading and profit and loss accounts for year ended 31 December Year 3

	HO £	Branch £		HO £	Branch £
Opening stock	7,570		Sales	78,100	50,900
Purchases	103,090		Stock in transit (2)		1,240
			Stock shortage (3)		280
	110,660				
(1) Goods to branch	(44,000)	44,000	Closing Stock (5)	4,180	1,760
	66,660	44,000			
(4) Gross profit	15,620	10,180			
	82,280	54,180		82,280	54,180
Stock shortage		280	Gross profit b/d	15,620	10,180
Expenses	12,490	8,110			
Net profit	3,130	1,790			
	15,620	10,180		15,620	10,180

Balance sheet as at 31 December Year 3

	£	£
Fixed assets		48,000
Current assets		
Stocks	5,940	
Goods in transit	1,240	
Debtors	11,690	
Bank	630	
Cash in transit	880	
	20,380	
Less		
Creditors	9,460	10,920
		58,920
Financed by		
Capital	57,800	
Add Profit	4,920	
		62,720
Less Drawings		3,800
		58,920

Note that the accounts of head office and all branches are combined into one figure for the balance sheet e.g. net profit is 3,130 plus 1,790 = 4,920. Current accounts are not shown on the balance sheet – only those items necessary to make them equal, in this case goods and cash in transit.

7.2   Branch accounts: Foreign branches

The main complication arises from differences in the **exchange rates** between the currency of the branch and that of the country in which the head office is located. No difficulty would arise if all the items in the branch trial balance could be converted at the same rate. However, remittances back to head office will have been converted at the rate of exchange ruling when the transfer actually took place and similarly fixed assets will have been entered into the account at the rate ruling when the asset was acquired. Goods transferred will have been at a variety of rates and, in addition to the problem of agreeing the current account, the situation poses problems in profit determination and asset valuation at the end of an accounting period. The objective is to distinguish gains or losses due to fluctuation in the exchange rates from real gains or losses due to the trading activities of the business. There are two main methods of valuation. With the **historic** (or temporal) method fixed assets are valued at the rate at date of purchase and current assets and liabilities at the rate at balance sheet date, except for stocks which may be at the estimated rate at acquisition. Revenue and expenditure items are deemed to have taken place evenly throughout the year and an average rate is used for conversion which reflects the whole period. Differences on conversion are treated on a conservative basis. A debit balance (loss) will be written off to the profit and loss account but a credit balance (gain) will probably be included in the balance sheet as a reserve.

The alternative method is the **closing rate** basis where balance sheet items are translated at the rate of exchange ruling at the balance sheet date. The revenue items may also be translated at the closing date or at the average rate ruling throughout the year. This method gives more realistic values and parallels the '**current cost accounting**' approach suggested as a better method of accounting under inflationary conditions.

7.3   Extended credit, hire purchase and leasing

The granting of credit facilities may range from short-term arrangements with individual customers for the purchase of more expensive durable goods to complex agreements for facilitating purchase by a company of very costly fixed assets. The legal implications must be considered in each case as these affect rights of ownership and operation. Depending upon fiscal policies governments may encourage such spending – low interest rate – or restrict it by imposing minimum deposits and repayment periods. Accountants are primarily concerned with the recognition of costs, income, ownership and liabilities at particular points in time. Although the principles may be consistent the degree to which they are applied depends upon whether the items are material i.e. significant in the accounting sense. If a company is engaged nationwide in large-scale trading on hire purchase (e.g. cars, electrical goods) then it is most important that profit attributable to a period is determined on a consistent and logical basis. On the other hand a one-man haulage business may have his main fixed asset purchased on HP to be accounted for on a basis which reflects continuing liability for repayment of the outstanding payment and degree of ownership.

The topic is extensive but for brief treatment and illustration of principles can be broken down into:

1 Businesses in retail activities conducting the majority of their sales over periods of a few months or years – each item of considerable value to the customer but a small element of total sales of the trader.
2 Businesses choosing to acquire their operating assets on a **hire purchase** or **leasing** basis probably because they are unable to raise cash for outright purchase or because they consider this method to be more beneficial cost wise or for operating efficiency. The financing may be through the supplier or through a third party (banks, finance houses) specializing in providing this facility. Since the 1960s there has been a huge expansion in this form of finance (sometimes referred to as '**off balance sheet**') and this has prompted publication by the accounting bodies of SSAP 21 – *Accounting for Leases and Hire Purchase Contracts*. This provides guidance on recommended treatment of large items from the point of the owner (lessor) and the user (lessee) particularly in respect of fixed assets.

Recognition of profit

When items are purchased by payments over intervals of time the total price paid is usually greater than if one immediate cash payment is made. From the point of view of the seller profit has not been fully realized until the final payment is made by the customer. Payments may extend over one or more financial periods and profit applicable to that period must be decided upon. Profits can be recognized at the time of the sale or over the life of the contract.

1 *In period of sale:* This procedure is normally only followed if the credit period is short term. The trade debtors are debited and sales credited with the full amount and, in the same period, the cost of sales is deducted to obtain gross profit. As payment is received the balance on debtors is reduced.
2 During term of contract
  Here the choices are:
  (a) Assume payments first received are recovery of the cost price and after this profit. This is a very conservative approach and could distort profit performances between years.
  (b) Assume payments first received are profit – the balance of payments considered to be recovery of cost. This is least favourable with accountants as full credit is taken for profit while the possibility of bad debts exist.

(c)   Instalment method – This is a compromise method between the previous two methods.

Instalment method

This method can be illustrated first by assuming – which is sometimes the case to boost sales – that no interest charge is being made. Assume a seller has an article that cost £175. A customer has agreed to buy the article paying an immediate deposit of £45 and the balance in twelve monthly instalments of £15 each. The total of the sale is £225 and would be recorded as follows:

Cash	£45	
Instalment contract receivable – 19x8	£180	
Instalment sales – 19x8		£225

The cost of sales entry would be:

Cost of instalment sales 19x8	£175	
Stock		£175

The entry to close the accounts would be:

Instalment sales	£225	
Cost of instalment sales		£175
Gross profit on instalment sales		£45

The rate of gross profit is $\frac{45}{225} \times 100 = 20$ per cent of sales over the whole of the transaction. Suppose the sale took place on 1 July with subsequent payments on the first of each month. At the end of 19x8 the deposit of £45 plus five payments of £15 will have been received making a total of £120. There is a balance outstanding on the instalments contracts receivable account of £105 (£180 less £75) paid. The amount of profit is considered to be 20 per cent of the amount collected, which in 19x8 was £120 so credit can be taken this year for £24.

The account would be as follows:

Gross profit on instalment sales

		£			£
Instalment sales			Instalment sales		
Gross profits realized		24	(total profit)		45
Balance	c/d	21			
		—			—
		45			45
		—			—
			Balance	b/d	21

The balance of £21 represents 20 per cent of the remaining balance in the instalment contracts receivable.

The above represents one item only and ignores the probability that interest would be charged but the same principles apply as illustrated in later examples. The items would be aggregated and shown on the balance sheet as instalment accounts receivable, and gross profits on instalment accounts receivable. The receivable account is shown by year and in total as follows.

	£000	£000	£000
Trade debtors		150	
Instalment contracts			
receivable			
19x6	20		
19x7	80		
19x8	160		
etc		260	
			410

Total debtors are £410,000.

The unearned gross profit may be shown in one of three ways:

1　As a current liability like any other unearned income.
2　As profit and part of net worth since only collection is required for profit to be realized.
3　As a reduction from the receivable account on the proposition that there may be some accounts which will not be collected.

Hire purchase – buyer

The above notes refer primarily to trading items affecting the revenue accounts. The other aspects of hire purchase accounting concern recognition of cost, ownership and liability in respect of assets which have been acquired or sold under long-term payment agreements. The account entries and principles involved from the point of view of the buyer, purchaser or lessee can be illustrated with the following example.

Example

On 1 January Year 1 Crabb Ltd purchased a machine on hire purchase, the cash price of which was £96,000. Under the agreement a total of £115,782 was payable, being a deposit of £32,000 on delivery, and two equal instalments of £41,891 on 31 December Year 1 and Year 2. Interest was included, calculated at 20 per cent per annum on outstanding capital balances.

As the machine's life was expected to be closely related to the amount of its use, it was decided that its annual depreciation would be calculated by using a rate based on its usage, assuming no residual value. For this purpose its useful working life was estimated at 25,000 hours.

The machine was delivered, and all payments made, when due. The machine was used for 6200 hours during Year 1 and for 7400 hours during Year 2. From this information prepare the relevant ledger accounts in the books of Crabb Ltd for its financial years ended 31 December Year 1 and 31 December Year 2 and show the balance sheet extracts at 31 December Year 1 and Year 2, showing how the machine would be recorded.

Source: LCCI

Notes
1　The cash price of the machine is £96,000 and this is the amount which should be debited to the asset account and on which any depreciation

calculations should be based. Any difference between this figure and the total payments represents financing charges which should be dealt with as below. It would of course be acceptable to capitalize any separate costs of installation such as concrete foundations.

2   Following from 1 any depreciation charge is computed by reference to the cash price figure less any anticipated allowance for value as scrap at the end of its useful life. In this example there is no residual value and depreciation is to be the unit method of operating hours. The depreciation rate per hour will therefore be $\frac{96,000}{25,000} = £3.84$. The charge for Year 1 will be 6200 times this amount and for Year 2 7400 times giving £23,808 and £28,416 respectively.

3   The HP seller (or vendor) has supplied a machine worth £96,000 and the credit is in this account from the asset account. There are a variety of ways of accounting for interest (see SSAP) but this is specifically on outstanding capital balances. The balance to which interest is applied for Year 1 is 96,000 less deposit of 32,000 = 64,000 and 20 per cent of this is 12,800 – the charge for Year 1. For Year 2 the interest is 20 per cent of 34,909 = 6,982. This exactly balances the second payment of 41,891. If there were other items they would be aggregated in the hire purchase interest account and the total charged (annually) to profit and loss. In other cases for simplicity the total interest is divided by the number of payments and spread to each year on the number of payments in the year. In this example that would have produced an annual (simple) interest charge of $\frac{115,782 - 96,000}{2} = 9,891$ per year.

Other methods include discounting the future payments and the greater the amount involved the more sophisticated the treatment.

Machine account

Year 1		£			
1 Jan	HP vendor	96,000			

Provision for depreciation

Year 1			£	Year 1			£
31 Dec	Balance	c/d	23,808	31 Dec	Profit and loss		23,808
			23,808				23,808
Year 2				Year 2			
31 Dec	Balance	c/d	52,224	1 Jan	Balance	b/d	23,808
				31 Dec	Profit and loss		28,416
			52,224				52,224
				Year 3			
				1 Jan	Balance		52,224

HP vendor

Year 1		£	Year 1			£
1 Jan	Bank	32,000	1 Jan	Machine account		96,000
31 Dec	Bank	41,891	31 Dec	HP interest		12,800
31 Dec	Balance c/d	34,909				
		108,800				108,000
Year 2			Year 2			
31 Dec	Bank	41,891	1 Jan	Balance	b/d	34,909
			31 Dec	HP interest		6,982
		41,891				41,891

HP interest

Year 1		£	Year 1		£
31 Dec	HP vendor	12,800	31 Dec	Profit and loss	12,800
Year 2			Year 2		
31 Dec	HP vendor	6,982	31 Dec	Profit and loss	6,982

Balance sheet extracts
Year 1 Assets include:

Machinery (at cost)	96,000
Less Provision for depreciation	23,808
	72,192

Liabilities include:

Amounts outstanding on hire purchase (not yet due)	34,909

Year 2 Assets include:

Machinery (at cost)	96,000
Less Provision for depreciation	52,224
	43,776

Hire purchase – seller

The accounts of a business conducting most, or all, of its sales on hire purchase contain problems of profit recognition similar to those described above. If the goods are consumable goods, however, the amount involved per item will, in most instances, be relatively small. More and more firms are now taking advantage of extended financing arrangements to overcome risk and cash flow problems. The time interval is extended and although the seller may retrieve the goods for partial payment only they may be worn out due to use or have limited second-hand value. Valuation of income and asset worth used in the seller accounts must reflect this.

Exercise 7.3

Higgin and Botham formed a partnership on 1 January Year 1 for the purpose of purchasing, and then hiring out, machinery. They had no formal partnership agreement.

The machinery was all purchased on an instalment basis. This involved a deposit of 20 per cent with the balance paid in five equal half-yearly instalments commencing six months after purchase. Interest was at the rate of 24 per cent per year payable with the half yearly instalments and calculated on the balance owing at the beginning of each half year.

The hire charges, payable in full in advance, upon hiring the machinery, were calculated as 45 per cent per year on the cost price of the machinery. Higgin and Botham paid all maintenance, transport, installation and removal expenses.

Their financial records for Year 1 showed the following:

	Date	Machine	Cost
1 Machines purchased:	1 January	A	£10,000
	1 March	B	£25,000
	1 July	C	£20,000
	1 December	D	£22,000

2   Machine A was replaced by a superior model, Machine D, on 1 December. Machine A was sold on that date for £9,000.
3   All machines are depreciated at the rate of 24 per cent per year on cost from the date of purchase to the date of sale.

	Date	Machine	Hire period
4 Machines hired out:	1 February	A	6 months
	1 March	B	12 months
	1 September	A	3 months
	1 September	C	9 months

5   Expenditure for the year consisted of: Machine maintenance £1,700; purchasing a ten-year lease on premises (from 1 January) £20,000; transport etc. £1,100; office expenses £430; and £6,000 paid in advance for a six-year advertising campaign which started on 1 January.

Required:
1   Calculate the depreciation expense, the instalment interest expense, and the hire charge income for the year.
2   Prepare the profit and loss account and appropriation account of Higgin and Botham for Year 1.

Source: LCCI

Workings

1   *Depreciation charges:*

Machine A	£10,000 × 24% × $\frac{11}{12}$ (to date of sale) =	2,200
B	£25,000 × 24% × $\frac{10}{12}$	= 5,000
C	£20,000 × 24% × $\frac{6}{12}$	= 2,400
D	£22,000 × 24% × $\frac{1}{12}$	= 440
		10,040

2 *Instalment interest:*

Machine A	£(10,000 − 2,000) × 24% × $\frac{6}{12}$	=	960
	(8,000 − 1,600) × 24% × $\frac{6}{12}$	=	768
B	£(25,000 − 5,000) × 24% × $\frac{6}{12}$	=	2,400
	(20,000 − 4,000) × 24% × $\frac{4}{12}$	=	1,280
C	£(20,000 − 4,000) × 24% × $\frac{6}{12}$	=	1,920
D	(22,000 − 4,400) × 24% × $\frac{1}{12}$	=	352
			7,680

3 *Hire charge income:*

Machine A	10,000 × 45% × $\frac{6}{12}$	=	2,250
B	25,000 × 45% × $\frac{10}{12}$*	=	9,375
A	10,000 × 45% × $\frac{3}{12}$	=	1,125
C	20,000 × 45% × $\frac{4}{12}$*	=	3,000
			15,750

* Period to end of Year 1

Machine A had a written down value of £7,800 (10,000 − 2,200). It was sold for £9,000 so there was a profit on sale of machinery of £1,200.

Higgin and Botham
Profit and loss account for year ended 31 December Year 1

	£	£
Hire charges received		15,750
Profit on sale of machine		1,200
		16,950
Less Depreciation	10,040	
Instalment interest	7,680	
Maintenance	1,700	
Lease (1 Year)	2,000	
Transport	1,100	
Office expenses	430	
Advertising (1 Year)	1,000	
		23,950
Loss*		(7,000)
Higgin share of loss		3,500
Botham share of loss		3,500
		7,000

* Shared equally in absence of partnership agreement

Leasing

Leasing of industrial plant and equipment is practised more widely now than in the times when ownership was deemed synonymous with profit making. Modern plant gets outdated quickly and technological advance means advantage is always with the possessors of the most up-to-date machinery and equipment. Leasing leaves the problem of obsolete equipment with the owner (**lessor**) rather than the user (**lessee**). A leasing agreement is entered into with the suppliers or a finance house for specific periods or the life of the equipment which remains the property of the lessor who obtains the appropriate tax allowances as owners. The leasing charge or rental is a tax deductible expense for the lessee who, although never owning the equipment, is required to keep it reasonably maintained. This is the main distinction between hire purchase and leasing. A hire purchase agreement usually contains some clause permitting ownership to be transferred at the end of a hire period whereas leasing may permit the lessee to withdraw at certain time periods but the length depends upon the versatility of the equipment. The expansion of this form of financing caused serious concern that a company's commitments might not be adequately indicated under existing methods in end-of-year reporting. If generally known, the 'off balance sheet' financial arrangements might change opinion as to the state of the business. Accordingly an Exposure Draft (29) *Accounting for Leases and Hire Purchase Contracts* was issued by the Accounting Standards Committee in 1981 and became SSAP 21 in August 1984. This applies to leasing of fixed assets and recommends that the amounts concerned be **capitalized**, thus bringing the figures into the published accounts. Among the requirements are that finance leases be distinguished from operating leases. Finance leases are defined as those that transfer, substantially, all the risk and rewards of ownership of an asset to the lessee. The word *substantially* is the key word as this does not include legal title which we have seen is usually transferred upon completion of a hire purchase contract. The transfer is deemed substantial if the present value of the lease payments at a rate of interest implicit in the lease (or estimated) is equal to 90 per cent or more of the fair value of the leased asset. The payments by the lessee to the lessor of the full cost of the asset together with a return on the finance provided by the lessor secure most benefits of ownership for the lessor. In an operating lease the lessee pays rental for the hire of an asset over a period of time – usually less than the economic life. There is no substantial transfer of risk and reward – as the lessor is likely to relet the equipment at the end of the period.

7.4   Investment accounts

As described in Section 2.1 **investments** represent assets which are intangible – they consist of legal claims of various descriptions and not physical assets. Individuals and companies invest surplus funds to achieve a return on the sum invested, capital appreciation and, in the case of companies, for expansion or protection. They are separated on the balance sheet into (a) **long-term investments** which include shares in group companies, loans to group companies, shares in related companies and other investments and (b) **short-term investments** which appear under current assets.

A further division is into **quoted investments** and **unquoted investments** – quoted investments being those quoted on a recognized stock exchange. Since the balance sheet is a summary, each total may contain a large number of items, each of which must be individually recorded. Accounts will normally be opened to aggregate income from quoted and unquoted investments. Because of this, and the considerable movements in value which occur daily on the stock exchanges, separate accounts are normally kept for each investment. Additionally it is necessary to separate income from the capital cost. This is particularly relevant where the gain in the form of interest on fixed-rate securities accumulates logically on a time basis. Thus, the nominal value to which the interest rate relates is separated from the income and the capital cost. Ledger accounts with three columns on each side or the equivalent are normally used to record these transactions, each account headed with the name of that particular security.

Example
A company acquires £6,000 nominal of 5% debentures in Y Ltd for £4,000 on 1 January the interest payable on 1 April and 1 October. The account would appear as follows:

19x8		Nominal £	Income £	Capital £	19x8		Nominal £	Income £	Capital £
1 Jan	Bank	6,000		4,000	1 Jan	c			75
					1 Apr	Bank		150	
					1 Oct	Bank		150	
31 Dec	Investment income (P and L)		300		31 Dec	Balance c/d	6,000		3,925
		6,000	300	4,000			6,000	300	4,000

The interest is paid every half year. On 1 January three months has elapsed since the previous October, therefore included in the price of £4,000 is interesting amount to $\frac{3}{12} \times 5\% \times £6,000 = £75$. The interest due at date of purchase is entered into the capital column (credit side) or alternatively the net figure can be inserted on the debit side for the 1 January entry. The 'capital' amount paid for the £6,000 nominal must therefore be £4,000 − £75 = £3,925. If the investment is subsequently sold for a higher price the difference would be a capital gain – if sold for a lower price it would be a capital loss. Separation is important both from the part of principle – as distinct from capital gains and losses and from the point of taxation since the rates of tax applicable to income may be different to those applicable to capital gains or losses. In this example taxation is ignored as are costs such as stockbrokers' commission which would be adjusted in the capital column. Unless otherwise stated investments are assumed to be purchased 'cum div' as above that the buyer is entitled to receive subsequent dividends or interest. Dividends do not specifically relate to times so are not usually apportioned on a time basis. If the time for payment of the dividend or interest is very close to that of the selling or buying transaction there is no time to record the change of ownership. This situation is specified as 'ex div' and indication is given by the financial press and institutions concerned when dealings are on this basis. In this event dividends or interest go to the previous owner and the purchase price is therefore entirely capital. Most companies also adjust the accounts at balancing dates to recognize that interest is due for the period from the date of the last payment, to the balancing date. Thus in the example above (credit side) £75 is due for the three months from 1 October 19x8 to 31 December 19x8. Since the investment has been held for a whole year the amount transferred to the investment income account (debit side) to the credit of that account and subsequently to the profit and loss account is £300, equal to a complete year's interest on the investment.

If the whole of the holding of a particular investment is subsequently sold at one date the ascertaining of profit and loss on sale is simply the difference between the price originally paid and that realized. If part only of the holding is sold or if there have been later purchases some basis of apportioning the original cost must be agreed upon and usually this is on the assumption of FIFO (first in first out) that the holding purchased first is assumed first to be sold as in stock examples.

Exercise 7.4 illustrates the procedure in respect of fixed interest terms.

Exercise 7.4

Funam Ltd, a manufacturing company, has for some years invested surplus funds in government 6% stock, on which interest is paid gross in equal instalments every 1 February and 1 August.

At 1 January Year 5, the company held £8,000 nominal of this stock, with a total book value of £7,080, including interest thereon accrued since the last payment.

The company's sales and purchases of this stock over the next two years have been as follows:

31 March Year 5	Purchased £5,000 nominal for £4,500.
1 December Year 5	Sold £4,000 nominal for £3,860.
1 March Year 6	Sold all stock remaining for £6,345.

There is no intention of investing further funds in this way. When calculating the profit or loss at the time of a sale of stock, the company applies the 'first in, first out' principle.

Required:

1 Show the investment account 'government 6% stock' in the books of Funam Ltd for the financial years ended 31 December Year 5 and 31 December Year 6. The account should be balanced off at both 31 December Year 5 and 31 December Year 6. Ignore brokerage and taxation.

2 Assuming that the amount is material, state how the profit or loss arising from the sale of stock in Year 6 should appear in the profit and loss account for that year.

Source: LCCI.

Workings

1 Interest due at opening date of account is $\frac{5}{6}$ of the half year interest due

on 1 February.

$= \frac{5}{6} \times \frac{1}{2} \times 6\% \times 8,000$ i.e. $\frac{5}{12} \times 6\% \times 8,000 = £200$

Total book value = £7,080 i.e. capital plus interest therefore capital value only = £7,080 − £200 − £6,880

2 On 1 February half year interest is £240 is received and credited to the investment account debiting interest received or bank.

3 On 31 March £5,000 nominal value purchased for £4,500. Interest

included in the £4,500 $= \frac{2}{12} \times 6\% \times £5,000 = £50$.

This can be entered as £4,500 on the debit side and £50 on the credit side (capital column). Alternatively the net figure of £4,450 could be shown on the capital side only but this is less informative as time goes on. In either case the interest of £50 must be posted to the debit side (interest column). This will reduce the balance to the correct figure for the time applicable when the interest is subsequently received.

4 The next transaction reflects the interest received on 1 August Year 5.

This is $\frac{6}{12} \times 6\% \times (£8,000 + £5,000) = £390$.

5 On 1 December Year 5 we sold £4,000 (nominal) value of our investment for £3,860. The interest due at this date was from 1 August i.e. 4 months =

$\frac{4}{12} \times 6\% \times £4,000 = £80$

therefore capital value = £3,860 − £80 = £3,780.

The £80 interest must be posted to the credit side of account (interest column).

6 At 31 December there is five months' interest due from 1 August on our

reduced total holding of 9,000 nominal (8,000 + 5,000 − 4,000) $= \frac{5}{12} \times$

$6\% \times 9,000 = £225$. The capital position is that on a first in first out basis 4,000 nominal of the oldest item was deemed sold on 1 December. This theoretically came entirely out of the £8,000 balance on 1 January

therefore proportionate capital cost remaining is $\frac{4,000}{8,000} \times £6,880 =$

£3,440 which, added to the £4,450 paid (capital) for the purchase of 5,000 units on 31 March is £7,890. When the credit sides have been totalled the differences between these and the debit side represents profit (in this case) or losses to be transferred in respect of interest and capital to the profit and loss account. Thus at the end of Year 5 the amount transferred to profit and loss will be the balancing figures of interest) £685 and capital £340.

7 £9,000 nominal of stock sold on 1 March Year 6 will include ($\frac{1}{12} \times 6\%$

$\times 9,000) = £45$. The amount received in respect of capital will be £6,345 less £45. The £45 must still be included in the interest column.

8   The balancing figure of £90 on the debit side for 31 December represents interest received during the year for the time (2 months) the stock was held prior to disposal $\frac{2}{12} \times 6\% \times 9,000 = £90$. This provides a check on the other calculations. Since in the capital column the debit exceeds the credit by £1,590 this must be the loss on sale.

Solution

Government 6% stock

Year 5		Nominal £	Interest £	Capital £	Year 5		Nominal £	Interest £	Capital £
1 Jan	Balance	8,000	200	6,880	1 Feb	Interest		240	
31 Mar	Bank	5,000		4,500	31 Mar	(c)			50
31 Mar	(c)		50		1 Aug	Interest		390	
1 Dec	(c)			80	1 Dec	Bank	4,000		3,860
31 Dec	Profit and loss			340	1 Dec	(c)		80	
31 Dec	Profit and loss		685		31 Dec	Balance c/d	9,000	225	7,890
		13,000	935	11,800			13,000	935	11,800
Year 6					Year 6				
1 Jan	Balance	9,000	225	7,890	1 Feb	Interest		270	
1 Mar	(c)			45	1 Mar	Bank	9,000		6,345
31 Dec	Profit and loss		90		1 Mar	(c)		45	
					31 Dec	Profit and loss			1,590
		9,000	315	7,935			9,000	315	7,935

(c) = contra entry

Even if the net figures are posted for capital and interest on a sale or purchase although the total is different the balances and transfers are unaffected as indicated in the alternative below.

Government 6% stock

Year 5		Nominal £	Interest £	Capital £	Year 5		Nominal £	Interest £	Capital £
1 Jan	Balance	8,000	200	6,880	1 Feb	Interest		240	
31 Mar	Bank	5,000		4,450	1 Aug	Interest		340	
31 Dec	Profit and loss		685		1 Dec	Bank	4,000		3,780
31 Dec	Profit and loss			340	1 Dec	(c)		80	
					31 Dec	Balance c/d	9,000	225	7,890
		13,000	885	11,670			13,000	885	11,670

Government 5% stock

Year 5		Nominal £	Interest £	Capital £	Year 6		Nominal £	Interest £	Capital £
1 Jan	Balance	9,000	225	7,890	1 Feb	Interest		270	
31 Dec	Profit and loss		45		1 Mar	Bank	9,000		6,300
					31 Dec	Profit and loss			1,590
		9,000	270	7,890			9,000	270	7,890

Note: Interest entries may be shown as 'bank' if not being posted via an 'interest received' account.

The profit or loss on investments would be shown as an exceptional item being disclosed and deducted before showing profit on ordinary items unless, that is, the business itself is an investment trust or something similar in which case its 'normal' activities would be gains/losses on sale of investments. As requested brokerage and taxation have been ignored but these items merely reduce capital gains and interest respectively. A typical illustration of investment groupings in a public company balance sheet is given on page 437.

7.5 Royalty accounts

Royalties are payments for the right to use a patented article, or to publish a copyright manuscript or reproduce records and videos. It is usually at a fixed rate per article or percentage of cost or retail price. The rate may be different for varying levels of sales. For example in the case of a book it may be 10 per cent of the published price for the first 25,000 copies sold and 15 per cent thereafter. The type of payment more common in accounting texts, as they usually require slightly more complex treatment, are royalties paid for the right to exhaust the resources of land as for example coal mines and oil wells. In this case the royalty would be per tonne, bushel, gallon etc. In some instances it may be some time before the mine or whatever comes into an economic scale of output or there may be some doubt as to whether the resources claimed are still there. In this case the owner, landlord or lessor may not be prepared to let the operator or lessee disturb and exploit the property without a guaranteed return. He may fix a minimum rent which must be paid if the achieved output at the royalty rate is less than this figure. This ensures a guaranteed minimum income to the landlord. When the royalties due are greater than the minimum the whole of the higher amount is paid. This means that as far as the operator is concerned the payment is the same as a fixed rental.

Example
Able Ltd have obtained the right to extract coal from the land of Baker. Under the agreement a royalty of £0.30 was payable per ton extracted. The tonnage extracted was as follows: Year 1 – 5000 tons, Year 2 – 6000 tons, Year 3 – 8000 tons, Year 4 – 9000 tons, Year 5 – 12000 tons. The accounts in Able's books to record the transactions would be as follows:

Notes

			£
Amounts due = Year	1	5,000 × 0.30 =	1,500
	2	6,000 × 0.30 =	1,800
	3	8,000 × 0.30 =	2,400
	4	9,000 × 0.30 =	2,700
	5	12,000 × 0.30 =	3,600

All that is required is a royalties account and a personal account for the landlord – Baker.

Royalties account

	£		£
Year 1 Baker	1,500	Year 1 Profit and loss	1,500
Year 2 Baker	1,800	Year 2 Profit and loss	1,800
Year 3 Baker	2,400	Year 3 Profit and loss	2,400
Year 4 Baker	2,700	Year 4 Profit and loss	2,700
Year 5 Baker	3,600	Year 5 Profit and loss	3,600

Baker account

	£		£
Year 1 Bank	1,500	Year 1 Royalties	1,500
Year 2 Bank	1,800	Year 2 Royalties	1,800
Year 3 Bank	2,400	Year 3 Royalties	2,400
Year 4 Bank	2,700	Year 4 Royalties	2,700
Year 5 Bank	3,600	Year 5 Royalties	3,600

Suppose the agreement is amended for a minimum rent to be payable in any year of the first five when royalties are less than £2,000. This applies to Years 1 and 2 and in this case the first two years of the above accounts would appear as follows (the latter Years 3–5 would be unaffected):

Royalties account

	£		£
Year 1 Baker	2,000	Year 1 Profit and loss	2,000
Year 2	2,000	Year 2 Profit and loss	2,000

Baker account

	£		£
Year 1 Bank	2,000	Year 1 Royalties	2,000
Year 2 Bank	2,000	Year 2 Royalties	2,000

The difference between the actual royalties for Year 1 of £1,500 and the amount paid of £2,000 is termed **shortworkings**. For Year 1 they are £500 and for Year 2 £200. Sometimes these are wholly or partly recoverable out of the higher output of future years. If they are not recoverable after a certain date then that excess will have to be left unrecovered. The reasons why shortworkings are recoverable are to allow for short-term fluctuations in output in the early years due perhaps to exploration and operating difficulties but at the same time provide a guaranteed return to the landlord. Suppose that the condition for minimum rent was amended in the agreement to the effect that the minimum rent would be £2,300 per annum and shortworkings would be recoverable up to Year 4 only, we now need a 'shortworkings' account to record the balances. It is simply a suspense account smoothing out the charges to profit and loss in line with the agreement. When the allowance for shortworkings is exhausted the balance remaining on the shortworkings account must be debited to the profit and loss. Ultimately the amount paid to the landlord in total and that charged against profits must be the same.

Royalties account

	£		£
Year 1 Baker	1,500	Year 1 Profit and loss	1,500
Year 2 Baker	1,800	Year 2 Profit and loss	1,800
Year 3 Baker	2,400	Year 3 Profit and loss	2,400
Year 4 Baker	2,700	Year 4 Profit and loss	2,700
Year 5 Baker	3,600	Year 5 Profit and loss	3,600

Baker account

		£				£
Year 1	Bank	2,300	Year 1	Royalties		1,500
				Shortworkings		800
		2,300				2,300
Year 2	Bank	2,300	Year 2	Royalties		1,800
				Shortworkings		500
		2,300				2,300
Year 3	Bank	2,300	Year 3	Royalties		2,400
	Shortworkings	100				
		2,400				2,400
Year 4	Bank	2,300	Year 4	Royalties		2,700
	Shortworkings	400				
		2,700				2,700
Year 5	Bank	3,600	Year 5	Royalties		3,600

Shortworkings account

			£				£
Year 1	Baker		800	Year 1	Balance	c/d	800
Year 2	Balance	b/d	800	Year 2	Balance	c/d	1,300
	Baker		500				
			1,300				1,300
Year 3	Balance	b/d	1,300	Year 3	Baker		100
					Balance	c/d	1,200
			1,300				1,300
Year 4	Balance	b/d	1,200	Year 4	Baker		400
					Profit and loss		900
			1,300				1,300

Over five years the total paid of £12,800 equals the total debits to profit and loss.

8
Taxation

Hitherto we have ignored taxation, apart from its appearance in the examples of published accounts to which we have referred. Taxation of profits is, however, a fact of life and it is necessary for us to consider how it affects a firm's accounts. The two taxes which we shall be concerned with are:

1 *Income tax*, which is a tax on personal incomes.
2 *Corporation tax*, which is a tax levied on the profits of companies in addition to the tax credit available to shareholders on the dividends which they may receive.

We shall consider these taxes in relation to the three types of business organization.

8.1   The sole trader

The total income of the sole trader, including his business profits, is assessed as a whole, taking into account any personal allowances to which he is entitled. The profits on his business which are included in his income for tax purposes will not necessarily be calculated on the same basis as in his accounts.

The assessment year for **income tax** purposes runs from 6 April to the following 5 April. This is the year of assessment and all income under the various schedules, e.g. Schedule A for rents and Schedule D Case 1/11 for profits, would be summed to provide the total income upon which the tax demand would be based.

8.2   The partnership

The profits of the partners form part of their individual total incomes, each of which is assessed as a whole, taking into account any personal allowances to which they are entitled. To make the necessary calculations it is necessary to have details both of the profits of the partnership and of the individual circumstances and other sources of income of each of the partners. The amount due from each partner will be debited to his drawings account and credited to a taxation account. When the amount involved is paid over to the Inland Revenue the taxation account will be closed. The applicable duties and schedules would be as described for the sole trader.

8.3   Aspects of company taxation

Companies pay **corporation tax** on their assessable profits. At the outset it is important to understand that assessable profit and net profit have different definitions. To arrive at assessable profit the net profit earned by a company is adjusted for certain items, e.g. depreciation charged against net profits is added back and substituted by capital allowances. It is not proposed to deal with the detailed rules relating to the calculation of assessable profits as this is a specialized topic best covered in a book dealing specifically with taxation. In this book we are more concerned with those aspects of company taxation which affect the **presentation** of companies' annual accounts.

The rate of corporation tax is fixed by the Chancellor of the Exchequer, usually in his annual budget. The tax year for companies runs from 1 April to the following 31 March. The rate fixed in the budget (usually in March or April) is applied to the assessable profits earned by companies during the twelve months previous to 31 March.

Example

In the budget announced in April 1984 the corporation tax rate was fixed at 50 per cent. Therefore assessable profits earned by companies from 1 April 1983 to 31 March 1984 (i.e. the Government's fiscal year) would be subject to a corporation tax rate of 50 per cent. Consequently, where a company's financial year spans two fiscal years then two rates of corporation tax may apply.

● Rate of corporation tax for the fiscal year ended 31 March 19x6 50%
● Rate of corporation tax for the fiscal year ended 31 March 19x7 40%

Company A Ltd: assessable profits for the financial year ended 31 December 19x6 £48,000.
Rate of tax applicable:

$$1 \text{ January 19x6 to 31 March 19x6: } 50\% \times \left(£48,000 \times \frac{3}{12} \right) = £6,000$$

$$1 \text{ April 19x6 to 31 December 31 19x6: } 40\% \times \left(£48,000 \times \frac{9}{12} \right) = £14,400$$

$$\overline{£20,400}$$

Payment of corporation tax

The dates on which a company pays corporation tax to the Inland Revenue depend on whether the payment relates to **advance corporation tax** or **mainstream corporation tax**.

Advance corporation tax (ACT)

When a company pays a dividend to its shareholders, a sum equal to a fraction of the dividend must be paid to the Inland Revenue within 14 days of the end of the quarter in which the dividend is paid. The fraction applied to the dividend payment depends on the standard rate of income tax applicable at the time, and is calculated as follows:

$$\frac{\text{standard rate of income tax}}{100 - \text{standard rate}}$$

Thus, if the standard rate is 30 per cent the ACT fraction applied to dividends will be:

$$\frac{30}{100 - 30} = \frac{3}{7}$$

Consequently, if a company pays a dividend of £21,000, and the standard rate of income tax is 30 per cent, the ACT payable within three months is $3 \div 7 \times £21,000 = £9,000$. It must be emphasized that the ACT is *not* deducted from the dividend paid to the shareholders, they will receive a total of £21,000 from the company. (*All* dividends are declared and paid *net*.)

The ACT paid is later deducted from the total corporation tax due on the assessable profits of the company's financial year from which the dividend was paid – up to an arithmetical maximum and any excess is available for carry forward or carry back.

Example

For the year ended 31 March 19x6 A Ltd had assessable profits of £200,000. During the year A Ltd paid a dividend of £42,000. The corporation tax rate is 50 per cent and the standard rate of income tax is 30 per cent.

Advance corporation tax payable = £42,000 $\times$ 3 $\div$ 7 = £18,000

Total corporation tax liability for the year £200,000 $\times$ 50% = £100,000
Less ACT already paid   18,000

Leaving mainstream corporation tax to pay of: £82,000

Mainstream corporation tax (MCT)

As shown in the examples above MCT is the amount of corporation tax owing to the Inland Revenue after deducting the ACT paid from the total tax liability. The date of payment of MCT depends on whether or not the company in question was trading before 1 April 1985.

For companies in existence before 1 April 1985 the date of payment of MCT is the 1 January following the end of the fiscal year in which the company's financial period ended. Thus if the financial year of A Ltd ended on 31 December 1985, then the end of the relevant fiscal year would be 5 April 1986. Thus the MCT is due for payment on 1 January 1987.

For companies who began trading after 1 April 1985 the mainstream corporation tax is due for payment nine months after the company's financial year end.

Income Tax – companies

As stated above, companies pay corporation tax on their assessable profits. In addition they may also make payments of income tax to the Inland Revenue. However, the income tax payments do not relate to the company's profits, instead they represent income tax deduction on certain payments made by the company. If, for example, a company pays debenture interest, income tax at the standard rate is deducted from the amount paid to the debenture holder and the tax so deducted is paid over directly to the revenue. This system simplifies the collection of taxes, although adjustments will have to be made directly between the revenue and the individual taxpayer if the standard rate of tax is not applicable to a particular taxpayer. Where a company receives income from which income tax has been deducted at source, the tax so deducted may be offset against the tax deducted and collected by the company itself, thereby leaving the balance only to be paid over to the Inland Revenue.

The imputation system

As explained in the earlier section on MCT when a company pays a dividend no tax is deducted from the amount paid to shareholders, although advance corporation tax is paid to the Inland Revenue by the company. The ACT so paid is regarded as a tax credit from the shareholders' viewpoint so that no additional tax liability will fall on the shareholder if the standard rate of income tax is applicable to his circumstances.

Example

A Ltd pays a dividend of £28,000; standard rate of income tax is 30 per cent.

The ACT fraction in this case is $\dfrac{30}{100 - 30} = \dfrac{3}{7}$

Therefore the ACT paid to the inland revenue by the company is $3 \div 7 \times £28,000 = £12,000$.

Thus if an individual shareholder receives a dividend of £70 he will disclose on his tax return an income of £70 plus £30 ($3 \div 7 \times £70$) tax credit. At a basic rate of income tax of 30 per cent the tax due on £100 is £30, but the shareholder is allowed to offset the tax credit against the tax charge. Clearly if the standard rate is not applicable to the shareholder a tax repayment or additional charge will be made.

Where a UK resident company receives a dividend from another UK resident company, the dividend received plus the tax credit is called **franked investment income**. Similarly the amount of dividend paid plus the tax credit is termed **franked payment**. During an accounting period a company receiving franked investment income can offset the tax credit against the advance corporation tax due on dividends paid, the balance only being paid over to the Inland Revenue. Where the franked investment income exceeds the franked payment the excess tax credit so arising can be set off against the advance corporation tax payable in the next accounting period.

8.4 Pay as you earn (PAYE)

In addition to deducting income tax from payments made in respect of dividends, interest on debentures and similar terms, a company (or any employer) is required to deduct income tax on payments of wages or salaries. But while the deduction of tax from dividends and interest is always made at the standard rate, the deduction from salaries and wages is related to the personal circumstances and total income of the employee.

This is achieved through the PAYE (pay as you earn) system. The Inland Revenue undertakes the work of assessing the tax-free allowances to which a person is entitled and the extent to which tax on income from other sources covers the tax liability of that person. This is estimated in advance for the fiscal year ending on 5 April. The results of these calculations are expressed in the form of a code number which is notified to the employer. Knowing the code number, the employer can, with the aid of tax tables supplied by the Inland Revenue, determine the tax-free pay to which the employee is entitled for that proportion of the fiscal year which has passed. Since certain amounts of income may be taxable at less than the standard rate, further tables are provided to indicate how much tax is due after making allowances for the reduced rate payable on part of the taxable pay.

This involves keeping certain information on a cumulative basis. The items are as follows:

1   Gross pay for the week or month.
2   Total gross pay since the beginning of the tax year.
3   Tax-free pay to date (from the tax tables).
4   Taxable pay to date.
5   Total tax due (from the tax tables).
6   Total tax paid since the beginning of the tax year.
7   Tax due or repayable for the week or month.

These items will be incorporated in the wages book and on each employee's tax record. So far as the accounts are concerned, the significant items is the tax due or overpaid at the end of the week or month, which is deducted or added when paying wages and salaries. The total amount involved is credited to a PAYE account, and the monthly remittance to the Inland Revenue is debited to this account. The entries for the last month of the company's financial year might well be:

PAYE account

			£				£
31 Dec	Balance	c/d	837.30	7 Dec	Weekly wages		128.25
				14 Dec	Weekly wages		132.50
				21 Dec	Weekly wages		130.40
				21 Dec	Monthly salaries		314.40
				28 Dec	Weekly wages		131.75
			837.30				837.30
15 Jan	Cash–Inland Revenue		837.30	1 Jan	Balance	b/d	837.30

When the balance sheet is prepared at 31 December the amount of £837.30 deducted from the December wages and salaries will not as yet have been paid over to the Inland Revenue. It will consequently appear on the balance sheet as a current liability.

8.5   Value added tax (VAT)

VAT is a tax goods and services which was introduced in 1973. Firms are required to add tax at the rate enacted to their sales when invoicing their customers. When remitting the tax to the Customs and Excise they are permitted to deduct the tax they have paid on their purchases of goods and services. It is necessary to accumulate the tax collected and paid either in analysis columns or in separate accounts and to transfer the totals to a VAT account in preparation for the payment of the tax each quarter. The VAT account might appear as follows:

VAT account

		£		£
Input tax			Output tax (tax charged on	
Imported goods		800	sales)	10,000
Purchase of UK goods		4,500		
Plant and equipment		600		
Telephone service		100		
Balance	c/d	4,500		
		10,000		10,000
			Balance being net amount pay-	
			able to Customs and Excise	£4,000

Certain businesses are zero rated which means that they are not required to add tax to their sales, but are entitled to reclaim tax paid on their 'inputs'. If this is applied in the above case, no tax would be charged and there would be no credit entry. The business is able to collect £6,000 from the Customs and Excise. Other businesses are exempt. As with zero rated businesses, these do not add tax to their sales, but are not able to collect tax paid on inputs from the Customs and Excise. If a business only makes exempt transactions it will not require to open a VAT Account; the amounts involved will be treated as expenses.

8.6   Foreign taxation

When a company receives income from abroad, the foreign country will normally have subjected the income to some form of taxation. There are double-taxation agreements with some countries whereby a company is permitted to set the payment of overseas taxation off in part against the corporation tax levied at home. There will, in any event, remain some foreign taxation which has to be borne by the company. This item is required to be shown separately in the profit and loss appropriation account or in the notes attached to it. The subject of double-taxation is a complex one and a matter for specialists.

Part Four
Management Accounting

9
The scope of management accounting

The accounting function provides data for both internal and external use. That part of the system which deals with the relationship of the business to outsiders and owners is normally termed **financial accountancy** and has been emphasized in previous chapters. Management accounting is concerned with providing information for planning, control and decision making. **Cost accounting** – or simply **costing** – is that part of the management accounting system which deals primarily with recording and analysis. Such a system would facilitate the establishment of past costs of products and functions but would not give maximum assistance to effective direction of the enterprise. Effective management accounting would require more sophisticated analysis of the data to provide other figures. For example, data would be required for comparison between budgets or standards and actual costs; for costs of processes or products to aid short-term control and long-term decision making. The fundamentals of cost accounting are covered in Chapters 9 and 10 while the wider scope of management accounting is described in Chapters 11 and 12.

9.1 Cost ascertainment: The elements of cost

Cost is a monetary measure of value consumed or acquired. The emphasis on money is important, as value can be expressed in terms other than money. The ascertainment of costs can best be explained in relation to a manufacturing or producing organization such as a car producer or maker of domestic electrical goods. There will be a variety of producing departments (foundry, drilling, assembly etc.) through which work actually passes, supported by a variety of essential services or functions which are also needed – such as design, stores, inspection, accounting and management.

The term **cost** may represent different ideas to different groups. The cost of a toothbrush to the person wishing to use it would be the price paid at the store from which it was purchased. The store, however, would consider the price at which it bought the toothbrush to be the cost. The toothbrush manufacturer would consider cost to be represented by the sum of expenditure on material, labour and expenses incurred in producing the toothbrush. It is the manufacturing situation which provides the challenge to the accountant as complex analysis will be required to furnish reliable figures. How the analysis is performed depends upon the objective. A cost objective is the name given to the purpose for which costs are measured. We may, for example, want to ascertain:

1   How much one particular item of **expense** is costing (e.g. material, labour, power, light).
2   How much one particular item of finished output is costing i.e. what is the **unit cost** of finished output (e.g. cost per toothbrush, bucket, motor car).
3   How much a particular department such as moulding, packing or machining is costing or alternatively what a particular **function** such as inspection or accounting is costing i.e. what are the costs of this or that cost centre.
4   How much a particular item of expense will change if we increase or decrease our production. i.e. what is the nature of degree of **variability** of the costs.
5   How efficiently a particular producing cost centre is operating e.g. what is the cost per unit of effort such as **standard** direct labour hour.

Build up of cost

Cost comprises expenditure which has been incurred and for costing purposes must be one of three elements – material, labour or expenses.

Material

This comprises items having a separate physical existence. The most common categories are:

● *Raw material:*   Natural resources such as coal, oil, iron ore.
● *Processed material:*   Wool, cotton, steel bars and sheets of plywood.
● *Components and assemblies:*   Tyres, engines, valves, screws, batteries.
● *Finished products:*   Refrigerators, cars, computers.

Note that the finished product of one entity or industry may be the raw material of another, from the point of view of that particular entity.

Labour

This represents the contribution to production made by personnel whether engaged directly in production or in a supporting function and the term covers all workers whether paid by output, hourly or salaried.

Expenses

These are costs other than material or labour which are nonetheless necessary to operate the business. Examples would be rent, rates and power costs incurred by the firm.

The elements described above can be further classified into **direct** and **indirect**. The objective of this subanalysis is to distinguish between those items of cost which relate specifically to, and vary with, the quantity produced and those which are not so related. Any item of expense incurred by the enterprise must be one of these elements:

- *Direct material:* The cost (including delivery) of materials and parts which can be identified with the physical units produced.
- *Direct labour:* The cost of employees engaged in converting raw or processed material into the finished product and whose earnings can be related to output achieved.
- *Direct expenses:* Items of cost other than that material or labour specifically incurred in producing a particular product or service.
- *Indirect material:* The materials which cannot be identified with particular units of production.
- *Indirect labour:* The cost of labour activities which cannot be measured or charged to specific cost units.
- *Indirect expenses:* Expenses other than indirect material and indirect labour which cannot be measured or charged to specific cost units.

All indirect expenses form part of what are termed **overhead costs** – the costs incurred in operating the production, administration, selling and distribution functions which cannot be directly charged to any one product or process. The subdivision of overhead and its incorporation into total cost can be represented by Figure 9.1.

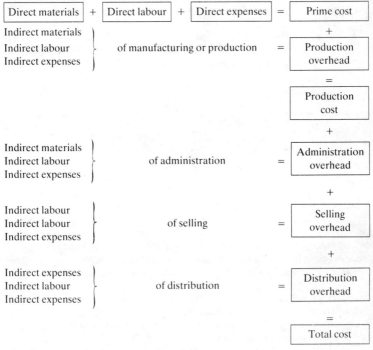

Figure 9.1

The production (or alternatively manufacturing) cost of goods produced may have to be adjusted by an change in stock levels between the beginning and end of an accounting period in order to find the cost of goods sold. The importance of overhead groupings shown in Figure 9.1 will vary with the products concerned and size of the organization. A company producing television sets on highly automated equipment will have low direct labour but high overhead costs relative to units produced, whereas a small building contractor will have – proportionately – high direct costs but low overheads. The manufacturer of soft drinks or tonic water has low unit production costs but high costs for selling (advertising etc.) and distribution. Note that the term indirect expenses is sometime used to refer to all overhead charges but this should be avoided where possible. We will now examine each cost element in more detail before considering the determination of product cost.

9.2   Cost ascertainment: Materials

Costing and control of materials can be divided into two aspects – the physical and the accounting. Physical aspects are concerned with the effective purchase, receipt, inspection, storage and handling procedures. Accounting aspects are concerned with ensuring quantities are purchased in the most economic numbers and prices; that effective records are maintained to ensure creditors are paid, stocks and losses accounted for and costs of consumption ascertained as accurately as possible. Material costs are the equivalent of cash and may – as for example in an extractive industry like sugar refining – form up to 90 per cent of total cost so that control of costs is essential for good management.

Purchasing routine

The purchasing routine should preferably be centralized to minimize the risk of fraud and locate responsibility. Although, by implication, the purchasing department has a general authority to make purchases it should receive specific authority before placing orders by means of a **purchase requisition**. This is a document signed by an authorized staff member requesting the purchasing department to place the goods on order. (*Note:* It should not be confused with a **materials requisition** which is a request to the stores to issue materials in stock to the producing departments.)

The objective of efficient purchasing is to obtain the right materials, at the right price, in the right quantities at the right time. If a material has not been previously bought an enquiry for quotation is sent to prospective suppliers. When quotations are received the most suitable is selected and a purchase order placed. The order must be signed, numbered and contain printed thereon the conditions upon which it is placed and by which responsibility for payment will be accepted.

Receipt of materials

Materials are usually received in a special department or section of a main stores unless required at a local site as in building contracts. This department has copies of the purchase orders and inspects goods received making out a **goods received note**. These help to provide records of all materials received, notice to particular storekeepers of items accepted, means of checking suppliers' invoices and advice to the requisitioning department of arrival of goods. The notes will normally include details of goods, supplier's name, order number, inspector's report and details of shortages or rejects. They will be signed by an inspector and clerk preparing notes and copies will be sent to the purchasing department, the accounts department, the requisitioner and the stores with one copy being retained.

Storage

As stated above, materials are the equivalent of cash. Some managements will go to great lengths to avoid pilfering of postage stamps or petty cash while tacitly condoning large-scale theft and wastage of material. Yet the material requisition is a 'cheque drawn on the stores' and every pound of material misappropriated is equivalent to withdrawing a pound from the bank without any gain. Storekeepers should be experienced, honest, orderly and tidy in nature. All materials create their own problems. Some are heavy and must be stored on ground floors, some are dangerous and subject to government requirements. Some have great bulk but relatively low cost value such as coal, while others take up little space but have high cost value and liability to theft such as precious metals and drugs. Conditions of temperature, ventilation and humidity may create problems. The study of material storage and handling is a specialized one but the accountant is involved, as satisfying the physical requirements will inevitably be a compromise between legal requirements, the ideal desirable and that which is possible by virtue of what the firm can afford.

Classification and coding

A coding system is essential with most systems of control and the system for materials should comply with normal desirable features. It should be simple, brief, precise and capable of extension. Examples would be:

● *Numeric:* Each section and bin numbered.
● *Decimal:* Each digit represents subsection of previous digit.
● *Alphabetic:* Letters chosen at random.
● *Mnemonic:* Letters chosen according to sound of word.
● *Compound:* Letters and figures.

Accounting routine

The accounting function will be responsible for the following:

1 Ensuring accurate records are kept in respect of all materials, of quantities received or rejected, issued or returned, the balance on hand and the cost value attributed to them.
2 The pricing and evaluation of all requisitions and stocks to obtain costs of production and profit determination and ensure minimum wastage or other losses.
3 Operating a system of internal control which willl minimize possibilities of fraud, theft, clerical error or inefficient system.

4   Cooperating with management in preparing budgets for purchases, creditors, stock levels, material requirements for production and all other aspects of efficient control of materials issuing from stores and pricing of issues.

No issues from stores should be made without a written or printed instruction known as a **material requisition**. These normally have to be signed by a person known to the stores as having authority to do so. For direct materials required by production departments such requisitions may in a small works be signed by the foreman but in larger engineering works they would be prepared by the progress or production control function – quite frequently on pre-printed forms prepared simultaneously with the works order. In continuous process and mass production industries such records are prepared, controlled and monitored by computers.

For indirect materials, items may be requisitioned by the department or function concerned. For example, standard cleaning materials may be requisitioned by the department foreman but maintenance materials by the maintenance engineer. Small items may be issued on an imprest system and the value of items may be related to the level of authority of the person signing – and accepting responsibility for the expenditure incurred by – the requisition.

Prior to posting the individual requisitions are collected, totalled and analysed by preparing summaries as frequently as the numbers of requisitions involved would suggest. This could be daily, weekly, monthly or some other time period, and will be by material code, job number, process or department as indicated later. Other documents likely to be involved are:

1   **Materials returns note:**   It is often necessary to issue approximate or bulk quantities to production departments and for the surplus to be returned to the stores when the job is completed. A note in a similar form to a requisition but possibly coloured red or otherwise distinguished is completed to provide the authority to record the return. This is also referred to as a materials debit note.
2   **Materials transfer note:**   The need for this arises when material is transferred between jobs or sites without being returned to the stores. The records can be adjusted by making out a requisition for the new job and a materials return note for the old job or making out a material transfer note which authorizes the debit to the new job and credit to the old.

Pricing issues from stores

The material costs used in ascertaining cost per unit of production must include all acquisition costs. The cost of transport must be added if not delivered carriage paid. Ideally the cost of acquiring the goods should be included but this frequently poses so many problems of apportionment that it is included in overhead costs. Trade discount is always deducted but cash discounts can be treated as a gain resulting from choice in financial operations. The distinction is that trade discount is a reduction from genuine or recommended final selling prices given to manufacturers, wholesalers or retailers whereas cash discount can be taken as an incentive for prompt payment.

There are several bases for pricing issues, for example, **actual cost methods**.

These have been discussed and defined in the section on stocks page 51. To recapitulate the most popular are **LIFO, FIFO** and **average cost**. These methods are simple to apply if items are bought in for specific jobs, but most materials are issued from stocks created by successive deliveries probably at different prices. The objective is to ascertain realistic costs of production as it is going on and this is a different challenge to determining one total cost of sales figure for a bygone period. An example is given below to illustrate the application of the methods as a means of pricing issues. The arithmetical processes were illustrated in detail on page 51–7.

Example

For the six months ended 31 October, an importer and distributor of one type of washing machine has the following transactions in his records. There was an opening balance of 100 units which had a value of £3,900.

Date	Bought quantity in units	Cost per unit £
May	100	41
June	200	50
August	400	51.875

The price of £51.875 each for the August receipt was £6.125 per unit less than the normal price because of the large quantity ordered.

Date	Sold quantity in units	Price each £
July	250	64
September	350	70
October	100	74

From the information given above and using weighted average, FIFO and LIFO methods for pricing issues:

1 Show the stores ledger records including the closing stock balance and stock valuation.
2 Prepare in columnar format, trading accounts for the period to show the gross profit using each of the three methods of pricing issues.
3 Comment on which method, in the situation depicted, is regarded as the best measure of profit, and why.

Source   CIMA

Weighted average method

Product No.		Description					Max stock Min stock			

	Receipts			Issues			Balance			Checked
Date	Qty	Price	£	Qty	Price	£	Qty	Price	£	
b/fwd							100	39	3,900	
May	100	41	4,100				200	40	8,000	
June	200	50	10,000				400	45	18,000*	
July				250	45	11,250	150	45	6,750	
August	400	51.875	20,750				550	50	27,500†	
Sept				350	50	17,500	200	50	10,000	
Oct				100	50	5,000	100	50	5,000	

* $18,000 \div 400 = 45$
† $27,500 \div 550 = 50$

Total value of issues = £11,250 + £17,500 + £5,000 = £33,750 − cost of goods sold.

FIFO (first in first out) method

	Receipts			Issues			Balance			Checked
Date	Qty	Price	£	Qty	Price	£	Qty	Price	£	
b/fwd							100	39	3,900	
May	100	41	4,100				100	39	3,900	
							100	41	4,100	
							200		8,000	
June	200	50	10,000				100	39	3,900	
							100	41	4,100	
							200	50	10,000	
							400		18,000	
July				100	39	3,900				
				100	41	4,100				
				50	50	2,500				
				250		10,500	150	50	7,500	
August	400	51.875	20,750				150	50	7,500	
							400	51.875	20,700	
							550		28,200	
Sept				150	50	7,500				
				200	51.875	10,375				
				350		17,875	200	51.875	10,375	
Oct				100	51.875	5,187.5	100	51.875	5,187.5	

Total value of issues = £10,500 + £17,875 + £5,187.5 = £33,562.5 – cost of goods sold.

LIFO *(last in first out method)*

	Receipts			Issues			Balance			Checked
Date	*Qty*	*Price*	*£*	*Qty*	*Price*	*£*	*Qty*	*Price*	*£*	
b/fwd							100	39	3,900	
May	100	41	4,100				100	39	3,900	
							100	41	4,000	
							200		8,000	
June	200	50	10,000				100	39	3,900	
							100	41	4,100	
							200	50	10,000	
							400		18,000	
July				200	50	10,000				
				50	41	2,050				
				250		12,050	100	39	3,900	
							50	41	2,050	
							150		5,950	
August	400	51.875	20,750				100	39	3,900	
							50	41	2,050	
							400	51.875	20,750	
							550		26,700	
Sept				350	51.875	18,156.25	100	39	3,900	
							50	41	2,050	
							50	51.875	2,593.75	
							200		8,543.75	
Oct				50	51.875	2,593.75				
				50	41	2,050				
				100		4,643.75	100	39	3,900	

Total value of issues = £12,050 + £18,156.25 + £4,643.75 = £34,850 – cost of goods sold

	Weighted average	FIFO	LIFO
	£	£	£
Sales	47,900	47,900	47,900
Less Cost of goods sold (total issues)	33,750	33,562.5	34,850
	14,150	14,337.5	13,050

This could be worked using stock valuation to determine cost of goods sold.

		£		£		£
Sales		47,900		47,900		47,900
Opening stock	3,900		3,900		3,900	
Add purchases	34,850		34,850		34,850	
	38,750		38,750		38,750	
Less Closing stock	5,000		5,187.5		3,900	
		33,750		33,562.5		34,850
Gross profit		14,150		14,337.5		13,050

The prices of materials purchased are rising and under this condition LIFO gives the best measure of profit. Production and sales are being charged with most recent prices being paid and the profit measure is more realistic. The other methods overstate profit performance and may lead to inaction and complacency in a long period of rising prices. Inflation – see later section on non-cost methods.

General comments on cost methods
The average cost method attaches no greater importance to recent price movements than to older prices, thus in slow-moving stocks the effect of earlier prices may have undue influence in managerial decision. If stocks turn over fairly rapidly it may be accepted as it smooths the effect of price fluctuation.

The FIFO method is the traditional and most popular method and closing stock valuation would be on the basis of more recent prices paid. This results in reasonable financial balance sheet figures but under rising prices the cost of goods sold (in the trading account) or manufactured (in the cost accounts) will be understated and profit declared will be higher.

The LIFO method means that current prices are being matched against current sales and is closer to the economic concept of real cost i.e. the cost of replacing an asset used up as opposed to merely recording its purchase price which for current and future decision making is largely irrelevant.

Other factors affecting the selection of the pricing method are:

1 Frequency and size of price fluctuations.
2 The proportion of total cost represented by material.
3 The frequency and quantity of ordering (see section on stock control below).
4 The time span of the accounts.
5 The objective i.e. FIFO may be used for published financial accounts but LIFO for management accounts.

Other pricing methods

Inflated cost

This is used in conditions such as when unavoidable losses occur. Liquids may evaporate during storage and other losses may occur on breaking bulk e.g. sawing standard lengths from random lengths of tubing, steel bars or timber.

An estimate of the rate of loss is made and the price inflated accordingly.

Example

Assume a liquid costs 19p per litre and 5 per cent loss due to evaporation and spillage is anticipated then each litre would result in only 0.95 litres being possible for production. The price of 19p is inflated to $19 \times \dfrac{100}{95} =$ 20p. It is more common to allow a normal loss at the basic rate and this method is illustrated in the section on process costs.

Standard price

Usually incorporated into a system of standard costing a fixed or standard rate per unit is applied to all quantities used. The difference between this and the purchase price paid is extracted (usually on purchase) into a material price variance account and disposed of separately. The advantages are simplicity, less computation and clerical labour required and material control made more effective through variance analysis. An example of the computation of the variances is postponed to the section on standard costing.

Market price

The purpose of using this method is to reflect current costs. It is more likely to be used in cost estimating than accounting. This is because large adjustments would frequently be necessary to stocks recorded in the books and current prices are not always available.

Stock control

Stock control means ensuring that sufficient materials or finished goods are retained in stock to meet stated requirements without carrying excessive stocks. Stores control should be distinguished from stock control as it is concerned with physical items such as space, safety, cleanliness and material handling. This puts constraints on stock levels in addition to the financial features discussed below. Any item in stock must be ordered, purchased and stored. The objective is to minimize the cost of carrying stock commensurate with satisfying customer demand or meeting manufacturing requirements. The factors involved in getting the best compromise are:

Q = Quantity ordered and delivered at any one time.
A = Annual demand for the product or material.
C = The costs incurred each time an order is placed. (This excludes the cost of the items themselves and refers to things such as purchasing function costs.)
P = Price paid per unit.
R = Cost of stockholding. (This represents the cost of holding each item in stock and can be expressed as a rate of interest on P since each item is an element of working capital or a unit cost of stockholding which is a combination of R × P.)

The simplest conditions are where items are sold or issued at a constant rate i.e. each period's demands are the same and the supplier can guarantee immediate replacement delivery upon receipt of order. In these conditions the quantity Q received would be exhausted over a constant period of time and a graph of the position would always show the characteristic sawtooth formation of Figure 9.2.

Under these conditions stock cannot exceed the quantity ordered since this is the maximum delivered. With a constant demand rate the stock will decline consistently as indicated by the downward sloping line. When stocks are zero a new consignment is delivered, stock returns temporarily to the maximum Q and the cycle is repeated. Further, it can be seen that in one half of the time period half of the batch purchased will have been consumed and therefore average stock overall will be half the quantity that is $\frac{Q}{2}$.

The number of deliveries required in the time period (year in this case) will be $\frac{\text{Annual demand}}{\text{quantity per order/batch}} = \frac{A}{Q}$ and this represents the number of orders which will have to be placed. Therefore if C is the cost incurred each time an order is placed the annual ordering costs will be $\frac{AC}{Q}$.

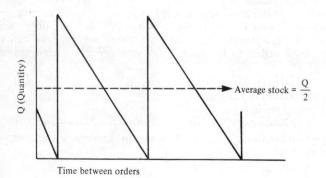

Average stock = $\frac{Q}{2}$

Time between orders

The average quantity in stock is $\frac{Q}{2}$. The stockholding costs per unit is equal to RP where R is the holding cost of stock (expressed as a percentage or fraction of the average stock) and P is the purchase price or manufacturing cost per item. If, for example, it costs 15 per cent per annum to borrow money from the bank and the unit price is £10 per unit then RP will be equal to 15% × £10 or 0.15 × £10 = £1.5 per annum. This would be multiplied by the average stock $\frac{Q}{2}$ to give the total annual cost of stockholding.

Economic order quantity

The total cost involved in maintaining stock levels is the sum of **ordering costs** and **stockholding costs**. As can be seen from Figure 9.2 the smaller the quantity kept in stock the lower will be the stockholding costs since warehouses could be smaller, insurance will be less and working capital to finance purchases will be lower. But this means that reordering will have to take place more frequently. The objective is to make the combined cost of these two functions as low as possible. The answer as to which batch quantity will make the total cost a minimum can be found by:

1 Drawing graphs of the variable costs concerned at a number of values for Q.
2 Simulation (or trial and error) i.e. computing costs at a variety of levels until the minimum figure can be obtained from inspection.
3 Using a basic formula derived from algebra or calculus.

Data from the following exercise will be used to illustrate all three methods.

Exercise 9.1

1 Explain what is meant by the term 'economic order quantity'. Your explanation should be supported by a sketch or graph, which need not be on graph paper.
2 Using the information stated below, you are required to prepare a schedule showing the associated costs if 1, 2, 3, 4, 5 or 6 orders were placed during a year for a single product. From your schedule, state the number of orders to be placed each year and the economic order quantity:
   ● Annual usage of product – 600 units
   ● Unit cost of product – £2.4
   ● Cost of placing an order – £6.0
   ● Stock holding cost as a percentage of average stock value – 20%
3 Comment briefly on three problems met in determining the economic order quantity.
Source: CIMA

Solution

A graph showing stockholding cost, ordering/delivery cost and combined cost of stockholding and ordering/delivery is shown in Figure 9.3.

The economic order quantity (EOQ) is indicated by the lowest point of the total (combined) cost of ordering and holding. This is also the point where the cost of stockholding and cost of ordering/delivery intersect. Data for plotting the curves are derived from columns 2, 4, 5 and 6 in the schedule shown below.

Number of orders p.a.	Batch size	Average stock	Stockholding cost £	Delivery costs £	Stockholding and delivery	
1	600	300	144	6	150	
2	300	150	72	12	84	
3	200	100	48	18	66	
4	150	75	36	24	60	
5	120	60	28.8	30	58.8*	Lowest
6	100	50	24	36	60	
(1)	(2)	(3)	(4)	(5)	(6)	

1   Number of orders per annum

2   Batch size $= Q = \dfrac{\text{annual demand}}{\text{Number of orders p.a.}} = \dfrac{A}{n} = \dfrac{600}{n}$

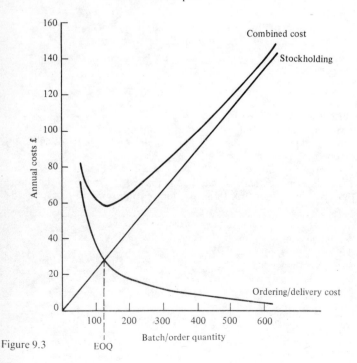

Figure 9.3

3   Average stock $= \dfrac{Q}{2}$

4   Stockholding cost $= \dfrac{Q}{2} \times R \times P = \dfrac{Q}{2} \times 20\% \times £2.4 = \dfrac{Q}{2} \times 0.48$

5   Delivery cost $=$ n $\times$ cost per order $=$ n $\times$ £6.0

6   Stockholding plus delivery = column 4 + column 5.

It can be seen that the lowest combined cost (lowest point of curve) coincides with the point at which the cost of stockholding equates with the ordering costs. This enables a general formula to be derived in accordance with traditional mathematical principles:

$$\text{Total cost} = \frac{RPQ}{2} + \frac{AC}{Q}$$

Using calculus and differentiating with respect to Q it can be shown that

$$\frac{d}{dQ} = \frac{RP}{2} - \frac{AC}{Q^2}$$

At the point of minimum cost this expression must equal zero

$$\text{i.e.} \; \frac{RP}{2} = \frac{AC}{Q^2} = 0$$

$$\therefore \; \frac{RP}{2} = \frac{AC}{Q^2}$$

$$\text{and } Q = \sqrt{\frac{2AC}{RP}}$$

For application it is only necessary to know the formula and incorporate the variables concerned. In the above example:

A = 600, C = £6.0, P = £2.4, R = 20% (or 0.20)

$\therefore$ economic order quantity will be when

$$Q = \sqrt{\frac{2 \times 600 \times 6}{0.20 \times 2.4}} = \sqrt{\frac{7200}{4.8}} = \sqrt{1500}$$

$$= 122.47$$

The theoretical ideal is 122 which compares with 120 obtained from the tabulation or graph method. In practice it may be necessary to consider other factors such as:

● Internal manufacturing conditions involving 'set up' costs as opposed to ordering costs.
● Variations in 'lead time' or what happens when suppliers cannot deliver immediately or when partially completed work is involved.
● Effect of quantity discounts offered by suppliers.
● The effect of 'stock outs' i.e. assessing the possible loss due on the one hand to not being able to satisfy customer's immediate delivery requirements and on the other hand carrying excessive safety stocks.

Stockholding costs include interest paid (or foregone) on capital tied up in stocks and this rate is not constant.

The reorder level is usually a compromise and is a point between maximum and minimum stock levels at which point it is necessary to initiate a purchase requisition. It is usually higher than nil or minimum stock to allow for things such as abnormally high rates of usage or delay in delivery.

Reference can be made to standard works on mathematical techniques and operational research for assistance in this complex field.

Stocktaking

Physical stock checks are performed at least once a year as part of the annual audit. This, however, is insufficient as any excessive losses would exist for too long without discovery. A system of **continuous stocktaking** is preferable. Under this system all stocks are counted at regular or (better) random intervals and the bins or other quantity confirmed. This should not be confused with the **perpetual inventory system** which is a clerical operation involving computing the theoretical balance after each issue or receipt illustrated in the example on page 238. If the stocktaker agrees the physical count with the recorded figures he can initial the card or otherwise set in motion means of investigating cause and value of differences.

9.3   Cost ascertainment: Labour

The term **labour** is used to reflect the human contribution to production and services. It is an all-embracing term including all personnel, from those working on production lines to the board of directors. Accounting for labour costs involves classification by employees – for payment, and by operation or function for control and assessment of productivity. More detailed records are usually required for analysis of direct labour costs as they are related directly to output volume achieved. The importance of the division between direct and indirect depends upon the type of production and size of organization. In jobbing works or individually controlled machine operations the longer the time spent, the greater will be the cost of that particular job but in large-scale car manufacture a worker on the line (or track) has to keep up a predetermined speed or all other operations are affected. In an oil refinery, car manufacturing plant or brewery even direct operations may be mainly automatic, robot or computer controlled. In the end, however, at some point human contribution is required and the greater the amount of capital behind each employee the more essential it is for production to be evenly maintained.

Employee records

Two kinds of records are required for labour control – **attendance** and **output**. Some employees are excused recording attendance time, particularly salaried workers, but for production – direct and indirect – workers' evidence of period of attendance is demanded. This is normally achieved by automatic time recorders or less frequently manually. There are various types of mechanical or electronic device which automatically record time of arrival and departure on a card operated at a 'clocking-in' point. Other workers such as administrative employees frequently 'sign in' on an attendance register.

The second record is a form of job card which refers to time and task. Job records may be filled in daily or weekly depending on length of task.

Frequently information is preprinted and internal clocks are used to record time 'on' and 'off' the particular task. Information which has to be entered will include the following – either preprinted or entered up by the employee.

● Production order number or job number.
● Batch number, part number and description.
● Operation number and description.
● Machine used or cost centre location.
● Date commenced and required completion date.
● Operator's name and clock number.
● Time started and time finished.
● Quantity produced and details of any scrap or rejects.
● Space for cost office to evaluate earnings.

The job cards are issued by planning or production control departments and when the job is completed cards go to the cost office or to the next worker depending on the system. Separate cards may be used to record lost time for all reasons. If the work is for other than production purposes cards are still required. For example, a direct worker may occasionally work on prototypes, maintenance or capital investment items such as a new machine. These, and the lost time cards, may be of different colours to facilitate analysis. The hours recorded as attended should be reconciled with hours recorded in the same period by job cards. This ensures that all time being paid for is being accounted for by some responsible person.

Wages may be analysed in a variety of ways – it depends on the objectives which include:

● Analysis by direct and indirect wages.
● Analysis by cost centre and functions.
● Analysis by production and lost time.
● Sex, age, occupational groups.
● Jobs and servicing (overhead) orders.

Whatever the system it is essential that all lost time is evaluated to cause and cost. Some losses are unavoidable and considered normal. This would include waiting for a machine changeover or changing a job. But if these delays are excessive they should be charged together with losses due to machine breakdown, waiting for orders, power cuts, strikes etc. to an **abnormal idle time account**. Allowances are also made for new workers to become familiar with the process and achieve the outputs expected.

Accounting for labour costs

The labour accounts have to serve two purposes:

1 *Financial records:* A record of total time worked and wages due is required for each worker. From this the payroll is prepared in convenient sections. The gross earnings are computed and standard deductions entered. There are compulsory deductions such as income tax (pay as you earn), earnings-related insurance contributions and contracted union subscriptions. Additionally there may be contri-

butions to a works pension or superannuation scheme and deductions for tools, sports club, savings schemes or holidays. The deductions are collected into suspense accounts and appropriate entries made when items are paid e.g. the PAYE total is usually paid monthly to the taxman and until it is paid it is a current liability. If employees are paid in cash a coin and notes analysis is prepared to facilitate putting up wage packets. Alternatively a pay advice is sent to the employee's bank.

2 *Cost records:*   From the clock cards, time cards and job records a **wage analysis sheet** is prepared. This summarizes the direct labour hours and costs by each production cost centre while indirect labour costs are transferred to various overhead accounts. This is usually done weekly to ensure reconciliation with the expenditure recorded on the payroll. Note that the costing records are concerned with gross pay analysis only. The fact that an employee does not receive all he earns – due to compulsory and other deductions is purely a financial or cashier function. In addition to the gross earnings of the employee there are additional related costs which have to be borne by the employer. These (in the UK) include the employer's contribution to Earnings Related National Insurance, provision for holiday payments, company share of superannuation payments and similar. Most countries impose similar additional costs including payroll taxes based on numbers and/or earnings of employees.

In the search for efficiency frequent special reports are requested from the accounting department in respect of labour performance. These include monitoring the performance of individuals and departments against standards predetermined by specialists in areas such as time study, methods engineering and in the case of office activities the organization and methods function. A regular request is for analysis of cost of **labour turnover**. When existing employees leave additional indirect costs are incurred. These include the following:

1 Advertising, recruitment, interview, selection.
2 Lost output – other employees idle unused capacity costs.
3 Training and instructing new employees.

Some turnover is unavoidable for reasons such as death, ill health or permanent removal of an employee to another area of the country. The firm may have to make some employees redundant due to lack of orders or may dismiss others for lateness or disciplinary reasons. These would be termed involuntary reasons as compared with voluntary severance by the employee. They may leave voluntarily for reasons such as promotion prospects, higher wages, job satisfaction or domestic circumstances. Attempts are made to assess the impact apart from costs by using a formal **ratio of labour turnover**. A typical format for this would be to relate (for the same period of time):

$$\frac{\text{Number of employees leaving and requiring replacement}}{\text{Average number of employees}} \times 100$$

The higher the percentage the less desirable the situation.

Methods of remuneration

The two extreme forms of remuneration are payment relative to **time attended** and payment entirely **by results**. Between these points there are literally thousands of schemes which attempt some compromise between the two. The main features of each will be given but emphasis in a brief text such as this is on cost effect and treatment. The arguments of history, suitability, psychological and other factors of incentive schemes are not dealth with. Payment by results is an ongoing study and the suggested reading includes wider-based texts.

Time-based systems

Frequently referred to as time or 'pay' rates the employee is paid a rate per hour. In the case of direct workers the incentive to produce has to be imposed by supervision or voluntarily by the worker. Overtime is usually paid at a higher (premium) rate but this is usually received only by manual and lower-salaried workers. The main advantage of time-based systems is simplicity both for control and budgeting. However, unit costs of production will vary with units produced as can be seen from the following tabulation.

John Smith is paid £4.00 per hour for a 40 hour week. The labour costs per unit in successive weeks when he produced 50, 70 and 60 units were as follows:

Week	Gross wages	Output units	Labour cost/unit (nearest p)
1	£160	50	£3.20
2	£160	70	£2.29
3	£160	60	£2.67

Payment by results

All businesses incur fixed costs which must be paid (e.g. rent) in a period irrespective of output produced. The greater the output the less the average cost per unit in respect of the fixed cost. The employer can afford to offer higher wages provided the increased labour cost is offset by these savings. This is the basic principle behind all payment by results – incentive – schemes.

Piecework systems

The simplest form of piecework is where a fixed price is paid per unit produced. The incentive is directly proportional to effort made, the unit labour cost is fixed but the total unit cost will fall because of the spread of the fixed overhead expenses. Suppose the firm employing John Smith introduces this system paying him £3.00 per unit and (theoretically) the only other costs involved are £100 per week rent, the costs would be as follows:

Week	Output units	Direct labour cost/unit £	Earnings £	Overhead per week £	Overhead cost per unit £	Total cost per unit £
1	50	3.00	150	100	2.00	5.00
2	70	3.00	210	100	1.43	4.43
3	60	3.00	180	100	1.66	4.66

Some systems pay higher rates either for different levels of output or for all output once a particular level has been reached. Earliest schemes of this type were named after their originators – mostly American management innovators such as Taylor, Merrick and Emmerson. In most modern variations minimum earnings, equivalent at least to time rates are guaranteed.

Premium bonus systems

These systems are mainly of historic interest as providing the first examples of schemes where time saved formed the basis of payment rather than work produced. The earnings were made up of two parts – time wages for hours attended plus a bonus proportional to the time saved out of the time allowed. There were a large number of schemes in use but only two principal bases were involved.

Halsey-type schemes

In these types of scheme a fixed proportion of the time saved was paid as bonus. In the original (Halsey) scheme this was 50 per cent but when introduced by Weir into the UK the proportion was reduced to between 30 and 33⅓ per cent. Assuming figures for output as in the previous example and a working week of forty hours then if the time allowed per unit was 1¼ hours and the rate per hour was £4.0 the costs would be as follows:

Week	Output	Hours worked	Hours produced	Time saved	Premium time	Hours earned	Earnings £	Direct labour cost/unit £
1	50	40	62.5	22.5	11.25	51.25	205	4.1
2	70	40	87.5	47.5	23.75	63.75	255	3.64
3	60	40	75	35	17.5	57.5	230	3.83
	(a)	(b)	(c) =	(d) =	(e) =	(f) =	(g) =	(h) =
			(a) × 1.25	(c) − (b)	50% × (d)	(b) + (e)	(f) × 4.0	(g) ÷ (a)

Under the Weir System Column (e) would be reduced to 30 or 33⅓ per cent of Column (d) or such proportion as the firm decided. Minimum earnings equal to day rates i.e. forty hours at £4 per hour would be guaranteed.

Rowan-type schemes

In the absence of efficient time and motion study the fixed ratios of Halsey-type schemes caused problems. If the time was loose i.e. generous employees could earn high bonuses with minimum effort whereas if time allowed was tight incentive to the employee was minimal. Rowan created a scheme with a built-in protection against excessive bonus by devising a

formula incorporating the elements concerned. A time allowed is determined and if a saving is effected by the worker a percentage equal to the
proportion of that saving is added to the time taken. Using the figures from
the previous example:

Time allowed per unit is 1.25 hours.
For output of 50 units total time allowed is 50 × 1.25 = 62.5 hours
Time taken is 40 hours
Time saved is 62.5 − 40 = 22.5 hrs

$$\text{Premium time} = \frac{\text{time saved}}{\text{time allowed}} \times \text{time taken}$$

$$= \frac{22.5}{62.5} \times 40 = 14.4$$

Hours to be paid for = time taken + premium hours
= 40 + 14.4 = 54.4
Earnings = 54.4 × £4.0 = £217.60

Readers may check for themselves computations included below for
output of 70 or 60 units when time taken remains at 40 hours.

Week	Output	Hours worked	Hours produced	Time saved	Premium time	Hours earned	Earnings £	Direct labour cost/unit £
1	50	40	62.5	22.5	14.4	54.4	217.60	4.35
2	70	40	87.5	47.5	21.71	61.71	246.84	3.52
3	60	40	75	35	18.66	58.66	234.64	3.91
	(a)	(b)	(c) =	(d) =	(e) =	(f) =	(g) =	(h) =
			(a) × 1.25	(c) − (b)	$\frac{(d)}{(c)} \times$ (b)	(b) + (e)	(f) × 4.0	(g) ÷ (a)

Other payment schemes

When individual output cannot be measured or the output is dependent
upon a team, group bonus schemes are used. Examples would be
continuous process industries, mass production assembly lines and a refuse
collecting gang. Some schemes relate to wages only but others are
combined with collective payment for savings in other costs such as
reducing material losses or energy consumption. The Rucker – share of
production – Plan was of this type and was one of the first to include direct
and indirect workers. The output of indirect and staff workers is much more
difficult to assess and so employers may be tempted to ignore them or resort
to profit-sharing schemes. The main disadvantags of such schemes are:

1 The bonus or share of profit is usually small.
2 Personnel are not rewarded relative to individual effort.
3 Profits are affected by external conditions and managerial ability.
4 Bonus is paid probably long after the period of effort concerned.
5 After a time such payments tend to be considered part of 'normal' wages
   or salaries.

Accounting for wages

The double entry in respect of wages is in the financial accounts. The wages
being analysed in the cost accounts are the same wages. To get a set of

double entry accounts into the cost records a system of control accounts are used. The figure may be entered into the cost records by means of journal entries, interlocking accounts or a completely integrated system.

The posting of the relevant accounts can be shown diagramatically as in Figure 9.4.

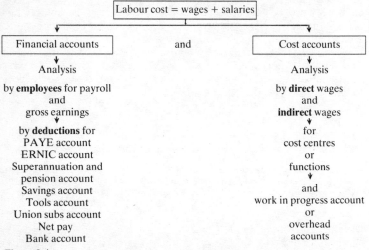

Figure 9.4

The following is an example using an integrated system.

Example

The following information is to be posted to the relevant accounts within an integral accounting system by means of double entry book-keeping.

		£
Direct labour:	Net wages	4,000
	Tax deducted	1,000
	National Insurance contributions	
	by employers	500
	by employees	200
	Overtime premium	500
Indirect labour:	Gross wages	3,000
	Tax deducted	750
	National Insurance contributions	
	by employers	375
	by employees	150

Source   LCCI

Note that direct labour is shown as **net** wages and indirect labour as **gross**. It is necessary to establish what the gross wages for direct labour were

		£
Net wages (cash paid)	=	4,000
Tax deducted		1,000
National Insurance (employees)		200
∴ Total direct wages		5,200

This includes £500 overtime premium. If it was known for which jobs this was incurred and if it was at the customer's request it would be debited to work in progress as direct labour. If, however, it is the result of spasmodic fluctuation in demand it would be unfair to charge extra to jobs which just happened to be operated on. In this case it would be treated as an additional overhead item. Note that it is already included in net wages paid. The wages control can now be built up and confirmed with the wages payable account. A cost journal voucher could be prepared as follows or the account posted direct.

A **wages payable account** may be opened to consolidate the financial transactions. Alternatively entries may be passed through the wages control direct. Journal entries using the first alternative would be as follows:

	£	£
Wages payable	8,200	
Bank (4,000 direct + 2,100 indirect)		6,100
Tax accrued (1,000 direct + 750 indirect)		1,750
National Insurance (200 direct + 150 indirect)		350
Gross wages due for period		
Production overhead	875	
National Insurance (500 direct + 375 indirect)		875
Employer's National Insurance		
Wages control	8,200	
Wages payable – direct		5,200
Wages payable – indirect		3,000
Wage analysis for period		

Using a wages payable account confirms immediately that the total wages (financial account) agrees with the wage analysis (management account) at £8,200. Care must be taken to distinguish gross wages from net wages when data is mixed. Employer's National Insurance is an additional cost to the total due to employees. At the appropriate time the taxation account and National Insurance account will be cleared by payment from the bank – until then they are current liabilities. The production overhead account will be increased by indirect materials and expenses. It will be credited with the overhead absorbed in the period which will be debited to work in progress.

Wages payable account

	£		£
Bank	6,100	Wages control – direct	5,200
Tax accrued	1,750	Wages control – indirect	3,000
National Insurance	350		
	8,200		8,200

Wages control account

	£		£
Wages payable – direct	5,200	Work in progress – direct	4,700
Wages payable – indirect	3,000	Production overhead O/T prem	500
		Production overhead – indirect	3,000
	8,200		8,200

Production overhead control account

	£	
Wages control O/T prem	500	
– indirect wages	3,000	
National Insurance – directs	500	
National Insurance – indirects	375	

Work in progress control

	£	
Wages control	4,700	

Taxation account

		£
	Wages payable	1,750

National insurance

		£
	Wages payable (200 + 150)	350
	Production overhead	
	(500 + 375)	875

9.4   Overheads: Classification and collection

The term **overhead** is used to refer to all those production, administrative selling and distribution costs which cannot be directly related to a specific job or product. It is the **summation of all indirect elements of cost** whether material, labour or expenses. In most costing systems production overheads are treated separately from the other groups such as selling, distribution administration and research. Reasons for this will be considered later but a major one is that an item should not incur selling and distribution costs until actually sold, therefore to get a correct unit cost for valuing production cost of goods sold subsequent costs should be excluded. There are four main stages in the treatment of overhead expenses.

1 Classify.
2 Collect.
3 Allocate and apportion.
4 Absorb.

Classify

Each item of expense is classified according to its nature as it is for financial accounting purposes. This means each item is classified on the original document – invoices, job cards, requisitions – according to whether it is for rent, rates, materials, wages or whatever. This is a **subject** analysis.

Collect

Once classified, items are collected into cost centre or cost unit totals for the accounting period concerned. In the case of overheads they must first be collected into cost centre totals since by definition above they cannot be directly related to the job or product – whereas direct elements could be so allocated. This process is an **objective** classification and the objective is at least twofold.

1 To establish both the total expenses incurred by a particular cost centre *and* whether they are reasonable when compared to production, past performance or budget.
2 To recover (absorb) the overhead costs so collected on some appropriate basis to establish a cost per unit of product or service.

Allocation and apportionment

There are two main problems in establishing the relevant overhead cost of the producing cost centres. In the first place not all indirect costs are incurred exclusively in respect of a particular cost centre. An expense such as rent is incurred for the benefit of the whole factory and a production manager's salary is paid for a person controlling all production cost centres. This creates the problem of **apportioning** or sharing such items – frequently termed common costs – between all the cost centres benefiting on some suitable base. The problems of absorption are dealt with separately in section 9.5.

Another problem is that not all factory cost centres are producing departments i.e. those departments through which the product actually passes at various stages of production. Such departments including, for example, maintenance, stores, toolmaking are essential to production but do not, in themselves, make products. They are normally termed **service departments** and problems of apportionment arise because they do varying amounts of work both for the producing departments and each other.

The base which is used for sharing the common overhead cost should be chosen carefully. The principle to be followed is that the base should have some relation to the amount of expense incurred. For example, the greater the number of employees the higher will be canteen and other personnel costs, therefore, number of employees in a cost centre would be a reasonable base of apportionment. Floor area could be used for rent and rates but if it is known that one particular building has a much higher valuation then this should be taken into account. It would appear at first sight that horsepower would be a reasonable basis of sharing power cost. However, we may have a sixty horsepower machine which only works twenty hours per month and a five horsepower machine which works every day for ten hours in a five-day week. In a month of four weeks this would be 200 hours running time. Power is charged on a basis of watts which relates to horsepower and time. Power cost ratio between these two machines would not be 60:5 but $(60 \times 20):(5 \times 200)$ i.e. not 12:1 but 6:5. Similarly area is not a suitable basis for lighting if lights vary in intensity or one department works a night shift. Frequently used bases are:

- Floor area for rent, lighting.
- Cubic capacity for heating.
- Value of plant and machinery for depreciation.
- Direct labour hours for supervision.
- Direct machine hours for machine running costs.
- Direct wages for pension contributions.
- Number of employees for canteen services.

Any basis will, of necessity, be arbitrary. Wherever possible the expense should be allocated. This is frequently referred to, particularly in American Literature, as the direct expense of a cost centre. This term is preferably not to be used as it causes confusion with a direct element of cost such as direct materials and direct labour.

When the costs of all manufacturing departments and services have been established it is necessary to reapportion the costs incurred by the service department to the production departments. This may become complex if service departments provide interdepartmental services (reciprocal service cost centres) and is dealt with later.

The most important document utilized in the overhead accounting process is the **overhead analysis sheet** or **overhead distribution summary**. An example of such a sheet is given on page 258 based on data taken from Exercise 9.2

Exercise 9.2

The Blackburn Company has a building, which houses three production departments A, B and C, and one service department D. The service department D is wholly involved in working for the three production departments and it is estimated that Department A uses 50 per cent, Department B uses 30 per cent and Department C uses 20 per cent of the services of Department D.

The actual costs for the four departments for a period were:

	£
Allocated costs	2,800
Insurance of building	600
Insurance of machinery	800
Rent	1,000
Heating	800
Pension fund (for employees)	850
General supervision	1,400
Electricity (lighting)	600
Electricity (power)	1,960
Depreciation	2,000

The following information is available in respect of the departments:

	A	B	C	D
Allocated costs	£800	£320	£1,200	£480
Value of machinery	£5,000	£5,000	£8,000	£2,000
Kilowatt hours (000s)	100	100	150	50
Number of employees	20	8	30	12
Area occupied (sq. ft)	2,000	1,000	4,000	1,000
Total wages	£2,500	£1,000	£3,200	£1,800

Required:

Apportion the costs to the departments on the most equitable bases.

Source: LCCI

Solution

It is necessary to relate each item of cost to the extra information given so that the most appropriate base is used. For example if you considered the insurance of buildings related to (i.e. tended to vary with) number of employees then this would be used. This would be rather irrational as rates are levied on buildings not people and the information most relevant to buildings is area occupied. The following bases are suggested:

Basis	Expense
Area	Insurance of building
Area	Rates
Area	Heating
Area	Electricity (light)
Value of machinery	Insurance of machinery
Value of machinery	Depreciation of machinery
Wages	Pension fund
Number of employees	General supervision
Kilowatt hours	Electricity (power)

The **allocated** costs do not require a basis as they have been recorded **specifically** for the cost centre. Expenses should always – in the interest of accuracy and control – be allocated if practicable. It may be possible to get the actual consumption of power recorded by meters installed departmentally but this would involve extra costs. The accountant has to assess the worth of extra precision obtained against the cost of obtaining the necessary statistics.

The second stage is to work out the proportions of the costs applicable. The proportion of area occupied by Department A is 2000 out of a total area of 8000 or 25 per cent. The value of machinery in Department C is $\frac{£8,000}{£20,000}$ or 40 per cent. The remaining calculations can be completed and summarized as follows:

	Dept A %	Dept B %	Dept C %	Dept D %	Total %
Area occupied	25	12.5	50	12.5	100
Value of machinery	25	25	40	10	100
Wages	29	12	38	21	100
Number of employees	29	11	43	17	100
Kilowatt hours	25	25	37.5	12.5	100

The next stage is to construct the overhead analysis sheet (or distribution summary). The total of each expense is shared over the departments in turn in that percentage represented by the most appropriate basis chosen from above. If minor differences occur they should be rounded off to the nearest pound, as the apportionment is approximate only and the total by expense should agree with the figures given. The basis used must be indicated on the analysis sheet so that all users may be aware of the foundation of the apportionment. When an expense is allocated this can be indicated by using the term 'allocated' or 'specific' in the basis column.

The Blackburn Company
Overhead analysis sheet for period ended XXX

Item	Basis of apportionment	Dept A £	Dept B £	Dept C £	Dept D £	Total £
Allocated costs	Allocated	800	320	1,200	480	2,800
Insurance of building	Area	150	75	300	75	600
Insurance of machinery	Value of machinery	200	200	320	80	800
Rent	Area	250	125	500	125	1,000
Heating	Area	200	100	400	100	800
Pension fund	Wages	250	100	320	180	850
General supervision	Number of employees	400	160	600	240	1,400
Electricity (light)	Area	150	75	300	75	600
Electricity (power)	Kilowatt hours	490	490	735	245	1,960
Depreciation	Value of machinery	500	500	800	200	2,000
		3,390	2,145	5,475	1,800	12,810
Apportionment of Service Dept D	Estimate	900	540	360	1,800	–
Total		4,290	2,685	5,835		12,810

Apportionment of service departments

All service departments have to be reallocated to production departments before the final stage of overhead absorption can be accomplished. This is fairly simple in an example such as the one above where an estimate of usage is supplied and there are not interservice transfers. Where there is more than one service department as for example stores, maintenance, canteens etc. they may service each other in addition to the production departments. This problem is known as interservice or reciprocal service costs. A number of techniques have been devised for dealing with this problem, the most utilized being the following:

1 *Elimination method:* This is sometimes referred to as specific order method. The order may be to apportion the department which serves the greater number of other departments first or start with those departments having highest cost. Once a department has been apportioned then other departments are apportioned without reallocation to those that have been used already.

2 *Continuous (repeated) distribution method:* Each department is apportioned in turn until the amount remaining on any service department balance is too small to be of significance. This method is manually time consuming but easily programmed for a small computer.

3 *Algebraic methods:* If there are only two service departments simultaneous equations may be used. This is a fairly common examination condition but one which rarely exists in practice. For more than two departments advanced mathematical programming can be used but the speed of computerized operations would render method 2 practically feasible.

The following exercise will be used to illustrate the above methods.

Exercise 9.3

In a factory with four production departments and two service departments, the operating costs for the month of October were as shown below. The cost of running the canteen is apportioned to each department on the basis of the estimated use of the canteen by the employees in each department. Similarly, the cost of the boiler house is apportioned on the basis of the estimated consumption of power used by each department:

Cost for October were:	£
Production department 1	200,000
Production department 2	500,000
Production department 3	300,000
Production department 4	400,000
Service department:	
Canteen	50,000
Boiler house	100,000
Total	£1,550,000

The service departments are apportioned as follows:

	Canteen %	Boiler house %
Production department 1	10	20
Production department 2	30	10
Production department 3	20	30
Production department 4	30	20
Service department:		
Canteen	–	20
Boiler house	10	–
	100	100

You are required to prepare a cost statement showing the costs of operating the four production departments after the costs of the service departments have been reapportioned to each production department and to comment briefly on the problems associated with apportioning service departments costs to production departments.

Source: CIMA

Elimination method

Since the boiler house serves four production departments and the canteen while the canteen serves four production departments and the boiler house the number of departments served with either is the same – five. The highest cost is incurred by the boiler house and this would therefore be apportioned first on the basis given.

		Production Dept			Canteen	Boiler house	Total
	1	*2*	*3*	*4*			
From overhead analysis (£000)	200	500	300	400	50	100	1,550
Apportion boiler house	20	10	30	20	20	(100)	–
	220	510	330	420	70		1,550
Apportion canteen*	7.8	23.3	15.6	23.3	(70)		
	227.8	533.3	345.6	443.3	–	–	1,550

* Note that the ratio is $\dfrac{10}{90}$ $\dfrac{30}{90}$ $\dfrac{20}{90}$ $\dfrac{30}{90}$

The 10 per cent of canteen costs allocated to the boiler house are automatically included in the inflated cost to the production departments.

Continuous (repeated) distribution method

		Production Dept			Canteen	Boiler house	Total
	1	*2*	*3*	*4*			
From overhead analysis (£000)	200	500	300	400	50	100	1,550
Apportion canteen	5	15	10	15	(50)	5	–
	205	515	310	415	–	105	
Apportion boiler house	21	10.5	31.5	21	21	(105)	
	226	525.5	341.5	436	21		
Apportion canteen	2.1	6.3	4.2	6.3	(21)	2.1	
	228.1	531.8	345.7	442.3	–	2.1	
Apportion boiler house	0.42	0.21	0.63	0.42	0.42	(2.1)	
	228.52	532.01	346.33	442.72	0.42		
Apportion canteen	0.042	0.126	.084	0.126	(0.42)	0.042	
	228.562	532.136	346.414	442.846	–	0.042	
Apportion boiler house	0.008	0.004	0.013	0.009	0.008	(0.042)	
	228.570	532.140	346.427	442.855	0.008	–	
Apportion canteen	0.002	0.002	0.002	0.002	(0.008)		
Total	228.572	532.142	346.429	442.857			1,550

Algebraic method

Let x = cost of canteen after charging part of boiler house.
Let y = cost of boiler house after charging part of canteen.
then x = £50,000 + 20% of y
then y = £100,000 + 10% of x
Equation (1) x = 50,000 + 0.20y
Equation (2) y = 100,000 + 0.10x
Multiply (2) × 10 we have 10y = 1,000,000 + x
   and therefore − x = 1,000,000 − 10y

Adding Equation (1) and (2) to eliminate x we have:

$$x = 50,000 + 0.2y$$
$$\text{plus} \; -x = 1,000,000 - 10y$$
$$\overline{0 = 1,050,000 - 9.8y}$$
$$\therefore 9.8y = 1,050,000$$
$$\therefore y = \frac{1,050,000}{9.8} = 107,143$$

Using (1) and substituting

$$x = 50,000 + 0.20 \,(107,143)$$
$$= 71,429$$

Reallocation	X Canteen		Y Boiler House	
Production department 1	10% of 71,429	7,143	20% of 107,143	21,429
Production department 2	30% of 71,429	21,428	10% of 107,143	10,714
Production department 3	20% of 71,429	14,286	50% of 107,143	32,143
Production department 4	30% of 71,429	21,428	20% of 107,143	21,429
		64,285		85,715

Note that the totals of £64,825 and £85,715 do not agree with £71,429 and £107,143 respectively. This is because the total percentages applied to the producing department are not 100 per cent. The interservice percentages have been taken care of by the formula. If we add £64,285 to £85,715 we get £150,000 which agrees with the total cost of canteen plus boiler house to be accounted for. The final distribution will now be:

Cost for October

	Production department				
	1 £	2 £	3 £	4 £	Total £
Ex question	200,000	500,000	300,000	400,000	1,400,000
Service departments					
Canteen	7,143	21,428	14,286	21,428	64,285
Boiler house	21,429	10,714	32,143	21,429	85,715
	228,572	532,142	346,429	442,857	1,550,000

The reader should compare the final line here with the result obtained by the repeated distribution method.

The objectives of the overhead analysis sheet have now been illustrated:

1   To provide cost centre totals as a basis for control.
2   To obtain total overheads by production cost centre to facilitate computation of overhead absorption rates.

9.5   Absorbing overhead costs

Once the steps of allocating and apportioning overheads to cost centres has been completed methods have to be devised for the fourth stage of treatment i.e. to **absorb** these costs into the cost of the products. A major distinction is made between the methods adopted for production overheads and those of the other main groups of overhead costs i.e. administration, selling and distribution, research and development.

Production overheads

As these are substantially related to factory activity separate rates should be devised for productive departments or even separate cost centres within departments. The rates are applied on some predetermined basis; that is a rate which is currently being applied is probably computed from some actual past cost period or preferably from a budget, which has computed the cost that should reasonably be incurred in relation to the level of productive activity chosen as the base. There is no single preferred method of computing overhead rates – it is part of the skill of the accountant to select the one most appropriate for the circumstances. Such circumstances would include:

1   Size of the organization, the total amount of overheads and the proportion of total cost represented by such overheads.
2   The number of manufacturing operations, processes and different machines within each department or cost centre.
3   The expense involved in continuous computation, revision and collection of necessary data and the extent of the use made of it by management.

A single rate may be used for the whole factory but will give unreliable results particularly if there is a mixture of labour and machine intensive operations. Such rates are sometimes termed **blanket** rates.

The main methods used will be illustrated by reference to Exercise 9.4.

Exercise 9.4
AC Limited is a small company which undertakes a variety of jobs for its customers.

**Budgeted profit and loss statement
for the year ending 31 December 19x6**

	£	£
Sales		750,000
Costs:		
Direct materials	100,000	
Direct wages	50,000	
Prime cost	150,000	
Fixed production overhead	300,000	
Production cost	450,000	
Selling, distribution and administration cost	160,000	
		610,000
Profit		£140,000

Budgeted data:

Labour hours for the year	25,000
Machine hours for the year	15,000
Number of jobs for the year	300

An enquiry has been received and the production department has produced estimates of the prime cost involved and of the hours required to complete job A57.

	£
Direct materials	250
Direct wages	200
Prime cost	£450
Labour hours required	80
Machine hours required	50

You are required to:

1 Calculate by different methods **six** overhead absorption rates.
2 Comment briefly on the suitability of each method calculated in 1.
3 Calculate cost estimates for job A57 using in turn each of the six overhead absorption rates calculated in 1.

Source: CIMA

Solution
(a) Percentage of direct materials

Formula: $\dfrac{\text{production overhead}}{\text{direct material cost}} \times 100$

$= \dfrac{£300,000}{£100,000} \times 100 = 300\%$

Production overhead applicable to Job A57 = 300% × £250 = £750

Production cost = direct material + direct wages + production overhead
= £250 + £200 + £750 = £1,200

Usually a blanket rate and unsuitable as little relationship between overhead and material cost. Easy to apply but can produce misleading results.

(b)   Percentage of direct labour

Formula: $\dfrac{\text{production overhead}}{\text{direct labour cost}}$

$= \dfrac{£300,000}{£50,000} \times 100 = 600\%$

Production overhead applicable to job A57 = 600% × £200 = £1,200
Production cost = £250 + £200 + £1,200 = £1,650.

Easy to apply and widely used. Some relevance to time but care required when used with incentive schemes or labour rates which are inflated by overtime premium.

(c)   Percentage of prime cost

Formula: $\dfrac{\text{production overhead}}{\text{prime cost}} \times 100$

$= \dfrac{£300,000}{£150,000} \times 100 = 200\%$

Production overhead applicable to Job A57 = 200% × 450 = 900
Production cost = £250 + £200 + £900 = £1,350

This method tends to combine the weaknesses of the direct materials and direct wages methods and is an improvement on neither as the time taken element is again ignored.

(d)   Direct labour hour rate

The number of direct labour hours for the period are divided into the production overhead for the factory or producing cost centre. This rate is then applied to the labour hours taken on each job.

Formula: $\dfrac{\text{production overhead}}{\text{direct labour hours}}$

$\dfrac{£300,000}{25,000} = £12 \text{ per DLH}$

Production overhead applicable to Job A57 = 80 × £12 = £960
Production cost = £250 + £200 + £960 = £1,410

This method takes into account the time factor and therefore – fairly – the longer a job takes the higher will be the overhead cost charged by absorption to the job. It eliminates the effect of wage differences between operators but records will be required of workers' time on individual jobs even with piecework systems.

(e)   Machine hour rate

Used where machine time rather than labour time is the dominant factor. The number of machine hours for the period is divided into the production overhead for the factory or production cost centre.

Formula: $\dfrac{\text{production overhead}}{\text{machine hours}}$

$= \dfrac{£300,000}{15,000} = £20$ per machine hour

Production overhead applicable to Job A57 = 50 × £20 = £1,000
Production cost = £250 + £200 + £1,000 = £1,450.

This method produces the most accurate results. Estimating and pricing are made easier and analysis of losses by virtue of underabsorption can be quickly analysed to amount, cause and responsibility. Large variations in machine running and depreciation costs are correctly reflected in the rate. Requires efficient production control, plant register and statistics for effective use.

(f) Cost unit rate

The output for the period in units is divided into the production overhead for the factory or cost centre for the period concerned.

Formula: $\dfrac{\text{production overhead}}{\text{number of units}}$

$= \dfrac{£300,000}{300} = £1,000$ per unit (job)

Production overhead applicable to Job A57 = £1,000
Production cost = £250 + £1,000 = £1,450

This method is easy to apply and adequate if a single product is made. It is most likely to be applicable to process industries as for example per kilogram of sugar, per tablet of soap, per tonne of coal or steel produced.

Comparison of production cost under alternative methods

	(a) £	(b) £	(c) £	(d) £	(e) £	(f) £
Direct material	250	250	250	250	250	250
Direct wages	200	200	200	200	200	200
Prime cost	450	450	450	450	450	450
Production overhead	750	1,200	900	960	1,000	1,000
Production cost	1,200	1,650	1,350	1,410	1,450	1,450

Note that there is a difference in cost of £450 between the lowest (a) and the highest (b) due solely to the absorption method used. A firm using (b) percentage of direct labour would always quote prices well below those using (a) percentage of direct material – assuming they sought similar profit margins. This does not mean they would always make profits for reasons discussed later. Methods (e) and (f) produce similar answers by virtue of the fact that all machine hours are efficiently utilized i.e. 300 jobs each taking fifty machine hours equals 15,000 machine hours.

The cost estimates above are incomplete to the extent that no addition has been made for selling, distribution and administration costs. In this exercise they are all grouped into one total and would most likely be absorbed as a percentage of production cost thus:

Formula: $\dfrac{\text{selling, distribution and administration overhead}}{\text{production cost}} \times 100$

$\dfrac{160,000}{450,000} \times 100 = 35.6\%$

The cost per unit under each of the methods above would be:

	(a)	*(b)*	*(c)*	*(d)*	*(e)*	*(f)*
Production cost (i)	1,200	1,650	1,350	1,410	1,450	1,450
Selling and distribution and administration (ii)	427	587	481	502	516	516
	1,627	2,237	1,831	1,912	1,966	1,966

Line (ii) = 35.6% of line (i)

If a selling price is required the final step would be to apply an appropriate profit percentage or mark up.

Absorption of non-production overheads

In the above example all the non-production overheads were grouped and absorbed under one heading. This is probable only in the smallest organization and each division of overhead would be separately considered in respect of amount and signficance. In a soft drinks industry such as Coca-Cola selling (including advertising) and distribution costs would be both large in amount and proportion of total cost. In engineering construction such as bridge building there would be small selling and distribution costs but high prime costs. Hence the necessity for skill in application of correct management accounting practice – identifying the correct objectives and techniques for the circumstances.

Administration overhead

This is the cost of managing and administering all activities other than production overhead or the groups listed separately below. It is mainly fixed in that it does not change substantially with fluctuation in outputs. It is recovered on a percentage basis, apportioned over other functions or charged as written off directly to the costing profit and loss account.

Selling overhead

This is the cost of securing orders and includes items such as advertising, salesmen's salaries and commissions. They are deemed to be incurred when goods are sold hence their exclusion from stock valuation figures. They may be segregated into fixed (salaries) and variable (commission) and absorbed on differing bases or recovered as a percentage of production cost or selling price or in the case of a single product on a per unit basis.

Distribution overhead

Sometimes treated jointly with selling overhead this is the cost of packing, storing and delivering finished products. Separate rates may be used for different expenses e.g. rate per mile for delivery and cost per unit for packaging.

Research and development

There are standard definitions of these items in SSAP 13. Such costs are likely to be significant in industries such as aerospace, petrochemicals and pharmaceuticals. **Applied research** is: 'The cost of original investigation undertaken in order to gain new or technical knowledge and directed toward a specific practical aim or objective'. **Basic research** costs are similar costs but without any specific practical aim or application. '**Development cost** is the cost of using scientific or technical knowledge in order to produce new or substantially improved material, devices, products, processes systems or services prior to commencement of commercial production.'

To allocate such cost to products is questionable and difficult and should be made the subject of specific study by accountants concerned with them. Failure to recognize their importance can have effects as serious as that which contributed to the failure of the original Rolls-Royce Aero Engine concern.

Actual and predetermined rates

Overheads may be computed from past actual costs and past levels of efficiency and performance but they are still applied to current operating activities. It would be rather single minded to use these figures when we were aware that prices or labour rates had changed. A predetermined rate is, therefore, usually employed. The figure used may be estimates of what costs and production levels are likely to be or – more scientifically – may be based on **budgets** to produce control figures. In any event the amount absorbed – charged to work in progress – in a period is unlikely to agree with the amount incurred or budgeted. The difference may be an overabsorption – more overhead absorbed than incurred or underabsorption – less overhead absorbed than incurred. In a formal standard cost and budgeting control system the difference will be split into a variety of reasons – spending more or less, producing more or less or not producing at the anticipated efficiency. (See Chapter 11.) In a non-standard system the difference would be debited or credited to the costing profit and loss account as illustrated in Exercise 9.5.

Also, in Exercise 9.5, the effect of using different rates for different departments or cost centres is illustrated. Exercise 9.4 showed only one (blanket) rate being used for the whole factory. In practice job or process costs would be accumulated using the method most appropriate for each cost centre.

Exercise 9.5

PQ Limited absorbs its production overhead by using predetermined rates – a percentage on direct labour cost for Department P and a machine hour rate (calculated to three decimal places) for Department Q.

The estimates made at the beginning of the financial year which ended on 31 October were as follows:

	Dept P £	Dept Q £
Direct labour cost	450,000	150,000
Production overhead	517,500	922,500
	Hours	Hours
Direct labour	172,500	40,000
Machines	20,000	180,000

For the month of October, the cost sheet for Job No. 186 shows the following information:

	Dept P	Dept Q
Materials used	£200	£800
Direct labour	£360	£190
Direct labour hours	120	47.5
Machine hours	20	260

Following the end of the financial year it was ascertained that actual production overhead incurred by Department P was £555,000 and that incurred by Department Q was £900,000.

Required:

1 Calculate the overhead absorption rates for each of the departments P and Q.
2 Determine the total production overhead cost to be charged to Job No. 186 for October.
3 Show the over/underabsorbed overhead for each department and for the company as a whole for the year ended 31 October assuming that actual direct labour cost and machine hours worked were as originally estimated.
4 Comment on the choice of an overhead absorption rate based on direct labour cost for Department P.

Source: CIMA

Solution
1 *Calculation of overhead absorption rates*

Key			Dept P	Dept Q
A		Production overhead	£517,500	£922,500
B		Direct labour cost	£450,000	–
$C = \dfrac{A}{B} \times 100$		Percentage on direct labour cost	115%	–
D		Machine hours	–	180,000
$E = \dfrac{A}{D}$		Rate per machine hour	–	£5.125

2   *Total production overhead cost of Job No. 186*

	£
Department P	
115% of £360	414
Department Q	
260 Machine hours @ £5.125	1,332.5
Total	1,746.5

3   *Over/underabsorbed overhead*

Key	**Department P**	
A	Direct labour cost incurred for year	£450,000
B	Overhead absorption rate	115%
C = A × B	Overhead absorbed	£517,500
D	Overhead incurred	£555,000
E = Q − D	Underabsorption of overhead	£37,500
	Department Q	
F	Machine hours worked for year	180,000
G	Machine hours absorption rate	£5.125
H = F × G	Overhead absorbed	£922,500
H	Overhead incurred	£900,000
J	Overabsorption of overhead	(£22,500)
K = E + J	Net under absorption for company as a whole	£15,000

Since time records are available it would be preferable to use a direct labour hour absorption rate rather than a percentage method. The percentage method ignores the time factor and would be affected by differing labour rates, incentive payments and overtime premiums.

The overhead account for the end of the period using the present method would appear as follows:

Production overhead account

	£		£
Sundry expenses (Material, wages Depreciation, etc. – overhead incurred)		Work in progress	
		Department P	517,500
		Department Q	922,500
		(overheads absorbed)	
Department P	555,000	Profit and loss	
Department Q	900,000	Underabsorption transferred	15,000
	1,455,000		1,455,000

Overhead expenditure is classified, collected, allocated, apportioned and absorbed to satisfy the following objectives:

- To ascertain the costs of cost centres and departments for accounting and control by means of comparison with targets, past actual performance or budgets.
- To ascertain overhead absorption rates to facilitate calculation of product unit costs for stock valuation, cost of sales and selling price determination.
- To assist in decision making by segregating fixed and variable costs to assess effects of volume changes.

10
Costing for various forms of enterprise

When the cost objective is the determination of product unit costs there are accepted basic costing methods which are used. The method of costing has been: 'Devised to suit the methods by which goods are manufactured or services provided.' There are two basic methods – **specific order costs** and **average unit costs** but these are frequently divided and given a special name according to the final end product as shown in Table 10.1.

Table 10.1

	Methods	Industry and examples
Specific orders	Job costing	Engineering – Garage repairs
	Batch costing	Shoe manufacture – more than one-off for an order but batches different
	Contract costing	Civil engineering – each job subject to special agreement. Roads, bridges, shipbuilding
Average unit	Process costing	Brewing, chemicals, oil refining
	Service costing	Electricity, gas
	Operating costing	Hospitals, theatres, transport

Large manufacturing organizations such as mass producers of cars would use a combination of the methods shown in Table 10.1. This is because although to the final purchaser a car would be a significant unit with individual characteristics such as colour, engine capacity and so on, it would represent a very small element of standardized output as far as the manufacturer was concerned. We are now aware of the main cost objectives and the main themes are illustrated in Figure 10.1. The ascertainment of product unit costs are dealt with in this chapter while analysis by function for cost control is covered in Chapter 11 and cost for decision making in Chapter 12. The 'methods' referred to should be distinguished from costing techniques. A technique is a system used by the organization for cost ascertainment and control. We may use absorption or marginal costing; historical costs or standard costs; actual figures or

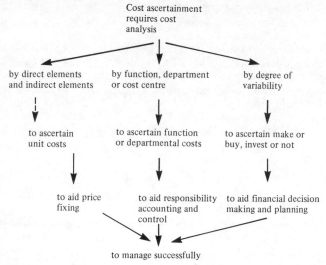

Figure 10.1

budgets etc. The costing method is determined by the process of manufacture and the **end product**. The particular technique(s) used are chosen by the accountant and management concerned. The interrelationships are illustrated in Figure 10.1.

Early costing development focused on analysis for ascertaining unit cost and it is to this aspect that attention will first be directed as, apart from its historical position, it is the most fundamental classification.

Data required to ascertain the costs of producing one unit is the expenditure in a period and the relevant output. Expenditure comprises the sum of the direct elements of cost i.e. direct materials, direct wages and direct expenses plus the indirect elements or overhead costs deemed applicable. As these are all items of expenditure they would be debits in any system of cost accounting. The credits must be represented by the value of work either fully or partially complete. The cost unit is the measure of completed work and is determined by the nature of the end product e.g. cars, dresses or soap tablets. The basic methods of ascertaining unit costs are therefore product determined (as opposed to techniques (see page 295) which are determined by the enterprise itself). Unit costs are of two basic types only, **specific order** costs or **average** costs.

10.1　Costing methods: specific order costing

The essential characteristic of this form of cost unit is that each order or job can be separately identified in its progress through the manufacturing cycle. In its extreme form when the single job is huge as, for example, in the building of a ship the order is the subject of a separate legal agreement and the method used is termed **contract costing** because contract costs normally extend over more than one accounting period – creating problems of work in progress and profit determination. At the other end of the range a small garage will carry out a variety of differing work on repairs to cars but each will have a **separate identity to which the direct costs can be allocated**. In between these two extremes we may have a specific order for a number of similar items but they will be processed as one **batch** hence batch costing is a form of specific order costing where the cost unit (batch) may be more than one item. The essential characteristics of the specific order system are however still there:

1   Each unit or batch is capable of separate identification at all stages of manufacture.
2   All direct elements of cost are capable of being allocated to the cost unit.
3   Overhead expenses are absorbed on a predetermined basis.

The essential documents of a job or specific order costing system are therefore:

1   *Material specification:* Detailing quantities and types of direct materials required for the job. It is from this that the **material requisitions** which provide the authority to withdraw materials from the stores are prepared.
2   *Operation or manufacturing layout:*   Detailing the route and nature of the direct operations to be carried out in converting the materials into components and assemblies. It is from this that **job cards** are prepared which provide authority for the direct labour to be recorded and paid.
3   *Overhead distribution summary:*   These are sheets on which are collected the **indirect** elements of cost that have been incurred in the period to which they relate and for which the accounts are being prepared. A portion of the overhead so collected is debited to the jobs on a basis of **absorption** which is arbitrarily determined in the manner described in Chapter 9.
4   *Weekly/monthly materials and wage cost analysis:*   These are convenient means of collating costs which are relevant to particular jobs in the accounting period. In a manual system they provide a means of reducing the actual number of postings but in a machine operated system are not so important as they are usually produced as by-products of the system.

The accounting system can now be illustrated and will comprise a minimum of six accounts.

Materials stock account (1)

	Folio			Folio	
Purchases (direct and indirect material)			Work in progress (direct materials issued)	4	
			Production overhead (indirect materials issued)	3	

Wages and salaries account (2)

	Folio			Folio
Bank			Work in progress	
Wage payments			Direct wages incurred	4
Salary payments			Production overhead	
			Indirect wages and	
			salaries	3

Production overhead account (3)

	Folio			Folio
Materials stock	1		Work in progress	4
(indirect materials)			Overhead *absorbed*	
Wages and salaries	2			
(indirect wages and				
salaries)				

Work in progress account (4)

	Folio			Folio
Material stock	1		Finished goods stock	5
(direct material issued)				
Wages and salaries	2			
Direct wages incurred				
Production overhead	3			
Overheads absorbed				

Finished goods stock account (5)

	Folio			Folio
Work in progress	4		Cost of sales	
(Cost of jobs completed)			(Cost of goods sold)	6

Cost of sales account (6)

	Folio			
Finished goods	5			

If the job is large enough or is made to a specific order then there may not
be a finished goods stock account. In the case of batch-style manufacture it
is likely that items may be completed but not despatched until the following
accounting period, hence the need for a stock account. Because of the large
number of entries the above accounts are frequently termed **control
accounts** as only the *total* figures are passed through them. Similarly a
purchases account may already have been debited with the cost of items
received and maintained in the nominal ledger of the financial accounts.
The wages account will have been similarly debited and bank credited when
these items have been paid. In order to avoid confusion the cost accounts
are frequently kept completely separate requiring a duplication of the
debits in the costing records. This is achieved by passing the information
through a cost journal which ensures that the *costs to be accounted for* agree
with items recorded in the financial books. Indeed the cost accounts are
merely an extension of the nominal ledger and later systems are described
whereby both sets of accounts are **interlocked** or indeed **fully integrated**.

Exercise 10.1

During May 19X7 a general engineering company undertook three jobs to which the following summarized details apply:

	Job 123	Job 456	Job 789
	£	£	£
Materials issued from stores	731	1,356	961
Direct wages	128	272	96
Special materials purchased	28	–	63
Materials returned to stores	7	15	–

In order to complete Job 123, materials valued at £43 were transferred thereto from Job 456, as the materials in question were not available in stores nor obtainable from suppliers in time to meet the promised delivery date.

The company's overhead for the year is estimated at £3,150 and the direct wages £8,400. Overhead incurred during May was £200.

Job 123 was completed and invoiced at £1,200 on 30 May. The other two jobs were not complete at this date.

Required:
(a) Prepare
    (i) cost accounts for each of the three jobs
   (ii) control accounts for work in progress and overhead
   (iii) the profit and loss account for May, and
(b) given that the quotation for Job 123 was based on estimates of £750 for materials and £112 for wages, prepare a statement reconciling expected profit with that shown by your cost account, and attach a brief report on Job 123 using imaginary but realistic explanations.

Note: Overhead is absorbed to jobs as a percentage of direct wages.
Source: CACA

Workings
   Overhead estimated for year   = £3,150
   Direct wages estimated for year = £8,400

$$\text{Overhead absorption rate*} = \frac{£3,150}{£8,400} \times 100$$
$$= 37.5\%$$

i.e. for every £100 spent on direct wages £37.50 must be added for overhead

* For fuller discussion of overhead absorption rates see page 262

Job No 123

	£		£
Material stock	731	Material stock	7
Job 456 transfer	43	Costing profit and loss	971
Direct wages	128	(cost of goods sold)	
Overheads	48		
Special purchases	28		
	978		978

Job no 456

	£			£
Material stock	1,356	Material stock		15
Direct wages	272	Job 123 transfer		43
Overheads	102	Balance	c/d	1,672
	1,730			1,730
Balance b/d	1,672			

Job No 789

	£			£
Material stock	961	Balance	c/d	1,156
Direct wages	96			
Overheads	36			
Special purchases	63			
	1,156			1,156
Balance b/d	1,156			

Work in progress control

	£			£
Materials stock control (issues)	3,048	Materials stock control (returns)		22
Direct wages control	496	Costing profit and loss Job 123		971
Special purchases	91	Balance	c/d	2,828
Overhead control	186			
	3,821			3,821
Balance b/d	2,828			

Overhead control

	£		£
Sundry expenditure	200	Work in progress control	186
		Costing profit and loss (underabsorbed overheads)	14
	200		200

Profit and loss

	£		£
Work in progress – Job 123	971	Sales	1,200
Overhead control	14		
Profit	215		
	1,200		1,200

Report on completion of Job no 123

	Quotation £	Actual £	Variance £
Direct materials	750	795	+45
Direct wages	112	128	+16
Overhead	42	48	+6
	904	971	+67
Profit	296	229	−67
Sales price	1,200	1,200	–

- *Materials:* The excess of £45 was due to price increase in general and underestimation of the quantity of steel required.
- *Wages:* The excess was due to an unanticipated increase in wage rates. The hours spent on the job were reasonably accurate.
- *Overhead:* As the overhead absorption rate was predetermined at 37.5 per cent the overhead reflects this percentage applied to the excess labour cost i.e. 37.5 × £16 = £6.

Tabular presentation of accounts

It is both quicker and more accurate in this kind of problem to prepare the accounts in a tabular form. The relevant entries form a self-balancing matrix and help to prevent misposting. It also avoids repeated description of the items. It does not matter whether the jobs are put in columns and the entries on horizontal lines or otherwise – it is a matter of whichever is most convenient. In practice each column (job) would be represented by a separate job and as items are entered on the card they are simultaneously posted to the control account. Alternatively all items concerned can be recorded on a minicomputer and individual records displayed on a VDU (visual display unit) as required.

Columnar control accounts using data from Exercise 10.1 would appear as follows:

	Work in progress control £	Job 123 £	Job 456 £	Job 789 £
Balance	–	–	–	–
Material stocks	3,048	731	1,356	961
Direct wages	496	128	272	96
Special purchases	91	28		63
Returns	(22)	(7)	(15)	
Transfer		43	(43)	
Overhead absorbed	186	48	102	36
	3,799	971	1,672	1,156
Transfer to P/L	(971)	(971)		
Balance c/f	2,828		1,672	1,156

The figures in brackets represent credits, to the particular account. The figures in the work in progress could be posted in total to provide quicker information hence **total** or control account.

10.2   Costing methods: average costs, process costing and service industries

There are a large number of products which do not have the characteristics listed for specific order costing. These are primarily products which are essentially the same in terms of specification and quality, the production of which is continuous and where great difficulty would be experienced in identifying a particular unit at all stages of manufacture. The cost period over which the costs are averaged need not be the same as the accounting period. It will probably be shorter e.g. a day, or a week – its length will be determined by convenience and the speed with which production statistics are collected.

There are two major types of manufacturing with which process costing is associated and they are **continuous** or **intermittent**.

Continuous processes

This is associated with production which, of necessity, is carried on continuously. Examples are steel manufacture, oil refining and brewing. The whole output from one process flows immediately into the next. (See Figure 10.2 showing the flow in the production of Guinness.) There are no interprocess stocks other than those actually in the system and the total cost of one process is carried forward (as all **material**) to the succeeding process. Since this results in an accumulation of costs by successive processes the finished product unit cost is given by the **final** process. Treatment of the elements of cost is the same as in the jobbing method. Direct materials, direct labour and direct expenses with the addition of overhead on some arbitrary basis is **debited** to the process account and the output to the succeeding process is **credited** at an average cost per unit determined by the costs and production statistics relevant to the cost period.

In most manufacturing processes all input is not represented by effective output. The processes may be of a chemical nature and varying losses occur depending on climatic conditions or the quality of the material input may vary thus causing consequent variations in the **yield**. This can occur even when only one main saleable product is produced and sold and these losses have to be accounted for. There are a variety of losses and the distinction suggested in the CIMA terminology is useful as an aid to the subsequent accounting treatment.

1   **Waste:**   *'Discarded substances having no value'.* In this case the total costs are divided by the 'good' output and the unit cost automatically inflated to absorb the loss.
2   **Scrap:**   *'Discarded material having some recovery value which is usually disposed of without further treatment (other than reclamation and handling) or reintroduced into the production process in place of the raw*

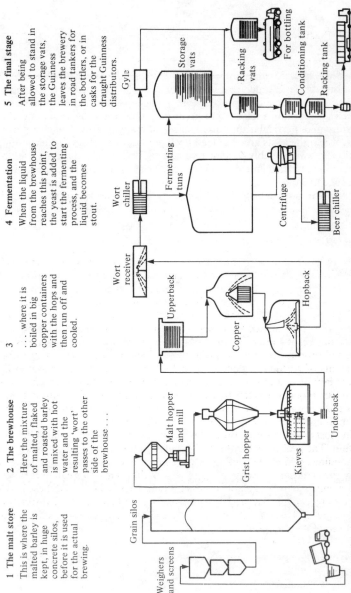

1 The malt store

This is where the malted barley is kept, in huge concrete silos, before it is used for the actual brewing.

2 The brewhouse

Here the mixture of malted, flaked and roasted barley is mixed with hot water and the resulting 'wort' passes to the other side of the brewhouse . . .

3

. . . where it is boiled in big copper containers with the hops and then run off and cooled.

4 Fermentation

When the liquid from the brewhouse reaches this point, the yeast is added to start the fermenting process, and the liquid becomes stout.

5 The final stage

After being allowed to stand in the storage vats, the Guinness leaves the brewery in road tankers for the bottlers, or in casks for the draught Guinness distributors.

Grain silos

Weighers and screens

Malt hopper and mill

Grist hopper

Kieves

Underback

Upperback

Copper

Hopback

Wort receiver

Wort chiller

Fermenting tuns

Centrifuge

Beer chiller

Gyle

Storage vats

Racking vats

For bottling

Conditioning tank

Racking tank

Draught

Figure 10.2 *How Guinness is made*

material'. In this case the value of the scrap is *credited* to the process concerned thus reducing the average cost per unit of the 'good' output.

3   **Spoilage:**   *'Units of output which fail to reach the required standard of quality or specification'*. Such faulty units may be capable of rectification, sold as substandard or disposed of as scrap. The net loss/gain due to additional costs incurred or revenue received will be debited or credited to the process account.

Example

Alpha produces a single product which involves two distinct processes A and B. The output of one process goes immediately into the next and there are no interprocess stocks. 10,000 kg of raw material was put into Process A at a cost of 25p per kg. Direct wage cost of the process amounted to £2,000 and overhead was 90 per cent of direct wages. In Process B additional materials were added at a cost of £4,000 and direct wages were £2,000. Overhead was 62.5 per cent of direct wages. 9000 kg of material was transferred from Process A to Process B in the period and 8400 kg from Process B into stock and the remaining units sold for scrap for £110.

Process A

19–		Qty	Unit cost £	£	19–		Qty	Unit cost £	Total £
	Material introduced	10,000	0.25	2,500		Transfer to			
	Direct wages		0.20	2,000		Process B	9,000	0.70	6,300
	Overhead		0.18	1,800		Waste	1,000	–	
		10,000		6,300			10,000	0.70	6,300

Process B

19–		Qty	Unit cost £	£	19–		Qty	Unit cost £	Total £
	Materials Process A	9,000	0.70	6,300		Finished stock	8,400	1.6	13,440
	Materials added			4,000		Scrap	600		110
	Direct wages			2,000					
	Overhead			1,250					
		9,000		13,550			9,000		13,550

The final unit cost is derived by dividing £13,440 by 8400 = £1.6 per unit. This includes all previous process costs. The £13,440 is derived by subtracting the scrap value of £110 from total costs incurred of £13,550.

Intermittent processes

In this situation the nature of the production cycle is such that material can be stocked in part completed form as work in progress. Thus in a product passing through four stages to completion there may be three work in progress stores and one finished goods store. There are distinctly separate operations which can be costed. The unit cost of each operation is determined without any cost from the preceding processes on an operation cost basis and total unit cost is the aggregate of the process unit costs.

Normal and abnormal losses

The **control** aspects of cost accounting are dealt with more fully later but most basic process cost systems – even on a historic costing basis – set targets for normal losses if these are to be expected. The reason for this is that since we are using average unit cost computed over differing periods and differing conditions we should attempt to distinguish between normal and abnormal losses in order to see how the work was performed in the immediate past period.

Example
20,000 kg of raw material which cost £0.25 per kilogram was put into a single process and the expected loss was 15 per cent. Scrap is sold for £0.10 per kilogram. The direct wage cost of the process was £4,000 and overhead is absorbed at 150 per cent of direct wages. Additional direct expenses amounted to £90. The weight of actual output produced in a period was 16,500 kg.

Workings

Expected yield = 85% × 20,000 kg	=	17,000 kg
Actual yield	=	16,500 kg
∴ Actual yield worse than expected:		
Expected or normal loss = 15% × 20,000	=	3,000 kg
Actual loss = 20,000 − 16,500	=	3,500 kg
∴ Abnormal loss	=	500 kg
Total costs to be accounted for:		£
20,000 kg of raw material @ £0.25 per kg	=	5,000
Direct wages		4,000
Direct expenses		90
Overhead (150% of £4,000)		6,000
		─────
		15,090
Less Normal scrap 3000 kg at £0.10		300
		─────
		14,790

Average cost of production $= \dfrac{£14,790}{£17,000} = £0.87$ per kg

The divisor is the **normal output expected**. This is in order that the full cost of producing scrap can be shown in the accounts. It may well be that the extra scrap can also be sold at £0.10 per kg but this is ignored in the cost calculation although it may ultimately be taken into account when it is sold. The first objective is to show what *should* have happened.

Process account

	Qty	Unit £	Total £		Qty	Unit £	Total £
Material introduced	20,000	0.25	5,000	Normal scrap	3,000	0.10	300
Direct wages			4,000	Abnormal scrap	500	0.87	435
Direct expenses			90	Finished stock	16,500	0.87	14,355
Overhead			6,000				
			15,090				15,090

Finished stock

	Qty	Unit £	Total				
Process account	16,500	0.87	14,355				

Normal scrap

	Qty	Unit £	Total				
Process account	3,000	0.10	300				

Abnormal scrap

	Qty	Unit £	Total				
Process account	500	0.87	435				

It may happen that *more* is produced than expected. The normal scrap would be computed in the same way. It would, however, be necessary to open an account for 'abnormal gains' to show the gain as opposed to the loss. This is shown in the consolidating example in Exercise 10.2 which should enable the distinction between the various terms to be clearly understood.

Exercise 10.2

MA Chemicals Limited process a range of products including a detergent 'Washo', which passes through three processes before completion and transfer to the finished goods warehouse. During April, data relating to this product were as shown:

| | Process | | | |
	1	2	3	Total
	£	£	£	£
Basic raw material (10,000 units)	6,000	–	–	6,000
Direct materials added in process	8,500	9,500	5,500	23,500
Direct wages	4,000	6,000	12,000	22,000
Direct expenses	1,200	930	1,340	3,470
Production overhead				16,500
(Production overhead is absorbed as a percentage of direct wages)				

	units	units	units
Output	9,200	8,700	7,900
	%	%	%
Normal loss in process, of input	10	5	10
	£	£	£
All loss has a scrap value, per unit, of	0.20	0.50	1.00

There was no stock at start or at end in any process.

Required: Prepare the following accounts:

1 Process 1
2 Process 2
3 Process 3
4 Abnormal loss
5 Abnormal gain

Source: CIMA

Workings

	Process 1		Process 2		Process 3	
To be accounted for	Units	£	Units	£	Units	£
Cost Incurred						
1 From previous process (units × Line 16)			9,200	23,000	8,700	43,500
2 Basic raw material	10,000	6,000	–		–	
3 Direct materials added		8,500		9,500		5,500
4 Direct wages		4,000		6,000		12,000
5 Direct expenses		1,200		930		1,340
6 Production overhead (75%)*		3,000		4,500		9,000
7	10,000	22,700	9,200	43,930	8,700	71,340
8 Abnormal gain (units × Line 16)	200	500	–		70	630
9 Total	10,200	23,200	9,200	43,930	8,770	71,970

	Units	£	Units	£	Units	£
Represented by						
10 Transfer to next process	9,200	23,000	8,700	43,500	7,900	71,110
11 Normal loss	1,000	200	460	230	870	870
12 Abnormal loss (units × Line 16)	–	–	40	200		
13	10,200	23,200	9,200	43,930	8,770	71,970
14 Normal cost Lines 7–11 (£)		22,500		43,700		70,470
15 Normal output Lines 7–11 (units)	9,000		8,740		7,830	
16 Normal cost per unit $\frac{\text{Line } 14}{\text{Line } 15}$		2.5		5.0		9.0

Line 6 is derived from $\frac{\text{total overhead}}{\text{total wages}} \times 100 = \frac{£16,500}{£22,000} \times 100 = 75\%$

Process 1 account

	Units	£		Units	£
Stores – basic material	10,000	6,000	Process 2	9,200	23,000
Stores – direct material		8,500	Normal loss	1,000	200
Direct wages		4,000			
Direct expenses		1,200			
Production overhead absorbed		3,000			
Abnormal gain	200	500			
	10,200	23,200		10,200	23,200

Process 2 account

	Units	£		Units	£
Process 1	9,200	23,000	Process 3	8,700	43,500
Stores – direct material		9,500	Normal loss	460	230
Direct wages		6,000	Abnormal loss	40	200
Direct expenses		930			
Production overhead absorbed		4,500			
	9,200	43,930		9,200	43,930

Process 3 account

	Units	£		Units	£
Process 2	8,700	43,500	Finished stock	7,900	71,100
Stores – direct material		5,500	Normal loss	870	870
Direct wages		12,000			
Direct expenses		1,340			
Production overhead absorbed		9,000			
Abnormal gain	70	630			
	8,770	71,970		8,770	71,970

Abnormal loss

	Units	£		Units	£
Process 2	40	200			

Abnormal gain

	Units	£		Units	£
			Process 1	200	500
			Process 3	70	630

By-products and joint products

Frequently in processing one or more basic raw materials the opportunity arises to produce more than one product. Usually the products are of less importance than the major reason for the existence of the business but they nevertheless make a significant contribution to overall profit. Such products are termed **by-products**. They can be formally defined as material recovered incidentally to the manufacture of a main product and having a realizable value. They differ from scrap in that the material usually requires further processing. When no one product is of sufficient size and importance to be designated the main product then the products are termed **joint products**. Such a situation would arise in a complex process such as oil refining where there would be a production of aviation spirit, petrol, diesel oil and thicker residues used as bases for lubricating oils, greases and petroleum jelly.

Problems of accounting arise in the treatment of costs accumulated to the point of separation (beyond this each product can be separately identified and charged with the identifiable direct costs). The treatment varies according to the nature and complexity of the production and is a specialized area of study. An outline of the more common bases together with a simple exercise are given to conclude this section:

1 *Average unit basis:* Cost up to separation are divided according to the quantity of output going forward into subsequent processes. Restricted to situations where all output is in the same physical unit e.g. kilogrammes, metres or litres.
2 *Physical unit basis:* Used where common units can be determined even where physical characteristics are different e.g. gases, liquids and solids could be converted to a common denominator of weight or calorific value.
3 *Selling price basis:* Joint costs are apportioned on the basis of weighted market values. Effectively it charges each product with what the market will bear, since the cost apportionment is related to sales. Because of its simplicity it is the most popular method.

Exercise 10.3

FPI Limited is in the food processing industry and in one of its processes, three joint products are manufactured. Traditionally, the company has apportioned work incurred up to the joint products pre-separation point on the basis of weight of output of the product.

You have recently been appointed cost accountant, and have been investigating process costs and accounting procedures.

You are required to prepare statements for management to show:

1 The profit or loss of each product as ascertained using the weight basis of apportioning pre-separation point costs.
2 The optimal contribution which could be obtained from the manufacture of these products.

The following process data for October are given:

Costs incurred up to separation point	£96,000			Line (c)
	Product A	*Product B*	*Product C*	
	£	£	£	
Costs incurred after separation point	20,000	12,000	8,000	(d)
Selling price per tonne: Completed product	500	800	600	(e)
Estimated, if sold at separation point	250	700	450	(f)
	Tonnes	*Tonnes*	*Tonnes*	
Output	100	100	80	(g)

The cost of any unused capacity after the separation point should be ignored

Source: CIMA

Workings

	A £	B £	C £	Total £	Workings
Sales	50,000	48,000	48,000	146,000	(1)
Joint costs	40,000	24,000	32,000	96,000	(2)
Contribution	10,000	24,000	16,000	50,000	(3)
Post separation	20,000	12,000	8,000	40,000	(4)
	(10,000)	12,000	8,000	10,000	(5)

The optimal contribution occurs when only Products A and C are processed further (see workings). The increase in profit is £16,000 − £10,000 = £6,000

This can be checked as follows:

Product B

	£	(6)
Gain per tonne if sold at separation point	700	
Revenue from 60 tonnes of B @ £700	42,000	
Add Costs after separation not incurred	12,000	
	54,000	
Less Revenue from B after separation not received	48,000	
Net increase in profit	6,000	

1 Sales = Line (e) × Line (g) from question
2 Line (g) total weight = 100 + 60 + 80 = 240 tonnes

$$\therefore \text{ Joint cost apportioned per tonne} = \frac{\text{Line (c)}}{240} = \frac{96,000}{240} = £400$$

		£
Cost apportioned to A = 400 × 100	=	40,000
Cost apportioned to B = 400 × 60	=	24,000
Cost apportioned to C = 400 × 80	=	32,000
		96,000

3 Gross margin or contribution = (1) − (2)
4 Post-separation cost = Line (d) from question
5 Profit (loss) = (3) − (4)
6

		A	B	C
Cost per tonne after separation $\dfrac{\text{Line (d)}}{\text{Line (g)}}$		$\dfrac{£20,000}{100}$	$\dfrac{£12,000}{60}$	$\dfrac{£8,000}{80}$
	=	£200	£200	100
Selling price per tonne Line (e)	=	500	800	600
giving total contribution of		300	600	500
If sold at separation we get		250	700*	450

* Since by further processing B we *lose* £100 per tonne it would be better to sell it at the point of separation. The cost of any unused capacity can be ignored and therefore profit would be increased.

			£
Proof	Product A	100 tonnes @ £500	50,000
	Product B	60 tonnes @ £700	42,000
	Product C	80 tonnes @ £600	48,000
			140,000

Less Costs incurred			
Up to separation			96,000
After separation	A	20,000	
	C	8,000	
			124,000
			16,000

Equivalent units

The examples given so far are relatively simple but unrepresentative of a large number of situations in practice. In most instances there are stocks in hand both at the beginning and end of the period for which the costs are being computed. It is necessary to take into account the **degree of completion** of the production in terms of the various elements of cost. This requires consideration of three stages:

1 Work required to complete units begun in a previous period.

288   *Accounting*

2   Work begun and completed in the period.
3   Work partially completed at the end of the period.

It is also necessary to be aware of, or assume the method of, stock pricing which is being used, i.e. FIFO, LIFO, average cost, standard cost or other basis. It will affect the unit cost computed for the period. On frequent occasions because the element of direct labour in the strict sense is small it is common for the labour and other costs to be combined and the sum of direct wages, direct expenses and absorbed overhead to be treated as one figure and referred to as **conversion cost**, which is the sum of the production costs of converting purchase materials into finished products i.e. direct wages, direct expenses and absorbed production overhead.

Exercise 10.4
The data given below relates to periods 5 and 6 in a department of a factory manufacturing a product by a continuous process.
You are required to calculate for the department:

1   For each period, using the present basis of average costs:
    (a)   The profit made.
    (b)   The value of closing work in progress.
2   For Period 5 only, using the proposed first in first out basis for charging out the finished products:
    (a)   The profit made.
    (b)   The value of work in progress at end of period 5.

Period 5

Opening work in progress:	400 units	
	Degree of completion	£
Direct materials	100%	462.80
Conversion cost	40%	186.20
Input:	Units	
Direct materials	2800	4,253.20
Conversion cost		5,485.80
Output passed by inspection	2690 units	
Closing work in progress	440 units	
	Degree of completion	
Direct materials	100%	
Conversion cost	30%	

Period 6

Input:	Units	£
Direct materials	3100	4,904.80
Conversion cost		6,760.60
Output passed by inspection	3110 units	
Closing work in progress	380 units	
	Degree of completion	
Direct materials	100%	
Conversion cost	25%	

Normal wastage is budgeted at 2 per cent of the physical input of materials and is regarded as comprising units on which both direct labour and full conversion costs have been expended.

The costs of the department are calculated at present on an average cost basis but the management is proposing to change to a first in first out basis.

The department is credited at £4 per unit with output passed by the inspection department.

Source: CIMA

Workings

1 Materials 400 units 100 per cent completed must be equal to 400 equivalent units.

   Conversion 400 units 40 per cent completed must be equal to 160 equivalent units.

2 Direct materials input of 2800 must have at least commenced conversion in period.

3 (1) + (2) must represent total full or partially completed work.

4 Output passed by inspection must be 100 per cent converted.

5 Normal waste has no value here and has no equivalent units as its cost is borne by good production.

6 Closing work in progress materials 440 units are 100 per cent completed and equivalent to 440 units. Conversion 440 units are 30 per cent completed equal to 132 equivalent units.

7 This is inserted after checking. The addition of lines (4) + (5) + (6) in the material units column do not equal the quantity to be accounted for (line 3). The difference is 14 and must represent abnormal waste since this is the quantity needed to balance. Were the sum of lines (4) (5) and (6) greater than line (3) it would imply more efficient production than expected and result in an abnormal gain. In the absence of information to the contrary it must be assumed that units of material lost are also 100 per cent lost in terms of equivalent units of conversion.

8 Sum of lines (4) (5) (6) and (7). Completion of opening work in progress is automatically included.

9 Value of opening work in progress as given.

10 Value of inputs as given.

11 Calculation of unit cost. On an average basis it is the total cost for the period divided by the equivalent completed units for the period.

   i.e. Materials $= \dfrac{£4,716}{£3,144} = £1.5$ per unit

   Conversion $= \dfrac{£5,672}{£2,836} = £2.0$ per unit

12 Units passed inspection valued at £4 per unit (sales).

13 Units passed inspection valued at £3.5 per unit (average cost).

14 Line (12) − (13) = normal profit.

15 Abnormal loss = 14 units valued at £3.5 each.

16 Profit = normal profit minus abnormal loss.

17 Closing work in progress material 440 units (complete) at £1.5.

18 Closing work in progress conversion cost 440 units 30 per cent complete = 132 @ £2.0

19 Sum of (17) + (18).

Solution

(1)
Period 5
Average cost basis
Calculation of closing stocks (units)

		Materials			Conversion	
Particulars	Units	Degree of completion (%)	Equivalent units	Units	Degree of completion (%)	Equivalent units
(1) Opening work in progress	400	100	400	400	40	160
(2) Direct materials input	2800	–	–	2800	–	–
(3) Total	3200	–	–	3200	–	–
(4) Passed by inspection	2690	100	2690	2690	100	2690
(5) Normal waste	56	–	–	56	–	–
(6) Closing work in progress	440	100	440	440	30	132
(7) Abnormal waste (gain)	14	100	14	14	100	14
(8)	3200		3144	3200		2836

Costs

	Equivalent units	Cost per unit £	Total cost £	Equivalent units	Cost per unit £	Total cost £
(9) Opening work in progress			462.8			186.20
(10) Input			4,253.2			5,485.80
(11)	3144	1.5	4,716	2836	2.0	5,672

Profit statement and stock valuation

	Units	Value/ unit £	Total £	
(12) Units passed inspection	2690	4.0	10,760	
(13) Average costs		3.5	9,415	
(14) Profit on average basis		0.5	1,345	
(15) Abnormal loss	14	3.5	(49)	
(16) Actual profit			1,296	
(17) Closing work in progress: material	440	1.5	660	
(18) Conversion cost	132	2.0	264	(440 units 30% complete)
(19)			924	

Period 6
Average cost basis
Calculation of closing stocks (units)

	Materials			Conversion		
Particulars	Units	Degree of completion %	Equivalent units	Units	Degree of completion %	Equivalent units
(1) Opening work in progress	440	100	440	440	30	132
(2) Direct material input	3100			3100		
(3) Total	3540			3540		
(4) Passed by inspection	3110	100	3110	3110	100	3110
(5) Normal waste	62	–	–	62	–	–
(6) Closing work in progress	380	100	380	380	25	95
(7) Abnormal waste (gain)	(12)	100	(12)	(12)	100	(12)
(8)	3540		3478	3540		3193

Costs

	Equivalent units	Cost per unit £	Total cost	Equivalent units	Cost per unit £	Total cost £
(9) Opening work in progress			660			264
(10) Input			4,904.80			6,760.60
(11)	3478	1.6	5,564.80	3193	2.2	7,024.60

Profit statement and stock valuation

	Units	Value/ unit £	Total £	
(12) Units passed inspection	3110	4.0	12,440	
(13) Average costs		3.8	11,818	
(14) Average profit		0.2	622	
(15) Abnormal gain			45.6	
(16) Actual profit			667.6	
(17) Closing work in progress material	380	1.6	608	
(18) Conversion cost	95	2.2	209	(380 units 25% complete)
(19)			817	

Period 5
First in first out basis
Calculation of closing stocks

		Materials			*Conversion*	
Particulars	*Units*	*Degree of completion %*	*Equivalent units*	*Units*	*Degree of completion %*	*Equivalent units*
(1) Opening work in progress	400	100	400	400	40	160
(2) Direct materials input	2800			2800		
(3) Total	3200			3200		
(4) Passed by inspection	2690	100	2690	2690	100	2690
(5) Normal waste	56	–	–	56	–	–
(6) Closing work in progress	440	100	440	440	30	132
(7) Abnormal waste	14	100	14	14	100	14
(8) Total	3200			3200		
(9) Completed this period =(4)+(5)+(6)+(7)−(1)			2744			2676

Costs	*Equivalent units*	*Costs per unit £*	*Total cost £*	*Equivalent units*	*Costs per unit £*	*Total cost £*
(10) Incurred this period	2744	1.55	4,253.2	2676	2.50	5,485.8

Profit statement and stock valuation

	Material			*Conversion*			*Total*		
(11) Units passed inspection	*Units*	*Per unit*	*Total £*	*Units*	*Per unit*	*Total £*	*Units*	*£*	*£*
(12)	–	–	–	–	–	–	2690	4.0	10,760
(13) Opening stock	400		462.8	160		186.2			
(14) To complete	2290	1.55	3,549.5	2530	2.05	5,186.5			
(15) Units passed inspection	2690		4,012.3	2690		5,372.7	2690		9,385
(16) Profit on FIFO basis									1,375
(17) Abnormal loss	14	1.55	21.7	14	2.05	28.7	14	3.6	50.4
(18) Actual profit									1,324.6
(19) Closing work in progress	440	1.55	682	132	2.05	270.6			952.6

The procedure for Period 6 is as for Period 5 with the following amendments.

Line

(7) The addition of lines (4) (5) and (6) is greater than line (3). The difference must therefore be abnormal gain and is a reduction.

(11) The average cost is worked out on the effective units of 3478 and 3193 respectively. By *deducting* the gain figure this does not mean it is a loss. We ascertain the average cost on the achievement to measure the value of gains or losses.

(15) To obtain the actual profit it is necessary to *add* the saving in costs not incurred in producing the abnormal gains. The selling value is part of the 3110 units sold but the average unit cost has been overstated on an actual basis. Contrast Period 5 when an abnormal loss was made then such costs were deducted.

The addition of lines (13) and (19) less (15) will confirm agreement with the cost incurred represented by the total of line (11) i.e. £12,589.40.

(2) Use of the FIFO basis means that the costs incurred in a period must be related to the equivalent units produced in that period. In the averaging method the value of an opening work in progress is amalgamated and its identity lost in the total used in computing the average. It is therefore necessary in FIFO to ensure that closing work in progress is valued on the costs incurred in the period and the transfers to subsequent processes or stock are the result of combining values brought forward with costs of completion in the current period.

On the first in first out basis:

Lines (1)–(8) are similar to the average basis.

Line 9 is computed as explained.

Line 10 – the effective units are transferred and cost per unit (this period) derived by dividing the cost information given by the equivalent units.

Line (13) is as given.

Line (14) – the balance necessary **to complete** the units passed inspection evaluated at rates determined in Line 10.

Line (15) – Lines (13) + (14) = cost of production on FIFO basis.

Lines (16)–(19) as previous.

The figures can be checked briefly in total as follows:

Period 5	Material £	Conversion £	Total £
Costs to be accounted for			
Opening work in progress	462.80	186.20	649
Input	4,253.20	5,485.80	9,739
	4,716	5,672	10,388

Represented by

Units passed inspection	4,012.3	5,372.7	9,385
Abnormal loss	21.7	28.7	50.4
Closing work in progress	682.0	270.6	952.6
	4,716	5,672	10,388

Other forms of average costs: Service industries

The principles and examples so far have been drawn from processes having one or more physical end product. Average costs are also used for **services** provided, in which case the method is usually termed **service costing** or **operating costing**. Examples would be theatres, hospitals and transport. In this case costs are collected under suitable cost centres and the average costs computed according to some reasonable basis of measurement e.g. per occupied bed/day or tonne/kilometre. Note that the cost unit in this situation is usually a combination – empty beds do not require attention and empty wagons provide no revenue hence distance is combined with load in the latter case to produce a reasonable **cost unit**. The word **operation costing** is frequently used in reference to assessing the costs of one stage of production and ascertaining the cost of that particular operation on an average basis. It should be distinguished from operating costing which applies to the average method when used in relation to service industries.

In concluding this section it should be reasserted that the methods of costing are primarily two – **specific order** and **average costing**. There are variations but the appropriate method is determined by the nature of the **end product** and does not therefore present much challenge in choice. The application of the techniques discussed in the following sections are more dynamic from the point of view of effective management accounting and control.

11
Cost control: Costing techniques

There are a variety of **techniques** available for use by the accountant in his efforts to provide the most effective information for managerial purposes and objectives. Unlike the **methods** discussed in Chapter 10 the choice is not decided by the nature of the product but by the size, systems, objectives and decisions of the management teams themselves. The techniques are not exclusive – one technique may be desirable for one particular purpose and one for another. Early distinction has to be made between the use of the techniques of **absorption costing** and **marginal costing**. Under an absorption cost system all costs – fixed and variable – are absorbed into unit costs according to the activity level upon which the absorption rate is based. This was the traditional approach and was utilized in application to the methods discussed in Chapter 10. It was much later that the alternative technique of marginal costing was developed. Linking with economist's studies some accountants argued that fixed costs related to time periods, not to quantity produced and should be charged into accounts as they are incurred. A fuller explanation of these two basic techniques and the contrast between them is given in Section 11.1.

The acceptance of marginal costing principles paved the way for **break-even analysis** and **profit volume studies**. The techniques became particularly useful in assessing the effect on profit of price and volume changes or alternative product mix. Concurrent with this, proponents of scientific management were developing **management by objectives** and application of the **exceptions principle**. This principle broadly states that managerial time is limited and expensive and should therefore be concentrated on what is wrong rather than what is going well. The construction of **budgets** and **standard costs** in advance of production enabled subsequent actual performances to be monitored against these and 'exceptions' (variances) to be extracted and hopefully acted upon promptly where unfavourable.

The common techniques utilized to assist cost control are analysed in this chapter. Combined with those explained in Chapter 12 they additionally provide essential information for decision making.

11.1   Costing techniques: Absorption and marginal costing

In the previous chapters emphasis was put upon the ascertainment of total unit cost by absorbing all the overheads in a period into the cost of the

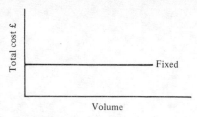

Figure 11.1   *Graph of total fixed cost*

product whether the costs were fixed or variable. We now need to examine the distinction between these costs and their relationship with the two techniques of **absorption** and **marginal costing**.

A **fixed cost** is a cost which, within certain limits of activity, tends to be unaffected by changes in volume or capacity employed. If fixed costs are related to time as, for example, rent, rates and insurance they are alternately referred to as **period costs**. If they are related to managerial decision such as advertising they are referred to as **policy costs**. These terms tend to be used interchangeably.

The characteristics are frequently illustrated graphically as shown in Figure 11.1.

The base line can be expressed in a number of ways such as volume in terms of number of units, labour hours, plant hours, £000 sales turnover or percentage of capacity employed. A graph can also be prepared to show how the cost per unit relates to volume in respect of fixed costs. (See Figure 11.2.) Assume fixed costs are £1,000 for a period in which production could range from zero to 500 units, then the cost per unit for selected outputs up to the maximum would be:

Output	1	2	10	50	100	200	300	400	500
Unit cost	1000	500	100	20	10	5	3.3	2.5	2.0

Note how the cost per unit declines steeply at the early stages of increased output but less reduction is achieved with successive units. This is true of all fixed costs relative to output and always produces a curve of the type shown in Figure 11.2.

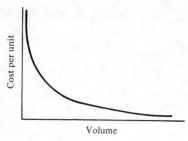

Figure 11.2   *Graph of total unit cost*

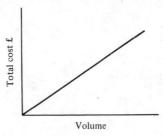

Figure 11.3   *Graph of total variable cost*

The other main type of cost behaviour is the pure **variable cost** which is a cost which tends to vary in total with the level of activity concerned. In theoretical examples direct material, direct labour and direct expenses are considered purely variable. Overheads provide the real challenge since they may be purely variable, purely fixed or between the two. The characteristics of a purely variable cost may be represented as shown in Figure 11.3.

If an expense is purely variable in total then the cost per unit is fixed. If the variable cost(s) were £2 per unit the total cost for output from zero to 500 units would be:

Output (units)	NIL	100	200	300	400	500
Total cost (£)	0	200	400	600	800	1,000

and would produce the line rising steadily from 0 to £1,000 as shown in Figure 11.3. Conversely, irrespective of the level of output the cost per unit would remain at £2.00 and would produce a graph such as that shown in Figure 11.4.

A **semi-variable cost** is one containing fixed and variable elements. Common examples are telephone charges where the total cost consists of a rental paid irrespective of the number of calls made and an additional cost related to time and distance of calls. Power costs of electricity are also frequently based on this principle.

If the two sets of figures from the previous examples are combined they would produce a semi-variable cost of this nature.

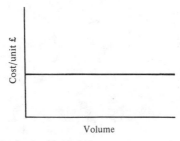

Figure 11.4   **Graph of unit variable cost**

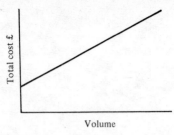

Figure 11.5   *Graph of total semi-variable costs*

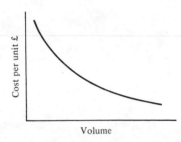

Figure 11.6   *Graph of unit semi-variable costs*

Exercise 11.1

Show by means of graphs the total cost and the cost per unit for a range of output from zero to 500 units for a period when fixed costs were £1,000 and a variable cost £2.0 per unit.

Total cost = fixed cost + variable cost per unit × number of units
At zero output total cost = £1,000 + 0
At 100 output total cost = £1,000 + (2.0 × 100) = £1,200
At 500 output total cost = £1,000 + (2.0 × 500) = £2,000

This can be tabulated:

Output	NIL	2	10	50	100	200	300	400	500
Total cost (£)	1,000	1,004	1,020	1,100	1,200	1,400	1,600	1,800	2,000
Cost per unit (£)	1,000	502	102	22	12	7	5.3	4.5	4.0

and graphed as shown in Figures 11.5 and 11.6.

Because the total variable cost is a straight line we would only need two points to plot it but if unit cost is required we need the additional calculations tabulated. If the graphs are superimposed upon each other we can produce a graph which shows the relationship of total costs to volume as shown in Figure 11.7.

The preceding graphs are subject to severe limitations and qualification:

1   It is assumed that all costs are linear and can be represented by straight lines. That this is not so is illustrated by the exercise showing graphs of

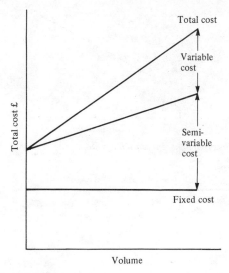

Figure 11.7 *Graph of total costs*

typical expenses on page 301. Frequently over a given range of output, expenses of a curvilinear relationship are assumed straight lines within acceptable limits of error purely for convenience.

2 It is assumed that fixed costs will remain the same. This requires the relevant range to be stated. A factory will always have a maximum capacity. Beyond this more machines, buildings and other fixed assets will be required. At this point the relevant range is being changed and fixed costs will increase.

3 Factors other than volume affect costs and to assume volume changes are the only factor can be an oversimplification.

4 The graphs represent either a single product situation or constant product mix.

Exercise 11.2 can be used to illustrate a few forms which particular expenses can take. The reader is invited to attempt to classify the expenses himself before referring to the answer.

Exercise 11.2

The following graphs reflect the pattern of certain overhead cost items in a manufacturing company in a year. The vertical axes of the graphs represent the total cost incurred, while the horizontal axes represent the volume of production or activity. The zero point is at the intersection of the two axes.

You are required to:

(a) Identify which graph represents the overhead cost items shown below:

(*Note:* A graph may be used more than once.)

Ref	Brief description	Details of cost behaviour
1	Depreciation of equipment	When charged on a straight line basis.
2	Cost of a service	£50 annual charge for subscription, £2 charge for each unit taken, with a maximum total charge of £350 per annum.
3	Royalty	£0.10 per unit produced, with a maximum charge of £5,000 per annum.
4	Supervision cost	When there is one charge hand for every eight men or less, and one foreman for every three charge hands, and when each man represents 40 hours of production, thus:

	Hours	
	Under 320	one charge hand
	321–640	two charge hands
	641–960	three charge hands
	etc.	plus one foreman.

Ref	Brief description	Details of cost behaviour
5	Depreciation of equipment	When charged on a machine-hour rate.
6	Cost of a service	Flat charge of £400 to cover the first 5,000 units:

Per unit
£0.10 for the next 3,000 units
£0.12 for the next 3,000 units
£0.14 for all subsequent units

7	Storage/carriage service	*Per ton*

£15 for the first 20 tons
£30 for the next 20 tons
£45 for the next 20 tons
No extra charge until the service reaches 100 tons; then £45 per ton for all subsequent tonnage.

8	Outside finishing service	*Per unit*

£0.75 for the first 2,000 units
£0.55 for the next 2,000 units
£0.35 for all subsequent units

(b) Give an example of an overhead cost item that could represent those graphs to which you do not refer in your answer at (a) above.

(c) Draw one graph of a pattern of an overhead item not shown and give an example of an overhead cost item that it would represent.

Source: CIMA

Solution

Reference	Graph
1	C
2	F
3	B
4	H
5	E
6	K
7	G
8	D

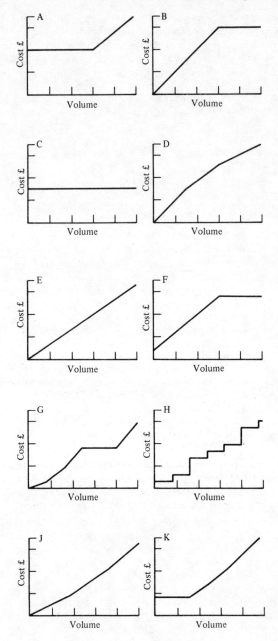

An example of an expense which would be reflected by Graph A would be car leasing on the basis of a fixed amount up to a limited mileage then a standard amount per mile thereafter. Graph J would be the same as for a service similar to Reference 6 without the initial fixed charge of £400.

Marginal cost

One definition is that marginal cost is the amount by which aggregate costs are changed if the volume of output is increased or decreased by one unit. This equates with the economist's conception of marginal cost but the term is frequently not interpreted in this manner in theory or in the practice of accounting as can be seen by the following example.

Example

Assume that items are purchased from a supplier at a cost of £10 each for quantities up to ninety-nine. For quantities of 100 or more the supplier is prepared to offer a 10 per cent discount then the total cost of 100 units will be (100 × £10) less 10% = £900. The marginal cost of the hundredth unit is £900 − (99 × £10) = £90 negative. This is the change in total cost caused by the addition of one extra unit. The hundredth unit is, however, physically indistinguishable from the previous ninety-nine and it would be impractical to say that ninety-nine units cost £10 each and one cost minus £90. It could be said that marginal costs were now £9 each where previously they were £10 each – but this would impart a different interpretation to that specified previously. £9 is the **average variable cost per unit** after ninety-nine units are purchased whereas below this quantity average variable cost per unit is £10. Frequently the word marginal cost per unit is used when strictly one should refer to average variable cost. On this basis marginal cost is preferably defined as the variable cost per unit. Such costs are not incurred if production does *not* take place.

Contribution

This is particularly important in the application of marginal costing. It can be defined as the difference between sales and marginal (or variable) cost. It can be expressed per unit or in total and is therefore **the amount available for fixed expenses and profit**. Fixed expenses are treated as period costs and charged against the sales for the period in which they are incurred. One advantage of this is that since the fixed expenses are charged in their entirety to the accounting period, work in progress and finished stock valuations contain no amount in respect of these. This is contrary to an absorption costing system where the amounts are added via the absorption rate for allocated overheads (including fixed) up to the degree of completion achieved. Direct material, direct wages and direct expenses can be identified and vary with a product or batch of products. Overhead costs are classified according to their behaviour relative to the volume of output or period concerned. A purely variable overhead will increase in total as the volume of output increases while a fixed overhead will tend to remain constant over a given range of output. In between these two extremes there are costs which are not wholly fixed or wholly variable. They are classified as semi-fixed (or semi-variable) but their degree of variability can be almost infinite.

When all expenses have been segregated into fixed and variable elements a marginal cost per unit can be produced. The following exercise illustrates the differences in reported profit when marginal costing is used as opposed to absorption costing.

Exercise 11.3
Using the information given below, prepare profit statements for the months of March and April 19x8 using:
(a) Marginal costing.
(b) Absorption costing.

	£
Per unit:	
Sales price	50
Direct material cost	18
Direct wages	4
Variable production overhead	3
Per month:	
Fixed production overhead	99,000
Fixed selling expenses	14,000
Fixed administration expenses	26,000
Variable selling expenses	
10% of sales value	

Normal capacity was 11,000 units per month.

	March units	April units
Sales	10,000	12,000
Production	12,000	10,000

Source: CIMA

Workings
(a) Production cost per unit – marginal costing basis:

	£
Direct materials	18
Direct wages	4
Variable production overhead	3
	£25

(b) Production cost per unit – absorption costing basis

	£
Direct materials	18
Direct wages	4
Variable production overhead	3
Fixed production overhead	9
	£34

Fixed production overhead is absorbed on the normal capacity of £11,000 units i.e. $\frac{£99,000}{11,000}$ = £9 per unit.

The production cost per unit is calculated rather than the cost of sales because stock is valued exclusive of cost incurred in selling the items concerned.

Solution

Marginal costing basis – Profit statement

	March £000	March £000	April £000	April £000
Sales	–	500		600
Opening stock	–		50	
Marginal cost of production	300		250	
Total	300		300	
Less Closing stock	(50)		–	
	250		300	
Variable selling expenses	50		60	
		300		360
Contribution		200		240
Less Fixed expenses				
Production	99		99	
Selling	14		14	
Administration	26		26	
		139		139
Net profit		£61		£101

No information is given in respect of any stock at the beginning of March, therefore, there must be no opening balance and the closing stock must equal production less sales i.e. 12,000 – 10,000 units = 2000. This valued at marginal cost of £25 per unit = £50,000.

Absorption costing basis – Profit statement

	March £000	March £000	April £000	April £000
Sales		500		600
Opening stock	–		68	
Cost of production	408		340	
	408		408	
Less Closing stock	68		–	
	340		408	
Under (over) absorbed overhead	(9)		9	
		331		417
		169		183

	March		April	
	£000	*£000*	*£000*	*£000*
Less Selling and administration costs				
Variable Selling Cost	50		60	
Fixed Selling Cost	14		14	
Fixed Administration	26		26	
		90		100
Net profit		£79		£83

In this exercise because the stock over the *two* periods are nil the cumulative profit under either system is the same:

Marginal £(61,000 + 101,000) = £162,000
Absorption £(79,000 + 83,000) = £162,000

The difference in the **period** profit is, however, quite significant. Under the marginal system it is (61–79) = £18,000 less in March and £18,000 greater in April. Protagonists of the marginal system claim that it gives a far clearer indication of profitability since the type of fluctuation illustrated under the absorption system and occasioned purely by the effect of overhead in the stock valuation is avoided. It is further claimed – with some justification – that the effect on profit of changes in prices, costs, volume or product mix can be easily identified and computed.

It should be evident that to determine marginal costs we need to separate the variable from the fixed elements for each item of overhead expense concerned. The addition of the direct elements (prime cost) will give the marginal cost and these can be used for assistance when making a decision. The other important factors in decision making on a marginal costing basis are capacity, time and the limiting factor. Contribution has been defined as the amount available for fixed expenses and profit but this has to be related to the limiting factor and, in general, it will be preferable to concentrate on an item which produces the greatest contribution per unit of the limiting factor. This need not necessarily be the highest contribution per unit of product. If skilled labour is the limiting factor the contribution is related to the hours of labour required to produce a unit of the product and the rate of contribution per labour hour is determined.

Examples of the situations in which marginal cost are relevant to decision making are given in Chapter 12.

11.2 Costing techniques: Break-even and cost/volume relationships

As with marginal costing **break-even analysis** is concerned with the effect on costs and profit of changes in volume either in total or in its make up. Break-even analysis is part of the wider study of **cost volume analysis** which assesses the interrelationship between costs, volume and profit. It measures how they are affected by changes in one or more of the constituents such as unit cost, fixed cost, sales revenue or mix of products.

Cost volume profit analysis embraces a number of techniques but the primary ones are marginal costing and break-even analysis. Fundamental to both are various basic assumptions upon which the validity of the results obtained depend. These include:

1 Separation of all costs into fixed and variable elements and aggregation into one or other group.
2 Over the relevant range unit costs, total fixed cost, selling prices and product mix will remain constant.
3 Volume is the main factor to which costs relate.
4 Where costs are of a stepped or non-linear nature, linear approximations made over the relevant range will not be gravely inaccurate.

Break-even chart

This is a chart which shows the profit or loss which can be expected at different levels of sales volume within a prescribed (relevant) range. It is essential that certain terms be clearly understood before proceeding to further development.

1 *Break-even point:*   This is the level of activity or sales volume at which neither a profit or loss is made, alternatively where total cost = total revenue.
2 *Margin of safety:*   This is the **sales in excess of the break-even point** at the level of sales being considered. It can be expressed in absolute numbers or expressed as a ratio over the sales volume concerned.

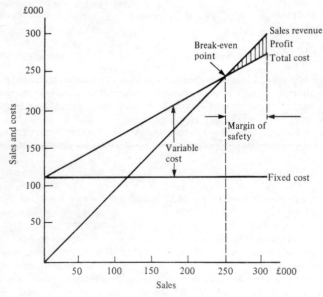

Figure 11.8   *Traditional break-even chart*

3   *Contribution:*   As defined in the section on marginal costing this is the **difference between sales and variable (marginal) costs** or alternatively the amount available for fixed expenses and profit.
4   *Product mix:*   Where a company produces and sells a variety of products, total volume may remain the same but the proportion of one product sold to the total may increase or decrease at the expense of another. Since each product will have a different contribution the results based on a constant mix will be invalidated.

Exercise 11.4
Using the following information in respect of B E Ltd. construct a break-even chart and indicate the break-even point and margin of safety.

Annual production and sales	10,000 units
Selling price	£30 each
Variable production cost per unit	£11
Variable selling cost per unit	£4
Total fixed cost	£120,000

The data must be reconstructed to provide the basic data required for the graph.

	£
Total sales (10,000 × £30)	300,000
Less Variable costs (10,000 × £11 + £4)	150,000
Contribution	150,000
Less Fixed costs	120,000
Profit	30,000

A traditional break-even chart is prepared with fixed cost plotted parallel to the horizontal axis and variable costs added thereto to provide the total cost line. Note that sales volume (£) is plotted on both vertical and horizontal axis. (See Figure 11.8.)

From Figure 11.8 we can see that the break-even point occurs where sales and total cost intersect at £240,000. The margin of safety is £300,000 less £240,000 = £60,000 or 20% as a percentage of sales.

It is claimed by some that more useful information is immediately apparent if variable costs are plotted first. The main advantage of this alternative format is that contribution can be read from the graph directly. (See Figure 11.9.)

In Figures 11.8 and 11.9 volume on the horizontal axis has been expressed in £ sales. It may alternatively be expressed in units of sales, some measure of activity such as direct labour hours or machine hours, or as a percentage of some relevant range. In the case of the former the break-even point and other information will be in the appropriate units (Figure 11.10) while in the latter it would be the appropriate percentage of capacity (Figure 11.11).

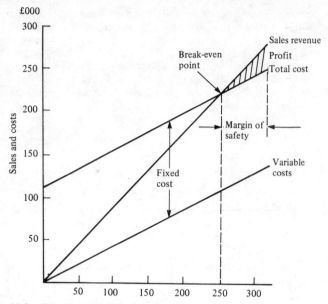

Figure 11.9   *Contribution break-even chart*

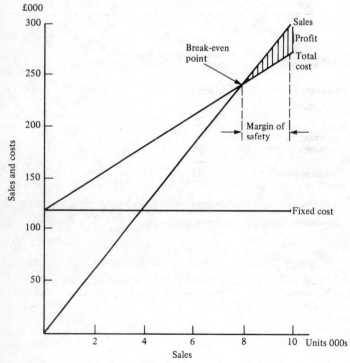

Figure 11.10   *Break-even chart – units*

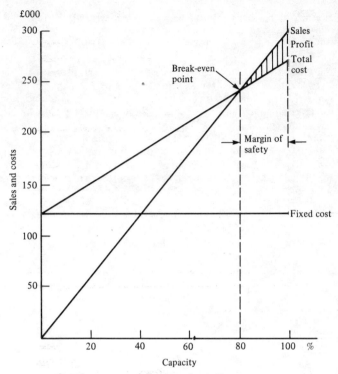

Figure 11.11   *Break-even point – percentage of capacity*

This can be confirmed by calculation:

Figure 11.10

	£
Selling price per unit	30
Less Variable cost per unit	15
Contribution per unit	15

At break-even point contribution must equal fixed cost since neither profit or loss is made. Units of sales required to break even $= \dfrac{\text{fixed cost}}{\text{contribution per unit}} = \dfrac{£120,000}{£15}$

$$= \quad 8,000 \text{ units}$$

The margin of safety with sales of 10,000 units equals 10,000 − 8000 i.e. 2000 units.

At a selling price of £30 each these figures would be £240,000 and £60,000 respectively which agrees with Figures 11.8 and 11.9.

Figure 11.11

100% capacity is represented by 10,000 units worth £300,000. Break-even point is at 80 per cent of this figure which is equal to £240,000 and margin of safety is (100 per cent − 80 per cent) equal to 20 per cent which is £60,000. In a particular problem 100 per cent capacity does not necessarily represent the maximum. It could be that proportion of maximum capacity considered for example most likely to be produced or sold.

Charts such as the ones illustrated can be used to assess the effect of changes in one or more of the factors concerned. Such data would have to be imposed on existing charts or a new chart drawn. Patented boards may be used or string diagrams i.e. coloured threads replace the drawn lines so that new data can be substituted quickly. By virtue of their simplified linear relationships it is easy to compile computer programs to cope with an infinite range of variations and the colourful presentation possible on visual display units can impress managers and others. Alternatively the effects can be computed by using the mathematical relationships of straight line graph calculations.

Calculation of break-even data

If the number of units and the contribution per unit are known then break-even point $= \dfrac{\text{total fixed cost}}{\text{contribution per unit}}$ as was shown in Figure 11.10. If this quantity is multiplied by selling price then we get break even in £s. If only total figures are known we can use ratios:

Let S = Sales at any capacity level (£)   Up to maximum of
Let V = Variable cost at any capacity level   the relevant range
Let F = Fixed cost
Let P = Net profit
Let C = Contribution

● Contribution (C) = fixed cost (F) + profit (P).
● At break-even point C = F since P is nil.
● The ratio of contribution to sales $= \dfrac{C}{S}$ and this is constant as long as selling prices and variable costs per unit remain unaltered.
● $\dfrac{C}{S}$ is termed the contribution volume ratio or profit volume ratio. (The term contribution volume ratio is preferable since profit could be interpreted as net profit but the term profit volume ratio is in such common usage in this context that it is used here.)

Profit volume (PV) ratio $= \dfrac{\text{total contribution}}{\text{sales}}$

At break-even PV ratio × sales = fixed costs

∴ break even sales $= \dfrac{\text{fixed cost}}{\text{PV ratio}}$

In Exercise 11.4:

PV ratio $= \dfrac{150,000}{300,000} = 50\%$

∴ break even sales $= \dfrac{£120,000}{50\%} = \dfrac{120,000 \times 100}{50} = £240,000$

An alternative formula is:

Break-even sales $= \dfrac{\text{fixed cost}}{\text{PV ratio}}$

$$\text{PV ratio} = \frac{\text{contribution}}{\text{sales}}$$

$$\therefore \text{Break-even sales} = \frac{\text{fixed cost}}{\dfrac{\text{contribution}}{\text{sales}}} = \frac{\text{fixed cost}}{\text{contribution}} \times \text{sales}$$

In Exercise 11.4:

$$\text{Break-even sales} = \frac{£120,000}{£150,000} \times £300,000$$

$$= £240,000$$

This approach can be developed by considering, say, a request from management to explain to them the effect on the original figures in Exercise 11.4 of the following alternatives:

1   An increase in fixed cost of £10,000.
2   A decrease in variable costs of £1 per unit.
3   An increase in selling price of 5 per cent.
4   Effect of decrease in sales volume of 5 per cent.

1   Effect of an increase in fixed cost
Suppose fixed costs increase by £10,000 then we get:

	£000
Sales	300
Less Variable costs	150
Contribution	150
Less Fixed cost	130
Net profit	20

1   An increase in fixed costs is accompanied by a decrease in the profit or (increase in a loss) of the same amount.
2   The profit/volume ratio of 50 per cent is unaffected.
3   Break even £(000) $= \dfrac{\text{fixed cost} \times \text{sales}}{\text{fixed cost} + \text{net profit}}$

$$= \frac{130 \times 300}{(130 + 20)} = £260,000$$

4   Margin of safety is reduced to £40,000.

2   Effect of a decrease in variable cost
If variable cost is reduced by £1.00 per unit then total costs will decrease by £10,000 at maximum sales of 10,000 units and we get:

	£000
Sales	300
Less Variable cost	140
contribution	160
Less Fixed costs	120
Net profit	40

1   A decrease in variable cost is accompanied by a similar *increase* in profit and contribution.
2   The profit/volume ratio has to be recomputed

$$\frac{\text{contribution}}{\text{sales}} = \frac{160}{300} = 53.5\%.$$

3   Break even (£000) $= \frac{FC \times S}{FC + P} = \frac{120 \times 300}{120 + 40} = \frac{36,000}{160} = £225,000.$
4   Margin of safety is increased to £75,000.

3   Effect of an increase in sales price
Suppose prices are increased by 5 per cent thus producing increased revenue of £15,000 at maximum sales we get:

	£000
Sales	315
Less Variable costs	150
Contribution	165
Less Fixed costs	120
Net profit	45

1   An increase in selling price will increase revenue and profit by the same amount.
2   The profit volume ratio has to be recomputed

$$\frac{\text{contribution}}{\text{sales}} = \frac{165}{315} = 52.38\%.$$

3   Break even (£000) $= \frac{FC \times S}{FC + P} = \frac{120 \times 315}{120 + 45} = \frac{37,800}{165} = £229,091.$
4   The margin of safety is increased to £85,909.

4   Effect of a decrease in sales volume
Assume a reduction of 5 per cent in the volume of sales i.e. 5,000 units at £35 per unit then the position will be:

	£000
Sales	285.0
Less Variable costs	142.5
Contribution	142.5
Less fixed costs	120.0
	22.5

1   A reduction in sales volume is accompanied by reduction in variable costs and net profit.
2   The profit/volume ratio is unaffected.

3 Break even (£000) = $\dfrac{FC \times S}{FC + P} = \dfrac{120 \times 285}{120 + 22.5} = \dfrac{34,200}{142.5} = £240,000.$

    i.e. the same as that with which we started.

4 The margin of safety is reduced to £45,000.

Some modifications to the basic charts

Very few business situations in the real world can be simplified to the extent theorized above but the technique can be modified. The most common complications are:

1 Fixed costs change over output range being considered. This can occur if, for example, it is envisaged that a large advertising programme can boost sales above certain limits. Once those limits have been reached additional warehousing facilities may be required to accommodate extra stocks or an additional assembly line may be required.

2 With a higher volume of sales the normal laws of economics may apply i.e. the extra quantity may only be sold at lower unit prices for all sales. Beyond an optimum point total profit will decline as the marginal costs of the increased output exceed the change in sales revenue.

Exercise 11.5

A company making and marketing a single product contemplates expansion of output. With the existing type of factory equipment the variable cost of £200 per unit of output is practically constant from 1000 to 8000 units but more equipment than at present will be required if output in excess of 3000 units annually is produced. This extension of equipment would increase total annual fixed costs from £900,000 to £1,200,000.

You are asked to provide management with a graph from which profit, or loss, for any level of sales, can be determined. The following figures should be used to plot the sales curve:

Units of output	Selling price per unit £
1500	1000
2000	950
2500	900
3000	850
4000	760
5000	700
6000	600
7000	500
8000	400

Read from the graph the output figure at which the sales curve overtakes total costs and the output figure at which profit is at its maximum.

Source: CIMA

Workings

Output units	Selling price £	Total sales £000	Variable costs £000	Fixed costs £000	Total costs £000	Profit loss £000
1500	1,000	1,500	300	900	1,200	300
2000	950	1,900	400	900	1,300	200
2500	900	2,250	500	900	1,400	850
3000	850	2,550	600	900	1,500	1,050
4000	760	3,040	800	1,200	2,000	1,040
5000	700	3,500	1,000	1,200	2,200	2,000*
6000	600	3,600	1,200	1,200	2,400	1,200
7000	500	3,500	1,400	1,200	2,600	900
8000	400	3,200	1,600	1,200	2,800	400

* Maximum profit occurs when 5000 units produced and sold.

Solution

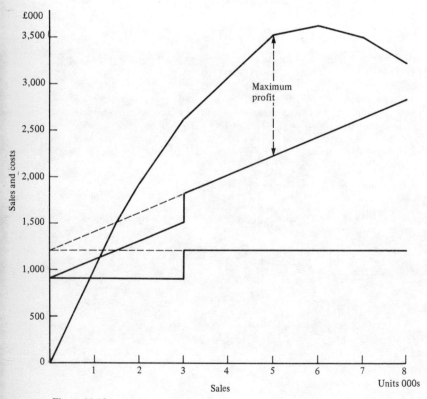

Figure 11.12

Profit/volume charts

Break-even charts show the effect of costs and revenues over a relevant range but the profit figure has to be read by taking the difference between two levels – sales and total costs. An alternative form of presentation is the profit/volume graph which is preferable when emphasis on profit is required or no information on cost structure is given. The data used in the break-even exercise can be used to show the relationship between the two. It is repeated here for convenience of reference.

Annual production and sales	10,000 units
Selling price	£30 per unit
Variable production cost	£11 per unit
Variable selling cost	£4 per unit
Total fixed cost	£120,000

A profit/volume graph shows the relationship between contribution, net profit and sales. It emphasizes that at **zero output the business will make a loss equal to the total fixed costs**. When sufficient contribution to equal the fixed costs has been made then **break even** will have been reached. To plot the graph under linear assumptions only two points need to be known – either the relevant net profit at two alternative sales levels or one profit figure and the volume of fixed costs. In plotting the profit volume graph, volume is recorded horizontally (x axis) and profit is recorded vertically (y axis). In graphical or mathematical terms a loss is a negative or minus profit. The greatest loss figure will equate with the fixed costs and the highest net profit with the maximum volume given.

Redrafting the information above we get as previously:

	£
Total sales	300,000
Total variable cost	150,000
Contribution	150,000
Total fixed costs	120,000
Net profit	30,000

The effect of changes can be illustrated by redrawing the graphs in lieu of the calculations (see Figure 11.13).

We can illustrate by means of revised profit/volume charts the following alternatives:

1 An increase in fixed costs of £10,000 (see Figure 11.14).
2 A decrease in variable cost of £1 per unit (see Figure 11.15).
3 An increase in selling price of 5 per cent (see Figure 11.16).
4 Effect of decrease in sales volume of 5 per cent (see Figure 11.17).

The graphs should be compared with the result (by calculations) on pages 311–3.

Typical cost volume structures

Break-even charts together with similar charts are useful for categorizing

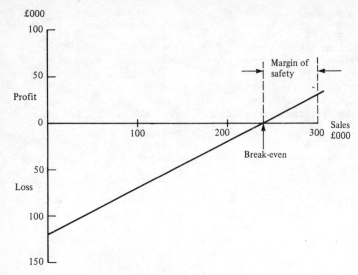

Figure 11.13   *Contribution/volume (P/V) graph*

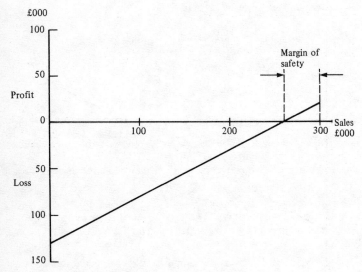

Figure 11.14   *Effect of increase in fixed costs*

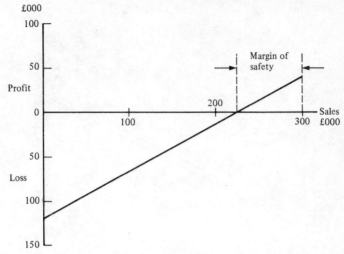

Figure 11.15 *Effect of a decrease in variable costs*

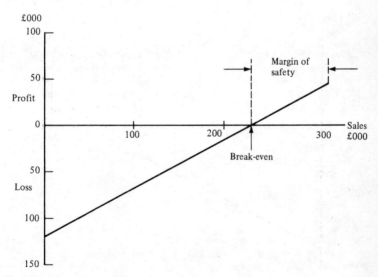

Figure 11.16 *Effect of an increase in sales price*

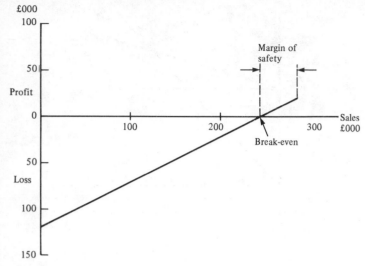

Figure 11.17   *Effect of a decrease in sales volume*

the problems of different industries or situations within a particular company. Consider Figures 11.18, 11.19 and 11.20 and what they could represent.

The company represented in Figure 11.18 has very high fixed costs but low variables. Break even is at a high proportion of sales and margin of safety is low. The graph could typify a railway company or air transport. In manufacturing it could be car manufacture. If the company is operating around break even relatively small volume changes could transfer a profit into a loss. On the other hand net profit can be greatly increased by small increases past the break even. Such firms are obviously vulnerable to strikes, disputes etc. for serious profit or operating circumstances.

Figure 11.19 represents a company or situation with low fixed costs but high variables. The total costs at any level could approximate to the situation represented by Figure 11.18 but the firms' problems would be different. Figure 11.19 could typify a retailing unit with leased premises such as a mail order house.

The break-even point is reasonable and the margin of safety satisfactory but the net profit achieved is small. If it is not possible to pass on increases in variable costs to the consumer the company could be under pressure.

The company represented in Figure 11.20 is in a good position. As with the company in Figure 11.19 break even and margin of safety is good. The lower variable costs mean that the profit/volume ratio is better. The company is making higher net profit than the companies in Figures 11.18 and 11.19 and will continue to make profit down to a reasonable volume of sales.

The advantages of break-even charts are that they demonstrate clearly – and particularly to non-accountants – the results of changed decisions,

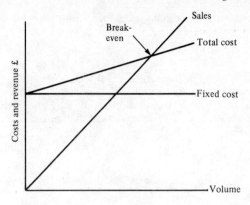

Figure 11.18

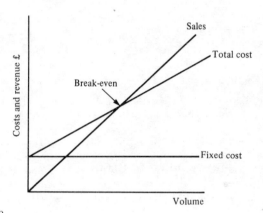

Figure 11.19

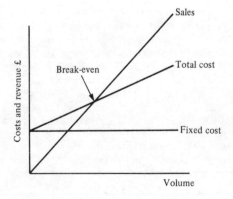

Figure 11.20

policies or circumstances due to cost price volume or mix changes. They demonstrate that:

1   The amount of fixed costs is the most significant factor in achieving or maintaining profits.
2   A business with low fixed costs is better equipped to face poor trading conditions than the alternatives.
3   Additional sales to offset increased fixed charges are lower than is the case if variable costs increase by the same amount.

Formulae

In sales value:

$$\text{Break-even point} = \frac{\text{fixed cost}}{1 - (\frac{\text{total variable cost}}{\text{sales}})}$$

In units:

$$\text{Break even} = \frac{\text{fixed costs}}{\text{contribution per unit}}$$

$$\text{Margin of safety \%} = \frac{\text{sales} - \text{break-even sales}}{\text{sales}}$$

Limitations of break even

1   If more than one product is concerned sales mix and prices must be constant. Separate charts or sequential product charts may be used to offset this.
2   All cost volume and price assumptions are linear. This may not reflect adequately the actual divergences in practice.
3   Changes in cost and prices occur faster than charts can adequately reflect.

11.3   Costing techniques: Budgetary control – master and subsidiary budgets

Most people are familiar with the idea of planning. They anticipate their holidays and plan accordingly. They invest in a major personal acquisition such as a car or house and have to think about allocating their income accordingly. They are conceiving a financial plan or **budget**. It may be done formally as in a commitment for regular saving to acquire the asset or pay off a loan or mortgage. All the essentials of a complex business budget are paralleled in this analogy – a budget is quite simply **a plan of future activities necessary to achieve specific goals or objectives**. Usually the plan is quantified in monetary terms but not always – we sometimes express labour in hours or personnel or materials in kilogrammes. The plan must have a stated objective – maximize profits from a given volume of sales, for example, and it must relate to a specific period of time. The definition suggested by the CIMA incorporates most of these points comprehensively.

A budget is a plan quantified in monetary terms, prepared and approved prior to a defined period of time, usually showing planned income to be generated and/or expenditure to be incurred during the period and the capital to be employed, to attain a given objective.

The determination of budgets ideally commences with the formation of a **corporate plan**. This is a formulation at top management level of the goals and objectives of the enterprise for the period under review. Such a goal may be in very broad terms – for example to obtain maximum profit commensurate with reasonable rewards and conditions for employees. Subsidiary goals would then be set involving optimum utilization of human, financial, physical and other resources. This provides the basis for the control process.

Budgetary control

The CIMA definition of **budgetary control** is as follows:

> This is the establishment of budgets relating the responsibilities of executives to the requirements of a policy and the continuous comparison of actual with budgeted results either to secure by individual action the objective of that policy or to provide a basis for its revision.

The second part of the definition – comparison – is concerned with monitoring and performance measurement. This is usually carried out by extracting variances between budgeted and actual performance.

The third part of the definition is what budgetary control should be all about – action. If managers do not act on feedback information they receive then nothing positive is achieved.

The final part of the definition can be interpreted as acceptance that no planning process is perfect. The budget is a prediction of quantities, prices, circumstances and is made by people – who are not infallible.

The basic steps can therefore be summarized as **plan, coordinate, measure, communicate** and **control**.

Setting of budgets

This requires coordination. It is useless planning for maximum production if that quantity cannot be sold. Similarly it is impractical to plan sales if production capacity is less than demand unless consideration is given to expansion and the financial implications associated with it. *Individuals* are responsible for action on budgets therefore they must:

1 *Participate* in their formation.
2 *Accept* their viability.
3 *Respond* to suggestion and feedback from subordinates.
4 *Cooperate* in achieving corporate and budget objectives.

Hence the alternative term of **responsibility accounting**. The prerequisite is a clear organization chart indicating the extent of each individual manager's responsibility. Officials will participate in the preparation of their own budget and **key factors** will be identified. A key factor, or alternatively limiting factor, is that factor which, over the relevant time period of the budget, will limit the activities. Examples of limiting factors are constraints on the supply of a particular material, the skilled labour available or sales demand. The policy may be to remove the obstacle as, for example, buying additional plant but the result would be to create or substitute another factor. When the key factor has been identified sectional budgets are created which are amalgamated into a **master budget**.

Time horizon

Time is a very relevant element in budget construction. Budget periods need not necessarily be identical. The length (or **time horizon**) is related to the objective of the budget. Capital expenditure involves long-term planning of source and use of funds and five years would be a reasonable time span. Annual budgets are usual for most accounting purposes – broken up into quarterly, monthly or even weekly periods for control purposes. They will normally be on a continuous or rolling basis i.e. as one period is completed another is added in similar fashion to moving averages. The advantages of budgetary control are that it forces managers to plan ahead, it provides the means by which performance can be assessed and helps to ensure coordinated effort. They are behavioural complications in the setting and use of budgets which are the subject of current study but at present they are still a primary management tool.

Constructing the master budget

Sectional budgets are prepared and aggregated to give the master budget. The same data may be utilized in various ways in budget preparation but they fall into three main categories as shown in Table 11.1.

Table 11.1

Category	Description
Operating or functional	Budgets in respect of sales, production, material and labour requirements. Expense budgets for production, selling, distribution, overhead etc.
Statistical	Quantified budget statements in appropriate units for labour (manpower) capacity (machine hours), stores (square metres) etc.
Financial	Budgeted profit and loss account, budgeted cash flow, source and application, capital expenditure budget.

The relationship between these categories is indicated diagrammatically in Figure 11.21.

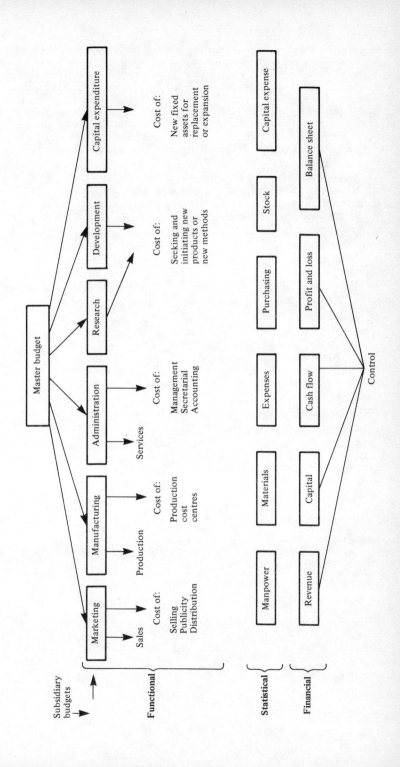

Preparation of budgets

The preparation of sectional budgets should not present great difficulty when the figures are comparatively small. The principles are illustrated in the following exercises. The main difficulty in practice is that various operating divisions in differing localities may be concerned, all with different key factors and priorities. Compromise must be used to get the best overall result and this is where the human factor dominates. A manager of strong personality may well succeed in getting his own position strengthened at the expense of the firm.

One fundamental point is that adjustments frequently have to be made in the opposite way to that which they are usually made. The manager may be aware of the sales he hopes to make in a period and the desirable stock level at the end. Production requirements could therefore be sales plus closing stock minus opening stock.

Exercise 11.6

R Limited manufactures three products: A, B and C. You are required:

1   Using the information given below, to prepare budgets for the month of January for:
   (a)   Sales in quantity and value, including total value.
   (b)   Production quantities.
   (c)   Material usage in quantities.
   (d)   Material purchases in quantity and value, including total value.
   (*Note*:   Particular attention should be paid to your layout of the budgets.)
2   To explain the term principal budget factor and state what it was assumed to be in (1) of this question.

Data for preparation of January budgets

Sales:

Product	Quantity	Price each £
A	1000	100
B	2000	120
C	1500	140

Materials used in the company's products are:

Material	M1	M2	M3
Unit cost	£4	£6	£9

Quantities used in:

	Units	Units	Units
Product: A	4	2	–
B	3	3	2
C	2	1	1

Finished stocks:

Product	A	B	C
Quantities			
1 January	1000	1500	500
31 January	1100	1650	550
Material stocks:	*M1*	*M2*	*M3*
	Units	*Units*	*Units*
1 January	26,000	20,000	12,000
31 January	31,200	24,000	14,400

Source: CIMA

Sales quantity and value budget

	Products			
	A	B	C	*Total*
Sales quantities	1,000	2,000	1,500	
Selling prices	£100	£120	£140	
Sales value	£100,000	£240,000	£210,000	£550,000

Production quantities budget

	Products		
	A	B	C
Sales quantities	1,000	2,000	1,500
Add Closing stock	1,100	1,650	550
	2,100	3,650	2,050
Deduct Opening stock	1,000	1,500	500
Units to be produced	1,100	2,150	1,550

Material usage budget: quantities

Production quantities	Materials					
	M1		M2		M3	
	Units per product	*Total*	*Units per product*	*Total*	*Units per product*	*Total*
A 1,100	4	4,400	2	2,200	–	–
B 2,150	3	6,450	3	6,450	2	4,300
C 1,550	2	3,100	1	1,550	1	1,550
Usage in quantities		13,950		10,200		5,850

Material purchases budget: materials in quantities

	M1	M2	M3	
Materials usage budget	13,950	10,200	5,850	
Add Closing stock	31,200	24,000	14,400	
	45,150	34,200	20,250	
Deduct Opening stock	26,000	20,000	12,000	
Purchases in quantities	19,150	14,200	8,250	
Price per unit	£4	£6	£9	Total
Value of purchases	£76,600	£85,200	£74,250	£236,050

The financial budgets are the formats most important for:

1 Assisting in controlling performance.
2 Ensuring financial resources are adequate.

In respect of assisting in controlling performance departmental operating statements, profit and loss statements and budgeted balance sheets are the main tools.

For ensuring financial resources are adequate detailed cash flow statements showing receipts, payments and balances and funds flow indicating non-cash sources are required. These are discussed in Section 11.4.

Profit budgets

These may be prepared for the usual twelve month financial period or shorter periods – quarterly or monthly – for monitoring and control purposes. The following figures all need to be budgeted relative to the appropriate volume of sales: sales revenue, cost of goods sold, gross profit, other overhead expenses, net profit, non-trading income or unusual losses.

Frequently past results are used as a basis for the forecast upon which the budget is based. Adjustments are made in respect of anticipated or known changes. Exercise 11.7 is fairly typical.

Exercise 11.7

The financial year of EFG Limited ends on 31 March and sales for 19x8–x9 are expected to amount to £1,680,000, while costs are expected to be as follows:

	Variable £000	Fixed £000
Direct materials	480	
Direct wages	360	
Production overhead	120	220
General administration		100
Advertising and selling	24	136
Distribution	60	30

The budget for 19x9–y0 is in course of preparation and the following factors are relevant:

1 Hourly wage rates are to be increased by 10 per cent as from 1 April 19x9.
2 Average prices of direct materials are expected to be 5 per cent higher than in 19x8–x9.
3 Factory management salaries are expected to be increased by £10,000 and office salaries by £12,000 as from 1 April 19x9.
4 Despite rising costs, selling prices are to be held at the 19x8–x9 levels in order to capture a larger share of the market and this objective is to be further supported by additional expenditure of £40,000 on advertising. An increase in sales of one-third is aimed at.

Required:
(a) Compile the budget for 19x9–y0.
(b) State whether the budgeted profit will be more or *less* than the expected profit for 19x8–x9 and by how much.

Source: LCCI

EFG Limited
Budgeted profit and loss account
for year ended 19x0

	19x8–x9	Changes	19x8–y0
Sales	£1,680,000	+ 1/3	£2,240,000
Costs			
Direct materials	480,000	+ 5%, + 1/3	672,000
Direct wages	360,000	+ 10%, + 1/3	528,000
Production overhead – Variable	120,000	+ 1/3	160,000
Fixed	220,000	+ 10,000	230,000
Factory costs	1,180,000		1,590,000
Gross margin	500,000		650,000
Selling and administration expenses			
General administration – Fixed	100,000	+ 12,000	112,000
Advertising and selling – Variable	24,000	+ 1/3	32,000
Fixed	136,000	+ 40,000	176,000
Distribution – Variable	60,000	+ 1/3	80,000
Fixed	30,000	–	30,000
	350,000		430,000
Budgeted profit	150,000		220,000

The budgeted profit for 19x9–y0 will be £70,000 more than that of 19x8–x9.

Exercise 11.8 below shows a similar but slightly more complex problem. You may wish to attempt to complete this exercise checking each step with the suggested answer.

Exercise 11.8

The trading results for the year ending 30 June 19x8 of D Ltd, a face cream manufacturer, are expected to be as follows:

	£000	£000
Sales (100,000 jars)		400
Costs:		
Material	50	
Wages: direct	82	
indirect, fixed	19	
Production expenses:		
variable	25	
fixed	30	
Administration expenses:		
fixed	24	
Selling expenses:		
variable	20	
fixed	22	
Distribution expenses:		
variable	18	
fixed	10	
	——	300
Profit		100

Forecasts for year ending 30 June 19x9 are given below:

1 A sales price reduction to £3 per jar will increase sales volume by 50 per cent.
2 Material prices will remain unchanged except that, because of increased quantities purchased, a 5 per cent quantity discount will be obtained.
3 Direct wage rates will increase by 10 per cent.
4 Variable selling costs will increase proportionately with sales value.
5 Inflation will increase variable production and distribution expenses by 10 per cent.
6 All fixed costs will increase by 20 per cent.
7 There will be no stocks or work in progress at the beginning or end of the year.

Required:

(a) Prepare a budget showing the profit for the year ending 30 June 19x9 on a marginal costing basis.
(b) Comment on the result forecast in your answer to (a) above.
(c) Prepare an alternative profit statement for the year ending 30 June 19x9 based on a sales price increase of 10 per cent on 19x7/x8 price and a sales volume of 100,000 jars.
(d) State the price increase per jar (and as a percentage to three decimal places) needed, above the current sales price, for year ending 30 June 19x9 to achieve a profit of £110,000.

Source: CIMA

Workings
A suggested procedure is to start with the existing situation; adjust for all volume changes at old prices, adjust for all price changes on new volume and extract the required final figure. For example, the increase of 50 per cent in volume at the old prices would increase 19x8 sales by 50,000 jars worth £200,000. The present price per jar is £4 so reducing all prices to £3 per unit, therefore total sales revenue would be reduced by £150,000. The total change in revenue is therefore plus £50,000. The remaining adjustments are summarized as follows:

	Fixed or variable	Present year	Volume change	Price change	Budget for 19x9 £000
Sales	V	400	+ 200	− 150	450
Material	V	50	+ 25	− 3.75	71.25
Wages – direct	V	82	+ 41	+ 12.3	135.3
Wages – indirect	F	19	–	+ 3.8	22.8
Production expenses	V	25	+ 12.5	+ 3.75	41.25
	F	30	–	6	36
Administration expenses	F	24	–	4.8	28.8
Selling expenses	V	20	+ 2.5	–	22.5
	F	22	–	4.4	26.4
Distribution expenses	V	18	9	2.7	29.7
	F	10	–	2	12

(a)
D Ltd
Budgeted profit statement for year ended 30 June 19x9

	£	£
Sales of 150,000 jars of cream		450,000
Less: Marginal costs		
Material	71,250	
Direct labour	135,300	
Production expenses	41,250	
Selling expenses	22,500	
Distribution expenses	29,700	
		300,000
Contribution		150,000
Less: Fixed costs		
Indirect wages	22,800	
Production expenses	36,000	
Administration expenses	28,800	
Selling expenses	26,400	
Distribution expenses	12,000	
		126,000
Profit		24,000

(b)   Although sales volume has increased by 50 per cent the price cut proposed to achieve this – from £4 to £3 per unit – has a drastic effect on the profit when combined with anticipated cost changes. The contribution to sales ratio is 33⅓ per cent. To maintain the existing profit of £100,000 would require a contribution of £100,000 (for profit) plus £126,000 for fixed expenses – a total of £226,000. If this is to represent 33⅓ per cent of sales then total sales would have to be £678,000 or 296,000 jars at £3 per jar.

(c)   As the volume is maintained at 100,000 jars only price changes need to be considered.

D Ltd
Alternative profit statement for year ended 30 June 19x9

	19x8 £	Change £	19x9 £
Sales	400,000	+ 40,000	440,000
Less Marginal costs			
Material	50,000	–	50,000
Wages direct	82,000	+ 8,200	90,200
Production expenses	25,000	+ 2,500	27,500
Selling expenses	20,000	+ 2,000	22,000
Distribution expenses	18,000	+ 1,800	19,000
			209,500
Contribution			230,500
Less Fixed cost			126,000
Profit			104,500

(d)   Variable selling costs increase with sales value which in turn depends upon unknown selling price. Variable selling costs are however at present:

$$\frac{£20,000}{£400,000} \times 100 = 5\% \text{ of sales}$$

Total variable costs (see part (c)) are forecast at	209,500
Less Variable selling cost	22,000
	187,500

Let S = sales required to achieve profit of £110,000

then Variable cost equals	£187,500 + 5% (S)
Fixed cost	£126,000
Required profit	£110,000
∴ S	= £423,500 + 5% S

$$S - 5\% \text{ of } S = £423,500$$
$$95\% \text{ of } S = £423,500$$
$$\therefore S = 423,500 \times \frac{100}{95} = £445,790$$

$$\text{Price increase per jar} = \frac{£445,790 - £400,000}{400,000} = \frac{£45,790}{400,000} \times 100$$
$$= 11.448\text{p}$$

Fixed and flexible budgets

When the main budgeting processes have been completed as described in the previous section we end up with a final plan in budgeted quantities and prices. But this is related to one level of activity only and is referred to as a **fixed budget**. (Note particularly that in this context a fixed budget does not refer to a budget of fixed expenses but the costs sales and profits anticipated when a fixed level of output and/or sales has been achieved.) Alternatively described as a **basic budget** this presentation is useful for planning and focusing managerial attention upon objectives but is limited in suitability for control purposes. Suppose, for example, the budget for producing 100 items in respect of the direct material content was £1,200. In the period for which it was prepared 110 items were produced at a cost of £1,350. Under the basic budget the figures would appear as follows:

Materials budget for period	£1,200
Actual expenditure on materials	£1,350
Difference (i.e. variance)	£150 Adverse

The manager might be criticized for having spent £150 more than the budget. Quite reasonably he could probably respond that since each item was costing £12 in the budget he could hardly be expected to produce 110 items for the same cost as 100. At the budgeted price of £12 each a more realistic budget would be £1,320 i.e. 110 units at £12. This could now be set out:

	£
Basic budget 100 items @ £12	1,200
Adustment for volume change	
10 items @ £12	120
Revised budget 110 items @ £12	1,320
Actual expenditure	1,350
Variance	30 Adverse

A **flexible budget** is one which reflects the different characteristics of fixed and variable costs and 'allows' differing amounts of expense according to the volume of output achieved.

Exercise 11.9

Examination of the power costs of Company A over an extended period indicates that the cost is of a composite fixed and variable nature such that the total cost is equal to a fixed amount of £500 per annum plus a variable element equivalent to £100 for every 200 units of product made. Compute the total power cost for a range of output from zero to 1400 units and indicate the budgeted amount for (a) 600 and (b) 1200 units under a fixed budget and flexible budget system when the activity level on which the fixed budget was based is determined at 800 units.

Solution
When estimating the expenditure for any item of expense it is preferable to attempt to determine a 'model' of its behaviour. Since in this example total cost is equal to a fixed cost plus a constant amount for each level of activity then the expense would follow a form of:

$$\text{Total cost} = \text{fixed cost} = \frac{£100}{200} \text{ units produced}$$

or TC = £500 + ½ × (where x = units produced)

The term activity or capacity is used to indicate the level of production achieved, or to which the budget is to be applied. It is sometimes expressed simply in units, hours, money etc., but quite frequently it is expressed as a percentage. In this event some predetermined level of production has been accepted as the **normal capacity** (or activity) and this is used as a basis of 100 per cent. The normal capacity is usually the level at which production and sales over a medium time span are reasonably matched, and as such will also become the activity to which the basic budget is related. The cost of power in the above example can thus be calculated and tabulated:

TC = FC + {(VC) × (x)}
i.e. Total cost = fixed cost + (variable cost per unit × number of units)

Power budget

Activity / Cost	Units	0	200	400	600	800	1000	1200	1400
	per cent	0	25	50	75	100	125	150	175
Fixed	£	500	500	500	500	500	500	500	500
Variable	£	–	100	200	300	400	500	600	700
Total		500	600	700	800	900	1000	1100	1200

The total power cost is given by the final line in the tabulation. The budgeted amount termed the **allowance under the flexible system** would be:

For 600 units of output (75 per cent activity) £800
For 1200 units of output (150% activity) £1,100

Under a fixed budget system the amount budgeted would remain at £900 since by definition this figure is *not* amended in respect of the actual output achieved.

Exercise 11.9 represents a simple example of an **expense budget** i.e. the budget is prepared from information classified by the nature of the expense. This is similar to the classification used in financial accounts e.g. wages, lighting, telephone, materials consumed. Such classification may be of little use for control purposes and expenses may be collected together into budgets for **cost centres**. These may be **locational** e.g. the foundry or machine shop or **functional** e.g. inspection, personnel. The main criteria is that the cost centre represents a convenient division to which costs can be allocated and related to a person for control responsibility. They may be referred to as **budget centres**. The setting of expense budgets usually precedes the determination of the flexible budget or allowance for a particular cost centre. There are three basic stages in setting an expense budget.

1   To determine the quantity and cost of expense which should be incurred at any reasonable potential level of output.
2   The budget is then expressed or computed in physical quantities since these are more stable than prices.
3   Attempts are made to anticipate or provide for amendment if serious changes are expected in the period.

The budget cost allowance

This is the fundamental notion of the flexible approach. It represents an analysis by nature of expense of the cost which the budget centre is expected to incur during the period to which it is applied. In a manual system separate lists for each type of expense would be prepared from which the 'allowed' amount could be read for the activity level concerned. The sum of all the individual expense allowances would provide the total which would represent the total allowance for the cost centre.

Exercise 11.10
Prepare a flexible budget for 19x6 for the overhead expenses of a production department at the activity levels of 80 per cent, 90 per cent and 100 per cent using the information listed below.

1   The direct labour hourly rate is expected to be £3.75.
2   100 per cent activity represents 60,000 direct labour hours.
3   Variable costs:
   Indirect labour   £0.75 per direct labour hour
   Consumable supplies   £0.375 per direct labour hour
   Canteen and other welfare   6% of direct *and* indirect labour
     services   costs
4   Semi-variable costs are expected to correlate with the direct labour hours in the same manner as for the last five years which was:

Year	Direct labour hours		Semi-variable costs £	
19x1	64,000		20,800	
19x2	59,000		19,800	
19x3	53,000		18,600	
19x4	49,000		17,800	
19x5	40,000	(estimate)	16,000	(estimate)

5   Fixed costs:

	£
Depreciation	18,000
Maintenance	10,000
Insurance	4,000
Rates	15,000
Management salaries	25,000

6   Inflation is to be ignored.

Calculate the budget cost allowance for 19x6 assuming that 57,000 direct labour hours are worked.

Source: CIMA

Workings

Note 1   Range of activity percentage – given
Note 2   100% = 60,000 ∴ 90% = 54,000 80% = 48,000
Note 3   Line 2 × £0.75
Note 4   Line 2 × £0.375
Note 5   6% of {Line 2 × £3.75 + Line 3}

$$= 6\% \text{ of } \left\{ \begin{array}{ccc} 180,000 & 202,500 & 225,000 \\ 36,000 & 40,500 & 45,000 \\ \hline 216,000 & 243,000 & 270,000 \end{array} \right.$$

=	12,960	14,580	16,200

Note 6   Semi-variable cost:

		£
19x1	64,000 hours	20,800
19x5	40,000 hours	16,000
Change	24,000	4,800

∴ each hour costs $\dfrac{4,800}{24,000}$ = £0.2 Variable

For 64,000 hours variable cost = 64,000 × 0.2 = £12,800
Total cost = £20,800
∴ Fixed part of semi-variable cost = £8,000

Check:
For 40,000 hours cost should be:
   £8,000 + 40,000 × £0.2 = £16,000

At any level semi-variable cost = £8,000 + £0.2 × hours.
Variable element of semi variable at 48,000 hours £9,600; 54,000 hours £10,800; 60,000 hours £12,000

Note 7   Fixed costs as given

Allowance = fixed cost plus variable cost for activity achieved. At normal (100 per cent) capacity, variable cost per direct labour hour

$$= \frac{£95.700}{60,000} = £1.595$$

$$\therefore \text{Allowance} = £80,000 + (£1.595 \times 57,000)$$
$$= 80,000 + 90,915 = £170,915$$

Solution

Flexible budget – Production Department

	80	90	100	Note
Activity level %	80	90	100	1
Activity: Direct labour (hours)	48,000	54,000	60,000	2
Direct wages (£)	180,000	202,500	225,000	
	£	£	£	
Variable costs				
Indirect labour	36,000	40,500	45,000	3
Consumable supplies	18,000	20,250	22,500	4
Canteen etc.	12,960	14,580	16,200	5
Semi-variable	9,600	10,800	12,000	6
Subtotal	76,560	86,130	95,700	
Fixed costs				
Semi-variable	8,000	8,000	8,000	6
Depreciation	18,000	18,000	18,000	7
Maintenance	10,000	10,000	10,000	7
Insurance	4,000	4,000	4,000	7
Rates	15,000	15,000	15,000	7
Management salaries	25,000	25,000	25,000	7
	80,000	80,000	80,000	
Grand total	156,560	166,130	175,700	

The budget cost allowance for 19x6 is total fixed cost plus variables for 57,000 hours:

$$= £80,000 + 90,915$$
$$= £170,915$$

Methods of calculating the allowance

As we can see from Exercise 11.10 the allowance is the total of each separate expense. Each expense may vary in a different fashion – see for example the graphs of typical overhead expenses in the exercise on cost behaviour (page 300). This is the most accurate method of compiling the allowance – from separate data in respect of each item of expense. Alternatively if most items are linear a graph of total expenses can be drawn and the allowance read from it. (See Figure 11.22.)

Budget variances

Actual performance is recorded against the budget by each cost centre to monitor performance. Any significant deviation is highlighted and an analysis given. Standard feedback procedures should ensure that management is made aware promptly of such movements and corrective action taken. In systems language the operation has been brought back into control. Standard reports or operating statements are fed as frequently as practicable to the various managerial levels. The lower the level the more frequent and detailed would be the report. Using the data from Exercise 11.10 and adding in some theoretical actual expenditure for 19x6 the format might be as shown below. As a control statement it is more likely to be for a month rather than a year but the layout would be similar.

Production overhead operating statement

Department	Department number	Cost centre		Period ended 31 December 19x6
		Budget	*Actual*	*Vari-ance*	
Activity level (%)	95			
Activity level (Direct hours)	57,000	57,000		*Comment*
	£	£	£	
Variable costs				
Indirect labour	42,750	43,400	+650	Overtime due to breakdown
Consumable supplies	21,375	21,200	−175	
Canteen	15,390	15,600	+210	Food price increase
Semi-variable	11,400	11,900	+500	Electricity cost
	90,915	92,100	+1,185	
Fixed costs				
Semi-variable	8,000	8,000	–	
Depreciation	18,000	20,000	+2,000	Changed basis
Maintenance	10,000	11,200	+1,200	Machine break-down
Insurance	4,000	4,000	–	
Rates	15,000	15,500	+500	Revised assessment
Management salaries	25,000	26,000	+1,000	Salary changes
	80,000	84,700	+4,700	
Grand total	170,915	176,800	+5,885	

General report:

In practice the variance report would be more detailed, particularly dealing with controllable and non-controllable elements. These descriptions apply to the level of supervision or responsibility of the person receiving the report. For example the £175 (favourable) variance on

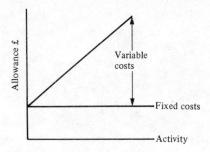

Figure 11.22

consumable supplies may be because less than the budgeted quantity have been used due to vigilance of the production supervision. On the other hand the production personnel may have used more than the allowance but the actual cost may be lower due to the buyer having secured more favourable prices than those in the budget. More examples of variance analysis are given under the standard cost section (see page 347) since detailed analysis presupposes the existence of standard costs in addition to budgetary control. The main distinction is that the flexible budget will not reflect any changes in amounts absorbed in respect of fixed costs since, by definition, fixed costs are allowed in full. In a standard cost system using absorption costs there will be volume variances in respect of fixed costs absorbed every time the actual production is different to that on which the standard overhead absorption rate is calculated.

11.4 Costing techniques: Budgetary control – cash flow

The format for a cash budget produced on receipts and payments was introduced and illustrated in Section 2.5. Exercise 11.11 shows that such statements are fairly stereotyped. They can be prepared manually but are more easily prepared on a simple computer program. Such programs enable easy substitution of data to see the result of alternative actions or events, and provide for constant updating with minimum effort.

Exercise 11.11
From the data given below, prepare a cash budget for each of the first three months of 19x8;

● Cash balance on 1 January 19x8 is forecast as £40,000.
● A new computer is to be installed in January 19x8 at a cost of £100,000 and will be paid for on 1 March 19x8.
● A sales commission of 2½ per cent on sales is to be paid within one month of the month of sale.
● Taxation of £180,000 is to be paid in February.
● In January a dividend of £40,000 is to be paid to ordinary shareholders (ignore taxation).

- £10,000 per month is payable under a leasing agreement.
- An issue of debentures is expected to be made in February, which will result in £50,000 being received during that month.
- The period of credit allowed by suppliers averages two months.
- Delay in payment of overhead averages one month.
- Delay in payment of research and development costs averages half a month.
- Delay in payment of wages averages a quarter of a month.
- To encourage payment of invoices, the company allows a cash discount of 5 per cent if payment is made within one week and of 2½ per cent if payment is made within one month. It is estimated that 25 per cent of the debtors of each month pay within one week, and a further 60 per cent of the debtors of each month pay within one month. The remaining debtors are expected to pay their invoices in full within two months.

A forecast of costs and revenues includes the following:

	October £	19x7 November £	December £
Direct:			
Materials	50,000	45,000	60,000
Wages	40,000	36,000	44,000
Overhead:			
Production	15,000	14,000	18,000
Administration	10,000	9,000	12,000
Selling and distribution	6,000	5,000	8,000
Research and development costs	4,000	5,000	5,000
Sales	160,000	200,000	240,000

	January £	19x8 February £	March £
Direct:			
Materials	40,000	30,000	35,000
Wages	32,000	24,000	28,000
Overhead:			
Production	20,000	16,000	18,000
Administration	10,000	11,000	12,000
Selling and distribution	6,000	5,000	7,000
Research and development costs	6,000	6,000	7,000
Sales	200,000	160,000	160,000

Source: CIMA

Workings

In the absence of information on stock levels it is assumed that the direct materials used in the month are the purchases of materials for that month. It is also assumed that all sales are invoiced at the end of the month concerned and credit periods allowed start from this date.

Commission:

	Sales	Commission	
	£000	*Earned*	*Month paid*
December	240	£6,000	January
January	200	£5,000	February
February	160	£4,000	March

Material creditors:

November	£45,000	paid in January
December	£60,000	paid in February
January	£40,000	paid in March

Overheads:

	December *£000*	*January* *£000*	*February* *£000*
Production	18	20	16
Administration	12	10	11
Selling and distribution	8	6	5
	38	36	32
Paid in	January	February	March

Research and development costs:

	Cost incurred *£*	*Paid* *£*	
December	5,000		
January	6,000	5,500	½ in December plus ½ in January
February	6,000	6,000	½ in January plus ½ in February
March	7,000	6,500	½ in February plus ½ in March

Wages:

	Cost incurred *£*	*Paid* *£*	
December	44,000		
January	32,000	35,000	¼ in December plus ¾ in January
February	24,000	26,000	¼ in January plus ¾ in February
March	28,000	27,000	¼ in February plus ¾ in March

Receipts from debtors from payments within one week of the end of the month:

If a cash discount of 5 per cent is allowed only 95 per cent of the value of the sales will be received in cash. The proportion of a month's sales subject to 5 per cent discount is 25 per cent so monies received will equal 95 per cent × 25 per cent equals 23.75 per cent.

Receipts from debtors from payments within one month of the end of the month:

If a cash discount of 2.5 per cent is allowed only 97.5 per cent of the value of the sales will be received in cash. The proportion of a month's sales subject to 2.5 per cent discount is 60 per cent so monies received will equal 97.5 × 60 per cent equals 58.5 per cent.

Remainder:

The proportion of debtors paying after two months and therefore receiving no discount will be the whole (100 per cent) less the above 85 per cent equals 15 per cent.

January (all figures £000):

23.7 per cent of December plus 58.5 per cent of December plus 15 per cent of November.
23.75 per cent of 240 plus 58.5 per cent of 240 plus 15 per cent of 200 equals 227.4.

February (all figures £000):

23.75 per cent of January plus 58.5 per cent of January plus 15 per cent of December.
23.75 per cent of 200 plus 58.5 per cent of 200 plus 15 per cent of 240 equals 200.5.

March (all figures £000):

23.75 per cent of February plus 58.5 per cent of February plus 15 per cent of January.
23.75 per cent of 160 plus 58.5 per cent of 160 plus 15 per cent of 200 equals 161.6.

The above figures are on the basis of common commercial practice, where irrespective of the actual invoice date of despatch, sales are deemed to arise on the last day of the month. If credit terms are literally – particularly in the case of weekly credit – dated from the actual time of invoicing then the timing would have to be adjusted to one-quarter of the previous month plus three-quarters of the current month, similar to the treatment of wages.

Cash budget
for three months January, February and March 19x8

	Jan £000	Feb £000	March £000
Receipts			
Debtors	227.4	200.5	161.6
Debenture issue		50	
	227.4	250.5	161.6
Payments			
New computer			100
Sales commission	6	5	4
Taxation		180	
Dividends payable	40		
Lease payment	10	10	10
Material creditors	45	60	40
Overheads	38	36	32
Research and development	5.5	6	6.5
Wages	35	26	27
	179.5	323	219.5

	Jan £000	Feb £000	March £000
Net cash gain/(loss)	47.9	(72.5)	(57.9)
Opening balance	40	87.9	15.4
Closing balance c/f	87.9	15.4	(42.5)

As stated in Section 2.5 statements such as the above do not, in themselves, result in control of the cash position. It is essential that the position be continuously monitored. To assist in this operation statements are prepared analysing the actual position in comparison with the budget. The following statement shows a specimen of such a statement using the budget illustrated in Section 2.5 for the Stoke Manufacturing Company as a starting point.

Stoke Manufacturing Company
Cash budget March 19x5

	Budget	Actual	Variance + gain − loss	Reason for variance	Action proposed/ taken
Receipts					
Cash sales 25%	19,000	18,500	−500	Lower volume	Advertising
Previous month 50%	32,000	30,920	−1,080	Slow payment	Chase debtors
Previous two months 20%	9,600	9,200	−400	Slow payment	
Three months or more 5%					
Total from debtors	60,600	58,620	−1,980		
Investment income					
Others					
Total	60,600	58,620	−1,980		
Payments					
Materials	26,100	25,500	+600	More favourable prices	
Wages	18,400	19,100	−700	Overtime plus rates	Correct machine breakdown
Variable overhead	8,200	8,150	+50	Minor price change	
Fixed overhead	2,000	2,100	−100	Rates increase	

	Budget	Actual	Variance + gain - loss	Reason for variance	Action proposed/ taken
Interest charges					
Loan repayments					
Purchase of assets					
Others		150	-150	Emergency plant repairs	Correcting machine breakdown
Total	54,700	55,000	-300		
Net cash gain/(loss)	5,900	3,620	-2,280		
Opening balance	10,500	9,600	-900	Previous months	
Indicated cash balance	16,400	13,220	-3,180		
Cash required					
Closing balance	16,400	13,220			Meeting for discussion 5 April 19x5

Budgeted funds flow statements

An alternative form of cash budgeting is the so called **balance sheet change** or **funds flow** method. This method does not require consideration of each item of expense but does assume a regular pattern of receipts and payments. It is less useful as a control budget that the receipts and payments method but useful for longer term projections. The basis is the profit budget but as this contains non-cash items such as depreciation these must be allowed for. Outstanding debtors and creditors as well as capital items such as new plant, repayment of loans or injection of new capital must also be allowed for. This type of budget is therefore used when the objective is to demonstrate a future cash position usually, but not necessarily, combined with a budgeted balance sheet. The format and principles of funds flow statements have been explored in Section 1.4. This treatment was, however, as part of stewardship requirements and as such influenced by SSAP 10. This can be modified or adapted as required when it is being utilized for future planning rather than past reporting as shown below:

Budgeted source and application of funds
Year ended 19xx

£   £

Sources of funds:
  Profit before taxation
  Depreciation
  Sale of assets
  Others (specify)

	£	£
Total internal sources		
Required from other sources		
	———	———
Total sources		
	=====	=====
Application of funds:		
Purchase of fixed assets		
Investments proposed		
Debentures/loans redeemable		
Taxation payable		
Dividends payable		
	———	———
Increase/(decrease) in working capital		
Increase/(decrease) in Stocks		
Debtors		
Creditors		
Cash		
	———	———
Total applications	———	———
	=====	=====

In a budget the total applications and internal sources would be compiled first and this line would be the balancing figure. In the event of no sources being necessary the figure would represent the surplus cash generated over the minimum cash balance considered reasonable. If funds are required from other sources the final stage would be to decide whether, and in what form, those capital requirements could be satisfied in a manner most profitable to the firm. If no changes in fixed assets or long-term sources are anticipated a simplified format such as this can be used:

Cash budget – total or funds flow format

	£	£
Profit for period		
Add Retained depreciation		
		———
Cash flow		
Increase in: Stocks		
Debtors		
	———	
Creditors		
	———	
		———
Increase/decrease in bank balance		
Opening bank balance		
		———
Project balance/(overdraft)		
		=====

Exercise 11.12

From the following information you are required, for year ending 31 December 19x1 to prepare:

(a)   By quarters, a cash budget, and
(b)   For the year, a budgeted source and disposal of funds statement.

It is expected that the working capital at 1 January, 19x1 will be as follows:

	£000s
Cash in hand and at bank	35
Stock	65
Debtors	50
Creditors	40

Budgeted profit statement:

	First quarter £000s	*Second quarter £000s*	*Third quarter £000s*	*Fourth quarter £000s*
Sales	150	135	165	150
Cost of sales	102	94	110	102
Gross profit	48	41	55	48
Administrative, selling and distribution expenses and interest	23	21	25	23
Net profit	25	20	30	25

Budgeted balances at the end of each quarter:

	31 March 19x1 £000s	*30 June 19x1 £000s*	*30 Sept 19x1 £000s*	*31 Dec 19x1 £000s*
Stock	65	75	60	65
Debtors	60	45	65	55
Creditors	50	40	55	48

Dividends amounting to £40,000 will be paid during the first quarter. Corporation tax amounting to £30,000 will be paid during the third quarter. Capital expenditure amounting to £88,000 is expected to be incurred during the fourth quarter and will be partly financed by a further issue of debentures amounting to £25,000 and the proceeds of the sale of old plant and equipment £5,000.

Depreciation amounting to £5,000 is included in the budgeted expenditure for each quarter.

Source: CIMA

Workings

	Quarter ending 31 March £000	Quarter ending 30 June £000	Quarter ending 30 Sept £000	Quarter ending 31 Dec £000	Total £000
Debtors at start	50	60	45	65	
Sales	150	135	165	150	
	200	195	210	215	
Budget debtors at end	60	45	65	55	
∴ Budget receipts	140	150	145	160	595
Cost of sales	102	94	110	102	
+ Closing stock	65	75	60	65	
	167	169	170	167	
− Opening stock	65	65	75	60	
Purchases	102	104	95	107	408
+ Opening creditors	40	50	40	55	
	142	154	135	162	
− Closing creditors	50	40	55	48	
Payments for goods	92	114	80	114	400
Administration, selling and distribution	23	21	25	23	92
Less Depreciation	5	5	5	5	20
	18	16	20	18	72
Dividends	40				40
Corporation tax			30		30
Capital expenditure				88	88
Debentures				+25	+25
Sale of plant				+5	+5

The movement for the increase or decrease in working capital is between 1 January 19x1 and 31 December 19x1. Movement between the quarters would only be shown if the statement were for a quarter.

Solution

(a)   **Cash budget by quarters (receipts and payments)**

	Quarter ending 31 March £000	Quarter ending 30 June £000	Quarter ending 30 Sept £000	Quarter ending 31 Dec £000
Receipts				
Total from debtors	140	150	145	160
Debenture issue				25
Sale of plant				5
Total	140	150	145	190
Payments				
Purchases	92	114	80	114
Administration, selling and distribution	18	16	20	18
Dividends payable	40			
Corporation tax			30	
Capital expenditure				88
Total	150	130	130	220
Net cash gain/(loss)	(10)	20	15	(30)
Opening balance	35	25	45	60
Indicated cash balance	25	45	60	30

(b)   **Source and application of funds statement**
                  Budget for year ended 31 December 19x1

	£000	£000
Sources of funds		
Profit before tax		100
Items not involving movement of funds		
Depreciation		20
Total from operations		120
Sale of plant		5
Issue of debentures		25
		150
Application		
Purchase of fixed assets	88	
Taxation payable	30	
Dividends payable	40	158
Decrease in working capital		(8)
Represented by		
Increase in stocks	–	
Increase in debtors	5	
Increase in creditors	(8)	(3)
Change in net liquid funds		
Decrease in bank		(5)
		(8)

The decrease in bank is confirmed by the fact that the bank balance has declined from £35,000 in January 19x1 to £30,000 at 31 December 19x1 as shown in the solution to (a). Alternatively the total figure shown in the final column of the workings might be used to produce a statement of cash flows.

Budgeted cash flow – year ended 31 December 19X1

	£000	£000	£000
Balance at 1 January 19x1			35
Sources			
Debtors	595		
Debenture issue	25		
Sale of plant	5		
	——	625	
Application			
Creditors	400		
Administration, selling and distribution	72		
Dividends payable	40		
Corporation tax payable	30		
Capital expenditure	88		
	——	(630)	
Excess of application over sources			(5)
Balance of cash at 31 December 19x1			30

11.5 Cost control: Standard costs and variance analysis

Historical costs suffer from the deficiency that they are not available until after the event and this, as was seen in the section on budgeting, makes them inadequate for control purposes. **Standard costs** are predetermined costs i.e. determined in advance of the period to which they are to be applied. They provide a basis for control through the exceptions principle, such exceptions being the **variances** or differences between the standard cost and the actual cost. The objective is to assist management by drawing attention quickly to significant variances – favourable or adverse – in order that investigation and action can be prompt and effective. The purpose of variance analysis is to answer four fundamental questions:

● Where did the variation occur?
● Why did the variation occur?
● To what extent is it controllable?
● Who was responsible?

Variance analysis can be extremely sophisticated or very simple. The degree of sophistication depends largely upon the number and type of standard costs in use. Some businesses make do with one standard only. The main types of standard are current, normal and ideal. The **current standard** should be related to current conditions. It will be applied in the short term and results in exposing variances which should be controllable at shop floor level. The **normal standard** will reflect a performance attainable over a longer time span and in an absorption cost system will usually correspond to the activity upon which standard overhead absorption rates are based. An **ideal standard** represents a target attainable only under most favourable conditions. Variances between current and normal standards would be the responsibility of middle and senior management while variances between normal and ideal standards would indicate the gains or losses attributable to fundamental policy and method changes in the long term.

Under any system the major variances can be isolated into two **primary** variances for each element of cost and they are:

1   Losses or gains due to paying higher rates for the material, labour or services concerned.
2   Losses or gains due to using more or less of the materials, labour or services specified.

Standard costs have to be related to the **actual** quantities produced or sold in order to assess the relative performance. In this respect they differ somewhat to budgets and although the budgets may incorporate standard costs this sometimes causes confusion, and the distinction must be kept clear. The budget is a plan and represents an objective to be attained under standard conditions. Budget variances therefore reflect failure to achieve or better the plan. Standard cost variances, on the other hand, measure the difference between actual cost and standard cost of the *actual* quantities produced or sold. In any situation it is necessary to ascertain the standard cost of the actual production/sales and compare it with the actual costs incurred. Once this has been established the total variance can be isolated and used as a check on the calculation of the subsidiary variances which follow. The breakdown of major variances as suggested by the Chartered Institute of Management Accountants is given on page 349. A second major difference between budget and standard cost variances is that the latter are incorporated into the accounting system, whereas the former may be incorporated into formal reports or statements but not the accounts themselves. In Exercise 11.13 which follows, a procedure is illustrated which can be followed in computing the major variances associated with production.

Exercise 11.13
SC Manufacturing Company Ltd manufactures a uniform product and operates a standard costing system.

Standard cost data are as follows:

● From each ton of raw materials consumed it is planned that forty units of product will be produced. The standard price per ton is £100.
● Twenty employees are engaged at a standard rate of £1.25 per hour. A forty-hour week is in operation and there are forty-eight working weeks per annum. The standard performance for the whole factory is set at a total of fifty units per hour.
● Budgeted production overhead for the year is £288,000.
● Budgeted output for the year is 96,000 units.

Actual data for the first week in May were as follows:

- Production was 2,020 units. Consumption of raw material was fifty-two tons at an actual price of £98 per ton.
- Three employees were paid at £1.30 per hour, two were paid at £1.20 per hour, and the remainder were paid at standard rate.
- Actual production overhead incurred was £6,200.

You are required to calculate the following variances:

(a)   (i)   Direct material cost
     (ii) Direct material price
     (iii) Direct material usage
(b)   (i)   Direct wages cost
     (ii) Direct wages rate
     (iii) Direct labour efficiency
(c)   (i)   Production overhead cost
     (ii) Production overhead expenditure
     (iii) Production overhead volume.

Source: CIMA

Workings
1 Calculate the standard cost per unit:

	Qty	Unit	Rate £	Unit cost £	Total for 2020 units £
Material ($\frac{1}{40}$ tons)	0.025	ton	100	2.5	5050
Labour 20 × 1/50	0.4	hour	1.25	0.5	1010
Overhead $\frac{£288,000}{96,000}$	1	unit	3.00	3.0	6060
				6.0	12,120

2 Calculate actual output at standard cost i.e. for May:
    2020 units at £6 =   £12,120

3 *Calculate actual cost incurred:*

		£
Raw material 52 tons at £98		£5,096
Labour	3 × 40 × 1.30 = 156	
	2 × 40 × 1.20 = 96	
	15 × 40 × 1.25 = 750	
		1,002
Overhead		6,200
		12,298

4 Determine production cost variance (2 − 3)   178 Adverse

The adverse variance indicates that the actual performance is poorer than the standard i.e. it has cost £178 more. If the reverse situation is the case the variance will be termed favourable. It is possible for the total adverse variance to be the result of various favourable and unfavourable variances in combination.

Solution

(a)   (i)   *Direct material cost variance:*

This is the difference between the standard cost of the direct materials specified for the production achieved and the actual cost of that input.

Consumption of raw material was:
52 tons × £98
∴. actual cost of production was 52 × £98 =   £5,096
Standard cost of actual production was:
2020 units @ £2.5   =   £5,050
                                ————
∴. *direct material cost variance*   =   £46 A

(a)   (ii)   *Direct materials price variance:*

Assuming materials are charged to production at standard prices this represents that part of the direct materials cost variance which is due to the difference between standard price and the actual price paid for materials purchased being different from standard – all *stocks* will therefore be at *standard* cost. When materials are charged to production at actual prices it represents the part of direct materials cost variance which is due to the difference between standard prices specified and actual prices paid for the materials *used* – all *stocks* will therefore be at *actual* cost. If stocks are slow moving then very large variances on large quantities purchased may be written off in one accounting period. This is, however, the more common method in practice as the administrative convenience of carrying stocks at standard cost is considerable. When figures for consumption only – as in this exercise – are given then price variances can only be worked out on the usage as no indication of purchases or stock value is given. The price variance is always worked out on the *actual* quantity used or purchased. Although there are some theoretical points against this it is standard practice and recommended for all practical purposes.

Actual cost of actual materials used
= 52 tons @ £98 per ton   =   £5,096
Standard cost of actual materials used
= 52 tons @ £100   =   £5,200
                                ————
∴. *Direct material price variance*   =   £104 F

or actual quantity (standard price − actual price)
  = 52   (£100 − £98)
  = £104 F

(a)   (iii)   *Direct material usage variance:*

This variance arises due to using more or less materials than the

standard quantity specified for the actual production achieved, both being valued at standard price. It therefore reflects the efficiency, or otherwise, achieved in control of materials.
Standard cost of actual materials used

= 52 tons at £100	=	£5,200

Standard quantity of material
specified $= \dfrac{2020}{40} = 50.5$ tons

Standard cost of standard quantity of materials specified = 50.5 @ £100	=	£5,050
∴ *direct material usage variance*	=	£150 A

or Standard price (actual quantity − standard quantity)
= £100 (52 − 50.5)
= £150 A

Check: Material cost variance = material price variance + material usage variance
i.e. £46 A = £104 F + £150 A

(b)   (i)   *Direct wages – cost variance:*
This is the difference between the standard direct wages specified for the production achieved and the actual direct wages incurred. As with the material cost variance it arises from two major sources – either paying more or less than the standard rate or working at a faster or slower rate than the expected norm.

	£	£
Actual cost of actual hours worked		
3 employees × 40 hours × £1.30 per hour	=	156
2 employees × 40 hours × £1.20 per hour	=	96
15 employees × 40 hours × £1.25 per hour	=	750
∴ Actual cost of actual production	=	1,002

In the absence of any information to the contrary it is assumed all employees worked the normal 40-hour week.

Standard cost of actual production was 2020 units @ £0.5	=	1,010
∴ *direct wage cost variance*	=	8 F

The total variance is favourable as the actual cost is *less* than the standard cost specified.

(b)   (ii)   *Direct wage rate variance:*
This is the part of the direct wage cost variance which is due to the actual rate paid being different to rates of pay specified. As with the material price variance it is calculated on the actual hours worked. This ensures that any subsequent variances are evaluated at the standard rate.

	£	£
Actual cost of actual hours worked		

3 employees × 40 hours × £1.30 per hour	156	
2 employees × 40 hours × £1.20 per hour	96	
15 employees × 40 hours × £1.25 per hour	750	
		1,002

Standard cost of actual hours worked
20 employees × 40 hours × £1.25   =   1,000

∴ *direct wages rate variance*   =   2 A

We need not compute the total again as above. A rate variance can only arise when the rate paid is different to the rate specified.

i.e. rates variance = actual hours (standard rate − actual rate)

17 employees were paid at the standard rate therefore we need consider only the exception

3 employees worked 40 hours each = 120 hours

∴ rate variance = 120 (£1.25 − £1.30)
                          = £6 adverse (they were being paid *more* per hour)

2 employees worked 40 hours each = 80 hours

∴ rate variance = 80 (£1.25 − £1.20)
                          = £4 favourable (they were being paid *less* per hour)

∴ total rate variance = £6 A + £4 F = *£2 A* as above

(b) (iii) *Direct labour efficiency variance:*

This is the portion of the direct wage cost variance which is due to the difference between the standard direct wage cost for the production achieved and the standard cost of the actual hours taken. It reflects the gain or loss due to not working the specified hours or not producing at the standard rate during the hours worked or the resultant combination of these factors.

Standard cost of actual hours worked   £

= 20 employees × 40 hours × £1.25   =   1,000

Standard cost of standard hours specified

Standard hours specified $= \dfrac{2020}{50} \times 20$ employees

Standard cost of standard hours specified

$= \dfrac{2020}{50} \times 20 \times £1.25$

= 808 × £1.25   =   1,010

∴ direct labour efficiency variance   =   10 F

The value at standard cost of the work is greater than the cost (at standard rates) of the hours taken to produce it and therefore the efficiency variance is favourable.

Check: Direct wages cost variance = direct wages rate variance + direct labour efficiency variance

i.e. £8 F = £2 A + £10 F

(c) (i) *Production overhead cost variance:*

This is the variance which is due to the difference between the standard cost absorbed in the actual production achieved and the actual cost of variable and fixed overhead attributed to the period concerned. In instances where a separate absorption rate in respect of the variable overhead is given, the amount of variable overhead under or overspent can be separated as part of the expenditure variance. Where the rate is not so separated the expenditure variance can only be isolated in total. The other major division of the production overhead variance is that attributed to volume change and this and its subdivision are described below.

Overhead differs in treatment from the direct elements of cost in that if an absorption system is used some budget and a related normal capacity must be used in determining the standard overhead absorption rate. This is because the nature of a fixed cost is fundamentally different to that of any variable element of cost.

Budgeted production overhead for year	£288,000
Budgeted output for year	96,000 units

$\therefore$ Standard overhead absorption rate per unit

$$+ \frac{£288,000}{96,000} = £3 \text{ per unit}$$

		£
Actual production overhead incurred in May	=	6,200
Standard overhead absorbed in actual output in May = 2020 (units) × £3 (per unit)	=	6,060
$\therefore$ Production overhead costs variance	=	140 A

We spent more than we absorbed therefore the variance is adverse (A)

(c) (ii) *Production overhead expenditure variance:*

The difference between the budget cost allowance for the actual production achieved and the actual overhead expenditure incurred for the period is termed the expenditure variance. The budget or standard allowance will normally comprise fixed cost as a proportion of the annual budget – such proportion being that appropriate to the period concerned – plus variable costs in proportion to the activity achieved. The term standard allowance should not be confused with standard cost. The former is an alternative term used in lieu of 'budget allowance' whereas the latter refers to the standard cost either of one unit or a quantity of output. If information is available on the split between variable and fixed overhead then this variance can be analysed into the gain or loss due to spending on fixed, as distinct from variable, overhead. If such information is not available – as in this exercise – the variance can be estimated only as one figure. (See section on flexible budgets for example of such a split.)

		£
Actual production overhead	=	6,200
Budgeted overhead for year	= £288,000	
Budgeted working weeks for year	= 48	
∴ Budget allowance	$= \dfrac{£288,000}{48} =$	6,000
∴ Production overhead expenditure variance	=	200 A

(c) (iii) *Production overhead volume variance:*
This variance relates to the difference between the standard cost absorbed in the actual production and the budgeted cost allowance. It measures, at a determined standard rate, the effect of producing more or less than the level of output (usually termed the normal capacity) on which the standard overhead absorption rate is based. If variable overheads are related to units produced then, because the allowance in respect of these will expand or contract at a standard rate, the volume variance *will relate exclusively to fixed overhead.*

		£
Standard overheads expected to be absorbed in one week $= \dfrac{£288,000}{48}$	=	6,000
Standard overhead absorbed in actual output = 2020 units × £3.0 per unit	=	6,060
∴ Volume variance	=	60 F

i.e. *more* overhead was absorbed than expected
Check: Production overhead cost variance = production overhead expenditure variance + production overhead volume variance
i.e. £140 A = £200 A + £60 F

This exercise can be used to demonstrate two important aspects of overhead cost variances – how they can be related to hours rather than units and the two major subdivisions of volume variance.

Relativity to direct labour hours

Most businesses are associated with more than one product and total output cannot effectively be expressed by adding units products. It is not logical, for example, to add chairs to tables in the case of a furniture manufacturer. Output can be expressed in homogeneous units such as sales value but this is subject to variation in selling prices. Units of effort are subject to less frequent change and the most common yardstick is the direct labour hours or alternatively machine hours taken to produce a unit of each type of product. In the computation of direct labour efficiency variance in Exercise 11.13 it was established that the time spent by each employee averaged $20 \times 1/50 = 0.4$ hours per unit

$\therefore$ Standard overhead absorption rate $= \dfrac{£288,000}{96,000 \times 0.4} = £7.5$ per hour

Check: 0.4 hours $\times$ £7.5 per hour $=$ £3 as standard cost card.

Production overhead cost variance is equal to the difference between the standard hours in the actual output and the standard hours in the budgeted output evaluated at the standard rate per hour:

$$\text{Standard overhead} \atop \text{absorption rate} \left\{ {\text{Standard hours} \atop \text{in actual output}} - {\text{Standard hours} \atop \text{in budgeted output}} \right\} \text{ for the period}$$

The period is one week

Budgeted output for one week $= \dfrac{96,000}{48} = 2000$

$\therefore$ Standard hours in actual output $= 0.4 \times 2020 = 808$
Standard hours in budgeted output $= 0.4 \times 2000 = 800$
Standard overhead absorption rate $= £7.5$ per hour
Volume variance $= £7.5 (808 - 800)$
       $= £60$ F as above

No information is given in Exercise 11.13 about the actual hours worked so it is assumed that all twenty employees worked for forty hours each i.e. the capacity used was exactly that which was budgeted. In this event what gave rise to the volume variance? The answer lies in examination of the direct labour performance. The workers produced 808 standard hours of work in (presumably) 800 hours. The standard overhead absorption rate is £7.5 per hour which is six times the standard direct labour rate of £1.25 therefore the production overhead volume variance was caused by the productivity of the direct labour force and since there was no change in the hours *worked* the volume and productivity variance would be the same.

Capacity variance

This is another major division of volume variance having particular reference to absorption systems. If an operator who is rated to produce one standard hour of work in one actual hour worked is absent for four hours then, unless substitute labour can be found, the machine will be idle and the capacity variance loss will be four hours at the appropriate overhead absorption rate. This will also be the volume variance. If, however, on his return the operator works sufficiently hard to make up the four hours lost production the efficiency variance will be four hours gain and the volume variance will be nil. This is why the elements of the volume variance need to be separated particularly into gains/losses caused by unused capacity as distinct from gains/losses caused by efficiency or productivity.

Calendar variance

A further subdivision of the volume variance is the calendar variance which, again as part of the volume variance, is only attributable to fixed overhead. This applies where a company uses traditional calendar months as the cost period. It will be necessary to decide on an average month of say twenty working days. When the actual months are longer proportional variances are added and when they are shorter such variances are deducted, thus over the year they will balance out. They can be avoided by using costing periods having equal numbers of working days. Weeks containing less than five, or whatever is the standard, working days per week due to holidays can be separately accounted for so that each comparable costing period contains, say, four weeks of five working days. In the following consolidating exercise the calendar variance is computed in order to show how it would be ascertained if required.

Exercise 11.14

Revenue accounts for May (financial books)

		£		£
Direct materials				
consumed		1,012	Sales 100 @ 36	3,600
Direct wages		1,672	Loss	24
Overheads				
Variable	240			
Fixed	700			
		940		
		3,624		3,624

The above results have been analysed in the traditional financial accounting form. Demonstrate how the technique of standard costing might be used to explain the reason for the loss given in the following additional information:

1. Budgeted output for a normal month of twenty-four working days is 1200 units and the cost allowance in respect of fixed overhead for this period is £720.
2. Standard cost per unit is made up as follows:
   Direct materials 4.5 kg at £0.20 per kg
   Direct wages 3.2 hours at £0.50 per hour
   Variable overhead £0.25 per unit

3 Actual number of working days in May were twenty-two.
 Actual materials used were 4400 kg.
 Actual cost of materials was £0.23 per kg.
 Actual direct labour was 3040 hours.
 Actual rate paid for labour 55p per hour.
4 Units produced and sold were 1000.

Workings
1 Calculate standard cost of one unit

	Qty	Unit	Rate £	Total £
Direct materials	4.5	kg	0.20	0.90
Direct wages	3.2	hrs	0.50	1.60
Overhead: Variable	1	unit	0.25	0.25
Fixed		unit	0.60	0.60
				3.35

Budgeted overhead is £720 per normal output of 1200 units.

$\therefore$ standard cost unit $= \dfrac{£720}{1,200} = 0.60$

or

Standard hours in normal budget period $= 1200 \times 32$ $=$ 3840
Standard allowance for budget period
for fixed overheads $=$ £720

$\therefore$ standard overhead absorption rate per hour $= \dfrac{720}{3840}$ $=$ £0.1875

and standard fixed overhead cost per unit $= £0.1875 \times 3.2 =$ £0.60

2 Calculate material variances
Direct material cost:
Actual cost − standard cost of actual output
440 kg × £0.23 − (100 units × 4.5 kg × £0.20)
£1,012 − £900 = £112 A

Direct material price:
Actual usage (actual price − standard price)
4400 (£0.23 − £0.20) = £132 A

Direct material usage:
Standard price (actual quantity − standard quantity)
£0.20 (4400 − 4500) = £20 F

Check: £112 A = £132 A + £20 F

3 Calculate labour variances
Direct wages cost:
Actual cost − standard cost of actual output
3040 hours × 55p − (1000 units × 3.2 hours × £0.50)
£1,672 − £1,600 = £72 A

Direct wages rates:
Actual hours (actual rate − standard rate)
3040 (£0.55 − £0.50) = <u>£152 A</u>

Direct wages efficiency:
Standard rate (actual hours − standard hours)
£0.50 (3040 − 3200) = <u>£80 F</u>

Check: £72 A = £152A − £80 F

4   *Calculate overhead variances*
Variable production overhead variance:
Actual cost − standard overhead absorbed in actual output
£240 − 1000 units at £0.25
£240 − £250 = <u>£10 F</u>

Fixed production overhead variance
Actual cost − standard fixed overhead absorbed in actual output
£700 − 100 units × £0.60
= £700 − £600 = <u>£100 A</u>

This comprises **expenditure** and **volume** and therefore entails:

1   Fixed production expenditure variance:
Actual cost − budgeted cost allowance
= £700 − £720 = <u>£20 F</u>

i.e. we *spent* less than the allowance

2   Fixed production overhead volume variance:
= Budget cost allowance − standard overhead absorbed in actual output
= £720 − (1000 units × £0.60)
= £720 − £600 = £120 A
Check: £100 A = £120 A − £20 F

The volume variance can be further divided into:

1   Calendar
2   Capacity
3   Productivity

Fixed overhead calendar variance

Number of days in budget period	24
Number days in actual month of May	22
Difference	2 days less

Assuming that normal hours were worked in all the days concerned there would be a proportional reduction in hours available in May compared with the budget period of $\frac{2}{24}$ i.e. $\frac{1}{12}$ of budget capacity.

This is equivalent to $\frac{1}{12}$ × 1200 units = 100 units less production than under standard conditions

∴. calendar variance

$= 100 \times £0.60$ per unit $= £60$ A

or $\dfrac{3840}{24} \times 2 \times 0.1875$

Costing profit and loss account for May

			£
Budgeted sales (1,500 @ £3.6)			5,400
Sales variances:			
Volume { Price		Nil	
Volume { Quantity (500 @ £3.6)		1800	
			1,800
Actual sales			3,600
Less Standard cost of sales (1000 @ £3.35)			3,350
Standard profit on actual sales			250

	Gains £	*Loss* £	
Variances			
Direct materials: Price		132	
Usage	20		
Direct wage: Rate		152	
Efficiency	80		
Variable overhead expenditure	10		
Fixed overhead: Expenditure	20		
Calendar		60	
Capacity		90	
Productivity	30		
	160	434	
Net variance (loss)			274
Loss as per financial accounts			24

Capacity variance

The hours available under normal conditions in twenty-two actual days compared with a budget period of twenty-four days would be $\dfrac{22}{24} = \dfrac{11}{12}$

Production expected would be $\dfrac{11}{12} \times 1200 = 1100$ units

or $1100 \times 3.2 \qquad = 3520$ hours

Actual hours worked $= 3040$ hours

∴. capacity variance

$=$ Standard rate (actual hours $-$ standard hours in period)

$= £0.1875 \times (3040 - 3520)$

$= £90$ A

Fixed cost productivity variance:

The hours worked were 3040

The hours *produced* were equivalent to
1000 × 3.2 hours per unit = 3200
We produced (3040 − 3200) = 160 *more* hours than expected
∴. direct labour productivity variance
Standard rate (actual hours − standard hours in actual output)
= £0.1875 (3040 − 3200) = £30 F

Check: Volume variance = calendar variance + capacity variance + productivity variance
         £120 A   =   £60 A   +   £90 A   +   £30 F

Most costing profit and loss accounts are presented in a vertical format. The first step is to show any adjustment to sales (volume and price) to arrive at the standard value of the actual sales. Such variances can be analysed to show the effect on *value of sales* or on *profit*. In the former case the selling price per unit is used while in the latter the profit (in an absorption cost system) per unit is used. Thus, in the figures used in the example:

Sales value variance due to sales volume:
The difference between budgeted and actual turnover for a specified period:
= (1,500 × £3.6) − £1,000 × £3.6
= £5,400 − £3,600
= £1,800 A

This is both the volume and value variance since the actual selling price was the same as the standard selling price

Operating profit variance due to sales volume:
The difference between budgeted and actual operating profit related to a specific period:
Budgeted profit − standard profit on actual sales
1500 (£3.6 − £2.35) − 1,000 (£3.6 − £2.35)
= 500 × 1.25
= £625 A

Summary of fixed production overhead variance

Units	Standard hours		£	Step
–	–	Actual fixed overhead	700	1
–	–	Expenditure variance (gain)	20	3 = 2 − 1
1200	3840	Budgeted fixed overhead	720	2
− 100	− 320	Calendar variance (loss)	60	5 = 4 − 2
1100	3520	Standard overhead in normal hours	660	4
− 150	− 480	Capacity variance (loss)	90	7 = 6 − 5
950	3040	Standard overhead in actual hours	570	6
+ 50	+ 160	Productivity variance (gain)	30	8 = 9 − 6
1000	3200	Standard overhead in actual output	600	9
(a)	(b)	(c)	(d)	(e)

Column (a)   Units at standard performance expected in direct labour hours listed.

Column (b)   Direct labour hours derived from, or giving rise to calculation of Column (a).

Column (c)   Abbreviated description of the subvariances the description and calculation of which are described in preceding pages.

Column (d)   With the exception of Line 1 which is derived from the actual accounts this column summarizes the budget allowance and the standard overheads absorbed in the various possible production hours.

Column (e)   Indicates the order in which these variances should be derived and that in which they would be entered. The variances are then given in the costing statement as on page 359.

11.6   Cost control: Non-manufacturing costs

These costs embrace all functions not directly related to the production or manufacturing function. They provide problems of absorption and control substantially different from the manufacturing cost.

Variable elements may not vary with quantities produced. Telephone costs are partly fixed (rentals) but the variable element varies with the number and distance of calls made – which may increase excessively in low volume production periods as efforts are made to drum up sales. Packing costs will vary with items sold, not produced, and distribution costs relate to the pattern of deliveries and distances as well as quantities. Fixed costs, also, are more truly period costs and, more importantly, relate to policies rather than output or sales. Management may decide on an intensive advertising programme – it may be entirely fixed, buying peak TV viewing time for a definite period or it may be partly variable as where prizes are offered or discount coupons are inserted in magazines. In the latter case the ultimate cost will depend upon customer response. Each main group of non-manufacturing cost will be briefly considered in turn.

Administration costs

This is defined by the CIMA as 'The cost of management, and of secretarial, accounting and administrative services which cannot be directly related to the production, marketing, research or development functions of the enterprise.' This raises issues of demarcation. For example, a production director is part of the cost of management but since his responsibilities are exclusively for the production function his salaries and associated costs might be classified as production overheads. A general manager or managing director oversees all functions and for absorption purposes must either be spread over all functions or treated wholly as administration costs. If such costs are not absorbed into product costs at the production stage they will either be added to production cost on a percentage or other basis or treated as period costs and charged in the period to which the relate. For control purposes budgets for the function will be produced by cost centre and some person will be held responsible for each item or group. The techniques advocated for control of production costs are not usually applicable but where there is an output capable of assessment, organization and methods personnel may use operational research techniques to assess performance and aid control. Exercise 11.15 shows how the flexible budget techniques developed for manufacturing can be applied to a secretarial operation.

Exercise 11.15

(a)   Prepare a flexible budget for a month at activity levels of 70 per cent, 80 per cent, 90 per cent, 100 per cent and 110 per cent for a purchasing department having the undernoted cost characteristics.

(b)   Calculate the average cost for processing a purchase order at each of the above levels.

The following information is given:

Staff and salaries:	
Department head	£5,400 per annum
2 Senior buyers	£3,000 each per annum
2 Junior buyers	£2,100 each per annum
1 Secretary	£1,800 per annum
2 Typists	£20 each per week
Employee benefits	20 per cent of salary payments
Space occupied	800 square feet
Rent	£5 per square foot per year
Heat and light	£840 fixed cost per year and £360 variable cost per year at 50 per cent activity, but thereafter proportionately variable
Office services	20 per cent of total rent, light and heat
Purchase orders issued at 100 per cent activity	2,100 per month
Average number of lines per purchase order	15
Average typing speed	90 lines per hour
Purchase orders cost	£0.15 per set and wastage amounts to 5 per cent of completed orders
Other typing and office supplies average	50 per cent purchase order cost

When not fully employed the typists have a fall-back job typing employee training records. Cost alloted to the fall-back job is confined to salaries only.

When extra typing is needed the first thirty-five hours is covered by overtime at time and one-half. Thereafter, agency typists are employed at an inclusive charge of £1.50 per hour. The agency typists only have a 70 per cent efficiency compared with the regular staff.

All staff work overtime proportionate to activity level above 100 per cent.

The senior salaried staff are not paid overtime but the junior buyers and the secretary get plain time for additional hours worked.'

You are to assume a month to be one-twelfth of a calendar year and to comprise of four weeks of thirty-five hours each.

(Work to nearest £1 in total costs and to two decimals of £1 for unit costs.)

Source: CIMA

Workings

Note			£
1	Departmental head	$\frac{1}{12} \times £5,400$	450
	2 Senior buyers	$\frac{1}{12} \times £6,000$	500
	2 Junior buyers	$\frac{1}{12} \times £4,200$	350
	1 Secretary	$\frac{1}{12} \times £1,800$	150
	2 Typists	4 weeks × £40	160
			1,610

2	Employee benefits 20% × £1,610	= £322
3	Rent 800 × £5 ÷ 12	= £333
4	Light and heat £840 ÷ 12	= £70
5	Office services = 20% (3) + (4) = 20% + £403	= £81
6	Sum of Lines 1 − 5 =	£2,416
7	Staff overtime	

Hours available = 2 typists × 4 weeks × 35 hours = 280 hours at 70% activity

$$\text{Hours required for typing orders} = \frac{\text{No. of orders} \times \text{lines per order}}{\text{lines per hour}}$$
$$= \frac{1470 \times 15}{90}$$
$$= 245$$

∴ hours spent typing employee records = 280 − 245 = 35

This is equivalent to 1 typist for 1 week i.e. £20 and this is a *credit* to the purchasing department.

There is a constant relationship between lines per order and lines per hour of $\frac{15}{90} = 1/6$ ∴ typing hours from our own staff will be equal to *number of orders divided by 6.*

Activity %	No. of orders	No. of hours	Own typists' hours For training	Own typists' hours Overtime	Agency hours required
70	1470	245	(35)	–	
80	1680	280	–	–	
90	1890	315		35	
100	2100	350		35	50*
110	2310	385		35	100*

* What our typist could do in 30 hours if available requires $35 \times \frac{100}{70} = 50$ hours as they are slower

Staff overtime

				Benefits @ 20%
100% activity	typist overtime			
	$= 35 \text{ hours} \times 1\frac{1}{2} \times \dfrac{£20}{35}$	= £30		6
110% activity	typist overtime	= £30		6
	+ Junior buyer's overtime			
	$10\% \times 2 \times \dfrac{£2,100}{13}$		£35	
	$+ 10\% \times \dfrac{£1,800}{12}$		£15	
			£80	16

8   Agency hours as computed in Note 7
   100% activity: 50 hours at £1.50 = £75
   110% activity: 100 hours at £1.50 = £150
9   Employee benefits – see Note 7
10 *Heat and light:*
   If the variable cost is £30 per year at 50% activity then the variable
   element is $\dfrac{10}{50} \times £360 = £72$ per annum for every 10% activity which

   is equivalent to $\dfrac{£72}{12} = £6$ per month per 10% activity

Level of activity	(%)	70	80	90	100	110
Variable cost	(£)	42	48	54	60	66

11 *Office services:*
   20% of line 10 = £8, £10, £11, £12, £13 to nearest £
12 *Purchase orders*

Level of activity	(%)	70	80	90	100	110
Number of orders		1470	1680	1890	2100	2310
Cost at 15p		£221	£252	£284	£315	£347
plus 5%	=	£232	£265	£298	£331	£364

13 *Other supplies:*

50% of Line 12	=	£116	£132	£149	£165	£182

14 Sum of Lines 7–13
15 Sum of Lines 6 and 14
16 Line 15 ÷ number of orders.

Solution

Flexible budget – purchasing department

Activity level (%)	70	80	90	100	110	
Number of orders	1,470	1,680	1,890	2,100	2,310	
	£	£	£	£	£	Note
Fixed costs						
Staff salaries	1,610	1,610	1,610	1,610	1,610	1
Employee benefits	322	322	322	322	322	2
Rent	333	333	333	333	333	3
Light and heat	70	70	70	70	70	4
Office services	81	81	81	81	81	5
Subtotal	2,416	2,416	2,416	2,416	2,416	6
Variable costs						
Staff overtime	(20)	–	30	30	80	7
Agency typist	–	–	–	75	150	8
Employee benefits	–	–	6	6	16	9
Heat and light	42	48	54	60	66	10
Office services	8	10	11	12	13	11
Purchase orders	232	265	298	331	364	12
Other supplies	116	132	149	165	182	13
Subtotal	378	455	548	679	871	14
Grand total	2,794	2,871	2,964	3,095	3,287	15
Cost per order	1.90	1.71	1.57	1.47	1.42	16

Marketing costs

These are: 'The costs incurred in researching the potential markets and promoting products in suitably attractive forms and at acceptable prices.' They include **selling costs** and **distribution costs** which are considered separately as the cost characteristics are very different.

Selling costs

These are costs incurred in securing orders including salesmen's salaries and costs. Sales promotion costs may also be included. Budgets would be prepared in a number of ways according to the size of amounts involved and the degree of control attempted. Budgets may be prepared by nature of expense – salaries, hotels, travelling etc. and analysed to individual salesmen, sales territories, groups of products and so on. Flexible techniques can be used for motor vehicle costs combining fixed costs such as licences, insurance and road funds with allowances related to mileage for petrol, diesel and tyres.

For advertising and similar items **appropriation budgets** are used. These are policy costs and once a figure has been determined the budget ensures it is spent on time and on the item for which funds were allocated.

Distribution costs

These are costs incurred in storing goods past the production stage and subsequently getting them into the hands of the consumer. In the case of wholesalers or processes such as brewing they may represent a most significant part of total cost. If the firm employs its own transport fleet then the major division will be storage and transport costs. Absorption into product cost may be on some percentage or unit basis. Alternatively they could be treated as period costs and deducted from the revenue in the period.

Research and development costs

In certain industries, as previously indicated, these costs may be very considerable. They are mostly policy costs in so far as the company decides how much it can afford (or not afford) to incur to remain progressive and competitive. Often success is closely related to the introduction and exploitation of new products or techniques. Lack of authority in accounting treatment can cause great disparity in assessing the relative performance between two companies. Attempts at standardizing an approach to accounting treatment (and hence control) have been made by the introduction of SSAP 13. This suggests a three part analysis based on the following definitions:

1 *Pure (or basic) research:*   Original investigation undertaken in order to gain new scientific or technical knowledge and understanding. Basic research is not primarily directed toward any specific practical aim or application.
2 *Applied research:*   Original investigation undertaken in order to gain new scientific or technical knowledge and directed toward a specific aim or objective. The statement recommends that expenditure on pure and applied research should be written off in the year of expenditure. If this is followed they would be treated for budgeting purposes as period costs. Budgets would be created in respect of cost centres such as various laboratories or specific projects such as design and construction of a new product or technique. The exception would be when fixed assets acquired for a number of accounting periods were acquired in which event they should be written off over their useful life.
3 *Development expenditure:*   The use of scientific or technical knowledge in order to produce new, or substantially improved, materials, devices, products, processes, systems or services prior to the commencement of commercial production.

It is recommended that such expenditure is written off in the year of expenditure except in the following circumstances when it may be deferred to future periods:

1 There is a clearly defined project.
2 The related expenditure is separately identifiable.
3 The outcome of such a project has been assessed with reasonable certainty as to technical feasibility and commercial viability.
4 If further development costs are to be incurred on the project the aggregate of such costs together with related production, selling and

administration costs is reasonably expected to be more than covered by related future revenues.

5   Adequate resources exist, or are reasonably expected to be available, to enable the project to be completed and to provide any consequential increases in working capital.

An arbitrary distinction is that basic and applied research is concerned with fundamentals and may, in fact, be costly and abortive. Examples would be the research into lasers for sound reproduction, terminating in the successful commercial application of the compact disc.

Attempts to find an alternative to the traditional forms of internal combustion engine such as the Wankel have not yet reached commercial application. Development costs occur after a product has been accepted by the company as commercially marketable. It may include all the costs from the successful demonstration of the first prototype to the first saleable edition coming off the production line.

Conclusion

The accounting and control treatments for all classes of non-manufacturing costs are governed by the type of industry and the size of the company. The above paragraphs give only brief indications of the characteristics of each major group of expense. Some industries such as oil exploration and refining, aerospace and telecommunications have problems requiring specialist studies. Any body of professional accountants would nominate specialist advisers or provide reading references for individual requirements.

12
Costs for decision making

Decision making is the process of choosing a course of action from a variety of alternatives. The factors affecting the choice may be personal or objective – capable of measurement, or subjective – a matter of opinion. The accountant's function is primarily to provide the objective data on which the decision would be made in the absence of any non-numerate elements. This may be the easier part of the decision. For example, it is comparatively simple to evaluate the costs of redundancy payments to a section of the workforce but more difficult to assess the reaction of remaining employees, the wider effect on the local community and thus, future consequences of the decision. The steps in the decision-making process comprise:

1 Definition of the problem – close examination of the situation may suggest the firm has only one course of action anyway and thus, there is no decision to be made. There must be at least one alternative course of action.
2 Identification and quantification of alternative course.
3 Study of the relevant costs and benefits of all possible alternatives.
4 Selection of final choice or priority order to enable correct managerial decision to be made.

It should be emphasized that there is a great deal of literature on managerial decision making, particularly in relation to environmental, human, psychological, tactical and facets other than costs or revenues. In this brief section, only financial techniques are considered but it should be appreciated that the manager's task of making the final decision is much more difficult and may not necessarily be the most profitable or least costly in monetary terms.

There are basically three types of decisions that the finance function is concerned with advising upon:

1 *Cost related decisions:* These usually involve short-run problems and the most typical examples are those of make or buy, pricing special orders or dropping a product line or department. (See Section 12.1.)
2 *Revenue and cost-related decisions:* These involve choice in situations where both revenue and costs have to be considered. Expansion of sales can usually only proceed indefinitely at lower prices. Maximum volume may not necessarily, therefore, equate with maximum profit, so at which volume should the firm aim to produce and sell? In addition to

marginal costing other examples of relevant costs are considered in Section 12.2.
3 *Investment decision making:* This is a special area of financial management. In addition to costs and revenues other issues involved are obtaining capital, risk and cost of the investments and problems concerned with long-term replacement or expansion projects. The remainder of Chapter 12 is devoted to these aspects of decision making.

A major difficulty in these situations is to identify and focus on **relevant costs** – that is costs relative to making the decision concerned. Costs which are relevant to one decision may not be relevant to another one – it depends, yet again, upon the objective of the analysis.

12.1 Marginal costs

Marginal cost in economic terms is the cost incurred by producing one more unit. As we have seen in costing this is the variable cost of one unit of product. When making a decision the unit may be something greater than a single unit – it may be an export order for several thousand, or closing down a branch, or cutting out one product line. **Incremental costing** is the name specifically given when: 'Consideration is given to a range of graduated or stepped changes in the level or nature of activity, and the additional costs or revenues likely to result from each degree of change are presented.' They can, therefore, be considered together. In most problems the change being considered is likely to involve more than one unit. Both techniques involve segregating those costs which change at any particular level. At some point in incremental analysis this will involve changes in semi-fixed and fixed costs as well as variables.

Marginal costing – make or buy

Example
XY manufacture car radios and a supplier has offered to provide a component for £9.00 per unit. A cost statement provided by the accountant reveals the following

		Per unit
		£
Direct material		2.50
Direct labour		4.00
Production overhead:	Variable	2.00
	Fixed	1.50
		———
		10.00
		———

The firm uses an absorption cost system and the normal capacity is considered to be 5000 units per annum. It would appear that there is a purchasing advantage of £1.00 but what are the relevant costs? The costs which will not be incurred if the firm buys out are direct material, direct labour and variable overhead – a total of £8.50 but fixed costs are equal to a total £1.50 × 5000 units = £7,500.

	£
Cost of purchase = 5000 × £9.0 =	45,000
+ Fixed cost still incurred	7,500
	52,500
Cost of production variable 5000 × £8.50	42,500
+ Fixed cost	7,500
	50,000

On this basis it is still cheaper to produce. It is not necessary to lay the data out as above. This has been done to emphasize that fixed costs here are irrelevant to the decision. All we need to do is to compare the variable cost of producing (£8.50) with the variable cost of buying (£9.00) and it can be seen that we would lose £0.50 per unit bought.

If, however, the fixed cost related entirely to the component then the situation would alter. Suppose the £7,500 represented a rental payable for all the plant involved in production of the component and cancellable immediately without penalty then that would be a relevant cost. By changing to purchasing we would save £50,000 less £45,000 = £5,000 per annum. In some make or buy decisions the concept of key factor is important. Exercise 12.1 is used to introduce the idea in a general fashion and Exercise 12.2 shows a more practical make or buy situation.

A key factor (or limiting factor) is that factor which over a period of time may limit the activity of an entity. It may be a particular material, class of labour, machine hours or a particular process and it may change from time to time. Profitability is maximized when contribution per unit of the limiting factor is optimized.

Exercise 12.1
From one basic raw material a company produces two different grades of a product known as 'Crude' and 'Refined'. The company's direct labour wage rate is £3 per hour and it absorbs overhead into the cost of its two grades of product by means of variable and fixed overhead rates per 100 kilogrammes produced. The budgeted costs and selling prices for each grade are as follows:

	Crude 100 kg £	Refined 100 kg £
Direct material	20.0	20.0
Direct wages	18.0	30.0
Variable production overhead	3.6	7.5
Fixed production overhead	24.0	40.0
	65.6	97.5
Selling prices	80.0	105.0

For the year ending 30 June 19x5, the company's effective annual production capacity is 120,000 labour hours and its estimated fixed production overhead costs total £480,000. Its sales policy is to sell 75 per cent of its capacity in the more profitable grade and 25 per cent in the less profitable grade.

You are required to:

(a) State on which grade of product the company should concentrate to obtain the highest profit – show your calculations.

(b) Present a statement for management which shows the expected sales, variable costs (by element of cost) and contribution for each grade of product together with the overall net profit which can be expected for the year ending 30 June 19x5, if the company's present sales policy is followed. Budgeted fixed selling and administration costs are £90,000.

(c) Comment on the principle you have followed to determine the highest profit in your answer to (a) above. Could this same principle be used in a retailing organization and if so, how?

Source: CIMA

Solution

	Crude per 100 kg		Refined per 100 kg	
	£	£	£	£
Selling price		80.0		105.0
Less Variable costs				
Direct material	20.0		20.0	
Direct wages	18.0		30.0	
Production overhead	3.6		7.5	
		41.6		57.5
Contribution		38.4		47.5

This suggests, initially, that since contribution is £47.50 per 100 kg of Refined compared with £38.40 of Crude the company should concentrate on the Refined product. The productive capacity is however restricted to 120,000 labour hours and since the direct labour hour rate is £3 per hour it means that each 100 kg of Crude requires $\frac{£18}{3} = 6$ hours and Refined requires $\frac{£30}{3} = 10$ hours.

	Crude	Refined
Contribution per 100 kg	38.40	47.50
Direct labour hours	6	10
Contribution per direct labour hour	£6.4	£4.75

The highest contribution **per unit of the limiting factor** is therefore Crude, and it would pay to produce as much as possible of this.

The labour hours available are 120,000 to be allocated (75 per cent) 90,000 to Crude and (25 per cent) 30,000 to Refined. This would mean $\frac{90,000}{6} = 15,000 \times 100$ kg of Crude and $\frac{30,000}{10} = 3,000 \times 100$ kg of Refined. The budget for 30 June 19x5 on this basis would be:

		Crude			Refined		Total
Sales (100 kg)		*15,000*			*3000*		
	£000	*£000*	*£000*	*£000*	*£000*		*£000*
Sales			1,200		315		1,515
Less Variable costs							
Direct material		300		60			
Direct wages		270		90			
Production overhead		54		22.5			
			624		172.5		796.5
Contribution			576		142.5		718.5
Fixed cost: Production	480						
Selling administration	90						570
Net profit							148.5

The principle is to maximize contribution per unit of the key factor. If it were possible to employ all the labour hours on Crude oil and market no Refined at all we could produce $\frac{120,000}{6} = 20,000 \times 100$ kg and this would increase contribution by $\frac{5,000}{15,000} \times £576,000 = £192,000$ less the contribution lost from refined – £142,500 = £49,500. As there would be no change in the fixed costs the contribution increase would correspond to the profit increase.

A further exercise involving plant capacity shows how the decision can be affected by alternative activity levels.

Exercise 12.2

Your company operates a factory which is working at full machine capacity producing the total requirements of three component parts: A, B and C used in equal proportions in an assembly type product. Data concerning one unit of the product is as follows:

	Machine hours	Costs		
		Variable £	*Fixed* £	*Total* £
Component parts:				
A	5	24	8	32
B	8	30	10	40
C	10	30	30	60
Assembly	–	50	20	70
Total	23	£134	£68	£202
Selling price				£250

In preparing a budget for the coming year an increase of sales and production is being considered. It is ascertained that the present machine capacity of the factory will be capable of producing the requirements of only two of the three component parts. No increase of machine capacity can be effected during the course of the next year although other facilities can be increased at very short notice.

In the circumstances it has been decided to consider purchasing supplies of one component part from outside suppliers and quotations have been received as follows:

Part	Each £
A	34
B	44
C	52

The sales manager feels that the minimum increase on existing sales and production that should be considered is 50 per cent and that he could sell up to an increase of 80 per cent provided the factory capacity is available.

You are required to prepare a report for management giving your recommendations as to which component part should be ordered from outside suppliers for the coming year if production is increased by 50 per cent and also if full factory capacity is utilised.

Source: CIMA

Solution
Since one component of A, B and C is required for each product capacity requirements must be in proportion of:

5:8:10 – First constraint

Existing capacity although not stated must be a multiple of:

5 + 8 + 10 = 23 – Second constraint

First option – Buy A:

We would then require 8 machine hours for component B and 10 machine hours for component C for every completed product. If we increased output by 50% this would be equivalent to 150% of A and 150% of B = (150% × 8) + (150% × 10) = 27 *but* total available is a function of 23. Since 27 is greater than 23 this solution is not practical therefore buy B or C.

Second option – Buy B:

This will save 8 hours per unit of complete product. Increasing output by 50% we would require proportionally 150% × A + 150% × C = (150% × 5) + (150% × 10) = 22.5. This is *less* than the total of 23 and therefore acceptable in terms of capacity. Existing contribution per *unit* = selling price − variable cost = £250 − £134 = £116. If we buy out B for £44 instead of producing it at a variable cost of £30 this will reduce contribution by £(44 − 30) = £14 therefore new contribution per unit of *product* = £116 − 14 = £102 but since we are increasing output by 50% contribution per unit of capacity will be $\frac{150\%}{100} \times 102 = £153$. Since 22.5 is almost equal to maximum of 23 we could only increase output by just over 50%.

Third option – Buy C:

This will save 10 hours per unit. Increasing output by 50% we shall require 7.5 for A and 12 for B = 19.5. 19.5 is less than 23 therefore we have capacity:

	£
Existing contribution	116
If we buy C at £52 instead of producing at £30 this will be reduced by	22
∴ new contribution per *product* is	94

but contribution per unit of capacity is $£94 \times \frac{150}{100} = £141$. This compares with a contribution per unit of capacity of £153 if we opt for B, therefore at 50% increase it is preferable to buy B. If full capacity is utilized we have a multiple of 23 hours available and for existing production of A and B we require a multiple of (8 + 5) = 13 hours. Maximum increase would be restricted to $\frac{23 - 13}{13} \simeq 77\%$. At this level the contribution per unit of capacity would be $94 \times \frac{177}{100} \simeq £166$ which is in excess of that achieved previously and it would therefore be preferable to buy C.

Summary

1   It is not practicable to buy out A by reason of production constraint.
2   It is preferable to buy B at a 50 per cent increase since the contribution in unit of capacity is higher than C.
3   The maximum possible increase in production is 77 per cent which is attainable by buying C outside. This gives a comparable unit contribution of £166 and is thus preferable at the higher level of production.

Pricing policies

If a company has temporary surplus capacity it may be prepared to use cost-based techniques to determine special prices for non-regular markets. It may be the opportunity to enter an export market or selling a non-competing segment of the existing one. The general rule is that all products must recover their variable costs. Above this, all contribution will increase total profits if the company is operating above break even or reduce losses if operating below break even.

Exercise 12.3

The capacity to produce a manufacturing unit is 15,000 units per annum. At present 10,000 units are being produced and sold at £20 each. Existing variable costs are £12.00 per unit and the company has received an invitation to supply 2000 items for export at a price of £15.00 each. Fixed costs are £60,000 per annum.

1   Should the firm accept the order?
2   Assuming a special finish was required for the export order which would involve hiring special spraying equipment for the duration of the order at a fixed rental of £5,000 and operating costs of £2.00 per unit what would be the minimum price the company could quote to avoid making a loss and what price would it have to quote to achieve the same profit as in Part 1?

Solution

1   The existing fixed costs of £60,000 per annum are irrelevant to the decision. Each item exported would provide a contribution of £15.00 less £12.00 which is £3 per unit. Contribution and profit would increase by £6,000.
2   The existing variable costs are £12.00 per unit which would increase to £14.00 to recover the increased finishing costs. The £5,000 rental would not be incurred if the order was not undertaken. This must be recovered exclusively on the export order and is equivalent to a $\frac{£5,000}{2,000} = £2.50$ increase in price. The minimum price is therefore £14.00 + £2.50 = £16.50. In Part 1 a profit of £6,000 has been made. To equal this the export order must contribute $\frac{6,000}{2,000} = £3.00$ per unit above the cost of £16.50 so the price must be £19.50. This can be checked by considering the figures relevant to the export order only:

	Unit	Total
		(for 2,000 units)
	£	£
Existing variable costs	12.00	24,000
Additional variable costs	2.00	4,000
Additional fixed costs (rent)	2.50	5,000
Required profit	3.00	6,000
Sales	19.50	39,000

Unprofitable products or departments

Quite frequently, as was illustrated in the section on overheads, it has been shown how fixed or period costs have been allocated over different products, cost centres or departments in a store on various arbitrary bases. This is legitimate when the objective is absorption costing or trying to indicate to a particular manager what proportion of a company's resources he is using but could be misleading for decision making.

Exercise 12.4

The Brierly company produces and sells three products, the results of which for a year's activities are as follows:

	Product X £	Product Y £	Product Z £
Sales	37,500	15,000	22,500
Variable cost	33,750	3,750	18,000
Contribution	3,750	11,250	4,500
Fixed cost	11,250	4,500	6,750
Profit/(loss)	(7,500)	6,750	(2,250)

The general manager suggests that on this basis the manufacture and sale of both Product X and Product Y should be discontinued as they are making losses. Would you agree with this statement if you were aware that the fixed costs in total were unavoidable and that they had been allocated on the basis of sales?

Solution

The total fixed costs are £22,500 (£11,250 + £4,500 + £6,750) and since unavoidable are irrelevant. The contribution at present is:

		£
£3,750 + £11,250 + £4,500	=	19,500
Fixed costs		22,500
Net loss		3,000

This agrees with the question above

	£
Loss on Product X	7,500
Loss on Product Z	2,250
	9,750
Profit on Product Y	6,750
Net loss	3,000

If the sales of X and Z are discontinued the position is:

	£
Sales (of Y)	15,000
Less Variable cost	3,750
Contribution	11,250
Less Fixed cost	22,500
Loss	11,250

The loss has increased by £8,250 to £11,250. This is equal to the lost contribution from Product X (3,750) plus the contribution lost from Product Z (£4,500). Product Y has a very high P/V ratio – $\frac{11,250}{15,000} \times 100$ equal to 75 per cent of sales while Product X is 10 per cent and Z is 20 per cent only. However, they are still making a positive contribution and the situation would only be worsened if their sales were discontinued.

12.2 Incremental, differential and opportunity costs

Incremental costs

The concept of marginal cost was borrowed from economists and adapted for business purposes by accountants. There is a similar history to the adaptation of techniques dealing with the notion of incremental costing. The term is defined by the CIMA as: 'A technique used in preparation of ad hoc information where consideration is given to a range of graduated or stepped changes in the level or nature of activity and the additional costs and revenues likely to result from each degree of change are presented.' Each increment represents the additional cost (and sometimes revenue) associated with specific volume changes or other conditions. Whereas, technically, marginal cost relates to one unit, incremental cost represents usually 'step' changes and includes associated increases in the fixed and variable costs.

Exercise 12.5

Demand for the output of a certain company is very elastic, and modern plant recently installed is capable of greatly increased production. Output at present is 80,000 units per year, and half a million units annually are estimated to be within the capacity of the new plant.

The present selling price per unit is £15.

The need for flexible budgeting is recognized and six alternative levels of output in addition to the present level are contemplated. Six equal increments in annual output level, up to a maximum of 500,000 units, would involve corresponding reductions of £1 each in unit price to £9 per unit at the maximum output.

The present variable costs amount to £400,000. Fixed costs which at present amount to £200,000 are not expected to increase for any of the six alternative output levels contemplated. Semi-fixed costs are expected to vary from the present annual figure of £230,000 to £320,000, the upward steps being to £260,000 at 220,000 units, £280,000 at 360,000 units, and £320,000 at 500,000 units. The costs classified as variable at the six projected levels of output are calculated to be as follows:

£750,000; £1,100,000; £1,500,000; £1,750,000; £2,050,000; £2,500,000

(a)   Tabulate the above data and show (i) total costs, (ii) incremental costs, (iii) total and incremental sales income at the various output levels.
(b)   Which volume should be set for budgeted output?
(c)   What is the selling price at that volume?

Source: CIMA

Solution

Statement showing incremental costs and revenues

1 Output (000s units)	80	150	220	290	360	430	500
2 Selling price/unit	£15	£14	£13	£12	£11	£10	£9
	£000	£000	£000	£000	£000	£000	£000
3 Total sales	1,200	2,100	2,860	3,480	3,960	4,300	4,500
4 Incremental sales income		900	760	620	480	340	200
5 Total variable cost	400	750	1,100	1,500	1,750	2,050	2,500
6 Incremental variable cost		350	350	400	250	300	450
7 Total semi-fixed	230	230	260	260	280	280	320
8 Incremental semi-fixed		Nil	30	Nil	20	Nil	40
9 Fixed costs	200	200	200	200	200	200	200
10 Total costs = (5) + (7) + (9)	830	1,180	1,560	1,960	2,230	2,530	3,020
11 Incremental costs = (6) + (8)		350	380	400	270	300	490
12 Incremental contribution = (4) − (11)		550	380	220	210	40	(290)

The volume at which the budgeted output should be set is 430,000 units, since at 500,000 units the incremental costs of £490,000 exceed the incremental sales of £200,000 by £290,000 and this would reduce *total* profit by the amount achieved at 439,000 units. Line 6 shows that equal increments of output are not accompanied by equal increments of costs i.e. variable costs are not directly variable.

The selling price per unit would be £10.

Differential costs

Differential costing has been defined by the CIMA as: 'A technique used in the preparation of ad hoc information in which only cost and income differences between alternative courses of action are taken into consideration.'

It would appear that from this view the only difference between incremental and differential costing is that the former presents the results of a range of movements whereas the latter is usually confined to changes between any two courses of action. The term differential cost is frequently used interchangeably with incremental cost and it does not matter which term is used providing the cost objective is kept, and made clear. Any cost or revenue which increases or decreases as a result of the decision taken or proposed is a differential or incremental cost to that decision i.e. they are the only relevant costs.

Exercise 12.6

The output of a mechanical operation is three tonnes per hour, saleable at £20 per tonne. Raw material costs £6 per tonne of product and operating wages, including payment for idle time amount to £700 per week. The normal working week is forty hours but, on average, ten hours per week are lost through mechanical breakdowns and sales are consequently being lost. Repairs to the plant are costing £400 per week.

Consideration is being given to the introduction of routine preventative maintenance to be carried out outside normal working hours and there are three alternatives.

1   A maintenance team to work on Saturdays at a weekly cost of £100 (this would be expected to halve the breakdown time and the repair cost).
2   A maintenance team to work on night shift at a weekly cost of £360 (this would be expected to save three-quarters of the present breakdown time and the repair cost).
3   To continue as at present.

You are required to prepare a statement indicating the best course of action.

Source: LCCI

Solution

A standard procedure for this type of problem is

1   Identify the alternative courses of action.
2   Estimate which (relevant) costs and revenues are affected.
3   Compare and select the most favourable alternative.

It may be easier to consider the present situation first (alternative 3) as a starting point.

Present arrangement:

Production hours = 40 less 10 = 30 per week
Output per week = 3 × 30 = 90 tonnes

			£
Sales	90 tonnes @ £20 tonne =		1,800
Less Costs:	Material 90 × 6 =	540	
	Wages	700	
	Repairs	400	
		——	1,640
Profit			160

Choice 1:

Differential costs	£	£
Change in revenue		
Savings in Repairs $\left(\frac{£400}{2}\right)$	200	
Additional Sales		
(5 hours × 3 tonnes @ £20)	300	
		500
Change in costs		
Material 15 tonnes @ £6	90	
Maintenance	100	
		190
Differential gain/(loss)		310

Choice 2:

Differential costs	£	£
Changes in revenue		
Savings in repairs (¾ × 400)	300	
Additional sales		
(7.5 hours × 3 tonnes × £20)	450	
		750
Change in costs		
Material 22.5 tonnes × £6	135	
Maintenance	360	
		495
Net gain/loss		255

Alternative 1 is preferable as the existing profit of £160 will be increased by £310 to £470.

A strict differential approach would be to examine the difference between 1 and 2 only.

	Action 1	Action 2	Differential cost
	£	£	£
Gain on repair costs	200	300	+ 100
Contribution (£14/tonne)	210	315	+ 105
	410	615	205
Cost of maintenance	100	360	− 260
	310	255	− 55

Action 2 produces a loss of £55 compared with 1 therefore 1 is more favourable.

Opportunity costs

Marginal costing, differential and incremental costing all examine the effect of changes in actual costs and revenues incurred or forecast as a result of alternative actions. Opportunity cost, similarly, is concerned with choosing between alternatives but the concept is unique to accounting in that it measures the extent of sacrifice made, when a course of action is chosen. It would not appear in the books and this sometimes creates difficulty in appreciation by accountants. Opportunity cost is the **benefit which could be obtained by pursuing an alternative course of action**. It is usually measured by way of the profit foregone (or least loss incurred) under the best available alternative. Suppose cost studies have shown that the results of three alternative trading policies would be an increase in profit of £5,000, £8,000 and £2,000. If we choose the first policy the opportunity cost would be £3,000. This is the profit foregone (£8,000 − £5,000) by choosing a policy which by comparison with the best available alternative would result in reduction in profit of £3,000. Similarly, if a person is offered a job abroad for £20,000 per annum and their present salary is £15,000 per annum should he choose for personal reasons to remain in his own country the opportunity cost of that choice is £5,000 per annum – the increased income foregone.

Exercise 12.7

A company has in stock 100 refrigerators which cost £4,000 to produce and which could be sold for scrap for £1,500. They have been damaged in storage and would require an additional £3,000 to put in saleable condition. They could then be sold at the same price as current sales and realize £5,000. To repair the refrigerators would, however, require the use of production facilities which would otherwise be engaged producing new refrigerators earning profits of £2,000. The alternatives are:

1   Sell for scrap value of £1,500.

	£
2 Rectify and sell	
Cost	3,000
Realizable value	5,000
	———
Net gain	£2,000

The opportunity cost of choosing 1 would be £500 profit foregone (£2,000 − £1,500).

3   Produce new refrigerators – if we chose 3 we gain the profit on new manufacture of £2,000. This is better than the previous choice as the scrap income will still be available. It must be reiterated that sunk costs – in this case the original costs of £4,000 to produce are irrelevant.

12.3   Investment appraisal: Payback and return on capital employed

Investment appraisal is providing information upon which long-term management decisions are made in respect of capital items. Most problems are marginal in the sense that we have to consider the effect on an existing structure of purchasing additional assets and finding the means of financing the purchase. This does not necessarily mean that the sums of money involved are small. We may at one end of the scale, be contemplating buying another factory and at the other replacing one of the company's cars. Ideally, each decision to invest or otherwise should be based on knowledge of what the future economic and political situation will be. These factors are inevitably unknown and the decision is made as much on a subjective basis as an objective one i.e. personal opinion as to future outcomes of every factor, in addition to the financial one. On the matter of finance, however, the manager relies heavily upon data provided by the accountant and he, in turn, should ensure the forecasts are as accurate as possible.

The financial factors which influence every investment decision are:

● The cost of the project.
● The source of funds for the project.
● The timing of the cash flows.
● The certainty of future cash flows.
● The existence of alternative opportunities for investment.
● Taxation and government policies.

Once this data has been gathered the methods available to assess the relative profitability of projects can be grouped into three major sections.

1   Techniques which evaluate the proceeds but ignore the timing of the proceeds and risk – these include **payback period** and the various accounting measures of **ROCE (return on capital employed)**.
2   Techniques which evaluate the timing of the proceeds but ignore the risk – these include the various discounted cash flow methods, in particular **NPV (net present value)** and **IRR (internal rate of return)**.
3   Techniques which are used to compel some quantitative assessment to be given to the risk associated with the project.

Exercise 12.8

The Alpha manufacturing plc is considering its capital investment programme. Table 12.1 indicates the net cash flow per year associated with five mutually exclusive projects each having the same capital cost of £20,000. (Mutually exclusive implies that only one project is possible and the choice eliminates the remainder.)

Table 12.1

Project	Capital cost £	Net cash flow (before depreciation)		
		Year 1 £	Year 2 £	Year 3 £
A	20,000	20,000	–	–
B	20,000	10,000	10,000	10,000
C	20,000	3,000	9,000	12,000
D	20,000	12,000	16,000	10,000
E	20,000	16,000	16,000	

Evaluate the ranking of the alternatives using the techniques described above. Note that net cash flow is profit with any provision for depreciation *added back*.

The payback period
This defined as the length of time required for the stream of cash flows produced by an investment to equal the original cash outlay required by the investment. Under this method the shorter the payback period, the more desirable the investment is said to be.

Workings
Project A: This produces a return of £20,000 after one year and this is the cost of the project. Payback period is one year.
Project B: This produces £10,000 per year so it will take two years to pay off the cost.
Project C: By the end of Year 2 proceeds are £3,000 + £9,000 = £12,000. This leaves £8,000 to make up the £20,000 and assuming an even cash flow per month in the third year it will take $\frac{8,000}{12,000} = \frac{2}{3}$ so the payback period is 2.66 years.
Project D: In Year 1 £12,000 is recovered. The annual inflow in Year 2 is £16,000 of which £8,000 is required which will take six months. Payback period is therefore 1.5 years.
Project E: Payback will be 1.25 years.
The ranking of the alternative projects is shown in Table 12.2.

Table 12.2

Project	Payback period (years)	Rank
A	1.0	1
B	2.0	4
C	2.66	5
D	1.5	3
E	1.25	2

The method is popular with managers because of its simplicity and emphasis on shorter repayment periods, providing opportunity for reinvestment at earlier dates. This is in spite of serious disadvantages which include:

1 Income arising after the payback period is ignored.
2 It is biased towards investments with high cash flows in the earlier years.
3 The method ignores the timing of the cash flow from the point of view of cost of funds.

Return on capital employed (ROCE)

Sometimes referred to as **Average rate of return** these rates may be computed gross or net.

Average* gross *annual rate of return

This is defined as the average proceeds per year over the whole of the life of the asset expressed as a percentage of the original capital cost. Under this method the higher the return the more desirable the investment is said to be. Using the data from Exercise 12.8 we can produce Table 12.3.

Project A: Cost £20,000, total income £20,000, life one year.

Annual average proceeds $= \dfrac{£20,000}{1} = £20,000$

% return $\qquad = \dfrac{£20,000}{£20,000} \times 100 = 100\%$

Project B: Cost £20,000, total income £30,000, life three years.

Annual average proceeds $= \dfrac{£30,000}{3} = £10,000$

% return $\qquad = \dfrac{£10,000}{£20,000} \times 100 = 50\%$

Table 12.3

Project	Capital cost	Cash flow (before depreciation)		Gross income % of capital cost	Rank
		Total	Average		
	£	£	£	£	
A	20,000	20,000	20,000	100	1
B	20,000	30,000	10,000	50	4
C	20,000	24,000	8,000	40	5
D	20,000	38,000	12,666	63.3	3
E	20,000	32,000	16,000	80	2

The advantages claimed for this (and other) average methods are:

1 They are easy to compute and for management to understand.
2 They emphasize profitability since – unlike the payback method – proceeds over the entire life of the asset are taken into account.
3 The concept of return on capital employed which the method uses is familiar to accountants and managers providing a yardstick for comparison which uses familiar notions of profit, cash flow and asset cost as a basis.

The disadvantages include the fact that the average methods smooth out the effects of irregularities in the cash flow and suggest that an investment which produces a cash flow which is built up gradually is just as preferable as one with large cash flows in the early years.

Consider the situation shown in Table 12.4.

Table 12.4

Project	Capital cost	Cash proceeds before depreciation			Total
		Year 1 £	Year 2 £	Year 3 £	£
X	10,000	3,000	5,000	7,000	15,000
Y	10,000	7,000	5,000	3,000	15,000

In both cases the average cash flow is $\frac{15,000}{3}$ which equals £5,000 per annum and the return will be $\frac{5,000}{10,000} \times 100 = 50$ per cent. However, inspection of Table 12.4 shows that Project Y has an income of £7,000 in Year 1 which can be reinvested, compared with only £3,000 from Project X. This ignoring of the timing of the cash flows can lead to errors of judgement because the greater the cash flow in the earlier years the quicker the payback, thus releasing money for reinvestment or reducing cost of borrowing and lowering risk of failure.

A further disadvantage is that once averaged, no indication is given of the time span of the ROCE and thus a return of 20 per cent per annum for one year would be equated with the same return for any number of years from an alternative.

Average net *annual rate of return*

This is defined as the average annual proceeds per year – after allowing for depreciation – over the whole of the life of the asset expressed as a percentage of the original capital cost. As above the higher the rate of return the more desirable the investment is said to be. In using this method depreciation is normally computed on the **straight line** basis i.e. charged in equal annual parts. Using the data from Exercise 12.8 Project A has a life of only one year therefore depreciation is £20,000 per annum. Projects B, C and D all have life of of three years therefore depreciation per annum is $\frac{£20,000}{3} = £6,666$ and Project E has a life of two years giving annual depreciation of £10,000. Procedure for computing averages is, thereafter, the same as for the average gross annual rate of return.

Table 12.5

Project	Capital cost £	Depreci- ation per annum £	Average cash flow per annum		Net income % of capital cost	Rank
			before depreciation £	after depreciation £		
A	20,000	20,000	20,000	NIL	–	5
B	20,000	6,666	10,000	3,334	16.6	3
C	20,000	6,666	8,000	1,334	6.6	4
D	20,000	6,666	12,666	6,000	30.0	1
E	20,000	10,000	16,000	6,000	30.0	1

In the case of the net method the disadvantage of averaging is heightened by the fact that the adjustment in respect of depreciation – when the straight line method is used – results in a fixed amount being charged each year against varying annual incomes and this exaggerates the distortion. Second, depreciation is both a policy and a non-cash charge and results in a contradiction of terms. The deduction of depreciation does not reduce the cash flow (unless immediately invested in an investment fund) and is thus a profit return rather than cash assessment. Arguments are advanced to use the average cost of the asset as the divisor when using this ratio on the grounds that reinvestment of the depreciation provision makes the asset self liquidating. It should be indicated when comparing investments on this basis which is the relevant capital cost being used – the total cost of the investment or the average capital employed over the life of the asset.

The advantages are familiarity to management and simplicity in computation. It demonstrates the rate of 'net' gain to the company i.e. after maintaining capital intact in terms of original cost. In this respect it tends to agree with the general notion of 'profit' and so finds general acceptance.

There are ways in which the above techniques – payback and ROCE – can be adapted to situations where capital costs are not the same or other complications are present. Such techniques are described in general texts on financial management.

12.4   Investment appraisal: discounted cash flow

A major disadvantage of the payback and return on investment methods is that they presuppose that money received at some future date is worth as much as money received now. This is a questionable concept for decision making as it is intuitively recognized that time is money. This is not due in this instance to the probable decline in the value of money in real terms i.e. inflation but simply to the fact that money – like all commodities – has a cost for its use. That cost is alternatively described as interest, dividends, profit etc. We have seen that opportunity cost measures the gain or loss due to an alternative course of action. If one chooses to keep savings of £100 under the bed rather than put them into a bank paying 10 per cent per annum the loss in interest is £10 per year. Similarly if excessive stocks are kept in the warehouse financed by a loan from the bank the cost of such holding is the amount paid in interest. From 1950 onwards, because of the large-scale financial resources required, the study of investment opportunity techniques intensified – particularly those developed from the familiar notion of compound interest.

If an investment such as a debenture is offering 10 per cent per annum then the value of every £1 invested will rise by the end of one year to £1.10. If the loan and interest is left to accumulate then the value at the end of the second year would be £1.10 plus 10% (£1.10) = £1.21. By the end of the third year the total sum accumulated would be £1.21 + 10% (£1.21) = £1.331. This is the notion of compound interest and can be generalized in the formula:

$$S_n = P(1 + r)^n$$

where S_n = Sum at the end of stated number of years (n)
      P = Original sum invested
      r = Rate of interest – as a decimal
      n = Number of years invested.

In the above example P = £1.0, r = 0.10 and n = 3, therefore:

$$S_n = 1 (1 + 0.3)^3$$
$$= 1 \times 1.331 = £1.331$$

In order to work out any sum, if we have access to tables giving the value for the expression $(1 + r)^n$ then we only need to multiply this factor by P – that is the original investment. Reference to the tables on page 564 will confirm that when interest rate (i) is 10 per cent and number of years (n) is 3 $(1 + r)^n$ is equal to 1.331. If one invested £200 then the value of P would be $(200 \times 1.331) = £266.2$.

Discounted cash flow

For some purposes such as forecasting the value of our savings at the end of some future number of years, or the value at the end of a period of a debenture investment fund, we need the compound interest tables. For most investment decisions, however, we wish to know if it is worth spending money on the project in the first place. Most proceeds from business investment arise over future periods of time – we have to wait for profits to turn into cash flows inwards. This means determination of whether the value of the future proceeds is worth more than its present cost. To repeat – this is not due simply to the erosion of inflation but the **time value of money as a commodity**.

If we have £1.00 available to invest and the opportunity to invest it at 10 per cent per annum then there are two options open to us – either to retain the £1.00 or invest it. Ignoring, for the present, the possibilities of risk and the effect of taxation, at the end of one year, if invested, the £1.00 would have increased to £1.10. That is the present value of £1.10 received in one year's time with interest rate of 10 per cent is the original £1.00. Every pound received in one year's time must therefore be worth $\dfrac{£1.00}{£1.10} = 0.9091$ or the present value of £1.00 for one year at 10 per cent is £0.9091 (to four decimal places).

This procedure of finding the present worth of future cash flows is termed **discounting** and is the basis of investment appraised methods termed **discounted cash flow (DCF)**. A check can be made on the above factor of £0.9091 by considering what happens if this sum is invested for one year at 10 per cent. The sum receivable at the end of the year would be equal to £0.9091 plus 10 per cent (£0.9091) = 0.9091 + 0.09091 = £1.00 (to four decimal places).

The present value of £1 receivable in two years' time can be similarly computed. The compound interest computation above showed the future value of £1.00 invested for two years at 10 per cent to be £1.21. If this is so the present value of each pound invested must be $\dfrac{1}{1.21} = £0.8264$.

It will be seen that in both the one and two year period the discounted figure is obtained by dividing into unity the figure previously computed for compound interest and this is true for the general case i.e. the value of £1.00 receivable in 'n' years' time at an interest rate of 'r' is the reciprocal of the compound interest figure for a similar period. This means that provided we have the compound interest tables available we can obtain the equivalent DCF figure by dividing this factor into unity. Most reference books contain both sets of tables for convenience but it is useful to realize that one can easily be derived from the other. If the compound interest table represents computations of the formalized expression $(1 + r)^n$ then the discounted cash flow represents the reciprocal of all these values i.e. the formalized expression $\dfrac{1}{(1 + r)^n}$ sometimes expressed as $(1 + r)^{-n}$. See tables on pages 564–9.

Use of the discounted cash flow techniques

There are a variety of methods which use DCF techniques for investment appraisal but they divide broadly into two groups.

1 Methods used when the cost of obtaining finance for a project is known and/or a minimum rate of return is given, usually referred to as the net present value method.
2 Methods used when alternative projects are competing for limited funds available for investment and it is desired to invest in that project which provides the highest rate of return usually referred to as the internal rate of return (or marginal efficiency of capital) method.

Net present value (NPV) method

Under this method a suitable discount rate is selected and the earnings forecast in any year are reduced to present value by applying the appropriate factor. These are aggregated and the cost of the project deducted from the total. Choice is then made on the basis of the highest net present value. Should the answer be minus this implies that one would be better off not investing at all so these projects could be rejected.

Consider now the projects referred to in Exercise 12.8 with the additional information that the cost of capital is expected to be 10 per cent per annum, then in respect of the first two investments we have:

	Year	Project A			Project B		
		Gross cash flow £	Discount factor	Present value £	Gross cash flow £	Discount factor	Present value £
	1	20,000	0.9091	18,182	10,000	0.9091	9,091
	2	–		–	10,000	0.8264	8,264
	3	–		–	10,000	0.7513	7,513
Gross present value				18,182			24,868
Less Cost				20,000			20,000
Net present value				−1,818			+4,868

Project A produces a negative net present value of £1,818 and should therefore be rejected. The reasoning behind this is that if I borrow £20,000 now at a cost of 10 per cent per annum in order to invest in a project which at the end of the year will result in an income of only £20,000 I will be out of pocket by the interest cost on the overdraft i.e. £2,000. Alternatively stated if every £0.9091 invested now at the start of the year is equivalent to £1.00 in a year's time, I need only invest (20,000 × 0.9091) = £18,182 now to accumulate £20,000 by the end of the year. This being so there is no merit in investing in Project A. On the other hand Project B has a positive net present value of £4,868.

The result of calculations for the remaining investments are as follows:

	Year	Factor	Project C		Project D		Project E	
			Cash flow £	NPV £	Cash flow £	NPV £	Cash flow £	NPV £
	1	0.9091	3,000	2,727	12,000	10,909	16,000	14,546
	2	0.8264	9,000	7,438	16,000	13,222	16,000	13,222
	3	0.7513	12,000	9,016	10,000	7,513		
Gross present value				19,181		31,644		27,768
Less Cost				20,000		20,000		20,000
Net present value				−819		+11,644		+7,768

These results can be summarized in ranking order as shown in Table 12.6.

Table 12.6

Project	Net present value £	Rank
A	−£1,818	5
B	+£4,868	3
C	−£819	4
D	+£11,644	1
E	+£7,768	2

In cases where the capital cost of the alternatives is not the same the NPV should be converted to an index by relating it to the original sum invested. Suppose the cost of Project B could be reduced by £5,000, the gross present value of the proceeds remaining unaltered then comparing Project B (as revised) with Project D (as existing).

Project B NPV = £24,868 − £15,000 = £9,868

$$\text{NPV index} = \frac{9,868}{15,000} = 0.658$$

Project D

$$\text{NPV index} = \frac{11,644}{20,000} = 0.582$$

Comparing the net present value, Project D is still higher at £11,644 than the revised Project B at £9,868. However, to produce a surplus of £9,868 only £15,000 has been invested i.e. each £1.00 has earned a surplus of 0.658 compared with £0.582 for Project D. On this basis the ranking would be reversed.

Equal annual cash flows

In Table 12.1 (see page 382) we can see that the income for Project B is the same for each year of its life and similarly for Project E. This is termed **equal annual cash flow** or an **annuity basis**. The income in respect of each period is constant and we can get the answer by multiplying the sum once only by the cumulative values of £1.00 received at the end of the year. i.e. £10,000 × (0.9091 + 0.8264 + 0.7513) = £10,000 × 2.4868 = £24,868. The figure agrees with the gross NPV previously computed and less the original cost of £20,000 gives the NPV of £4,868. Figures for annuity calculations are common to a variety of tasks in banking, insurance and other activities and tables exist which make it unnecessary to add single year factors together.

Internal rate of return

This method has a variety of alternative names, the most likely being **marginal efficiency of capital**. It is based on an economics approach and is used when the cost of providing capital is unknown, or, particularly when finance available is restricted, to indicate the most profitable alternative.

We must have available:

1   The initial cost of the project.
2   The value of future cash flows in each period.
3   The total life of the project.
4   Tables of DCF for reference.

The objective is to determine the rate of interest which equates the present value of future cash flows with the capital cost of the project. The preference will be for the project producing the higher rate of return. Computation under this method is more difficult than with the NPV method as with no rate given progress may have to be made on a trial and error basis.

Method of calculation (using data for Project C in Table 12.8)

Capital cost   £20,000
Cash flows   Year 1 £3,000, Year 2 £9,000, Year 3 £12,000

Assuming rates of 7 per cent, 8 per cent and 9 per cent alternatively and proceeding to calculate NPV as previously we get:

Year	Cash inflow £	7% Factor	7% Present value £	8% Factor	8% Present value £	9% Factor	9% Present value £
1	3,000	0.9346	2,803.8	0.9259	2,777.7	0.9174	2,752.2
2	9,000	0.8734	7,860.6	0.8573	7,715.7	0.8417	7,575.3
3	12,000	0.8163	9,795.6	0.7938	9,525.6	0.7722	9,266.4
			20,460		20,019		19,593.9

The above computations indicate that the present value of the cash flows at 7 per cent is £20,460 and at 8 per cent £20,019. Both these are higher than £20,000 so it is necessary to continue up the table and try 9 per cent. This produces an aggregate of £19,755.9 which is less than £20,000. The absolute rate therefore lies between 8 per cent and 9 per cent. For all practical purposes 8 per cent would be accepted since a difference of £19 in excess of £20,000 would be insignificant. Should it be necessary to adjust for the difference it can be approximated by linear interpolation.

$$£$$
Present value at 8% = 20,019
Present value at 9% = 19,594

Difference   425

The difference of £425 represents 1 per cent.

The figure required is $(20,019 - 20,000) = \frac{19}{425} \times 1$

more than the 8% rate (or $\frac{406}{425} \times 1$ less than the 9% rate)

$\frac{19}{425} \times 1 = 0.045$

∴ actual rate = 8.045%

Such computation would be regarded as spurious accuracy in practice but the interpolation technique is useful when tables, for instance, are in intervals greater than 1 per cent. Assuming that only 5 and 10 per cent tables were available then we would have:

$$£$$
Present value at 5 per cent per annum = 21,386
Present value at 10 per cent per annum = 19,181

Difference   2,205

Present value at 5 per cent   = 21,386
Capital cost   20,000

                              1,386

The difference of £1,386 is equivalent to an increase of $\frac{£1,386}{£2,205} \times 5 = 3.14$ above the 5 per cent rate i.e. 8.14 per cent.

This is slightly different to the 8.045 per cent calculated when figures are computed in 1 per cent increments. This is because the function is not a linear one but a curve. The difference is not significant in the above case and in others it would depend on the size of the figures required.

The computations can be repeated on a trial and error basis when the following should be the results of the alternative projects in Exercise 12.8.

Project A:
There is no rate of interest which will enable the same sum received in one year's time to equal the present cost – the rate of interest is in effect negative so this would be the least favourable choice.

Project B:
This is an annuity of £10,000 per year for three years.

£10,000 × a_n for three years must equal £20,000

$$\therefore a_n = \frac{20,000}{10,000} = 2.0$$

From inspection we can see that the interest rate which is nearest to 2.0 for value a_n when n = 3 is 23 per cent.
When the value of the annuity is £2.0114.
£10,000 × 2.0114 is £20,114 – slightly above £20,000.

Project C – already illustrated

Project D

Year	Cash inflow £	Factor	Present value £	Factor	Present value £
		40%		45%	
1	12,000	0.7143	8,572	0.6897	8,276
2	16,000	0.5102	8,163	0.4756	7,610
3	10,000	0.3644	3,644	0.3281	3,281
			20,379		19,167

Present value at 40% p.a. = 20,379
Present value at 45% p.a. = 19,167

Difference   1,212

The difference of 1,212 is equivalent to an increase of (20,379 − 20,000) = $\frac{379}{1212} \times 5\% = 1.56$ above 40% = 41.56%.

Project E:
This is an annuity situation again but for two years only

£16,000 × a_n for two years must equal £20,000

$$\therefore a_n = \frac{20,000}{16,000} = 1.25$$

From inspection we see that the interest rate which is nearest to 1.25 for value a_n when n = 2.0 is 38%
when a_n = 1.2497 (1.25 to two decimal places)

The ranking is shown in Table 12.7.

Table 12.7

Project	Internal rate of return %	Rank
A	–	5
B	23.0	3
C	8.14	4
D	41.55	1
E	38.0	2

Summary

Table 12.8 shows the ranking of the projects in Exercise 12.8 by the alternative methods discussed in this section.

Table 12.8

		Method			
		Return on capital		DCF	
Project	Payback	Gross	Net	NPV	IRR
A	1	1	5	5	5
B	4	4	3	3	3
C	5	5	4	4	4
D	3	3	1	1	1
E	2	2	1	2	2

It can be seen from Table 12.8 that there is a great disparity between some methods and this is even more noticeable when more practical situations involving different capital costs, irregular lives, taxation and other factors are considered. One may well question the usefulness of any of the techniques.

The answer is that no single technique is best for all purposes. The examples and methods given above are based on the following assumptions.

- All costs and revenues are known with certainty.
- Costs are assumed to arise at the beginning of the period.
- Revenues are assumed to arise at the end of the period.
- No taxation benefits or losses apply.

The following section gives a brief indication of techniques used when one or more of the above conditions are relaxed.

12.5   Investment appraisal: Risk analysis and other factors

All decisions to invest involve anticipation of future conditions. Risk is defined by *The Concise Oxford Dictionary* as: 'Hazard, chance of bad consequences, loss, exposure to mischance.' While uncertainty is defined as: 'Not certainly knowing.' The more uncertain the future conditions, the greater the degree of risk attached to any investment. Gamblers are aware of this – the more likely a horse is to win the lower the odds. If everything about a future project – initial cost, future costs and incomes over a perfectly predicted life span – were known then there would be little, if any, risk in undertaking the project.

If people are asked to forecast information about the outcome of a particular course of action they are likely to qualify their opinion. Remarks such as 'If such and such happens then the outcome will be . . . but if this does not occur then the result might be . . .' and so on. This opinion reflects the degree of information available, the expertise of the individual and also – most important – the personality of the manager or other official concerned. The advice may be coloured by a personality band between the extremes of optimism and pessimism. The techniques which follow are mostly based on probability theory and attempt to evaluate in quantitative terms what is otherwise purely subjective i.e. a matter of opinion.

Most probable outcome

This suggests that the alternative which is chosen should be the one most likely to occur. If a six-sided die is thrown each outcome is equally likely and the probability of any particular number being turned up would be one in six of $\frac{1}{6}$. If the die were deliberately loaded, however, so that the probability of a two being thrown was twice that of any other number then the most probable outcome would be two. Advocates of this technique would always choose two.

Expected value

The term **expected value**, when used in the statistical sense, has a particular meaning. It is defined as: 'The sum of the values of possible outcomes, each outcome being weighted by the probability of its occurrence.' In the cases of throwing a die the possible numbers (results) are one to six inclusive. If the die is properly balanced each result has a probability (P) of 1/6. The expected value if the throws were repeated continuously would be:

Possible outcome ×	Probability (P) =	Expected value
6 ×	1/6 =	1.00
5 ×	1/6 =	0.83
4 ×	1/6 =	0.67
3 ×	1/6 =	0.50
2 ×	1/6 =	0.33
1 ×	1/6 =	0.17
Total	1.0	3.50

The expected value is a weighted average. This can be confirmed by contrasting the above result with the simple average which would be:

$$\frac{6+5+4+3+2+1}{6} = 3.50$$

In this case the result is the same but this is because each outcome was equally likely. If we take the previous situation where the die was loaded so that the probability of a two being thrown was twice that of any number then in a continuous series of throws there are seven possibilities – two with the same result i.e. 6,5,4,3,2,2,1. On two out of seven occasions the probable result is 2 and so the probability of this result is $\frac{2}{7}$ compared with $\frac{1}{7}$ for any of the alternatives and the expected value will be:

Possible outcome ×	Probability (P) =	Expected value
6 ×	1/7 =	0.88
5 ×	1/7 =	0.71
4 ×	1/7 =	0.57
3 ×	1/7 =	0.43
2 ×	2/7 =	0.57
1 ×	1/7 =	0.14
		3.30

This is less than the simple average of 3.50 because of the higher frequency of the lower score. If the die is biased to result in a six on twice as many occasions as any other number the expected value is 3.85.

When faced with evaluating alternatives executives may use such phrases as there is a 'good chance', 'reasonable chance', 'very little chance' and so on. Use of probability techniques requires that these opinions be evaluated on a scale between 0 (no possibility whatsoever) and 1.0 (absolute certainty). In application to investment decision the techniques are illustrated by Exercise 12.9.

Exercise 12.9

Beta Manufacturing Company has two alternative projects under consideration. The opinions of various executives in marketing, development and engineering etc. have been assessed and the following is the resultant data.

Life of project	Project A 3 years		Project B 3 years	
Cost of project	£9,000		£8,000	
	P	*£*	*P*	*£*
	0.05	3,000	0.10	3,000
Possible average	0.10	4,000	0.80	4,500
Annual cash flows	0.80	5,000	0.10	5,000
	0.05	6,000	–	–
	1.0		1.0	

Advise Beta Manufacturing as to which alternative would be the better choice using probability analysis.

Workings
Note that the cash flows are average annual cash flows i.e. in the case of Project A there is 0.05 probability that the annual income will be £3,000 per annum for three years. Note also that the probability has deliberately been expressed here as a decimal 0.05. It could have been expressed as in the die example as a fraction i.e. $\frac{1}{20}$. Alternatively it could be expressed as a percentage i.e. 5 per cent. All results would be the same. The main thing is that the total of all probabilities must equal 1.0 or 100 per cent.

Solution
1   *Using most probable outcome:*

	Project A	Project B
Most probable average annual cash flow	£5,000	£4,500
Life	3 years	3 years
∴ Total income	£15,000	£13,500
Capital cost	£9,400	£8,000
Surplus	£5,600	£5,500

∴ recommend A

2   *Using expected value:*

	Project A			Project B		
	(P)	*£*	*£*	*(P)*	*£*	*£*
Weighted possible outcomes	0.05 × 3,000 =		150	0.10 × 3,000 =		300
	0.10 × 4,000 =		400	0.80 × 4,500 =		3,600
	0.80 × 5,000 =		4,000	0.10 × 5,000 =		500
	0.05 × 6,000 =		300			
			4,850			4,400
Expected proceeds over 3 years	3 × 4,850 =		14,550	3 × 4,400 =		13,200
Capital cost			9,400			8,000
			5,150			5,200

These techniques can be combined with the discounting methods of the previous section. If it was known that the cost of financing was 10 per cent per annum then the timing of the proceeds may offset or emphasize particular probabilities.

The discount cash flow rate is 10 per cent. From Tables present value of £1.00 per annum for three years at 10% $(a_n) = 2.4869$

	Project A	*Project B*
Weighted average annual proceeds (from above)	£4,850	£4,400
Present value of £1 for 3 years @ 10%	2.4869	2.4869
	£	£
Gross present value	12,061	10,942
Capital cost	9,400	8,000
Net present value	2,661	2,942

Still recommend Project B as the difference in net present value is even greater than before discounting.

There are other techniques which are used when the probabilities of alternative outcomes are unpredicted. They involve mathematical solutions such as game theory, linear programming, mathematical programming, simulation studies and criteria of optimism developed by Hurwicz and Savage. The intention of this section was to make the reader aware of the nature and complexity of the main variables in the decision.

Other factors affecting the decision in practice

Most business investment decisions are much more complex than the simplified examples above. We assumed all alternative investments had the same cost and in most instances lives were the same. What is more likely is:

1 Projects will have different capital cost.
2 Projects will have different lives.
3 Residual values of plant will have to be considered.
4 A package of more than one investment is likely.
5 Some necessary projects will have a nil return e.g. money spent on welfare.

Taxation and grants

In addition to the factors mentioned, one worthy of considering separately is the effect of taxation. In most countries relief from taxation in respect of profits reinvested is given to a greater or lesser extent. The amount of relief varies with the state of the economy and the philosophies of the government of the day. In computations the timing has to be allowed for. In most cases relief on one year's profits will not be received until the following year. This will be reflected in the discounted figures since having to wait for the benefit reduces its value in present-day terms. More positive incentives come from grants which are direct injections of cash into the business by the authorities to promote investment and employment.

Part Five
Miscellaneous and
Contemporary Issues

The boundaries of the accounting function are always changing. While the nucleus of common knowledge required for preparation and interpretation of basic records remains constant, areas of emphasis and present concern reflect the circumstances of the day. In the 1960s and 1970s inflation was rife in the UK and the resultant deficiency of historical cost accounts was emphasized and criticized. Academic research was almost entirely directed to the problem. Now in the late 1980s interest has declined reflecting lower inflation rates. The issue is still fundamental however, and the major aspects are outlined in Chapter 13.

A second major area of importance is the development and application of accounting standards. Some authorities are now beginning to question the validity of these practices and the future will see increasing debate on their desirability and effectiveness. A complete volume would be required to endorse or refute the applicability of each particular standard but again it is desirable in a brief volume such as this that one is made familiar with what SSAPs are.

Finally, it is always desirable to contrast theory with practice and for this reason the accounts of the Transport Development Company have been reproduced. As more people invest in shares the published accounts of at least the recently privatized UK companies are delivered to more individuals. Unions are also interested in financial positions and the increasing practice of publishing simplified reports for employees shows the greater degree of communication effected.

13
Accounting for inflation

It would perhaps be better for this section to be entitled 'Accounting for changing price levels' since the validity of reported accounts is affected whether prices are rising – **inflation** – or falling – **deflation**. The effects of **rising** prices, however, are so much more of consequence to the preparers and users of financial and other accounts that the problem has been almost exclusively tackled from this point of view. Further, as a world phenomenon inflation is much more prevalent than the alternative so that more attention is bound to be given to the aspect of rising prices. The outward characteristic of inflation is a general increase in the price of goods and services, though not necessarily at the same rate. Fundamentally it is caused by an excessive increase in the amount of money in circulation relative to the goods or wealth created. Lack of control – by the government concerned – of the money supply, or an increase in borrowing, will increase potential purchasing power without a comparable increase in wealth produced. Too much money will chase too few goods and prices will rise.

Inflation has been recognized as a progressive phenomenon through the ages, with aggravated phases occurring in times of calamity, particularly wars. During wartime national output is concentrated upon production essentially for destruction. This is admirably illustrated in the graphical interpretation of price levels from 1661 to 1975 (in log scale to indicate **rate** of change) reproduced in Figure 13.1.

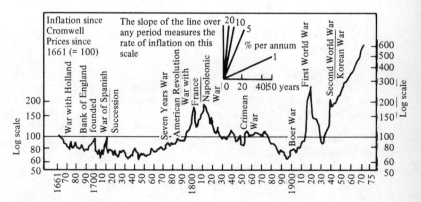

Figure 13.1 Getting inflation in perspective reproduced with permission of *News of the Week*

13.1   The impact of inflation upon a business

The main effects of inflation upon a business can briefly be described as distorting reported profit performance and capital valuation. The objective of all investors and entrepreneurs is to show **real**, not merely **monetary**, gains. These can only be measured if changes due to performance are distinguished from monetary or fiscal changes. If prices remain stable reported profit is **actual profit**. If prices are unstable the unit of measurement (money) is in itself changing and periodic comparisons are confused and unrealistic. Academics have long been aware of the difference between the economic concept of profit and that of the accountant. The CIMA researched the problem in 1949–50 and produced a basic work *The Accountancy of Changing Price Levels* in 1952. It may be useful to consider the problem briefly under three headings and then to consider the problem of communication and modification of financial statements.

Working capital

An early effect of inflation is to divert more cash into working capital in that increases in costs – stocks, labour and expenses – have to be met as incurred and before compensating increases in income are received. If there is strong market resistance to price increases by virtue of competition or government price control then the time span will be extended and the inflationary effect intensified. The longer the manufacturing cycle the more intense the situation. This may require action by management to reduce costs, improve productivity, maximize capacity utilization, tighten credit control and simplify products and processes. Failure to take action will result in liquidity problems and possible bankruptcy or liquidation.

Fixed assets

There are two main aspects to the problem. First that general increases in costs reduce the cash available for investment and second that the replacement cost of an asset will probably greatly exceed the purchase price of the original. In order to maintain its **capacity to produce** the business must find increasing amounts from a source upon which there is already pressure for extra working capital. The practical solution is adequacy of profit and depreciation, with the latter geared to replacement value instead of historic cost. This approach is not new and has been used for a long time by certain larger organizations such as Philips Industries. Providing higher depreciation does not ensure cash is available for replacement but does indicate more clearly real product prices and profits. A side benefit is that revaluation ensures management is more aware of the true net worth of the business at current prices.

Profits

Inflation increases costs and thus erodes profits. A relevant consideration is what it will buy at present prices – namely its purchasing power. A prerequisite for comparable judgement is to reduce the data to a common unit of purchasing power thus:

	Year 1	Year 2	Year 3
Index	100	120	135
Profit	£150,000	£160,000	£190,000
Adjustment	–	$160,000 \times \frac{100}{120}$	$190,000 \times \frac{100}{135}$
Profit (index adjusted)	£150,000	£133,333	£140,740

This demonstrates that contrary to monetary interpretation of profit in each year the profits in Years 2 and 3 were lower than Year 1 in terms of equivalent purchasing power although Year 3 showed some improvement over Year 2.

The effects of inflation upon a large international manufacturing company were well illustrated in a speech delivered in London by the Chairman of Unilever Ltd (now PLC) at the annual general meeting in May 1975. He pointed out that profit provides for:

1   The replacement and renewal of existing resources.
2   The financing of additional cost of stocks.
3   The payment for research which brings about technological change and improvements necessary to meet new environmental standards which society demands, at the same time bearing in mind that scientific discovery has usually to be incorporated into new physical assets in order to produce results.

In viewing the world situation he demonstrated the seriousness of decreasing investments in that in many major countries real profits have shown a continuous tendency to decline over the past decade or more. In the UK this decline was as much as 40 per cent and in the USA 19 per cent. Since capital employed increased considerably, yields on capital employed in industry went down much more; comparing the early 1950s with the early 1970s the net pre-tax profits on net assets in Swedish and British manufacturing virtually halved. Although not the only reason, inflation is adjudged to be the most important reason especially when accompanied by severe price control, and certainly the decline in corporate profitability has been most marked in recent years when world inflation has dramatically accelerated.

In this connection the chairman revealed that in Unilever Ltd the difference between historical cost depreciation and replacement cost depreciation was almost £30 million in 1974 and £50 million in 1975. Furthermore, the extra working capital to find out of profits was even more devastating. To do approximately the same amount of business at the end of 1974 as at the end of 1973 the company needed £289 million of extra working capital, three times the retained profits in sterling for the year.

If the business cannot find the funds then it contracts and unemployment results. To some extent it is possible to bridge the gap by borrowing providing the business is sound and has good prospects of profitable growth, but borrowing is a short term remedy only, not a permanent one. For a prudent management it has strict limits, particularly as interest rates are usually high when inflation is rampant. All of this means that when inflation is high, profits expressed in current terms have to rise. (With acknowledgements to the Information Division, Unilever Ltd.)

13.2   Adjusting accounts based on historic cost

Published financial statements reflect a company's financial position on the basis of **historic cost** i.e. the amounts reported are based on the actual amounts – pounds, dollars or whatever – spent or received without regard to changes in the purchasing power of the monetary unit. While this may be more acceptable for stewardship purposes, and even this is doubtful, it is not a good basis for decision making. There are a number of ways in which figures can be adjusted to reflect price changes but they fall into two main categories – **current purchasing power (CPP)** and **current cost accounting (CCA)**

Current purchasing power

Sometimes referred to as **constant purchasing power** this method attempts to measure the effect that **general** inflation has on historic cost financial data. In economic terms no profit is made unless the value of the original capital is maintained. In this approach the value of the original capital is adjusted to CPP before accepting that real profit has been made, thus maintaining the financial value of original investment.

Example

Consider a first year of trading in which, theoretically, one type of product only was sold and all stock was exhausted at the end of the period. The summarized historic cost accounts are as follows:

	£000
Sales	500
Less Cost of sales	400
Operating profit	100

During the year the general rate of inflation measured by changes in the Retail Price Index is 10 per cent. Then in order to maintain the general purchasing power of the original investment – in this case the £400,000 used to provide the original goods for resale – 10 per cent of £400,000 is required and this can be shown in the CPP adjusted account, thus:

	£000	
Sales	500	
Less Cost of sales	400	
Operating profit	100	
Less Capital maintenance adjustment	(40)	(10 per cent × £400,000)
Adjusted profit	60	

The firm has made a real profit of £60,000 but had the cost of sales been, for example, £460,000 original investment would require £46,000 from an operating profit of £40,000 giving an adjusted loss in real terms of £6,000. This method formed the basis of development of ED 8 and SSAP 7 described below.

Current cost accounting

Sometimes referred to as **current value accounting** this method attempts to measure the effect of **individual** rates of change on all assets and liabilities i.e. stocks, plant, machinery, investments, loans, creditors etc. It recognizes that there are great differences in the various rates of inflation and by using specific indices for items or groups of items, attempts to match the current cost of the assets used against current income generated by them. In this approach the objective is to ensure that operating capital is maintained at the appropriate level. If the trader in the example above is to continue operations the physical stock must be replaced for resale in Period 2. If the price of this commodity has risen, meanwhile, by 20 per cent (compared with the general rate of 10 per cent) the position under CCA accounts will be:

	£000	
Sales	500	
Less Cost of sales	480	(400,000 × 120 per cent)
Operating profit	20	
Adjustment	–	
Adjusted profit	20	

In this case the operating profit is automatically adjusted by the fact that the replacement cost of the asset has been charged in full against revenue. It can be seen that this profit is insufficient to maintain the purchasing power of the original investment by reason that the inflation rate for the particular asset is twice that of the general collection of retail prices. To this extent it was argued that this approach would be more realistic for business purposes than CPP and the method formed the basis for development of SSAP 16 – *Current Cost Accounting*.

13.3 Development of accounting standards

Because of the high rates of inflation in the 1960s and 1970s continuous pressure was put upon the accounting bodies to develop a uniform approach to the problem. A vast amount of literature was generated which can only be summarized here. An exposure draft ED 8 published in January 1973 led to publication of a provisional standard SSAP 7 in May 1974. This adapted the current purchasing power (CPP) method. The basis of conversion was the Retail Price Index and the statement was required to be audited. A special feature was the distinction between monetary and non-monetary items:

1 *Monetary items:*   Amounts fixed by contract regardless of changes in purchasing value such as cash, debtors, creditors and loan capital. A business gains on liabilities during inflation because the pound sum is fixed so that subsequent repayment in the same pound sums is in terms of lower purchasing value. (The converse of course applies to debtors and outward loans.)
2 *Non-monetary items:*   These are items such as fixed assets and stocks contracted at specific original cost but whose value in terms of pounds can have improved to reflect their equivalent purchasing power.

A great deal of controversy centred upon the use of the Retail Price Index and the treatment of monetary and non-monetary items. The government-sponsored Sandilands Report subsequently summarized the objections and recommended the introduction of a system of current cost accounting. For the time being the purchasing power approach was out of favour.

In December 1976 ED 18 was published, calling for companies to produce current cost accounts. The requirements were complicated and a majority of members of the English Institute of Chartered Accountants rejected them and asked for simplification. This resulted in the Hyde Guidelines, a further exposure draft in April 1979 and finally the introduction of SSAP 16 to be operative from 1 January 1980.

The stated objective was to achieve more useful information in the accounts regarding:

1 The financial viability of the business.
2 Return on investment.
3 Pricing policy, cost control and distribution decisions.
4 Gearing.

The objectives were to be achieved in stages. Current cost operating profit were to be calculated by making three adjustments to historic profit before interest and net borrowing and taxation. These adjustments were:

1 *Depreciation:*   The difference between the charge based on an asset's current cost and that based on its historic cost as charged in arriving at historic profit.
2 *Cost of sales:*   The difference between the current cost of stock consumed and the cost charged in the historic profit and loss account.
3 *Monetary working capital:*   Adjustment in respect of items of working capital such as trade debtors, prepayments creditors and accruals. Bank and cash balances were generally excluded.

The three adjustments, when computed, were totalled and applied to historic profit to determine (before interest) the current cost profit.

The gearing adjustment is part of the current cost adjustment attributable if a proportion of the net operating assets is financed by net borrowing. It is computed by:

1 Expressing net borrowing as a proportion of the net operating assets using average figures for the year from current cost balance sheets.

2 Multiplying the total of charges or credits made to allow for impact on the net operating assets of the business by the proportion determined at 1.

Finally a current cost balance sheet is prepared, similarly stated in current cost terms. This is achieved by revaluing assets at their value to the business defined as net current replacement cost – *or* if a permanent diminution to below net current replacement cost has been recognized then recoverable amount (disposal value).

The chief advantages claimed for CCA were:

1 Permitting returns on capital employed to be more usefully assessed.
2 Separating various classification of gains (losses) distinguishes productive from fortuitous results.
3 Recognizing present achievements at present prices.
4 Some firms already revalue assets and therefore have anticipated CCA.
5 Preventing excessive profit distribution.

The standard asked for changes to be implemented in company annual reports after 24 December 1977 in respect of:

1 Listed companies.
2 Others with a turnover exceeding £10 million per year.
3 Others with assets exceeding £10 million.
4 Nationalized industries.

In 1980 SSAP 16 was published and accepting the need for experiment was required from large companies and for a period of three years. It was never popular or universally recognized and pressure for its implementation relaxed as inflation rules generally became lower.

13.4 The present position regarding published accounts

The SSAP 16 was never universally received or endorsed and some company chairmen chose to ignore some, or all, of its requirements, even where this meant qualification of the accounts by auditors. The slowing down of the rate of inflation in the UK in the 1980s removed some of the impetus to distorting results. The position at the end of August 1987 was that compliance with SSAP 16 was no longer mandatory for companies within the criteria referred to above. A new exposure draft EP 35 was being issued while a new approach was formulated. The Accounting Standards Committee has also issued a *Handbook on Accounting for the Effect of Changing Prices*. Not much greater progress has yet been made internationally. In the USA the Financial Accounting Standard Boards Statement 33 – *Financial Reporting and Changing Prices* has been amended to remove the requirement to disclose historical cost/constant dollar information. The problem of dealing with accounts in unstable monetary units still remains and until – if at all – a generally accepted method of dealing with this phenomenon is achieved, the controversy will continue.

Summary of main UK developments

1974   ASC publish provisional standard on current purchasing power (CPP) method of accounting for inflation.
1975   Government rejects CPP and sponsors Sandilands committee with brief to examine adjustment on basis of replacement costs termed current cost accounting (CCA).
1976   ASC accept CCA principle and Morpeth committee publish Exposure Draft 18 calling for all companies to produce current cost accounts. Withdrawn after criticism of complications.
1977   ED 18 modified gearing adjustment, added Hyde guidelines, developed as encouragement to use ED 24, refined existing ideas and Hyde guidelines adding requirement for CCA balance sheet.
1980   SSAP 16 published – mandatory for large companies.
1987   Mandatory requirement withdrawn and position under review.

The results of a MORI survey of attitudes of preparers and users of accounts towards accounting for inflation (commissioned by the Chartered Association of Certified Accountants) tended to confirm the above thus:

● At current levels of inflation nine out of ten of both preparers and users of accounts believe that historic cost accounts present a reliable picture.
● Over three-quarters of the surveyed believe that at current levels of inflation it does not matter which system is used.
● Ten per cent is considered to be the rate needed before there would be great concern.
● A small majority of users and preparers agreed a new practice statement was needed from the Accounting Standards Committee.

13.5   Inflation and management accounting

The basic purpose of management control information is to demonstrate management performance against planned objectives and to isolate the differences into causes and under responsibilities so that management can make decisions and implement action to alter the adverse causes, counter them and improve upon the beneficial trends.

In comparing actual performance with plan in financial terms the impact of inflation can adversely affect results and distort interpretation, so that it becomes highly desirable to ensure that the data under comparison be similarly constituted as to money values. This then confines differences to aspects of performance. To make this possible the plan can be adjusted for inflation so that plan and actual performance each contain their elements of inflation, or alternatively the plan avoids any inflation content and the actual performance information is reduced net of price and wage rate increases by the normal process of variance accounting.

If inflation is anticipated in the budget, practitioners find that the only aspect about which there is certainty is that the degree and timing of the inflation content will be wrong and for this reason it is not encouraged for fixed budgets. Improved accuracy is forthcoming from adjustments to short-term budgets such as the rolling next quarter (updating the next three months progressively), when the rates and timing of inflation would be more informed. However, experts are confounded when forecasting inflation even in the short term, so that a more reliable method is to rely only upon published data of actual changes in the value of money. This invites a process of introducing the known degree of inflation into a flexible budget as a separate operation from that of adjusting for output volume.

Critics can advance the point that any published index of prices such as the Retail Price Index does not necessarily reflect the effect of inflation upon a particular business, and the Sandiland's Report and ED 18 endorsed this view. This criticism directs attention to the advantages of isolating the price variances from the performance data as they occur, as this would then demonstrate the actual impact of inflation upon the business. These price variances can be analysed under suitable categories and the degree of change related to nationally monitored changes within similar categories by government or trade associations. In such a manner the ability to shield the business from the full impact of price increases relative to it can be demonstrated. An efficient buying function deserves its contribution to be recognized if it is able to keep the impact of prices down to, say, half the national rate.

The actual expenditure, now devoid of price variance, provides a more adequate means of reflecting performance and the segregation of price variances of costs can be monitored against price variances of sales. Businesses subject to control of selling price changes by the Price Commission have to demonstrate the extent of cost increases incurred and a properly analysed price variance control can be of immense assistance in substantiating claims for compensating sales increases.

As a budget year progresses a price variance account can assume very generous proportions and in the later stages appear somewhat incongruous. However, the purpose of the procedure should be recognized as that of isolating the impact of inflation so as to reveal the actual performance data so vital for effective management.

The establishment of price standards for standard costing and budgeting will require careful consideration especially as to the degree of price change which should, or should not, be anticipated. Replacement values at the opening date of the budget would be the more advisable basis. It should perhaps be realized that standard costing is a means of facilitating control accounting and not of demonstrating product costs from time to time. The procedure for maintaining current product costs in a standard costing system is a separate operation from the accounting processes. It will be important to monitor and demonstrate the effects of progressive price changes upon current costs within the standard cost model as for all other changes such as methods, design, material substitutes, so that changes of product contribution are under regular management review in so far as they may affect pricing, product mix and marketing policies.

14
Standard accounting practices

Up until the late 1960s the preparation of accounts was required to be in conformity with the requirements of the Companies Acts from time to time in force, or in agreement with professional accounting practice for sole traders and partnerships. To the uninitiated the general requirement to present a 'true and fair view' would appear to preclude serious differences in published results. But as discussed in Section 1.6 the concepts allowed a choice of policies and bases which could be deliberately chosen to provide results with a bias toward a particular objective. The application of accepted principles was stretched to the limit in a number of widely publicized instances which reflected badly on the accounting profession. Laymen could see the results yet the policies were endorsed in the audit reports by some of the best-known public accountants. Hints were given that the government itself might have to intervene in the accounting profession. This led to the formation, in the UK, of the Accounting Standards Committee and the subsequent work of this body is discussed in the following two sections.

There has always been an interchange of accounting knowledge between Europe and the UK and particularly between the UK and the USA. A common language has made it easier for American texts, particularly on management accounting to be absorbed. The growth of the multinationals has meant harmonization of accounting practice and this has resulted in informal exchange and formalized action such as the International Accounting Standards Committee.

14.1 Statements of Standard Accounting Practice (SSAPs) – history

In order to achieve a rationalization of principles and practice in contentious areas of accounting the Accounting Standards Committee (ASC) was set up in 1969/70 comprising:

- The Institute of Chartered Accountants in England and Wales
- The Institute of Chartered Accountants in Scotland
- The Institute of Chartered Accountants in Ireland
- Chartered Association of Certified Accountants*
- Chartered Institute of Management Accountants*
- Chartered Institute of Public Finance and Accounting

The bodies marked with an asterisk were not at the time chartered and also joined the original bodies in membership of the ASC in 1971. CIPFA joined in 1976. The terms of reference were basically: 'To advance accounting standards and to narrow the areas of difference and variety in accounting practice by publishing authoritative statements on best accounting practice.' The procedure for the development of Statements of Standard Accounting Practice (SSAPs) is as follows:

> Research of a particular area is undertaken by a group of accountants, academics, industrialists etc. who prepare preliminary drafts which are studied by various committees appointed by the ASC. An exposure draft (ED) is then distributed as widely as possible, so that comments can be collected and assessed. After further consultation a final draft is agreed by the ASC and issued as an SSAP.

The format of the Statement is in a standard form and constructed in the following parts:

- Part 1 Explanatory note
- Part 2 Definition of terms
- Part 3 Standard Accounting Practice
- Part 4 Note on legal requirements in Great Britain and Northern Ireland
- Part 5 Note on legal requirements in the Republic of Ireland
- Part 6 Compliance with any International Accounting Standard
- Appendices illustrating application of the Standard

Some authorities consider the development of standards to be regrettable. They claim that they encourage a rigidity which may prevent development of better financial reporting. On the other hand the advocates of the standards refer to the practices which brought along the necessity for some alignment in the 1960s – the Pergamon Press and GEC-AEI merger and the activities of asset strippers. One can sympathize with both viewpoints and in any event directors of companies can override the standards and risk qualification of the accounts by the auditors. The typical example is where the directors do not concede the recommendation to depreciate the value based on historical cost still further when the property has increased in value. Some standards have proved so unworkable in practice as to be withdrawn or amended as described in Section 14.2 and the chapter on inflation. Among questions at present being debated are whether the ASC should have more power to impose SSAPs on its members and/or whether government regulation is necessary. A common criticism is that standards have been developed piecemeal and in a lot of instances have merely endorsed existing practice. The committee is already issuing Statements of Recommended Accounting Practice (SORPs) on some topics. As implied in the title these are not mandatory but it is hoped that members will follow their recommendations. One can sympathize to some extent with the view that if 'mandatory' standards are not complied with then it is doubtful that voluntary compliance will be any more effective. As stated in the foreword to the SSAPs (paragraph 5): 'In applying accounting standards it will be important to have regard to the spirit and reasoning behind them. They are not intended to be a comprehensive code of rigid rules.' Nevertheless, the paragraph goes on to state that significant departures should be disclosed and explained in the financial statements. This is an attempt to get the best of both worlds and inevitably on occasion fails by accident or design. The major objective is to present a true and fair view. To the extent that compliance with a particular standard endorses this then there is no conflict. If it does not then the accountant must look to the spirit of the standard and if necessary resist attempts by the Board not to comply or explain their stand in the qualification to the accounts.

14.2   Statements of Standard Accounting Practice at present in use

From the date of the inauguration of the Accounting Standards Committee many Exposure Drafts have been issued and resulted in a considerable number of standards being finalized. The position at present is as shown in Tables 14.1 and 14.2.

Table 14.1

SSAP number	Title	Date issued	Latest revision
1	*Accounting for Results of Associated Companies*	June 1973	1982
2	*Disclosure of Accounting Policies*	June 1973	
3	*Earnings Per Share*	February 1972	
4	*Accounting Treatment of Government Grants*	April 1974	
5	*Accounting for Value Added Tax*	April 1974	
6	*Extraordinary Items and Prior Year Investments*	April 1974	August 1986
7*	*Accounting for Changes in Purchasing Power of Money*	May 1974	Withdrawn 1978
8	*Treatment of Taxation under the Imputation system in the Accounts of Companies*	August 1974	December 1977
9	*Stocks and Work in Progress*	May 1975	
10	*Statements of Source and Application of Funds*	July 1975	
11	*Accounting for Deferred Taxation*	August 1975	Replaced by SSAP 15
12	*Accounting for Depreciation*	December 1977	November 1981/January 1987
13	*Accounting for Research and Development*	December 1977	
14	*Group Accounts*	September 1978	
15	*Accounting for Deferred Taxation*	October 1987	May 1985

SSAP number	Title	Date issued	Latest revision
16*	*Current Cost Accounting*	March 1980	
17	*Accounting for Post Balance Sheet Events*	August 1980	
18	*Accounting for Contingencies*	August 1980	
19	*Accounting for Investment Properties*	November 1981	
20	*Foreign Currency Translation*	April 1983	
21	*Accounting for Leases and Hire Purchase Contracts*	August 1984	
22	*Accounting for Goodwill*	June 1985	
23	*Accounting for Acquisitions and Mergers*	April 1985	

* Mandatory status withdrawn July 1985

Table 14.2

Exposure draft	
38	*Accounting by Charities*
39	*Accounting for pension costs*
40	*Stocks and Long-Term Contracts*

The exposure drafts reflect matters of latest interest and concern. In addition, at the time of writing, there are proposals to amend SSAP 13 – *Research and Development* and for a review of SSAP 14 – *Group Accounts* by virtue of European regulation. Goodwill and depreciation are a continuing source of discussion, SSAP 7 was the first response to the inflation conflict and was replaced by SSAP 16 – *Current Cost Accounting*. Even this was so antagonistically received that it was modified by the Hyde guidelines issued as provisional and finally withdrawn as mandatory in 1987 (see Section 1.3).

Failure to get general consensus has led to the creation, in 1986, of a further category of Statements of Recommended Practice (SORPs). As previously stated these are not mandatory on members of the governing bodies of the ASC. The aim is to narrow the areas of difference and variety in the accounting treatment of matters with which they deal. At present there is one statement only SORP 1 – *Pension Scheme Accounts*. The individual professional bodies also issue their own publications as, for example, *Guidelines in Management Accounting, Auditing and Investigation Standards and Guidelines*.

14.3   European and international standards

The first instance of international cooperation by the UK with Europe was on the occasion of entrance into the European Economic Community (EEC). The mechanism of this has been the issue of directives by the EEC council of ministers which are binding on member countries. The main directives, the fourth, seventh and eighth cover the preparation of accounts and auditing.

International standards

A further step towards standardization was undertaken following the International Accounting Congress held in Sydney, Australia, in 1973, when the International Accounting Standards Committee (IASC) was set up, as a result of an agreement by the leading professional accounting bodies of the following founder countries:

- Australia
- Canada
- France
- Germany
- Japan
- Mexico
- Netherlands
- United Kingdom
- Ireland
- United States of America

The following year six further countries were admitted as associate members:

- Belgium
- India
- Israel
- New Zealand
- Pakistan
- Rhodesia

The objectives of the IASC as set out in the agreement are: 'to formulate and publish in the public interest, basic standards to be observed in the presentation of audited accounts and financial statements, and to promote their worldwide acceptance and observance.'

As with EEC directives the IASC requirements tend to be at a somewhat insignificant level as compared with the UK Companies Acts requirements.

Founder and Associate members also undertook the following obligations:

1   To support the standards promulgated by the Committee.
2   To use their best endeavours:
    (a)   To ensure that published accounts comply with these standards or that there is disclosure of the extent to which they do not, and to persuade governments, the authorities controlling securities markets and the industrial and business community, that published accounts should comply with these standards.
    (b)   To assume that the auditors satisfy themselves that the accounts comply with these standards. If the accounts do not comply with these standards the audit report should either refer to the disclosure of non-compliance in the accounts, or should state the extent to which they do not comply.
    (c)   To ensure that as soon as practical, appropriate action is taken in respect of auditors whose audit reports do not meet the requirements of (b) above.
3   To seek to secure similar general acceptance and observance of these standards internationally.

The above agreement refers to financial statements, prepared for use by persons other than internal management, such as shareholders, creditors, employees, and the public at large.

The Standards at present issued are shown in Table 14.3.

Table 14.3

IAS number	
1	*Disclosure of Accounting Policies*
2	*Valuation and Presentation of Inventories in the context of the Historical Cost System*
3	*Consolidated Financial Statements*
4	*Depreciation Accounting*
5	*Information to be disclosed in Financial Statements*
6	*Accounting treatment of changing prices*
7	*Statement of Changes in Financial position*
8	*Unusual and prior period items and Changes in accounting policies*
9	*Accounting for Research and Development Activities*
10	*Contingencies and Events after the Balance Sheet Date*
11	*Accounting for Construction Contracts*
12	*Accounting for Taxes on Income*
13	*Presentation of Current Assets and Current Liabilities*
14	*Reporting Financial Information by Segment*
15	*Information Reflecting the Effect of Changing Prices*

Authority and the Standards

The authority of the SSAPs is described in the explanatory foreword issued in 1973 which states that the accounting bodies expect their members 'Who assume responsibilities in respect of financial accounts to observe accounting standards'.

The Stock Exchange expects the accounts of listed companies to be prepared in conformity with SSAPs and since 23 October 1974 accounts must conform with the standards issued by the IASC.

Member countries of the EEC are required to comply with the directives issued from time to time. If a directive is not covered by SSAPs, the Accounting Standards Committee would raise either a new SSAP or revise an existing one in order to cover the requirement of any EEC directive or failing that, they would require accountants to note on the accounts the extent to which a directive had not been complied with.

Generally the standards issued by the IASC, do not override the provisions of the Companies Act from time to time in force, or the Statements of Standard Accounting Practice. If the International

Accounting Standards (IAS) conform with the Companies Acts or the SSAP on any particular topic, they will obviously comply with the IAS in respect of that subject. If, however, they either differ from one another or are in direct conflict, the accounts and the auditors, report must indicate in what respect the IAS has not been observed, though numerical data is not obligatory.

In order to assist UK and Irish accountants to comply with the IAS, a preface is attached to each IAS to make clear the extent to which the standard is already covered by an SSAP, and the effect on the content of the accounts and of the audit report of any conflict between the two.

15
Published company accounts

The following pages reproduce most of the information from the published accounts of Transport Development Group PLC. The accounts are included to give the reader an idea of content, style and good presentation. Although greater conformity to a prescribed layout is continually being imposed by the latest legislation there is still an art in presenting data and the Institute of Chartered Accountants award annual prizes for what are judged to be the best examples of this art.

The aim is to present a certain body of financial information, the contents of which are closely defined by laws and accounting practice in a form which is easily assimilated and pleasing (if such a term can be applied to company accounts).

It will be noticed that a considerable amount of statistical information is included in the accounts. Most of this is now required by law. We have not dealt with this in this book as it does not present any accounting problems within the scope of the text. The only omissions from the accounts as published are the directors' report and list of subsidiaries which are omitted by virtue of pressure on length of the text. Readers should, however, make a practice of reading the comments made by directors and executives on company performance, since they frequently draw attention to accounting, environmental and economic practices and difficulties.

15.1   Transport Development Group PLC Annual Report and Accounts 1986

Transport Development Group PLC is the parent of approximately 100 subsidiary companies operating in the United Kingdom, Europe, North America and Australia. Each company is commercially independent. The main activities are road haulage, storage, and distribution. Other activities include plant hire, industrial removals, export packing, exhibitions, and the manufacture of steel reinforcement.

Contents

The year in brief

	1986 £000	1985 £000
Turnover	543,164	481,462
Profit before tax	39,362	29,665
Capital employed	253,583	232,567
Operating profit % of turnover	8.9%	7.9%
Operating profit % of average capital employed	19.8%	16.1%
Net tangible assets per ordinary share	111.3p	101.6p
Earnings per ordinary share	17.2p	12.4p
Dividends per ordinary share	7.5p	6.2p

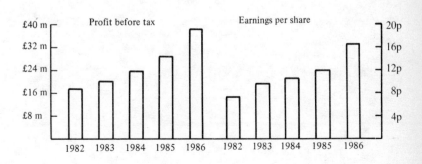

Board of directors

Sir James Duncan Chairman and Chief Executive	Joined the Group in 1953. Appointed a director in 1960. Chairman since 1979. A former president of the Chartered Institute of Transport. President of the Institute of Road Transport Engineers. Chairman of the London Chamber of Commerce and Industry. Aged 59.
J. D. Lockhart Managing Director	Joined the Group in 1958. For some years Managing Director of a major haulage and warehousing subsidiary in the Midlands. Director of TDG 1971. Managing Director 1979. A former chairman of the National Association of Warehousekeepers. Aged 53.
J. Wishart Executive Director	Joined the Group in 1961. Now Chief Executive of TDG Southern Limited. A director of TDG since 1969. Aged 49.
D. S. Horner Finance Director	Formerly Group Accountant of Lombard Banking Limited. Joined TDG in 1971. Appointed Finance Director 1973. Aged 52.
J. G. Lithiby Non-executive Director	Appointed 1977. Chairman of Panmure Gordon & Co. Limited, stockbrokers. Also a director of Fortnum and Mason Limited. Aged 56.
J. G. Davis Non-executive Director	Appointed 1984. A director of Kleinwort Benson Limited and of Associated British Ports PLC and Chairman of DFDS Limited. A former president of the Chartered Institute of Transport and of the Institute of Freight Forwarders. Aged 58.

Secretary	R. D. Garwood FCIS
Accountant	M. A. Hodge CA
Registered office	Windsor House, 50 Victoria Street, London SW1H 0NR. Telephone 01-222 7411. Fax 01-222 2806. Telex 919369
Transfer office	Bourne House, 34 Beckenham Road, Beckenham BR3 4TU. Telephone 01-650 4866
Auditors	Dearden Farrow *Chartered Accountants*
Solicitors	Slaughter and May

Appendix to the report of the directors:
Year ended 31 December 1986

Directors' interests

The following were directors of the company during the year. They and their families had interests in shares of the company and of its subsidiary Transport Development Australia Limited (TDA) as shown below. Unless otherwise stated all interests are beneficial.

	1 January 1986	31 December 1986
Sir James Duncan		
Ordinary shares	45,214	45,214
Ordinary share options	25,000	75,000
Ordinary shares of 50 cents of TDA*	5,850	–
J. D. Lockhart		
Ordinary shares	31,228	31,228
Ordinary share options	20,000	60,000
Ordinary shares of 50 cents of TDA*	6,542	–
J. Wishart		
Ordinary shares	22,279	22,279
Ordinary share options	17,500	57,500
Ordinary shares of 50 cents of TDA*	2,248	–
D. S. Horner		
Ordinary shares	10,221	10,871
Ordinary shares (non-beneficial)	–	5,500
Ordinary share options	17,500	48,000
Ordinary shares of 50 cents of TDA*	2,114	–
J. G. Lithiby		
Ordinary shares	5,000	5,000
J. G. Davis		
Ordinary shares	3,500	3,500

* These shares were acquired by Transdev Pty. Limited on 11 February 1986 pursuant to its offer to the minority shareholders of TDA.

There was no change in the interest of any director in the shares of the company or of its subsidiaries between the end of the year and 16 March 1987.

Material contracts

No contract of significance subsisted during or at the end of the financial year in which a director of the company is, or was, materially interested.

Political and charitable contributions

	£
Centre for Policy Studies	4,000
Conservative Party	4,250
Aims of Industry	600
Charitable contributions	13,338

Ownership of ordinary share capital at 31 December 1986

	Number of accounts	% of total shares
Category of holding		
Private holders	11,973	16.2
Banks and nominees	493	38.5
Insurance companies	87	22.3
Pension funds and charities	120	16.6
Investment trusts	80	3.6
Other corporate bodies	123	2.8
	12,876	100.0
Size of holding		
1– 1,000 shares	7,011	2.1
1,001– 5,000 shares	4,724	7.3
5,001–10,000 shares	526	2.5
10,001 shares upwards	615	88.1
	12,876	100.0

Throughout the financial year the close company provisions of the Income and Corporation Taxes Act 1970 did not apply to the company. The Provident Mutual Life Assurance Association has notified an interest in 8,380,272 ordinary shares representing 5.81% of ordinary shares in issue. So far as the company is aware, no other person during the year held, or was beneficially interested in, any substantial part of the share capital of the company. There was no change in the position at 16 March 1987.

Employee involvement

A principal objective of the decentralized Group structure is to ensure that communication is direct and simple. Each Group trading company is commercially independent, most are relatively small. In many cases, there is a direct relationship between the chief executive of the company and individual employees. In these conditions, complex consultative procedures are seldom needed to ensure that there is an understanding of the purpose of the business, and the commercial realities which determine its success. However, some of the larger and more scattered subsidiaries have recently developed company newspapers to keep their employees better informed. Every effort is made to ensure, wherever practicable, that pay is linked to results.

In recruiting, training, career development or promotion, Group companies make no distinction between disabled and able-bodied persons, provided the disability does not make the particular employment impractical or the employee unable to conform to the stringent statutory regulations which apply to the operations of many of the companies.

Report of the auditors

To the members of Transport Development Group PLC

We have audited the accounts on pages 425–42 in accordance with approved auditing standards. In our opinion the accounts, which have been prepared under the historical cost convention as modified by the revaluation of certain assets, give a true and fair view of the state of affairs of the company and the group at 31 December 1986 and of the profit and source and use of funds of the group for the year then ended and comply with the Companies Act 1985.

Dearden Farrow
Chartered Accountants, London, 16 March 1987

Consolidated profit and loss account: Year ended 31 December 1986

	Notes	1986 £000	1985 £000
Turnover	2	**543,164**	481,462
Operating expenses	3	**494,937**	443,228
Operating profit		**48,227**	38,234
Net interest payable	4	**8,865**	8,569
Profit on ordinary activities before tax	2	**39,362**	29,665
Tax	5	**14,304**	11,218
Profit after tax		**25,058**	18,447
Minority interests		**300**	615
Profit on ordinary activities after tax attributable to shareholders		**24,758**	17,832
Extraordinary items	6	**38**	(153)
Profit for the financial year		**24,796**	17,679
Dividends paid and proposed	7	**10,870**	8,980
Transfer to reserves	17	**13,926**	8,699
Earnings per ordinary share (before extraordinary items)	8	**17.15p**	12.37p

Consolidated balance sheet: 31 December 1986

	Notes	£000	1986 £000	£000	1985 £000
Fixed assets					
Tangible assets	9		**232,869**		209,696
Investments	10		**2,114**		108
			234,983		209,804
Current assets					
Stocks	11	**14,280**		14,872	
Debtors	12	**107,315**		95,328	
Deposits		**3,453**		6,578	
Cash at bank and in hand		**1,903**		2,639	
		126,951		119,417	
Creditors: due within one year					
Borrowings	13	**9,777**		12,771	
Other creditors	14	**102,995**		87,437	
Net current assets			**14,179**		19,209
Total assets less current liabilities			**249,162**		229,013
Creditors: due after one year					
Borrowings	13	**64,549**		57,436	
Corporate tax		**7,377**		4,804	
Provisions for liabilities	15	**11,533**		13,279	
Investment grants		**2,831**		1,981	
			86,290		77,500
			162,872		151,513
Capital and reserves					
Called up share capital	16		**37,434**		37,366
Share premium	17		**6,788**		6,633
Revaluation reserve			**10,406**		10,406
Other reserves	17		**107,150**		93,138
			161,778		147,543
Minority interests			**1,094**		3,970
			162,872		151,513

Parent company balance sheet: 31 December 1986

	Notes	£000	1986 £000	£000	1985 £000
Fixed assets					
Tangible assets	9		769		797
Investments	10		51,717		41,336
			52,486		42,133
Current assets					
ACT recoverable after one year		3,238		2,775	
Debtors	12	138,289		123,529	
Deposits		1,583		1,165	
Cash at bank and in hand		156		26	
		143,266		127,495	
Creditors: due within one year					
Borrowings	13	8,112		5,508	
Other creditors	14	40,575		21,716	
Net current assets			94,579		100,271
Total assets less current liabilities			147,065		142,404
Creditors: due after one year					
Borrowings	13		38,118		38,536
Corporate tax			1,482		1,635
			107,465		102,233
Capital and reserves					
Called up share capital	16		37,434		37,366
Share premium	17		6,788		6,633
Revaluation reserve			10,611		10,611
Other reserves	17		52,632		47,623
			107,465		102,233

The accounts were approved by the Board of Directors on 16 March 1987

James Duncan   J. D. Lockhart

Source and use of funds

	1982 £000	1983 £000	1984 £000	1985 £000	1986 £000
Source of funds					
Profit before tax	18,329	20,980	24,060	29,665	39,362
Deduct:					
Tax paid	8,335	8,345	7,033	7,246	9,802
	9,994	12,635	17,027	22,419	29,560
Depreciation	21,287	22,545	25,247	28,159	31,776
Generated from trading operations	31,281	35,180	42,274	50,578	61,336
Extraordinary items	(185)	451	(1,115)	(239)	(67)
Net movements on investment grants and pension provision	80	145	218	226	440
Share capital subscribed	–	33	8,863	486	223
	(105)	629	7,966	473	596
	31,176	35,809	50,240	51,051	61,932
Use of funds					
Expenditure on tangible assets	27,691	39,160	53,725	45,292	58,890
Deduct: Sales thereof	5,460	6,424	6,486	9,840	9,347
	22,231	32,736	47,239	35,452	49,543
Expenditure on investments	(22)	279	33	(578)	(13)
Subsidiaries acquired/(sold)	3,373	1,021	11,130	(2,487)	2,425
Minority interests acquired	93	76	–	120	4,289
Investment in associated company	–	–	–	–	55
Dividends paid to:					
Minority and preference shareholders	187	233	332	204	81
Ordinary shareholders	5,648	5,982	6,798	8,178	9,357
	31,510	40,327	65,532	40,889	65,737
Increase/(decrease) in working capital:					
Stocks	(1,280)	(655)	455	240	(668)
Debtors	4,992	7,737	8,953	9,965	9,918
Creditors	1,103	(8,766)	(3,032)	(4,805)	(7,808)
	4,815	(1,684)	6,376	5,400	1,442
	36,325	38,643	71,908	46,289	67,179
(Increase)/decrease in net borrowings	(5,149)	(2,834)	(21,668)	4,762	(5,247)
	31,176	35,809	50,240	51,051	61,932

The movement in net borrowings during 1986 may be reconciled with the opening and closing balance sheets as follows:

	£000
Movement as above	(5,247)
Exchange rate adjustment	(2,733)
Balance sheet movement	(7,980)

The acquisition of subsidiaries and the disposal of a subsidiary with subsequent reinvestment in the associated company during the year comprised:

	Acquisitions £000	Disposal £000
Fixed assets	1,524	(1,810)
Net current assets	107	(454)
Tax due after one year and other items	17	152
Goodwill	777	–
Reinvestment in associated company of proceeds of disposal of subsidiary	–	2,167
	2,425	55

Notes on the accounts

1   Accounting policies

Basis of accounting
The accounts have been prepared under the historical cost basis of accounting as modified by the revaluation of certain fixed assets.

Basis of consolidation
The accounts consolidate those of the company and its subsidiaries together with their share of the results of associated companies.

An associated company is one in which the group has a substantial shareholding not exceeding 50 per cent and where the group is in a position to exert a significant influence over its commercial and financial policy decisions.

The accounts are made up to 31 December except that for administrative reasons the accounts of the overseas subsidiaries are made up to 30 September.

The goodwill or discount on consolidation, being the difference between the fair value of attributable net tangible assets at the date of acquisition and the cost of shares acquired, is taken to reserves in the year of acquisition.

All amounts denominated in overseas currencies are translated into sterling at the rates ruling at 31 December.

Exchange differences arising from the restatement of opening balance sheets of subsidiary companies are dealt with through reserves, net of differences on related currency borrowings. All other currency differences are dealt with through the profit and loss account.

Depreciation
Freehold and long leasehold land is not depreciated. Depreciation is provided on the cost or subsequent valuation of other tangible assets over their estimated useful lives on a straight line basis as follows:

Freehold and long leasehold buildings	20–50 years
Short leaseholds (less than 40 years to run)	Amortized over remaining life of lease
Motor vehicles	4–6 years
Trailers	8 years
Cranes, plant and furniture	4–10 years
Insulation and refrigeration plant	10–20 years

Investment grants are credited to revenue in equal annual amounts over the expected life of the asset.

Finance leases
Assets obtained under finance leases are recorded in the balance sheet as fixed tangible assets, initially at fair value, and depreciated over the shorter of the lease term or their estimated useful life. Future rental obligations are included with borrowings. The interest element of the rent payable is charged to the profit and loss account over the period of the lease using the actuarial method.

Deferred tax
Deferred tax is provided when it is expected that the potential tax liability will be payable in the foreseeable future.

Stocks
Stocks and work in progress are stated at the lower of cost and net realizable value. The cost of work in progress includes a proportion of overhead.

Pensions
Group companies contribute to a variety of pension schemes and arrangements appropriate to the circumstances and countries in which they operate. The funds of the principal schemes are administered by trustees and are completely separate from the funds of the companies concerned. The schemes are reviewed every three years by independent actuaries and were fully funded at the last review; contributions paid in the light of such actuarial advice are charged as incurred against profits. Pensions in the course of payment are regularly reviewed.

Extraordinary items
Extraordinary items derive from events or transactions outside the ordinary activities of the business. They include the profit or loss on disposal of properties and investments and the costs of permanent alterations in capacity.

2   Turnover and profit before tax

Turnover comprises sales to external customers excluding sales taxes and customs duties.

	Turnover £000	1986 Profit before tax £000	Turnover £000	1985 Profit before tax £000
Geographical				
United Kingdom	303,279	29,493	275,423	23,639
Europe	118,991	11,074	93,041	7,740
Australia	21,694	2,065	23,420	2,396
North America	99,200	5,595	89,578	4,459
	543,164	48,227	481,462	38,234
Net interest payable		8,865		8,569
		39,362		29,665
Functional				
United Kingdom				
Road haulage	166,175	11,192	153,696	8,316
Storage	53,465	12,655	48,826	12,680
Other services	83,639	5,646	72,901	2,643
	303,279	29,493	275,423	23,639
Overseas				
Road haulage	164,142	11,965	140,128	7,860
Storage	14,001	3,668	12,283	3,674
Other services	61,742	3,101	53,628	3,061
	239,885	18,734	206,039	14,595
	543,164	48,227	481,462	38,234
Net interest payable		8,865		8,569
		39,362		29,665

Turnover includes income from operating leases amounting to £33,929,000 (1985 £29,958,000).

3   Operating expenses

	1986 £000	1985 £000
Raw materials, consumables and other external charges	217,990	202,188
Staff costs:		
Wages and salaries	153,428	133,030
Social security costs	22,974	19,994
Other pension costs	1,944	2,733
Redundancy costs	289	616
	178,635	156,373
Other operating charges	67,093	56,847
Depreciation:		
Provision for year	33,607	29,595
Amounts over provided in previous years	(1,831)	(1,436)
Release of investment grants	(557)	(339)
	31,219	27,820
	494,937	443,228

Operating expenses include:		
Operating leases		
Hire of plant and equipment	7,723	4,563
Rent of land and buildings	4,691	2,798
Auditors' remuneration	686	632
and income from:		
Listed investments	1	11
Unlisted investments	27	14

The average weekly number of employees in the group during the year was:

	1986 Number	1985 Number
Road haulage	6,644	6,293
Storage	1,257	1,182
Other services	1,520	1,497
Office and management	3,406	3,253
	12,827	12,225

	1986 £000	1985 £000
Directors' remuneration comprised:		
Management salaries	341	289
Performance related commission	100	16
Pension contributions	30	69
Fees	19	19
Past directors' pensions	4	34
	494	427

The emoluments of the Chairman, excluding pension contributions, were £145,774 (1985 £92,006).

The emoluments, excluding pension contributions, of the other directors of the company and of employees of the group in the UK were within the following ranges:

	Directors		Employees	
	1986	*1985*	**1986**	*1985*
£1– £5,000	**1**	1		
£5,001– £10,000	**1**	2		
£30,001– £35,000	–	–	**11**	18
£35,001– £40,000	–	–	**12**	12
£40,001– £45,000	–	–	**10**	4
£45,001– £50,000	–	–	**5**	5
£50,001– £55,000	–	–	**3**	2
£55,001– £60,000	–	–	**3**	–
£60,001– £65,000	–	1	**2**	1
£65,001– £70,000	–	–	**1**	–
£70,001– £75,000	–	1	**1**	1
£75,001– £80,000	–	1	–	–
£85,001– £90,000	**1**	–	–	–
£90,001– £95,000	**1**	–	–	–
£115,001–£120,000	**1**	–	–	–

At 31 December 1986 one officer had a loan outstanding of £2,500 (1985 £7,815)

4 Net interest payable

	1986 **£000**	*1985* *£000*
Interest payable on:		
Short-term borrowings and bank overdrafts	**2,458**	2,533
Other borrowings:		
Repayable within 5 years	**3,499**	2,535
Repayable after 5 years	**3,498**	3,940
	9,455	9,008
Deduct:		
Short-term interest receivable	**590**	439
	8,865	8,569

5 Tax

	1986 **£000**	*1985* *£000*
The tax charge based on the profit on ordinary activities for the year is made up as follows:		
Corporation tax at 36.25% (1985 41.25%)	**12,222**	8,267
Double tax relief	**(60)**	(34)
	12,162	8,233

	1986 £000	1985 £000
Overseas tax	3,578	3,484
Deferred tax	(1,436)	(499)
	14,304	11,218

If full deferred tax had been provided the tax charge for the year would have been £14,220,000 (1985 £11,607,000).

6   Extraordinary items

	1986 £000	1985 £000
Net surplus/(loss) on sale of:		
Properties	208	462
Investments including shares in subsidiaries	19	(185)
Restructuring costs	(294)	(516)
	(67)	(239)
Tax relief	105	86
	38	(153)

7   Dividends paid and proposed

	1986		1985	
	p per share	£000	p per share	£000
Ordinary shares:				
Interim	2.0	2,882	1.7	2,446
Proposed final	5.5	7,929	4.5	6,475
	7.5	10,811	6.2	8,921
Preference shares		59		59
		10,870		8,980

8   Earnings per ordinary share

Earnings per ordinary share are calculated on the basis of the weighted average of 144,023,000 (1985 143,691,000) ordinary shares in issue and earnings before extraordinary items attributable to ordinary shareholders of £24,699,000 (1985 £17,773,000). There is no material dilution of earnings per share as a result of the existence of the shares under option.

9   Tangible assets

	Land and buildings £000	Vehicles £000	Plant and equipment £000	Total £000
Cost or valuation:				
At beginning of year	115,123	152,868	76,953	344,944
Exchange rate adjustment	2,405	6,859	1,546	10,810
Companies acquired/(sold) during year	(206)	(1,214)	(219)	(1,639)
Purchases	8,239	34,167	16,484	58,890
Sales	(4,006)	(16,706)	(4,020)	(24,732)
Cost or valuation at 31 December 1986	121,555	175,974	90,744	388,273
Depreciation:				
At beginning of year	12,727	86,017	36,504	135,248
Exchange rate adjustment	196	3,994	928	5,118
Companies acquired/(sold) during year	(16)	(1,279)	(58)	(1,353)
Provision for year	2,587	21,805	9,215	33,607
Relating to sales	(458)	(13,653)	(3,105)	(17,216)
Depreciation at 31 December 1986	15,036	96,884	43,484	155,404
Book value at 31 December 1986	106,519	79,090	47,260	232,869
includes assets leased to customers under operating leases	16,462	7,174	8,227	31,863
Cost or valuation at 31 December 1986 includes assets valued at 1 January 1978	50,560	–	–	50,560

Assets obtained under finance leases included above are not material.
It is not practical to identify the original cost to the group of those assets which are included at valuation at 1 January 1978.

Land and buildings at 31 December 1986 comprise:

	Cost of valuation £000	Accumulated depreciation £000	Net book value £000
Freehold	109,010	12,458	96,552
Long leasehold	6,880	1,141	5,739
Short leasehold	5,665	1,437	4,228
	121,555	15,036	106,519

The tangible assets of the parent company at a cost of £1,341,000 (1985 £1,244,000) and accumulated depreciation of £572,000 (1985 £447,000) are included above. During the year net additions amounted to £139,000 and depreciation of £167,000 was provided. The book value at 31 December 1986 was £769,000 (1985 £797,000).

10   Investments

	Group		Parent		
	Associated company *£000*	*Other* *£000*	*Associated company* *£000*	*Listed* *£000*	*Subsidiary companies* *£000*
Cost or valuation:					
At beginning of year	–	108	–	13	41,323
Exchange rate adjustment	–	14	–	–	–
Additions	1,793	2	1,793	2	10,222
Share of losses	(162)	–	–	–	–
Advances	374	–	374	–	–
Sales	–	(15)	–	(3)	(1,972)
Provision	–	–	–	–	(35)
Cost or valuation at 31 December 1986	2,005	109	2,167	12	49,538
includes assets valued at 1 January 1978	–	–	–	–	23,996

The amounts dealt with in the consolidated profit and loss account in respect of the associated company were:

	1986 *£000*	*1985* *£000*
Loss before tax	190	–
Tax relief	(28)	–
Loss after tax	162	–

Other group investments at 31 December 1986 comprise listed investments of £20,000 (1985 £24,000) with a market value of £34,000 (1985 £36,000) and unlisted investments of £89,000 (1985 £84,000). The market value of the investments held by the parent company at 31 December 1986 is £23,000 (1985 £25,000).

The historical cost less provisions of the investments in subsidiaries at 31 December 1986 amounts to £37,632,000 (1985 £28,487,000).

11   Stocks

	1986 £000	1985 £000
Raw materials	5,783	6,205
Work in progress	2,811	3,118
Finished goods	2,138	1,727
Consumable supplies	5,476	5,491
	16,208	16,541
Deduct:		
Receipts on account of work in progress	1,928	1,669
	14,280	14,872
Reinforcement steel	8,076	8,244
Transport and others	6,204	6,628
	14,280	14,872

12   Debtors

	1986 Group £000	Parent £000	1985 Group £000	Parent £000
Trade debtors	91,615	–	81,361	–
Amounts due from subsidiaries	–	137,865	–	123,304
Other debtors	5,058	215	3,877	111
Prepayments and accrued income	10,642	209	10,090	114
	107,315	138,289	95,328	123,529

13   Borrowings

Analysis of loan stocks, bank loans and overdrafts by year of repayment:

	1986 Group £000	Parent £000	1985 Group £000	Parent £000
Over five years	38,635	21,644	33,858	26,920
From two to five years	25,633	16,474	18,937	9,700
From one to two years	281	–	4,641	1,916
Amounts falling due after more than one year	64,549	38,118	57,436	38,536
Amounts falling due within one year	9,777	8,112	12,771	5,508
Borrowings	74,326	46,230	70,207	44,044
Deduct:				
Deposits	3,453	1,583	6,578	1,165
Cash at bank and in hand	1,903	156	2,639	26
Net borrowings	68,970	44,491	60,990	42,853

		1986		1985	
		Group £000	*Parent* £000	*Group* £000	*Parent* £000

Amounts falling due for repayment after more than one year comprise:

Rate	Repayable				
Sterling					
7%	1982/87	**150**	**150**	150	150
6¾%	1989/94	**2,204**	**2,204**	2,267	2,267
8¼	1993/98	**1,179**	**1,179**	1,184	1,184
9¼%	1995/2000	**5,000**	**5,000**	5,000	5,000
12½%	2008	**10,000**	**10,000**	10,000	10,000
10%	1990	**625**	**625**	–	–
Variable	1991	**2,500**	**2,500**	2,500	2,500
Variable	1986	**–**	**–**	121	–
American and Canadian dollar					
Variable	1987/91	**3,247**	**3,247**	5,474	5,474
9.1%–12.45%	1988/96	**15,873**	**13,851**	12,764	10,690
8½%–10%	1987/92	**332**	**–**	413	–
Australian dollar					
Variable	1987/96	**5,046**	**3,251**	2,120	–
Dutch guilder					
9¼%	1989/93	**7,692**	**–**	6,266	–
French franc					
8½%	1993	**9,692**	**–**	–	–
8½%–14.1%	1989/93	**3,514**	**–**	3,159	–
Variable	1986/92	**–**	**–**	3,709	–
Deutsche mark					
10¾%	1987	**–**	**–**	1,271	1,271
Variable	1989	**678**	**–**	–	–
Other currencies					
Variable	1987/91	**1,425**	**–**	1,430	–
13¼%	1989	**254**	**–**	211	–
		69,411	**42,007**	58,039	38,536
Deduct: Repayments due within one year		**4,862**	**3,889**	603	–
		64,549	**38,118**	57,436	38,536

The borrowings set out above are unsecured except for £467,000 (1985 £711,000) which is secured over the tangible assets of the subsidiary companies concerned.

14   Other creditors

	1986 Group £000	1986 Parent £000	1985 Group £000	1985 Parent £000
Trade creditors	40,046	–	38,170	–
Amounts due to subsidiaries	–	23,639	–	8,557
Corporate tax	10,889	5,277	7,145	4,454
Other creditors	5,526	119	7,156	99
Accruals and deferred income	24,095	3,418	16,616	1,987
Sales and payroll taxes	14,510	193	11,875	144
Proposed ordinary dividend	7,929	7,929	6,475	6,475
	102,995	40,575	87,437	21,716

15   Provisions for liabilities

	Deferred tax £000	Overseas pension provision £000	Total £000
At beginning of year	15,606	448	16,054
Exchange rate adjustment	367	(11)	356
Companies acquired/(sold)	(176)	–	(176)
Transfer for the year	(1,436)	108	(1,328)
Payments made during year	–	(135)	(135)
	14,361	410	14,771
Advance corporation tax recoverable (1985 £2,775,000)	3,238	–	3,238
At 31 December 1986	11,123	410	11,533

	1986 £000	1985 £000
No provision has been made for:		
Tax deferred principally by capital allowances	12,734	12,334
Tax deferred on properties sold	2,466	2,132
	15,200	14,466

The amounts included above for United Kingdom deferred tax have been calculated at 35%. It is not practical to quantify the notional tax liability which might arise if all the properties were sold at their book value. No provision has been made for any tax which may be payable on the distribution of reserves by overseas subsidiaries.

16   Share capital

	Author- ized £000	Allotted & fully paid £000
Ordinary shares of 25p each:		
At beginning of year	49,056	35,972
Shares issued under the 1973 share option scheme	–	68
At 31 December 1986	49,056	36,040
4.2 per cent cumulative preference shares of £1 each	1,394	1,394
	50,450	37,434

The total consideration received by the company in respect of the 270,000 ordinary shares issued during the year amounted to £223,000. Under the 1973 share option scheme there remain options exercisable between 1987 and 1989 to purchase 280,000 ordinary shares at 82½p per share. In addition under the 1986 share option scheme there are options, granted on 10 June 1986, existing for 2,218,500 ordinary shares exercisable between 1989 and 1996 at 174p per share.

17   Reserves

	Share premium £000	Other reserves	
		Group £000	Parent £000
At beginning of year	6,633	93,138	47,623
Exchange rate adjustment net of tax	–	2,282	(1,955)
Arising on shares issued during the year	155	–	–
Goodwill on consolidation arising in the year written off	–	(2,196)	–
Surplus for the year retained	–	13,926	6,964
At 31 December 1986	6,788	107,150	52,632

Other reserves include a capital redemption reserve of £435,000 (1985 £435,000). The profit dealt with in the accounts of the parent company was £17,834,000 (1985 £15,402,000).

18   Capital commitments

	1986 £000	1985 £000
Outstanding contracts for capital expenditure	6,790	8,588
Capital expenditure authorized but not con- tracted for	19,131	14,741
	25,921	23,329

19   Operating lease commitments

The group has commitments under operating leases to make payments in
the following year as set out below:

	Plant & equipment	1986 Land & buildings	Plant & equipment	1985 Land & buildings
	£000	£000	£000	£000
Operating leases which expire:				
Within one year	319	454	829	103
Between two and five years	2,094	1,439	846	894
After five years	18	2,095	21	2,185
	2,431	3,988	1,696	3,182

20   Exchange rates

Assets, liabilities and profits of the year in overseas currencies have been
translated into sterling at rates ruling at 31 December. The principal
exchange rates used were:

	1986	1985
American dollar	1.48	1.45
Australian dollar	2.23	2.12
Canadian dollar	2.05	2.02
Dutch guilder	3.25	3.99
French franc	9.29	10.78

Five year record

	1982 £000	1983 £000	1984 £000	1985 £000	1986 £000
Turnover	347,786	367,653	434,651	481,462	543,164
Operating profit	23,568	26,351	31,534	38,234	48,227
Net interest payable	5,239	5,371	7,474	8,569	8,865
Profit before tax	18,329	20,980	24,060	29,665	39,362
Tangible assets	166,581	177,420	216,102	209,696	232,869
Investments	801	1,067	679	108	2,114
Net current assets (excluding cash and short term borrowings)	15,503	15,142	24,204	22,763	18,600
Net assets employed	182,885	193,629	240,985	232,567	253,583
Ordinary shareholders' funds	127,192	134,579	142,040	146,149	160,384
Preference share capital	1,394	1,394	1,394	1,394	1,394
Minority interests	3,074	3,196	4,742	3,970	1,094
Deferred liabilities and provisions	6,551	6,239	18,724	20,064	21,741
Net borrowings	44,674	48,221	74,085	60,990	68,970
Capital employed	182,885	193,629	240,985	232,567	253,583
	%	%	%	%	%
Operating profit as a percentage of average capital employed	13.5	14.0	14.5	16.0	19.8
	p	p	p	p	p
Earnings per ordinary share	7.9	10.1	10.8	12.4	17.2
Dividends per ordinary share	4.45	5.0	5.6	6.2	7.5
Net tangible assets per ordinary share	95.7	101.2	99.1	101.6	111.3

Statement of value added

	1982 £000	1983 £000	1984 £000	1985 £000	1986 £000
Turnover	347,786	367,653	434,651	481,462	543,164
Deduct:					
Cost of services and materials purchased	185,210	192,052	230,897	258,696	284,526
Value added	162,576	175,601	203,754	222,766	258,638
Applied as follows:					
Employees	117,721	126,705	146,973	156,373	178,635
Governments (corporate tax)	7,338	7,211	9,075	11,218	14,304
Providers of capital:					
Net interest payable	5,239	5,371	7,474	8,569	8,865
Minority and preference shareholders	539	319	252	674	359
Ordinary shareholders	5,914	6,651	7,874	8,921	10,811
Reinvestment in the business:					
Depreciation	21,287	22,545	25,247	28,159	31,776
Profit retained (excluding extraordinary items)	4,538	6,799	6,859	8,852	13,888
	162,576	175,601	203,754	222,766	258,638

The above figures showing the application of value added may be expressed in percentage terms as follows:

	%	%	%	%	%
Employees	72.4	72.2	72.1	70.2	69.1
Governments	4.5	4.1	4.5	5.0	5.5
Providers of capital	7.2	7.0	7.7	8.2	7.7
Reinvestment in the business	15.9	16.7	15.7	16.6	17.7
	100.0	100.0	100.0	100.0	100.0

Notice of meeting

Notice is hereby given that the thirty-eighth annual general meeting of Transport Development Group PLC will be held at Glaziers Hall, 9 Montague Close, London Bridge, London SE1 9DD on Friday 1 May 1987 at twelve noon for the following purposes.

1   To consider the accounts for the year ended 31 December 1986 and the reports of the directors and auditors thereon.
2   To declare a dividend on the ordinary shares.
3   To elect a director.
4   To appoint auditors.
5   To authorize the directors to fix the remuneration of the auditors.

As special business to consider and if thought fit pass the following ordinary and special resolutions.

Ordinary resolution

6   That the Board be and it is hereby generally and unconditionally authorized to exercise all powers of the Company to allot relevant securities (within the meaning of Section 80 of the Companies Act 1985) up to an aggregate nominal amount of £10 million provided that this authority shall expire on the date of the next annual general meeting of the Company after the passing of this resolution save that the Company may before such expiry make an offer or agreement which would or might require relevant securities to be allotted after such expiry and the Board may allot relevant securities in pursuance of such offer or agreement as if the authority conferred hereby had not expired.

Special resolution

7   That subject to the passing of the previous resolution the Board be and it is hereby empowered to allot equity securities pursuant to the authority conferred by the previous resolution as if sub-section (1) of Section 89 of the Companies Act 1985 did not apply to any such allotment provided that this power shall be limited:

   (a)   to the allotment of equity securities in connection with a rights issue in favour of ordinary shareholders where the equity securities respectively attributable to the interests of all ordinary shareholders are proportionate (as nearly as may be) to the respective numbers of ordinary shares held by them, and
   (b)   to the allotment (otherwise than pursuant to sub-paragraph (a) above) or equity securities up to an aggregate nominal value of £2.45 million.

and shall expire on the date of the next annual general meeting of the Company after the passing of this resolution save that the Company may before such expiry make an offer or agreement which would or might require equity securities to be allotted after such expiry and the Board may allot equity securities in pursuance of such an offer or agreement as if the power conferred hereby had not expired.

Any member of the Company entitled to attend and vote at the meeting is entitled to appoint one or more proxies to attend and vote instead of him. A proxy need not be a member.

By order of the Board

R. D. GARWOOD, *Secretary*.

Windsor House,
50 Victoria Street, London SW1H 0NR
1 April 1987

Copies of the contracts of service of the directors are available for inspection at the registered office of the Company during usual business hours and also at the place of meeting from 11.45 a.m. until its conclusion.

Financial calendar

Final ordinary dividend payable on 8 May 1987 to shareholders registered on 10 April 1987.

Half-year results expected to be announced on 10 August 1987.

Interim ordinary dividend normally payable in the first week of November.

Form of proxy

I/We ....

of ....

....

being a member of TRANSPORT DEVELOPMENT GROUP PLC hereby appoint the chairman of the meeting*

....

as my/our proxy to vote for me/us on my/our behalf at the annual general meeting of the company to be held on 1 May 1987 and at any adjournment thereof. In the event of a poll I/we desire our votes to be cast as follows:

(Please indicate with a tick ∨ how you wish your votes cast)	For	Against
To adopt the report and accounts		
To declare a final dividend		
To re-elect Mr J. Wishart as a director		
To re-appoint Binder Hamlyn as auditors		
To authorize the directors to fix the remuneration of the auditors		
To authorize the directors to allot securities up to a maximum amount		
To authorize the directors to allot securities as if Section 89(1) of the Companies Act 1985 did not apply		

Dated this ....day of.. 1987

Signature ....

*If you wish to appoint a proxy other than the chairman of the meeting please insert his or her name and address and delete the chairman of the meeting.

Notes
1 Proxies must be lodged at the address overleaf not later than 48 hours before the meeting.
2 In the case of a corporation the form of proxy must be under its common seal or under the hand of an officer or attorney duly authorized.
3 In the case of joint holdings the signature of one holder will suffice.
4 Unless otherwise instructed the proxy will vote or abstain as he thinks fit in respect of your total holding.

15.2 Communicating to employees

It is only since the 1960s and 1970s that the United Kingdom has made any real attempt to secure the provision of information in an accounting form to employees. This has been brought about by the changing social and political attitudes of that period, the main work in the field being the Royal Commission on Trade Unions and Employers Association 1968 (The Donovan Report), which contained no specific proposals, other than to state that management should: 'Make available to worker representatives (presumably trade union officials etc.,) such information as they may reasonably require, to develop policies on such matters as recruitment, promotion, training and retraining.'

The Report on Industrial Democracy by the National Executive Committee of the Labour Party (1967) suggested that information should be disclosed:

1   To government – to extend effective social accountability and forward planning.
2   To trade unions – to enable them to protect their members' interests through collective bargaining and through participative processes, to include:
    (a) Manpower and training plans, management emoluments, labour turnover statistics, labour costs and details of accidents.
    (b) Control information of holding, subsidiary and associated companies; directors' shareholdings and decision-making responsibilities.
    (c) Development, production and investment information, including changes in work methods, investment plans, research and development, and order book details.
    (d) Cost and pricing structures, sales turnover, and details of investment financing methods.

These two reports lead to the introduction of a White Paper on Industrial Relations being introduced in 1969 entitled *In Place of Strife*. This did not detail information disclosure proposals, but stated that 'adequate information to allow an independent judgement to be made on management proposals, policies and decisions' would be required to ensure informed participation on equal terms with management in the extension of collective bargaining and consultation at company or plant level.

The Labour Government were, however, replaced by a Conservative Government in 1970, before legislation could be introduced. The Industrial Relations Act 1971 and the Employment Protection Act of 1975, both contained provisions on Disclosure of information to employees, but both became non-operative, mainly due to the considerable criticism from both trade unions and employers; the first claiming too many loopholes justifying a refusal to disclose information and the latter claiming that too much information was called for. A second code of practice, *Disclosure of Information to Trade Unions for Collective Bargaining Purposes* was, however, approved by Parliament on 22 May 1977, so that trade unions are now empowered to call for information relevant to collective bargaining in line with the guidelines of Code of Practice 2, the main provisions of which are as follows. During collective bargaining between an employer and a recognized trade union the employer is under a general duty to disclose to trade union representatives information:

1   Without which the representative would be materially impeded in carrying out negotiations.
2   Which it would be in accordance with good industrial relations to disclose.

The information *must* be requested by the trade union representative and the employer is not required to disclose any information which:

1   Would be against the interests of national security.
2   Would contravene a prohibition imposed by, or under, an enactment.
3   Was given to an employer in confidence, or was obtained by the employer in consequence of the confidence reposed in him by another person.
4   Relates to an individual unless he has consented to its disclosure.
5   Would cause substantial injury to the undertaking (or national interest in respect of Crown employment) for reasons other than its effect on collective bargaining.
6   Was obtained for the purpose of any legal proceedings.

The employer is also under a general duty to disclose information to the trade union representative if the trade union considers that an employer has failed to disclose to its representatives information required to be disclosed by section 17 of the Act.

Because of the variety and complexity of collective bargaining issues which may have to be dealt with, it has not been possible to specify the exact information which must be disclosed by employers, only to state that the employer must disclose information concerning his undertaking, without which trade union representatives would naturally be impeded during collective bargaining. The following examples of information which could be relevant are listed in the Code of Practice:

● Pay and benefits
● Conditions of service
● Manpower
● Performance
● Financial

By this Employment Protection Act the strength of the union in the collective bargaining situation is clearly being enhanced, by the provision of information hitherto denied to the union's side of the negotiations, but the limits of disclosure will become clearer as 'case law' and 'appeals' come before the authorities.

From the above legislation it can be seen that the time is right for drastic improvements in the 'disclosure of information to employees and unions, and the British Institute of Management's survey Report 31, *Keeping Employees Informed* indicates that voluntary disclosure is becoming increasingly common. Should workers achieve representation on boards of directors as suggested by the Bullock Committee Inquiry Report of 1972, in any form, disclosure of information to employees or employee representatives would be essential to effective participation.

Part Six
Exercises

Exercises:
First series

No. 1

Certain mistakes have been made in drawing up the following balance sheet of M. Rose:

Balance sheet
(as at 31 December 19xx)

	£	£		£
Capital Account:			Freehold Premises	3,000
1 January 19xx	6,000		Stock, 31 December 19xx	2,845
Add Loan Received			Plant and Machinery	2,560
from H. Glass	1,000		Cash in Hand	78
		7,000	M. Rose, Drawings	702
Net Profit for Year	1,368		Bank Overdraft	349
Sundry Debtors	1,412		Sundry Creditors	1,880
Stock, Jan. 1st, 19xx	1,634			
		£11,414		£11,414

Show the balance sheet as it should be.

No. 2

From the following trial balance and the account 'Wilkinson, Capital', prepare a balance sheet, statement of proprietor's capital, and profit and loss account for the Golden Gate Landscaping Company.

Golden Gate Landscaping Company
Trial balance
(31 December 19xx)

	£	£
Cash	562	
Debtors	2,116	
Garden supplies	402	
Lorry	2,100	
Accumulated depreciation – Lorry		560
Gardening tools	317	
Prepaid insurance	109	
Creditors		107
Contracts payable		
(11 payments @ £60/mo.)		660
Wilkinson, capital		4,500
Wilkinson, drawings	3,600	
Income from landscaping		7,350
Telephone	50	
Garden supplies used	2,516	
Depreciation – lorry	560	
Petrol and oil	373	
Office supplies	27	
Insurance	207	
Sundry expenses	238	
	£13,177	£13,177

Wilkinson, capital

	19xx	£
	January Balance	3,500
	6 May Cash	1,000

No. 3

Using the same data as in the previous example show only the liabilities and owner's equity sections of the balance sheet when no separate statement of proprietor's capital is used.

No. 4

The balance sheet of the ESBA Bookshop at the start of 19x8 was as follows:

ESBA Bookshop
Balance sheet
(as at 1 January 19x8)

Claims	£	Assets	£	£
Ownership interest	2,600	Shop fittings: cost	1,500	
Trade creditors	850	Accumulated		
Rent owing	250	Depreciation	450	
Bank overdraft	750		—	1,050
		Stock of books		2,600
		Trade debtors		800
	£4,450			£4,450

Transactions for 19x8 were:

		£
(i)	Sale of books	10,000
(ii)	Cost of books sold	7,000
(iii)	Wages and general expenses	850
(iv)	Depreciation of shop fittings	150
(v)	Payment to landlord for rent (see note)	1,500
(vi)	Withdrawal of capital by owners	500

At 31 December 19x8 the values of certain items in the balance sheet were:

(i)	Stock of books	2,300
(ii)	Trade debtors	650
(iii)	Trade creditors	1,200

Note: Rental payment: The annual rent of the bookshop is £1,000. This payment represented rent for the period from 1 October 19x7 to 31 March 19x9.

Required:

(a)   Prepare for the firm for the year 19x8:
   (i) Profit and loss report, and
   (ii) Flow of funds statement giving the causes of the change in the cash balance over the year.
(b)   Indicate briefly the use which the firm's management might make of (a(i)) and (a(ii)), distinguishing between the function of each report.

Examples from Chapter 2

No. 5

A machine costing £5,000 is purchased and shipped to the San Antonio plant of Penexco. The freight charges are £105, insurance while the machine is in transit is £75, and installation charges are £200. What is the total cost of the machine?

No. 6

A machine costs £10,600 installed **and ready to use**. Bay Machine Co. pays £2,000 down and agrees to assume **contract** obligations to pay £400 per month for twenty-four months. **Prepare the journal** entry for this transaction.

No. 7

A machine costing £9,800 is installed on 2 January. It is intended to be used for eight years and will have a scrap value of £200. What is the yearly amount of depreciation charge using the straight line method?

No. 8

The auditor for DERINI Products finds the following after an analysis of trade debtors:

Age of account	Amount £
0–30 days	170,000
31–60 days	80,000
61–90 days	40,000
over 90 days	30,000

On analysis of past experience it is found that the loss ratios for overdue accounts are as follows:

31–60 days	2 per cent
61–90 days	5 per cent
over 90 days	10 per cent

(a)   What should be the balance in the provision for bad debts account?
(b)   If the balance in the provision for bad debts account is £2,200 prior to the calculations made in (a) above, prepare the journal entry required.

No. 9

It is decided to sell the trade debtors to our bank at a discount of 4 per cent with no recourse. Under this plan we give £200,000 of debts to the bank.
    Prepare the required journal entry.

No. 10

Under an arrangement with Factors Ltd we pledge £150,000 of trade debtors as security for a loan of £100,000. The accounts are to be collected by us and are to be maintained at our office. At the end of each month a photostat is to be made of each account on which a collection has been made and these copies are to be forwarded to Factors Ltd with a cheque for the amounts collected and interest on the loan balance at the beginning of the month at 5 per cent.

(a) Prepare the entry (entries) required on transfer of the accounts to Factors Ltd on 1 February.
(b) In February £20,000 is collected. Prepare the required 28 February entry (entries).
(c) In March £50,000 is collected. Prepare the required 31 March entry (entries).
(d) In April £30,000 is collected. Prepare the required 30 April entry (entries).

No. 11

A business purchases merchandise on account. The amount of the invoice is £6,742.90. Terms are 2 per cent/10 days; net 30 days.

(a) Prepare the entry for the purchase. (Debit merchandise purchases.)
(b) Prepare the entry for payment made during the discount period.
(c) Prepare the entry for payment made after the discount period.

No. 12

In reviewing shipments of merchandise and the invoices covering these shipments, the following are found:

(a) Goods shipped FOB shipping point on 28 December 19x8, arrive on 5 January, 19x9. The invoice for £8,200 is received on 6 January 19x9, and is recorded on that date.
(b) Goods shipped FOB destination on 28 December 19x8, arrive on 5 January 19x9. The invoice for £3,500 is received on 6 January 19x9, and is recorded on that date.

Prepare any entry (entries) required in 19x8.

No. 13

A machine costing £15,000 is installed on 2 January 19x8, and is used for special jobs on an intermittent basis. It will have a scrap value of £1,000 after 2000 hours of use. Time records of machine usage are kept as follows:

| 19x7 | 175 hours |
| 19x8 | 62 hours |

(a) What is the hourly depreciation rate?
(b) What amount should be charged to depreciation expense in the calendar years 19x7 and 19x8?

No. 14

A company buys a machine costing £40,000 on 2 January 19xx. It has an expected life of eight years. Assuming a scrap value of £400, determine the yearly depreciation expense using the sum-of-the-years-digits method.

No. 15

On 1 July 19x0, a business buys a machine costing £25,200 having an estimated life of ten years and a scrap value of £1,200. Management depreciates the machine on a straight line basis. The accumulated depreciation at 31 December 19x7 was £18,000. On 1 October 19x8, the company part-exchanges the asset for a new and larger machine of the same type. This asset costs £30,000 and the dealer agrees to allow a trade-in of £1,800 for the old machine if it is used as a down payment on the new one.

(a) Prepare the entry to record the depreciation of the machine to 1 October 19x8.
(b) Prepare the entry to record the purchase of the new machine on 1 October 19x8.
(c) Prepare the entry to record the depreciation expense of the new machine to 31 December 19x8, using the straight line method. Assume a scrap value of £1,600 and an eight-year life.

No. 16

Mr Overstreet, the owner of an apartment house that cost £75,000 and has now depreciated to a book value of £32,000, wants to present a statement to the bank to secure credit. The building has a current value of £125,000 and is insured for £90,000. The balance owing on the mortgage is £60,000. What entry should be made to present the facts of current value to the bank?

Examples from Chapter 3

No. 17

From the following trial balance of Santini & Casey, Insurance Brokers, and the two capital accounts shown, prepare a balance sheet (showing a detailed equity section) and an income statement.

Santini & Casey, Insurance Brokers
Trial balance
(as at 31 December 19x8)

	£	£
Cash	4,015	
Debtors	700	
Commissions receivable	5,603	
Office supplies	1,210	
Office furniture	9,315	
Accumulated depreciation – Office furniture		3,702
Motor vehicles	7,600	
Accumulated depreciation – Motor vehicles		3,300
Prepaid insurance	570	
Prepaid rent	600	
Premiums payable		2,950

	£	£
Creditors		111
M. Santini, capital		10,000
M. Santini, drawings	5,200	
W. Casey, capital		10,000
W. Casey, drawings	5,200	
Commissions income		29,585
Wages	9,050	
Rent	2,400	
Telephone	1,100	
Office supplies used	560	
Insurance	210	
Vehicle running expenses	2,300	
Depreciation – Office equipment	955	
Depreciation – Motor vehicles	2,010	
Sundry expenses	1,050	
	£59,648	£59,648

M. Santini, capital

	19x8	
		£
	1 January Balance	8,000
	3 March Cash	2,000

W. Casey, capital

	19x8	
		£
	1 January Balance	10,000

No. 18

From the data given in the previous example prepare a separate statement of partners' capital and show how the liability and equity sections of the balance sheet would appear.

No. 19

The partnership agreement between Messrs Brick, Bat and Rubble contained the following provisions:

	Brick		Bat		Rubble
Fixed capital	£16,000		£12,000		£10,000
Salaries	–		£1,000		£900
Interest on fixed capital	7%		7%		7%
Profit-sharing ratio	3	:	2	:	2
Current account balance, at 1 January	£500		£400		£450
Drawings during year	£2,000		£1,400		£1,100

The year's profits of the partnership before charging items included above was £7,430.

Show the profit and loss appropriation account and the current accounts of the partners for the year in question.

No. 20

The following is the balance sheet of Messrs Hit and Miss, who share profits in the ratio of 3:2.

Balance sheet

	£	£		£
Capital: Hit	8,000		Assets	20,000
Miss	5,000			
	——	13,000		
Liabilities		7,000		
		£20,000		£20,000

The business has been valued and the net worth is £18,000. It is decided to introduce a new partner, Target, who has £6,000 to contribute. The profits are to be shared in the ratio of 4:3:3.

(a) Show the balance sheet after goodwill has been entered in the accounts, and Target has been introduced into the partnership.

(b) Show the balance sheet when the goodwill has been eliminated after the admission of Target.

(c) Show the balance sheet and the payment made to the other partners if Target pays a premium for admission to the partnership.

Examples from Chapter 4

No. 21

From the information contained in the following two balance sheets, prepare a consolidated balance sheet of Shark Ltd and its subsidiary as at 31 December.

Shark Ltd
Balance sheet
(as at 31 December 19xx)

	£		£
Share capital	150,000	Fixed assets	120,000
Reserves	40,000	30,000 shares in Minnow	
Liabilities	75,000	Ltd (acquired on	
		1 January)	45,000
		Current assets	100,000
	£265,000		£265,000

Minnow Ltd
Balance sheet
(as at 31 December 19xx)

	£		£
Share capital		Fixed assets	40,000
40,000 £ shares	40,000	Current assets	33,000
Reserves at 1 January	12,000		
Profit for year	6,000		
Liabilities	15,000		
	£73,000		£73,000

No. 22

From the information contained in the following two balance sheets prepare a consolidated balance sheet of House Ltd and its subsidiary Hut Ltd as at 31 December.

House Ltd
Balance sheet
(as at 31 December 19xx)

	£		£
Share capital	200,000	Fixed assets	160,000
Reserves	50,000	40,000 shares in Hut Ltd	
Liabilities	60,000	(acquired on 1 January)	54,000
		Loan to Hut Ltd	6,000
		Current assets	90,000
	£310,000		£310,000

Balance sheet of Hut Ltd
(as at 31 December 19xx)

	£		£
Share capital		Fixed assets	50,000
50,000 £ shares	50,000	Stock bought from House	
Reserves at 1 January	5,000	Ltd for £750	1,000
Profit for year	7,500	Other current assets	51,500
Loan from House Ltd	6,000		
Other liabilities	34,000		
	£102,500		£102,500

Examples from Chapter 5

No. 23

Below is a very rough draft of the balance sheet of Shaky Grounds Ltd, at 31 December 19x8:

	£		£
Creditors	9,000	Plant – cost	26,000
5½% Debentures	12,000	Depreciation	6,000
General reserve	2,500		
Unappropriated profit	1,560		20,000
Bank	2,250	Debtors	10,510
Tax due immediately	1,200	Patents, at cost *less* amounts	
Capital:		w/o	5,000
10,000 6% preference		Stocks	17,000
shares of £1	10,000		
14,000 Ordinary shares of			
£1	14,000		
	£52,510		£52,510

The preference shares have priority for both dividends and repayment at winding up. No dividends have been declared for 19x8. No adjustments have so far been made for:

(i)   A bad debt of £320.
(ii) Accrued charges of £1,500.

Required:
(a)   Redraft the balance sheet in good style.
(b)   Suppose that (as the patents have been superseded and the company's main product will no longer sell) the company is liquidated at the start of 19x9. The assets realize £34,450 in cash. Draw up a statement to show how much in the £ each class of creditors, shareholders, etc. will receive.

Examples from Chapter 6

No. 24

The total sales of Departmentalized Stores Ltd for the financial year ended 31 March 19x9, are £360,000 from the following sources:

	£
Department 1	85,000
Department 2	72,000
Department 3	93,000
Department 4	110,000

The opening stock in each department is:

	£
Department 1	7,000
Department 2	6,000
Department 3	7,000
Department 4	11,000

The net purchases in each department are:

	£
Department 1	74,000
Department 2	68,000
Department 3	81,000
Department 4	99,000

The closing stock in each department is:

	£
Department 1	6,000
Department 2	7,000
Department 3	8,000
Department 4	10,000

The selling expenses in each department are:

	£
Department 1	7,000
Department 2	4,000
Department 3	6,000
Department 4	4,000

The total administrative expense is £8,000.

Prepare a departmentalized trading and profit and loss account with percentages.

No. 25

T. Jones and H. Higgins were partners in a manufacturing business trading under the provisions of the Partnership Act, 1890.

Trial balance at 30 September 19x2

	£	£
Stocks 1 October 19x1: Raw materials	8,000	
WIP	16,000	
Finished goods	14,000	
Capital: T. Jones		28,000
H. Higgins		40,640
Drawings: T. Jones	14,800	
H. Higgins	12,000	
Creditors		7,600
Debtors	20,800	
Sales of finished goods		210,500
Purchases of raw materials	80,000	
Factory wages	50,000	
Office salaries	9,850	
Rent and rates (factory ⅔, office ⅓)	15,000	
Factory power	6,000	
Heat and light (factory ⅗, office ⅖)	5,000	
Returns outwards	500	
Salesmen's commission	2,100	
Delivery expenses	4,000	
Postage, stationery, printing	1,800	
Bank charges and interest	800	
Advertising	500	
Plant and equipment (cost)	50,000	
Provision for depreciation		20,000
Office furniture (cost)	5,000	
Provision for depreciation		3,000
Office machinery (cost)	3,000	
Provision for depreciation		1,800
Insurance	390	
Bank		20,000
Factory manager's salary	12,000	
	£331,540	£331,540

Additional information

1   Stocks on hand September 30th, 19x2:

Finished goods	£16,000
Raw materials	£12,000
Work in progress	£18,000

2   At the end of the year the following adjustments have to be made: factory wages due £2,000; office wages due £159, and insurance prepaid £40.

3   During the year Mr Jones had taken finished goods for his personal use valued, at cost, at £200.

4   Depreciation is to be provided as follows:

Plant and equipment	10 per cent	⎫
Office furniture	5 per cent	⎬ on cost
Office machinery	20 per cent	⎭

5   A bad debt provision equal to 5 per cent sundry debtors is to be provided.

From the trial balance and additional information provided, you are required to prepare the manufacturing account, the trading and appropriation account for the year ended 30 September 19x2 and a balance sheet as at that date.

Source: SCCA

Examples from Chapter 7

No. 26

Trunk Ltd opened a branch at Southend on 1 January. All merchandise is provided by the head office and is invoiced to the branch at selling price. The following is a summary of the transactions for the first year:

		£
Goods from head office	(cost price)	6,000
Goods from head office	(selling price)	8,000
Goods returned to head office	(cost price)	600
Goods returned to head office	(selling price)	800
Proceeds from cash sales remitted to head office		6,500
Stock-in-hand, 31 December 19xx	(selling price)	600
Stock-on-hand, 31 December 19xx	(cost price)	450

Show in summary form the entries that would appear in the head office books if the selling price entries were treated as memorandum entries.

No. 27

From the information in the previous example, prepare the summarized entries if the goods were transferred at selling price, and the selling price were recorded in the branch account. Include the adjustments necessary at the end of the year.

No. 28

100 units were consigned by Senders Ltd to Sellers Ltd at £10 each. Expenses amounting to £180 were paid by Senders Ltd, and £250 by the consignee, Sellers Ltd. Seventy units have been sold by Sellers Ltd for £1,800, their commission being 10 per cent on sales. £1,000 has been remitted back to Senders Ltd.

Show the entries in the books of Senders Ltd and balance the consignment account.

No. 29

From the details in the previous example, show the entries in the books of Sellers Ltd.

No. 30

An abbreviated profit and loss statement for REMCO Ltd, follows:

	£
Sales	200,000
Cost of goods sold	170,000
Gross profit	30,000
Operating expenses	12,000
Net profit	£18,000

The business is contacted by a credit card company with a proposal to redeem all credit card sales slips at 6 per cent discount. It is estimated that sales will increase by 25 per cent but that 20 per cent of the current business will convert to credit card sales. The gross profit percentage would remain the same but operating expenses (excluding credit card discounts) would increase by 5 per cent of new sales.

Should REMCO Ltd, make credit card sales? Why?

No. 31

What factors might a company selling on credit in the following circumstances look at?

(a)   Houses
(b)   Cars
(c)   Mail order
(d)   General retail goods (department store)

No. 32

Goods costing £300,000 are sold for £500,000 on instalment contracts in 19x8. Prepare the required entry (entries).

No. 33

In 19x8, collections on the goods sold in the previous example amounted to £70,000. Prepare the necessary entry (entries).

No. 34

In 19x9, collections on the goods sold in Example 32 amounted to £180,000. Prepare the necessary entry (entries).

No. 35

At the beginning of 19x9 there are credit balances in these accounts:

Gross profit on instalment sales – 19x6:   £20,000
Gross profit on instalment sales – 19x7:   £160,000
Gross profit on instalment sales – 19x8:   £500,000

The gross profit percentages in these years were as follows:

19x6:   32 per cent
19x7:   37 per cent
19x8:   35 per cent

The balances in the accounts at the end of 19x9 are:

Gross profit on instalment sales – 19x6:   0
Gross profit on instalment sales – 19x7:   £30,000
Gross profit on instalment sales – 19x8:   £220,000

What were the collections on the 19x6, 19x7, and 19x8 instalment sales?
Answer to the nearest pound.

No. 36

A customer wants to trade in a used machine for a new one priced at
£15,000 that cost £13,000. The salesman allows £3,000 on the used machine
and accepts an instalment contract for £12,500. The used machine can be
sold for £4,500 after spending £800 to recondition it. The mark-up for used
equipment is 20 per cent of the selling price.

(a)   Prepare a schedule showing the value of the trade-in merchandise.
(b)   Prepare the entry (entries) for the sale.

No. 37

Statham designed a new football boot, with a special protective pad for the
heel, and granted a licence to Regis Ltd for the manufacture and sale of
these boots.

Under the terms of the agreement the company were to pay Statham a
royalty of 50p for each pair sold up to 9000 in any one year, with 40p for
each pair sold above this number, subject to a minimum payment of £4,000
per annum. In any year that royalties came to less than the minimum of
payment, the deficiency could be set off against excess royalties in either of
the next two, succeeding years.

Payment was to be made at the end of the company's financial year, on
31 March.

The number of pairs of boots sold in the first four years of the agreement
was as follows:

Year to 31 March 19x9   3,000
Year to 31 March 19x0   9,200
Year to 31 March 19x1   11,000
Year to 31 March 19x2   17,000

Royalty payments were made on the correct day.

   You are required to record the entries for the above transactions in the ledger accounts of Regis Ltd.

Source: SCCA

Examples from Chapter 8

Taxation systems and rates are continually changing and questions quickly date. Details can be obtained from current specialist texts, professional magazines and revenue offices of the country concerned.

Examples from Chapter 9

No. 38

Mention (a) some advantages, and (b) some disadvantages of using the periodic inventory method.

No. 39

From the following figures in the accounts of Traders Ltd, prepare a cost of goods sold statement for the year to 31 March 19x9:

	£	£
Stock at 31 March 19x9	150,000	
Stock at 1 April 19x8	130,000	
Purchases	1,600,000	
Purchase returns and allowances		30,000
Purchase discounts		31,000
Carriage inwards	12,000	

No. 40

When the re-order point for Item 3XB is reached, the count of the items shows 150 units but the perpetual inventory card shows 140 units. The unit price is £1.25. Prepare the adjusting entry.

No. 41

A sale is made for cash (200 units costing £1.50 each are sold for £2 each). The periodic inventory method is used.

(a)   Prepare the sales entry.
(b)   Prepare the cost of sales entry.

No. 42

A count is made of Item 66–329B, and 297 units are counted. The perpetual inventory card shows 325 units. The unit price of the item is £1.60. Prepare the adjusting entry.

No. 43

Concerning the perpetual inventory method:

(a) Mention some advantages of using this method.
(b) Mention some disadvantages of using this method.

No. 44

A sale is made for cash (300 units costing £4 each are sold for £5 each). The perpetual inventory method is used.

(a) Prepare the sales entry.
(b) Prepare the cost of sales entry.

No. 45

The following information is taken from the perpetual inventory card for Item 49–3B127:

Balance, 1 January 19xx	1,000 units	£5.70 each
Received, 31 January	2,000 units	£6.20 each
Received, 15 February	2,000 units	£6.40 each
Received, 18 March	2,000 units	£6.60 each
Sold, 20 April	3,000 units	£7.40 each
Sold, 15 May	1,500 units	£8.00 each

Complete the following table:

	LIFO	Average	FIFO
Sales			
Cost of goods sold			
Gross profit			
Stock, 31 May			

No. 46

Below is a table of items showing the invoice price and current market price for each item. What is the value of the stocks using cost or market, whichever is lower?

Item		Invoice price	Cost price
		£	£
A1	100 units	60	67
A2	120 units	120	110
A3	600 units	210	200
A4	210 units	300	290
B1	430 units	400	410
B2	10 units	75	72
B3	25 units	450	430
C1	900 units	790	810
C2	42 units	575	560
C3	150 units	815	804
C4	200 units	615	627

No. 47

From the figures: cost = £4 each and selling price = £5 each, what is the gross profit:

(a)   As a percentage of the selling price?
(b)   As a percentage of the cost?

No. 48

In analysing storeroom requisitions, the following is found:

Storeroom requisition number	Total	Job 16	Job 19	Job 22	Dept. A	Dept. B
	£	£	£	£	£	£
615	19.20	19.20				
616	42.50		20.50	12.00		10.00
617	53.15				53.15	
618	109.30	19.00	80.00	10.30		
619	41.70					41.70

Prepare an entry to record the above data. (Assume that the departments mentioned are service departments.)

No. 49

Using the formula given on page 245, determine the economic order quantity for Item 335, given:

Annual requirement	2,000 units
Cost per unit	£6.40
Inventory holding cost	30 per cent
Ordering cost per order	£14.00

No. 50

Assuming 250 working days a year, how often must Item 335 (in the previous example) be ordered?

No. 51

Determine the minimum stock for Item XB–222, given the following:

Daily usage	30 units
Lead time	2 calendar weeks

The plant is on a five-day-per-week schedule.

No. 52

The time analysis for Department 1 is:

	Monday	Tuesday	Wednesday	Thursday	Friday
Jones	8	8	8	8	8
Smith	7	9	8	8	8
Blue	8	8	7	7	9
Green	8	9	9	6	10
Acme	3	11	8	6	10

The hourly rates of pay are as follows:

Jones	£1.75
Smith	£2.10
Blue	£2.05
Green	£1.95
Acme	£1.52

Compute gross pay, assuming:

(a) Overtime of 50 per cent is paid for all hours over forty worked in one week.

(b) Overtime of 50 per cent is paid for all hours over eight worked in one day.

No. 53

The piecework rate for Part 632 is:

First 100 pieces	17.5p each
Next 50 pieces	18p each
All over 150 pieces	19p each

Jones produces 70 pieces; Smith, 110 pieces; Blue, 180 pieces. Compute the week's wages for each worker.

No. 54

Would any of the answers to the previous example have been different if the minimum weekly wage was £16?

No. 55

What would the week's wages be if the piece rate in Example 53 had read:

0–100 pieces	17.5p each
0–150 pieces	18p each
over 150 pieces	19p each

No. 56

To the production overhead account post data from the following facts:

(a) An analysis of the payroll summary shows work in progress £18,629; production overhead £2,302; sales salaries £5,621; office salaries £8,897.

(b)   An analysis of the materials requisition shows:

	£
Work in progress	42,915
Plant maintenance	297
Equipment repair orders	623
Production office supplies	105

(c)   The ledger shows purchases as follows:

	£	
Materials	62,336	
Telephone	128	50% sales / 30% office / 20% factory
Sundry expenses	215	10% sales / 10% office / 80% factory
Rent	1,450	5% sales / 5% office / 90% factory

(d)   An analysis of the prepaid accounts shows:

	Opening balance	Additions	Closing balance
	£	£	£
Insurance	3,900	9,000	3,600
Production supplies	4,200	5,000	4,800

70 per cent of insurance expenses chargeable to production.
(e)   The depreciation is computed to be £15,320.

No. 57

The 19x8 production overhead is £152,310. It is estimated that in 19x9 this will increase 10 per cent. Determine the various overheads:

(a)   Per direct-labour hours (assuming 16,750 direct-labour hours in 19x9).
(b)   Per direct-labour pounds (assuming an average of £0.75 per hour).

Examples from Chapter 10

No. 58

Part of the debit side of the payroll entry for November 19x8 is:

Work in progress – Job 16	£7,387
Job 17	7,622
Job 20	9,468
Job 21	763

Part of the debit side of the payroll entry for December 19x8 is:

Work in progress – Job 17	£7,341
Job 20	2,901
Job 21	2,538
Job 22	806

Part of the debit side of the payroll entry for January 19x9 is:

Work in progress – Job 20	£203
Job 21	4,742
Job 23	1,542

Part of the debit side of the materials requisition analysis entry for November 19x8 is:

Work in progress – Job 16	£6,802
Job 17	2,121
Job 20	2,253
Job 21	968

Part of the debit side of the materials requisition analysis entry for December 19x8 is:

Work in progress – Job 17	£8,591
Job 20	905
Job 21	6,437
Job 22	8,807

Part of the debit side of the materials requisition analysis entry for January 19x9 is:

Work in progress – Job 20	£347
Job 21	8,642
Job 23	3,763

The overhead rate is computed anew each month based on the performance of the two previous months:

November:	47 per cent of direct-labour pounds
December:	44 per cent of direct-labour pounds
January:	46 per cent of direct-labour pounds

Job 20 is completed in January 19x9. What is the value of Job 20 on:

(a)   30 November 19x8?
(b)   31 December 19x8?
(c)   31 January 19x9? (Before transfer to finished goods stock)

No. 59

In a situation where process cost accounting is used, the following facts are determined:

3000 lb of Material A and 2000 lb of Material B have been put into production at the beginning of the job. Material A costs £3/lb; B costs £15/lb. Direct labour expended in processing this material is £18,400. Overhead burden is 1.4 times direct labour. No shrinkage of material is involved in the process. At the end of the month 4000 lb of the end product are completely finished and 1000 lb are 60 per cent complete as to direct labour (100 per cent complete as to material).

Determine the value of:
(a)   Completed production.
(b)   Work in progress at the end of the month.

No. 60

In a process situation there is an opening inventory whose cost for completion to the present stage is:

	£
Direct labour	6,000
Direct materials	14,000
Overhead	12,000

To complete this inventory would take £9,000 of direct labour. (The overhead is expressed as a percentage of labour, and this percentage has not changed.) How much will the completed inventory cost?

No. 61

In Department 6 there is both opening and closing inventory for January 19xx. Details concerning the status of production in the department are as follows:

	Units	Percentage completion	
	Units	*Direct labour and overhead*	*Direct materials*
Opening inventory	300	50%	75%
Started in production	2,000		
Closing inventory	500	60%	100%

Determine the equivalent units of production for labour, materials and overhead. (Check your answer before going on to Example 62.)

No. 62

The value of the opening inventory in Example 65 is as follows:

	£
Direct labour	1,050
Direct materials	2,250
Overhead	2,100

The value of additions to production during the month is as follows:

	£
Direct labour	13,845
Direct materials	20,542
Overhead	27,495

Determine the value of the equivalent units of production.

No. 63

In a joint production situation, it costs £40,000 to manufacture Products A and B to point of separation. When completed, the sales value of A and B will be £60,000 and £40,000 respectively. It will cost £10,000 and £20,000 respectively to complete A and B. Determine the valuation of A and B at point of separation, using:

(a) Market value of the end product.
(b) Market value of the end product less further conversion.

No. 64

A batch of 700 units in production is inspected. Twenty units are found to be defective. The cost sheet up to the point of inspection shows:

	£
Labour	2,114
Materials	4,228
Overhead	1,057

How much is the cost of defective items, assuming:

(a) Defective goods and accepted goods should be valued the same at point of separation?
(b) Defective goods are valued at present worth (assume completed value to be £18.00; it costs £9.75 to complete) with all costs chargeable to work in progress?
(c) Defective goods priced at present worth and accepted goods priced at cost to point of inspection?

No. 65

Prepare entries for parts (a), (b), and (c) of the previous example.

Examples from Chapter 11

No. 66

From the following information for producing 60,000 units, prepare a break-even chart and check by calculating the break-even point.

	Variable £	Fixed £	Total £
Direct labour	13,000	–	13,000
Direct materials	12,000	–	12,000
Factory overhead	4,000	7,000	11,000
Selling expenses	6,000	3,000	9,000
Administration expenses	–	5,000	5,000
Total	£35,000	£15,000	£50,000

The price per unit is £1 irrespective of the level of sales.

No. 67

Prepare a second break-even chart to show the effect of the following changes in the information given in the previous example:

(a) An increase of 10 per cent in direct labour cost.
(b) An increase of 2 per cent in all other variable costs.
(c) An increase of £3,260 in fixed costs.
(d) An increase of 5 per cent in selling price.

No. 68

The income statement for the year 19x8 of the Progressive Company is shown below:

	£	£
Sales		200,000
Cost of goods sold		
Labour	80,000	
Materials	46,000	
Overhead	14,000	140,000
Gross profit		60,000
Selling expenses	25,000	
Administrative expenses	20,000	45,000
		£15,000

Prepare a budget for 19x9, assuming:

(a) Sales increase 20 per cent
(b) Labour increases 15 per cent
(c) Materials increase 20 per cent
(d) Selling expenses increase 15 per cent
(e) Administrative expenses increase 10 per cent
(f) Overhead maintains the same ratio to sales.

No. 69

In 19x7 it was determined that 19x9 plant production would involve 42,700 direct-labour hours, that factory overhead would be £623,950, and that the plant would operate at 80 per cent of capacity. However, the plant operated at 85 per cent capacity, using 45,000 direct-labour hours. The actual production overhead was £651,259. Determine the total variance.

No. 70

Analyse the variance determined in the previous example as to:

(a) Budget variance
(b) Volume variance
(c) Efficiency variance

No. 71

In a company using a standard costing system, the following facts are found:

● The standard labour rate for drilling is £2 per hour.
● The standard labour time required to complete 100 units of Part X34B is 7 hours.
● The actual time it took to complete 100 units of Part X34B was 7.1 hours and the pay rate of the operator was £2.10 per hour.

(a) How much was the actual cost of direct labour to produce the 100 units of Part X34B?
(b) How much was the standard cost of direct labour to produce the 100 units of Part X34B?
(c) Analyse any variance.

No. 72

The latest annual accounts for Wholesalers Ltd are:

Wholesalers Ltd
Balance sheet
(as at 31 December 19x8)

	£	£		£	£
Claims			*Assets*		
Capital			*Fixed Assets*		
Share capital 20,000			Motor vans: cost	5,000	
Shares of £1	20,000		Accumulated		
Profit and loss a/c	2,500		depreciation	3,000	
		22,500			2,000
Current liabilities			*Current assets*		
Trade creditors		9,000	Trade debtors	10,000	
			Stock	18,000	
			Prepaid rent	1,000	
			Cash at bank	500	
					29,500
		£31,500			£31,500

Profit and loss account for 19x8

	£	£
Sales		100,000
Less Cost of goods sold		90,000
Gross profit		10,000
Less Expenses		
Rent of warehouse	4,000	
Depreciation of motor vans	1,000	
Wages and general expenses	4,000	
		9,000
Net profit		£1,000

You are given the following information about the company's plans for 19x9:

(i) The lease on the present warehouse will expire on 31 March 19x9. In its place the company will purchase a freehold warehouse currently under construction that is due to be completed late in March. It will cost £15,000 payable on completion.

(ii) In order to finance the purchase, the company will issue for cash 15,000 £1 ordinary shares at par.

(iii) Sales in 19x9 are expected to be 30 per cent higher than in 19x8.

(iv) The gross profit margin (as a percentage of sales) in 19x9 will be double that of 19x8.

(v) In 19x9 the following expenses, depreciation of motor vans, wages and general expenses, will be the same absolute amount as in 19x8.

(vi) In all other respects the same pattern of trading that the company experienced in 19x8 will be repeated in 19x9.

Required:
(a) State, giving your reasons, what you would expect the level of stock, trade debtors, and trade creditors to be at 31 December 19x9.
(b) Prepare for Wholesalers Ltd:
   (i) The budgeted profit and loss account for 19x9.
   (ii) The budgeted balance sheet at 31 December 19x9.

Note: Ignore tax.

Examples from Chapter 12

No. 73

There are two types of machine available to a firm. The details are as follows:

	Machine A	Machine B
Output per year	6000 units	8000 units
Cost	£75,000	£60,000
Scrap value	£5,000	£5,000
Life	8 years	6 years
Annual running costs	£3,430	£8,610

The annual output required is 24,000 units. Disregarding the effect of any change in the price level, and assuming that the funds required will be borrowed at 6 per cent per annum, indicate which type of machine the firm should purchase.

No. 74

The One-shot Company Ltd owns the freehold interest in a plot of land which it may develop.

The plot was purchased five years ago for £5,000. Its market value has now appreciated to £10,000. A development scheme has been prepared by an architect: his fee, 1,000 guineas, is payable forthwith. The scheme requires the demolition of a building on the site, at a current cost of £2,000 (payable at the commencement of the development). Building costs, at current prices, would amount to £20,000, payable in equal instalments on the first and second anniversaries of the commencement. The development would be completed on the second anniversary and it is expected that the finished building and land could be sold in two years' time for £40,000. The company's cost-of-capital is 7 per cent per annum.

If the commencement were delayed for one year:

(a) It would be necessary to spend £500 at once to make the site safe and tidy during the interim.
(b) Each payment for demolition and building would be 5 per cent higher and
(c) The sale price would increase by 10 per cent.

There are three possibilities worth considering:

(i)   The undeveloped site could be sold immediately.
(ii) The site could be developed immediately.
(iii) The site could be developed, commencing in one year's time.

There is no advantage in selling the undeveloped site at a future date or in delaying the development by more than one year. The directors have ruled out the possibility of an immediate development followed by a delayed sale because they believe that the building would deteriorate if it were unoccupied for a year or more.

Required:

Calculation showing whether the development should be commenced immediately.

No. 75

Mini-Motors Ltd, is drawing up its production plan for the coming year. It deals in four types of motor vehicle: the 'Mouse' and the 'Rat' are saloon cars, and the 'Beatle' and the 'Bee' are vans. There is complete flexibility as regards product mix. The selling price of each model has been set having regard to competitive considerations, and it will be maintained whatever the level of output of the model. The firm can buy all the parts which are required for its vehicles in sufficient quantities for any likely needs.

The firm has two divisions; in one the vehicles are assembled, and in the other they are sprayed. Next year, whatever the volume or mix of production, the costs of the assembly division are likely to be labour £100,000 and overheads £50,000, and 200,000 man-hours will be worked: the costs of the spraying division are likely to be labour £60,000 and overhead £45,000 and 120,000 man-hours will be worked. General overhead expenses of the firm are likely to be £51,000.

The accountant has prepared the following statement to assist management in deciding what products to manufacture:

	Mouse	*Rat*	*Beatle*	*Bee*
Estimated demand for the year (units)	900	1,600	1,900	1,100
Number of man-hours to process one vehicle:				
in assembly division	100	66	34	50
in spraying division	32	20	36	28

Profit per unit sold	£	£	£	£
Costs of assembly division:				
labour	50	33	17	25
overheads – 50% of labour cost (say)	25	16	8	12
Cost of spraying division:				
labour	16	10	18	14
overheads – 75% of labour cost (say)	12	8	14	11
Total divisional costs	103	67	57	62
General overheads – 20% of divisional cost (say)	21	13	11	12
	124	80	68	74
Cost of parts and materials	220	197	172	188
Total costs	344	277	240	262
Selling price	410	340	280	310
Profit	£66	£63	£40	£48
Ranking	1	2	4	3

Required:

Criticize the accountant's statement as a basis for management's deciding what to produce in the coming year. If you think some other calculations would be more appropriate, describe the method and include a formulation of the problem; a numerical solution is not required.

Examples from Chapter 13

No. 76

The following is a summary of the accounts of a company over a period of 23 years:

Balance sheets at year end

	1944	1951	1958	1966	1967
	£000	*£000*	*£000*	*£000*	*£000*
Fixed assets at cost	200	200	317	504	519
less depreciation	25	132	148	235	243
	175	68	169	269	276
Trading assets, net	200	300	460	560	580
Quick resources	35	66	(5)	3	1
Equity capital and retained profits	410	434	624	832	857

Profit and loss accounts for the year

Trading profit	80	120	184	224	232
Depreciation	25	10	24	39	40
Profit before taxation	55	110	160	185	192
Taxation	15	56	80	95	97
Dividend, gross	24	30	50	70	70
Retained	16	24	30	20	25
	55	110	160	185	192

Index numbers

Wholesale prices	100	150	230	280	290

A financial commentator suggests that, because of the changing value of money, the company has in effect been paying dividends out of capital. You are asked to comment on this statement, saying whether:

(a) You agree with the commentator's calculations and with his interpretation of the facts.
(b) In your view the company has fulfilled its obligations to its shareholders.

Source: CIMA

No. 77

A newspaper recently reported that a manager had stated that, under conditions of inflation, businessmen were unwilling to undertake plans for expansion because rapid increases in sales and profits could cause cash flow problems.

Do you consider this to be a fair statement of fact?

Source: CIMA

No. 78

The financial manager in his day-to-day decisions must take into consideration the impact of inflation. However, for long-term decisions such as the appraisal of capital projects he can ignore this because in the long run an average inflation rate applied to all the variables will produce the same answer as if inflation had been ignored.

Comment.

Source: CACA

No. 79

'The figures shown in the balance sheet for long-term assets and for stocks of goods are in most cases based on historical costs, which may represent the purchasing power of many months or years ago. The capital figures

Discuss the problems of adjusting for the effects of inflation in reporting results to shareholders and other external parties. Give your own views on the desirability of making such adjustments.

Source: SCCA

Exercises:
Second series

No. 1

Timber Chests Ltd is a public company and its shares are quoted on the
London Stock Exchange. Its most recent results are as follows:

Balance sheet
(as at 31 March 19x9)

	£000	£000		£000	£000
Ordinary share			*Fixed assets*		
capital			Land and		
Authorised			buildings at		
issued, and			cost		26,700
fully paid		38,600	Plant and		
Capital reserves		11,900	machinery		
Profit and loss			at cost	51,000	
Account		13,600	*Less* Depreciation	26,600	
		———			24,400
		64,100			———
6% Debentures		15,000			51,100
Future taxation		1,500	*Trade investments*		
Current liabilities			at cost		3,700
Creditors	23,700		*Current assets*		
Current taxation	5,600		Stocks	34,300	
Proposed dividends	1,900		Debtors	17,800	
	———	31,200	Quoted		
			investments	2,400	
			Cash at bank	2,500	
				———	57,000
		———			———
		£111,800			£111,800

Profit and loss account
(for the year ended 31 March 19x9)

	£000	£000
Trading profit		15,850
Less Directors' emoluments	150	
Depreciation	4,600	
Debenture interest	900	
	———	5,650
Profit before taxation		10,200
Less Taxation		4,900
Profit after taxation		5,300
Less ordinary dividend, paid and proposed (gross)		4,600
		700
Add Balance as at 1 April 19x8		12,900
		£13,600

Required:

Define and calculate, from the figures in these accounts, the five accounting ratios which you think would be most helpful to a prospective investor in the company. Explain the significance and limitations of each.

No. 2

You are the treasurer of the Polecon Cricket Club, whose latest annual accounts are set out below. The club is planning to build a new pavilion at an estimated cost of £5,000. Recently you received the following letter from the chairman of the committee:

Dear—,

I see from the club's balance sheet that we have £1,200 in the general fund, £2,000 in the building reserve, £1,900 in investments and £125 in the bank: that makes £5,225 in all, £225 more than we need for the new pavilion. I suggest that we place the contract at once. What is your opinion?

Yours sincerely,
J. Bowler.

Polecon Cricket Club
Balance sheet
(as at 31 March 19x9)

Claims	£	Assets	£	£
General fund	1,200	Cricket ground: at cost		6,500
Building reserve	2,000	Equipment: cost	750	
Mortgage loan	5,400	Accumulated		
		depreciation	675	
			—	75
		Investments: at cost		1,900
		(Note: market value		
		£1,450)		
		Cash at bank		125
	£8,600			£8,600

Income and expenditure account
(for the year ended 31 March 19x9)

	£	£
Subscriptions		490
Less General expenses	400	
Depreciation of equipment	75	
	—	475
Surplus carried to general fund		£15

Required:

Your reply to the chairman's letter.

No. 3

Galvin Ltd commenced business on 1 January 19x1. The following ratios were extracted from the information contained in the first year's accounts.

Share capital:	
36,000 £1 ordinary shares, issued and fully paid	
Working capital	£6,000
Ratio of turnover to capital employed (at end of year)	2 to 1
Ratio of turnover to stock	12 to 1
Current ratio	1.6 to 1
Liquid (or acid test) ratio	1.1 to 1
Ratio of debtors to sales	0.075 to 1
Ratio of general expenses to sales	0.2 to 1

Notes:

1 Current assets are made up of stock (unchanged throughout the year), debtors and cash.
2 Capital employed is share capital plus revenue reserve.
3 Ignore depreciation and profit appropriations.

You are required to prepare, a far as is possible from the above figures:

(a)   A trading and profit and loss account for the year ended 31 December 19x1.

(b)   A balance sheet as at 31 December 19x1.

Source: SCCA

No. 4

Mr Green started in business as a retail grocer on 1 January. He opened a bank account for his business and paid into it £500, borrowed from Mr White, and £1,000, drawn from his personal bank account; the bank agreed that he might borrow up to £500 on overdraft to help finance his trading stock requirements. He immediately purchased a delivery van for £300 and initial trading stock for £1,476.

You are given the following additional information:

1   On 31 December Mr Green's trading stock had a value, at cost prices, of £2,204. Included in this sum was £143, the cost of 3000 tins of corned beef, purchased some months ago in response to a special offer; this product has not been selling well and so all 3000 tins will have to be sold for £75.

2   Several customers have weekly accounts with Mr Green and, on 31 December they owed him £86.

3   On 31 December the business bank account is overdrawn by £196 and trade creditors are owed £876 for goods supplied.

4   The delivery van has a market value of £220 at 31 December. Mr Green believes that his best policy will be to keep the van for another two years, after which time he expects to be able to sell it for £120.

5   Mr Green receives all his takings in cash. From these, he meets small business expenses and his own 'wages' of £15 per week. He pays the remainder into his business bank account.

6   However at one time during the year, the business bank account had reached the allowed overdraft limit and so Mr Green had to pay £94, a wholesaler's account for groceries supplied, from his personal bank account. He has not subsequently made any adjustment for this item.

7   During the year, Mr Green repaid £150 to Mr White, by cheque drawn on his business account.

Required:

Calculation of Mr Green's profit for the year ended 31 December 19xx, according to normal accounting conventions.

Examples from Chapter 2

No. 5

A firm buys a lorry for £10,000. The expected costs, etc. are:

Year	1	2	3	4	5	6
	£	£	£	£	£	£
Maintenance during year		100	800	500	1,000	1,200
Scrap value, end of year	7,000	5,300	3,200	2,400	1,000	200
Miles run during year	10,000	30,000	30,000	20,000	10,000	10,000

Required:

(a) Calculation of optimum life.

(b) On the assumption that actual mileages prove to be the same as those in the budget, draft ledger accounts (over the optimum life) for:

  (i) The asset; and
  (ii) Depreciation provision

using the service-unit method of depreciation.
  Ignore tax and interest.

No. 6

(a) In relation to stock evaluation a business man nearly always has to make certain assumptions about the movement of stock:

  (i) Why does he have to do this?
  (ii) Describe the assumptions that can be made, and explain the effect that each would have on the final accounts of a business.

(b) Accounting for depreciation is a process of allocation, and not of valuation.'

  (i) What does this statement mean?
  (ii) Do you agree with it?
  (iii) Give four methods which can be used for the calculation of depreciation.

Source: SCCA

No. 7

Among the items appearing in the balance sheet of Wan Ltd at 31 March 19x2 are the following:

	S$000
Share premium account	80
Capital redemption reserve fund	200
Debenture redemption reserve	100

Explain the nature of each of the above items, describing how and why they arise, and the purpose for which each may be used.

Source: LCCI

No. 8

The following items appear on a limited liability company's balance sheet:

  (i) Goodwill.

(ii)   Capital redemption reserve fund.
(iii) Profit and loss account (debit balance).

In respect of each of these suggest:

(a)   Circumstances in which the balance might have arisen.
(b)   Circumstances in which the balance might be reduced or eliminated.

Source: LCCI

No. 9

On 1 January 19x1 Jones and Co. drew a bill of exchange upon DJ Traders for £2,000 at two months for goods supplied. The bill was accepted and then immediately discounted by Jones and Co. at a cost of £15. At maturity the bill was dishonoured and Jones and Co. agreed to accept £500 in cash and another bill of exchange for £1,600 at three months from DJ Traders, which amount included interest charged by Jones and Co. This bill was not discounted and was duly met at maturity.

You are required to record these transactions in the books of Jones and Co.

Source: SCCA

No. 10

Giving illustrations where appropriate, distinguish carefully between each of the following:

(i)   Current liabilities and long-term liabilities.
(ii)   Liabilities and reserves.
(iii) Reserves and provisions.
(iv)   Provisions and contingent liabilities.

Source: LCCI

Examples from Chapter 3

No. 11

Old and Middle are partners. They share all profits in the ratio 3:2 (but get no salaries or interest). Their 19x8 accounts run:

Balance sheet
(as at 31 December 19x8)

	£		£
Old, Capital	12,000	Net tangible assets	19,000
Middle, Capital	7,000		
	£19,000		£19,000

Profit and loss account
(year ended 31 December 19x8)

	£		£
Workshop expenses	8,000	Sales	14,000
Bad debts	500		
Profit: Old	3,300		
Middle	2,200		
	£14,000		£14,000

Old retires at 31 December 19x8. The agreement provides that, on the death or retiral of either partner, assets are to be revalued at current figures, and 'goodwill' is to be calculated at two years' purchase of the average profits ('to be computed by an independent expert in accordance with normal accounting practice') of the last three years. You find that:

(i) Profits before adjustment were shown in the firm's accounts for 19x6, 19x7, and 19x8 as £4,800, £5,200, and £5,500.
(ii) Actual bad debts charged against profits were £300, £700, and £500.
(iii) In 19x6, a £1,700 loss due to fire was charged against profit.
(iv) In 19x7, an £800 loss on realization of property was charged against profit.
(v) The net tangible assets have a current value of £20,000.

Required:

(a) Calculate the sum due to Old.
(b) Advise Young, a potential new partner not at present connected with the firm, what capital and premium he should pay for a one-quarter share of profits.

No. 12

(a) A company's balance sheet runs:

	£		£
Ordinary shares of £1:		Net assets	4,000
Mr *A*	1,000		
Mr *B*	3,000		
	£4,000		£4,000

A and *B* are directors, each getting a salary of £2,400 p.a. Profit is £1,200 p.a.

A retires. He sells all his shares to *C* for £2,400 (their full market value). *C* becomes a director, with a salary (at his current market rate) of only £2,000 p.a., so that profit rises to £1,600 p.a.

Required:

Table showing the balance sheets, before and after the sale, on the alternative assumptions that:

(i)   Book values of assets are written up (and bonus shares issued) just before the sale, to reflect the shares' full market value; and

(ii) The old book-values are instead retained.

(b)   Suppose instead that the firm is a partnership, owned again by *A* and *B* with capitals of £1,000 and £3,000, and sharing profits 1 : 3 after crediting salaries of £2,400 each. *C* buys out *A* in return for a direct private payment of £2,400, and agrees with *B* that profits be shared:

B – 60 per cent
C – 40 per cent

(no salaries being allowed).

Otherwise the facts resemble those in (a) as closely as possible.

Required:

Extension to the table under (a) to show the firm's post-sale balance sheets at (i) full values, (ii) the old values.

No. 13

Summarized accounts of Cornucopia Ltd, for 19x8 are shown below:

Cornucopia Ltd
Accounts for year ended 31 December 19x8
Income statement

	£000	£000
Operating profit		53
Less Debenture interest		6
		—
		47
Less Corporation tax		21
		—
		26
Less Ordinary dividend (gross)	15	
Transfer to reserve	10	
	—	25
		—
Increase in carry forward		1
		═

Balance sheet

	£000		£000
Ordinary shares of £1	200	Fixed assets – cost	430
Reserve	150	*Less* Depreciation	53
Profits undistributed	18		—
6% Debenture stock, 19y4	100		377
Creditors, etc.	120	Stocks	126
		Debtors	64
		Cash	21
	—		—
	£588		£588
	══		══

Required:

Calculate *any five* of the following from the given data:

(a)   Balance sheet value of £1 ordinary share of Cornucopia.
(b)   Market value of a £1 ordinary share, on the basis that the price: earnings ratio of similar shares is eleven.
(c)   Market value of a £1 ordinary share, on the basis that the current dividend yield on similar shares is 6 per cent.
(d)   Market value of £100 debenture stock *ex div*, if the appropriate yield is 7 per cent and this stock is redeemable at par in exactly six years. (Interest is paid on 31 December each year.)
(e)   The company's liquid asset ratio.
(f)   The annual instalment of a sinking fund at 7 per cent, to redeem the debentures at 31 December 19y4 (the first instalment being invested at 31 December 19x8, and the last set aside on 31 December 19y4).

No. 14

(a)   For a small businessman, what are the advantages and disadvantages of taking a business partner?
(b)   For a partnership, what are the advantages and disadvantages of converting into a limited company?

Source: SCCA

Examples from Chapter 4

No. 15

The following balances appeared in the books of Poon Ltd and Sing Ltd at 31 December 19x1 after the trading and profit and loss accounts for the year had been prepared.

	Poon Ltd		Sing Ltd	
	Dr	*Cr*	*Dr*	*Cr*
	S$000	*S$000*	*S$000*	*S$000*
Trading profit for the year 19x1		160		100
Retained profits at 1 January 19x1		58		90
Ordinary shares of S$1 each		920		400
Current liabilities		180		254
Fixed assets (net of depreciation)	470		312	
Investment in Sing Ltd at cost	400			
Current assets	448		532	
	1,318	1,318	844	844

Notes:

1   The investment in Sing Ltd comprises 320,000 shares acquired on 1 January 19x8 when Sing Ltd had a *credit* balance of S$40,000 on retained profits account.

2   At 31 December 19x1:
  (a)   The directors of Poon Ltd proposed a dividend of S$184,000.
  (b)   The directors of Sing Ltd proposed a dividend of S$50,000.

Required:
Prepare for Poon Ltd and its subsidiary Sing Ltd:
  (i)   Consolidated profit and loss account for the year ended 31 December
         19x1.
  (ii)   Consolidated balance sheet at 31 December 19x1.

Source: LCCI

No. 16

Martin Ltd agreed to buy all the shares of Norman Ltd and Oracle Ltd on 1
April 19x2 for a total consideration of 270,000 ordinary £1 shares in Martin
Ltd to be divided in proportion to the agreed net asset values. The Balance
Sheets of the three companies at that date were as follows:

	Martin Ltd	Norman Ltd	Oracle Ltd
	£000	*£000*	*£000*
Ordinary shares of £1 each	300	150	45
Share premium	60	20	8
Retained profits	90	10	7
Creditor: Norman Ltd	–	–	18
Other current liabilities	75	57	54
	525	237	132
Fixed assets	375	150	90
Debtor: Oracle Ltd	–	18	–
Other current assets	150	69	42
	525	237	132

For the purposes of the takeover it was agreed that:
1   The fixed assets and 'other current assets' of Norman Ltd and Oracle
     Ltd should be revalued at:

	Norman Ltd	Oracle Ltd
	£000	*£000*
Fixed assets	164	104
Other current assets	77	39

2   Goodwill should be valued at four years' purchase of the average
     trading profits of the past three years after deducting, for each year,
     'normal profit' equal to 15 per cent of the equity shareholders' interest
     at 1 April 19x2 as shown by the balance sheets of Norman Ltd and
     Oracle Ltd *before* the revaluations mentioned above had taken place.

Trading profits have been:

	Norman Ltd	Oracle Ltd
	£000	£000
Year ended 31 March 19x0	31	18
Year ended 31 March 19x1	38	20
Year ended 31 March 19x2	45	28

Required:

(i)   Explain what you understand by 'equity shareholders' interest'; calculate the goodwill of Norman Ltd and Oracle Ltd, and calculate the *number* of shares to be issued by Martin Ltd to the shareholders of Norman Ltd and Oracle Ltd respectively in exchange for their existing shares.

(ii) Prepare a summarized balance sheet of Martin Ltd immediately after the takeover.

Source: LCCI

No. 17

The draft balance sheet of Stroke Ltd at 30 September 19x1 was presented to you in the following form:

	£		£
Share capital authorized		Property at valuation	250,000
issued and fully paid		Plant and machinery at	
ordinary shares of £1 each	500,000	book value	184,000
Profit and loss account	160,000	Investments at cost	188,000
12% Debentures	140,000	Stocks	152,000
Creditors	180,000	Debtors	270,000
Corporation tax	64,000		
	1,044,000		1,044,000

You subsequently discover that:

1   The property valuation had been made by an expert during the financial year. The original cost was £196,000 and the surplus on revaluation had been credited to the profit and loss account.

2   The accumulated depreciation in respect of plant and machinery was £88,000.

3   Stocks have been valued at the lower of cost or net realizable value but include goods at branches at the cost to the branches of £48,000. Goods are invoiced by head office to branches at cost plus 50 per cent.

4   The debtors figure includes £15,000 owed by the managing director and a short term loan to an employee of £6,000.

5   Stroke Ltd originally issued debentures with a nominal value of £300,000 but has subsequently reduced the company's long term indebtedness by purchasing them on the open market. During the last financial year £20,000 at par value were so purchased at a discount of 5 per cent. These have been included (at cost) in investments at cost. *All* debentures purchased are available for reissue.

6   The remaining investments comprise: shares costing £46,000 currently listed on a recognized stock exchange and having a market value of £41,000; shares purchased several years ago for £123,000 in an unlisted company in which Stroke Ltd both owns more than 20 per cent of the equity share capital and over whose policies Stroke Ltd exercises considerable influence. The unlisted shares are considered by the directors to be worth £160,000.

7   Creditors include net indebtedness to the company's bankers of £25,000. According to Stroke Ltd's accounting records, the overdraft at North Bank was £40,000, whereas it had a balance in hand at South Bank of £15,000.

8   The corporation tax figure comprises £28,000 payable 1 January 19x2 and £36,000 due 1 January 19x3.

Required:

In so far as you are able, from the data available, prepare a revised balance sheet for Stroke Ltd at 30 September 19x1 in a form suitable for publication.

Source: LCCI

No. 18

Look through the information given below about Scallions Ltd. Then answer *any three* of sub-questions (a), (b), (c), (d) and (e) below, from that information. Ignore tax.

(a)   The figures for the 'shareholders' interest' section of the 19x8 balance sheet are not complete. Draft a statement showing, in detail, all the figures that should go in this section. (You can assume that all figures already shown in the balance sheet are correct.)

(b)   Show the 19x8 appropriation account as it would appear in order to be consistent with the balance sheets. (The directors take the view that goodwill should be written off as far as possible, but regard any such amounts written off as 'appropriations of profit', not as 'business expenses'.)

(c)   Explain to what extent, and how, the bonus issue in 19x8 will be of advantage to the shareholders.

(d)   Suppose that the debentures must be redeemed at par by annual instalments over a period of seventeen years, beginning on 1 January 19x0. The amount of money to be used in redemption each year is the annual instalment of a sinking fund (which is assumed to earn interest at 4 per cent *per annum*) plus the annual interest added to the fund. What is the amount of the annual instalment?

(e)   A prospective purchaser of all the ordinary shares in Scallions requires a valuation per share as at 31 December 19x9. It is agreed that:

(i)   The asset values shown in the balance sheet are good approximations of the saleable value of the assets (the figure for goodwill being excepted), and

(ii)   If a stock market quotation were obtained for the ordinary shares they would be quoted on the basis of a 5 per cent dividend yield (dividend/price ratio) applied to the 19x8 dividend.

What is the maximum price that could reasonably be offered, *per ordinary share*? Show your calculations.

Scallions Ltd
Simplified balance sheets, at 31 December

	19x7 £	19x8 £		19x7 £	19x8 £
Shareholders'			*Fixed assets*		
interest			Goodwill –		
Ordinary shares			cost, *Less*		
of £1	20,000		written off	5,370	3,000
7% Preference			Plant and		
shares of £1	14,000		buildings – cost	36,800	51,800
Revenue reserves	19,087	9,570	*Less* Depreciation	14,350	17,600
				22,450	34,200
	53,087				
6% Debentures	10,000	10,000			
Current liabilities			*Current assets*		
Dividends payable			Stocks	17,415	17,900
to shareholders	3,980	5,180	Debtors	18,585	19,415
Creditors	9,173	7,830	Bank	12,420	17,065
	13,153	13,010		48,420	54,380
	76,240	91,580		76,240	91,580

In January 19x8:
A one-for-two bonus issue was made to the ordinary shareholders by capitalizing reserves.

In February 19x8:
The plant of a retiring competitor was bought, and the full price of £15,000 was added to 'plant and buildings' (and was met by the issue to him of 12,000 ordinary shares, then valued at £1.25).

In December 19x8:
The directors decided to recommend the payment of the whole year's dividends (i.e. the preference dividend and a dividend on all ordinary shares at £0.10 per share); this is already allowed for in the balance sheet above. 19x8 trading results:

   Sales revenue   £55,000   Net profit   £8,033 (against £6,500 in 19.7)

In a liquidation the preference shares and debentures are repayable at par.

Examples from Chapter 5

No. 19

Xanthus Ltd's latest balance sheet, in summary form, was as follows:

Xanthus Ltd
Balance sheet at 30 June 19x2

	£000
Share capital (authorized £2,000,000), issued and fully paid:	
7% Redeemable preference shares of £1 each	
(redeemable at par on 1 July 19x2)	600
Ordinary shares of £1 each	1,000
	1,600

Reserves:	£000	
Share premium account	100	
Retained profits	500	600
Sundry net assets		2,200

The redeemable preference shareholders were offered the following options with regard to the redemption of their shares (as specified in the original terms of issue):

Either: (1) accept 100 new ordinary shares of £1 each, fully paid, in exchange for each 150 preference shares,

Or: (2) accept £100 of 12 per cent unsecured loan stock, at par, in exchange for each 100 preference shares.

Holders of 330,000 redeemable preference shares agreed to accept ordinary shares, the remainder accepted loan stock. Both the new shares and the loan stock were issued on 1 July 19x2, on which date the preference shares were redeemed.

Required:

(i)   Journal entries to record the above transactions.
(ii) Xanthus Ltd's balance sheet, immediately after the transactions had occurred.
(iii) Explain briefly:
   (a)   The purpose of creating a capital redemption reserve fund.
   (b)   The use(s) to which it can be put, as compared with a share premium account.

Source: LCCI

No. 20

On 1 January 19x8 Pyramid Ltd acquired 100 per cent of the equity capital of Y Ltd and 70 per cent of the equity capital of Z Ltd. The accountant of Pyramid Ltd is unable to determine the appropriate treatment in the accounts of the company and the group for the year ending 31 December 19x8 of certain items arising in connection with the subsidiaries, viz.:

(a) Cash remitted by Y Ltd in December 19x8 was received and recorded by Pyramid Ltd in January 19x9.
(b) On 1 January 19x8 Y Ltd had a debit balance on profit and loss account. (The accountant reminds you of the normal accounting convention of conservatism in writing off losses.)
(c) Pyramid Ltd paid for the shares in Y Ltd more than the book value of the net assets acquired. (The accountant hesitates to record a cost for 'goodwill' on purchase of a company with accumulated losses.)
(d) During 19x8 Z Ltd paid a dividend out of profits earned in 19x7.
(e) During 19x8 Pyramid Ltd has sold goods to Z Ltd at cost plus 25 per cent. Z Ltd has resold most of these goods, but some are still in stock at 31 December 19x8, and are recorded in the books of Z Ltd at the cost to that company.

Required:

In respect of each item, a clear statement of the accounting problems involved, and a recommendation, with reasons, as to their most appropriate solution.

Examples from Chapter 6

No. 21

Messrs E. Crouch and C. Cook run a retail newsagents and tobacconist business. They do not have a partnership agreement and do not maintain current accounts, but are content to work within the provisions of the Partnership Act of 1890. In the past they have not separated the results of the different activities of their business, but this year they wish the accounts to show the profit margin made on tobacco sales separately from that made on newspaper sales, and the percentage profit margins are also to be shown. The partners inform you that tobacco purchases and sales are consistently three times greater than the amounts for newspapers, but the stock figures relate exclusively to tobacco.

From the following trial balance and notes you are required to prepare the trading and profit and loss accounts for the year ended 31 December 19x1, in the form requested by the partners, together with a balance sheet as at that date.

Trial balance as at 31 December 19x1

	£	£
Capital accounts: E. Crouch		25,200
C. Cook		42,000
Drawings accounts: E. Crouch	3,500	
C. Cook	4,600	
Leasehold premises	60,000	
Stock	14,800	
Purchases	300,000	
Fixtures and fittings	20,000	
Motor vehicles	15,000	
Debtors and creditors	28,000	20,000

Continued over.

	£	£
Interest paid	1,000	
Cash	500	
Loan at 10% (repayable in 8 years 1 January 19x1)		20,000
Sales		356,000
Motor expenses	2,000	
Heat and light	3,000	
Miscellaneous expenses	2,000	
Wages and salaries	4,400	
Rates and insurance	4,400	
	£463,200	£463,200

Further information:

1 Closing stock was valued at £30,000.
2 A general provision for bad debts should be made, equal to 10 per cent
   of sundry debtors.
3 Depreciation should be provided as follows:

Leasehold premises	20%
Fixtures and fittings	25%
Motor vehicles	20%

4 The following amounts were due but were not paid as at 31 December
   19x1:

	£
Motor expenses	400
Wages and salaries	600
Interest on loan	1,000

5 Rates and insurance were prepaid by £400 at the end of the year.

Source: SCCA

No. 22

Falco, the manager of a small grocery shop owned by Perryman Ltd,
decided to go into business on his own account, and agreed to buy from the
company the goodwill, fixtures and fittings of the branch shop for £5,000,
plus stock at valuation.

The fixtures and fittings were valued at £500. Falco arranged a new lease
with the owner of the premises for seven years at £800 per annum, payable
quarterly in arrear.

Falco opened a business bank account with £12,000, paid Perryman Ltd
the agreed amount including the stock, and opened for business on 1 April
19x1.

He failed to keep proper records. A cash payments notebook showed the
following details for the year:

	£
Drawings	1,248
Cash purchases for resale	316
Wages and national insurance	1,194
Sundry shop expenses	208

A summary of his bank account for the year showed:

		£
Deposits	Cash introduced	12,000
	Takings banked	24,100
Withdrawals	Perryman Ltd	7,500
	Purchases for resale	20,000
	Rent	600
	Rates	196
	Electricity	98
	Additional fixtures 1 April 19x1	200

At 31 March stock valued at cost was £2,912, cash in hand £224, trade creditors £534 and electricity £34.

Depreciation on fixtures is to be provided at 10 per cent.

Required:

(a) A trading and profit and loss account for the year ended 31 March 19x2.

(b) A balance sheet as at that date.

Source: SCCA

No. 23

Singh and Pereira are in partnership sharing profits equally, their accounting year end being 31 December. On 1 March 19x2, a company (SP Ltd) was incorporated in order to take over the trading activities of the partnership as from 1 January 19x2. The purchase consideration was settled by the issue to the partnership of 420,000 M$1 ordinary shares in exchange for the following assets: goodwill, land and buildings, plant and machinery, and stocks.

The business was carried on by the partnership on behalf of the new company from 1 January 19x2 to 31 March 19x2 and no recognition of the change in ownership appeared in the accounting records during this period.

The following trial balance was extracted from the partnership books as at 31 March 19x2:

	M$	M$
Goodwill	54,000	
Land and buildings	150,000	
Plant and machinery	132,000	
Stock (1 January 19x2)	30,000	
Debtors and creditors	48,000	33,000
Purchases and sales	138,000	273,000
Wages and salaries	105,000	
Discounts allowed and discounts received	3,600	1,800
Directors' remuneration	3,000	
Other expenses	13,200	
Company formation expenses	11,000	
Bank	4,000	
Capital accounts: Singh		223,800
Pereira		160,200
	691,800	691,800

Stocks on 31 March 19x2 were valued at M$21,000 and all revenues and expenses accrued evenly over the three month period. Depreciation is to be ignored.

It had been agreed that the partnership would be responsible for collecting money from customers, and paying suppliers, in respect of the period ending 28 February 19x2. During March 19x2 all sales and purchases were made under the company name. The debtors and creditors above include M$24,000 and M$18,000 respectively relating to March 19x2.

Required:

 (i) Prepare the trading and profit and loss account of SP Ltd for the three months ending 31 March 19x2, distinguishing between the pre- and post-incorporations profits (or losses).
 (ii) Prepare the account of SP Ltd in the books of the partnership for the three months ending 31 March 19x2.
 (iii) Prepare the balance sheet of the partnership at 31 March 19x2.

Source: LCCI

Examples from Chapter 7

No. 24

Hotspur Ltd, whose head office was in London, opened a branch in Newcastle on 1 January 19x1. Head office kept all the books, except for local debtor records. All purchases were made by head office and transferred to branch for sale on credit as required, the transfer price being cost plus 25 per cent.

During 19x1:

	£
Goods sent to Newcastle (at cost to head office)	34,000
Returns to London (at invoice price to branch)	1,660
Branch sales, all on credit	36,780
Cash received from branch debtors and remitted to head office	31,240
Debtor balances written off as bad	1,470

Stock of goods held at the branch on 31 December 19x1, at invoiced price to branch, totalled £3,535.

The branch manager agreed to accept personal responsibility for all pilferages at the branch over and above an allowance of 1 per cent of goods received.

You are required to write up the following ledger accounts as they would appear in head office books for the year ended 31 December 19x1:

(a)   Goods to branch account
(b)   Branch stock account
(c)   Branch adjustment account
(d)   Branch debtors account

Source: SCCA

No. 25

(a)   The Birmstol Trading Co. Ltd has a head office in London and a
branch in Surrey. All books are kept at head office and goods are
invoiced to the branch at cost. From the following information you are
required to write up the Branch Stock Account.

	£
At 1 January 19x2	
Stock at branch	8,000
Debtors of branch	2,000
Imprest balance	100
Cost of goods sent to branch	28,000
Cash sales made by branch	31,000
Cash paid by branch debtors	6,000
Credit sales made by branch	5,000
Return of faulty goods to head office	100
At 31 December 19x2	
Stock at branch	10,000
Debtors of branch	1,000
Cash imprest at branch	100

(b)   The company prices its products to achieve a gross profit margin of 25
per cent on selling prices. What could account for the discrepancy
between the actual results achieved by the branch and the normal,
anticipated results?

Source: SCCA

No. 26

Slice and Hook entered into a joint venture in order to purchase, and resell,
the stock of a company in liquidation. This was acquired on 1 September for
£35,000 of which Slice contributed £20,000 and Hook contributed £15,000.

They agreed that profits (or losses) of the venture should be shared
equally after charging interest equal to 5 per cent of the amount each had
contributed initially (regardless of the length of time the venture existed)
and a commission of 10 per cent in respect of each party's sales. All sales
were to be on a cash basis.

Relevant transactions were as follows:

2 September	Hook purchased a delivery van for £2,300.
5 September	Slice incurred advertising expenses £130.
7 September	Slice collected £6,000, and Hook collected £9,000 in respect of sales.
11 September	Hook hired a market stall for £160.
14 September	Slice collected £20,000, and Hook collected £7,500, in respect of sales.
17 September	Hook paid £430 in respect of van repairs.
24 September	Slice collected £2,500, and Hook collected £4,200, in respect of sales.
30 September	Hook took over the delivery van for his own use at an agreed value of £2,000 and Slice took over the small amount of stock remaining unsold at an agreed value of £600 in the hope of selling it on his own behalf. Debts between them were then settled in cash.

Required:

  (i) Show in Slice's books – joint venture with Hook account.
 (ii) Show in Hook's books – joint venture with Slice account.
(iii) Show the memorandum joint venture account.
(iv) Briefly outline the advantages (and disadvantages) of such arrangements as compared with more formal partnership agreements.

No. 27

Clemence was in the transport business. His accounts were made up to 31 December each year. His depreciation policy was to provide for 20 per cent per annum on a straight line basis, charging a full year in the year of purchase but none in the year of sale.

On 15 February 19x9 he bought two lorries for £4,300 each. He paid a deposit of 10 per cent and took out an agreement with a hire-purchase company to pay the balance, plus total interest of £2,160, over a period of 36 months, starting on the last day of the month following the month of purchase. Clemence could terminate the agreement at any time by payment of the capital amount owing, plus a penalty of £100. Interest is deemed to accrue evenly over the life of the agreement.

On 1 January 19y1 one of the lorries became involved in an accident, and was written off as a total loss. Clemence immediately terminated the agreement with the hire-purchase company on that lorry. On 27 January he received £2,100 from his insurance company.

You are required to write up the following ledger accounts for the period from 15 February 19x9 to 31 December 19y1.

(a) Lorry account
(b) Hire-purchase company account
(c) Depreciation account
(d) Disposal account

Source: SCCA

Examples from Chapter 8

Taxation systems and rates are continually changing and questions quickly date. Details can be obtained from current specialist texts, professional magazines and revenue offices of the country concerned.

Examples from Chapter 9

No. 28

Mr Nova and his wife own all the shares in the Widget Manufacturing Corporation Ltd, a business which they started just over a year ago. You have prepared the accounts for the first year and they run as follows:

Profit and loss account

Direct manufacturing costs:	£
Materials	54,000
Labour	72,000
Cost of 2000 widgets	126,000
Less Stock of 1000 finished widgets	63,000
	63,000
Depreciation of plant and machinery	55,000
Other factory overheads	34,000
General overheads	21,000
Research and development expenditure written off	17,000
	190,000
Sales – 1000 units @ £130	130,000
Net loss for the year	£60,000

Balance sheet

	£		£
Ordinary shares	500,000	Plant and machinery – Cost	500,000
Less Profit and loss		*Less* Depreciation	55,000
account	60,000		
			445,000
	440,000	Stocks	63,000
Creditors, etc.	29,000	Debtors	26,000
Bank overdraft	65,000		
	£534,000		£534,000

Depreciation is provided at 11 per cent per annum by the reducing-balance method. This rate will reduce the book value of the plant approximately to £50,000, its residual value, at the end of its life of twenty years.

Mr Nova writes the following letter to you:

Dear Sir,

Thank you for sending me the accounts.

I was very surprised to see that these showed a loss of £60,000 for things seem to have been going rather well. I had planned to produce many more widgets than I could sell in the first year. At maximum capacity, I can only produce 3000 widgets per annum with this plant and I expect to be able to sell a larger number once my product becomes known. In fact the sales of 1000 widgets during the first year were slightly better than I expected. In addition, the research department have been working on an improved model with excellent results. It should be possible to produce this soon and make a much higher profit per unit than with the current model.

At the end of the first year, someone offered to buy all the shares of my wife and myself in the company for £750,000. Since we only invested £500,000 in the business, this proves that we have made a profit.

A friend of mine has suggested three alterations which might improve the accounts of the first year:

(a)   Production overheads (including depreciation) should be included as a cost of production in the valuation of stock.

(b)   Depreciation of plant and machinery should be on a straight line basis.

(c)   Research and development expenditure should be treated as an asset.

Please let me know what profit (or loss) would be shown if these adjustments were made and whether you agree that they are desirable.

> Yours faithfully,
> S. Nova.

Required:

Your reply.

No. 29

Moonshine Ltd, manufacturer of plastic nameplates, operates a job costing system in which actual costs incurred on jobs are recorded and accumulated daily on job cards from source documents. Batch totals of the various source documents are posted monthly to the work in progress and other control accounts. On the day a job is completed and transferred to finished goods stock the accumulated cost on the job card is posted to the detail stock ledger account but the total of all transfers is not posted to the nominal ledger control accounts until the end of the month.

On 30 April 19xx. Moonshine Ltd made a routine quarterly physical stock check at which all jobs actually found to be in progress in the factory were listed on stock sheets and then valued by the accountant at the accumulated cost shown on the individual job cards as at 30 April. The stock sheets for uncompleted jobs were totalled as £6,320 for 148 kg. The balance shown by the work in progress control account (WIPCA) was £6,598 for 158 kg. When the difference was investigated only the following discrepancies came to light:

(i)   5 kg of raw materials in excess of requirements and valued at £155 had been returned to stores by production departments. The transfers had been recorded on the job cards but omitted from the batch totals posted to the control accounts.

(ii)   There was an overaddition of £30 in the stock sheet total for uncompleted jobs at 30 April.

(iii) Job No. 253 had been in progress on 31 January but was still not finished at 30 April. Although included in the April stocksheet total the job had been completely overlooked at stocktaking on 31 January and therefore excluded from the adjusted opening balance on the WIPCA for 1 February even though there was an accumulated cost of £92 for 2 kg on the job card.

(iv) Direct costs of £68, correctly charged to WIPCA in April for Job No. 371, were not recorded on the job card until 4 May.
(v) On 10 April direct labour of £18 had been incorrectly charged against Job No. 310 which was still in progress at stocktaking when it should have been charged against Job No. 311 which had been transferred to finished goods stock on 26 April but had not been sold at the end of the month.
(vi) Job No. 298 with an accumulated cost of £250 for 5 kg had been totally destroyed in a fire in March. The insurers agreed to meet a claim for £300 in respect of the job but the appropriate entries had not been made in the WIPCA.
(vii) The total of £460 for a batch of documents recording scrap material arising in production and deducted individually from job costs was incorrectly posted as £640 in the scrap stock account and WIPCA.

It is the policy of the company to adjust the WIPCA balance to agree with the corrected total sheet total if there is any difference between the two.

Required:

(a) A statement showing the quantity and value of work in progress which should appear in the balance sheet at 30 April 19xx.
(b) The reconciliation of this value with the figures shown in the work in progress control account (£6,598) and stocksheets (£6,320) before the errors were corrected.

No. 30

Hooks & Crooks Ltd make one type of power bicycle. You find the following figures for the year 19xx.

	£
Raw materials, 1 January	25,000
Raw materials purchased	125,000
Finished goods, 1 January, 3,200 bicycles at £30	96,000
Direct labour	165,000
Manufacturing expenses (including foremen's wages £19,000)	46,000
Selling costs	240,000
Depreciation, plant, and machinery	11,000
Administration (including depreciation on office equipment (£950)	80,000
Bad debts	16,000
Sales, 12,000 bicycles	1,080,000
Raw materials, 31 December	8,000
Finished bicycles, 31 December, numbered 1,600	

Required:

Suitable income statement. Show also (in extra columns, or separate notes):

(a) The number of bicycles manufactured.
(b) The manufacturing cost per bicycle (on FIFO assumptions).

Examples from Chapter 10

No. 31

The following figures are taken from the books of Welkin Ltd:

		£
Stock on hand at 1 January 19x8: Raw materials		700
Work in progress		1,300
Finished goods		500
Materials purchased		3,000
Wages: Direct		2,000
Indirect		400
Direct expenses		300
Rent, lighting, etc.: Factory		650
Office and administrative		400
Salaries (general office)		600
Depreciation, factory plant		450
Selling value of completed contracts invoiced during year		8,000
Stock on hand at 31 December 19x8: Raw materials		800
Work in progress		1,000
Finished goods		1,500

Required:

(a) Draw up an income account for the year, in a form suitable for use in costing. Work in progress and finished goods are valued at works cost.

(b) Prepare a cost estimate for a contract in respect of which it is computed that material will cost £300, direct wages £400, and direct expenses £60. Assume that the 'direct wages' basis is in use for allocating production overhead, and apply the rate found from (a). Select your own method for allocating other cost and profit.

(c) Comment briefly on the theoretical and practical justifications for the use of the method of cost estimating in (b).

No. 32

At the end of its first year of business a manufacturing company's accounts include the following ledger balances:

	£	£
Raw materials stock	11,000	
Work in progress stock	15,600	
Finished goods stock	18,900	
Cost of goods sold	65,700	
Sales		88,000
Office and selling expenses	6,000	

The work in progress account has, throughout the year, been debited with the direct-labour cost, the direct-material cost, and the general expenses of the factory. These amounted in total to:

	£
Direct-labour cost	40,200
Direct-material cost	26,600
Production overhead	33,400

The balances of work in progress and finished goods at the end of the year contain these three cost components in the same proportion.

Required:

(a) Accounting report showing the profit for the year.
(b) The same report if, instead of valuing work in progress and finished goods on the above basis, they had been valued at prime cost (direct labour and material cost only) throughout the year, cost of sales being computed accordingly.
(c) The end-year balance sheet values of stocks on the same assumption as in (b). Show calculations.

Examples from Chapter 11

No. 33

(a) The master budget of Mercanti Ltd, for the year ending 30 September 19xx, runs as follows:

		£000
Direct costs: Materials		80
Labour		70
		150
Production overhead		60
Total works cost		210
General overhead		70
Total cost		280
Sales		315
Profit		35

After this budget has been drawn up, Mercanti Ltd is offered an additional job, a special contract to manufacture military equipment for the government of Ruritania. The government agrees that the price of the contract is to be found by:

(i) Calculating the total production cost of the job by adding to its direct costs a percentage to cover production overheads.
(ii) Calculating the total cost of the job by adding to its total production cost a percentage to cover general overheads.
(iii) Adding a profit margin equal to $12\frac{1}{2}$ per cent of total cost.

The overhead absorption rates are to be found from the corresponding total figures in the above master budget. The equipment would require £9,500 of direct materials and £12,000 of direct labour.

Required:

Calculation of the price which Mercanti Ltd would receive if it accepted the contract.

(b)   The direct materials cost of the contract includes £2,750, the cost of 100 units of Part QX 9, already in stock. These parts are not likely to be required for any other future jobs. However if £75 were spent on conversion, they could be used as substitutes for 100 parts of ML 9 which would otherwise have to be bought in at a cost of £22 each. Or they could be sold (without conversion) for £19 each. The direct materials cost of the contract also includes £1,500, the cost of the required quantity of material PX 8, which is also in stock. This material is used frequently by the company and, because it is in short supply, its current cost has risen to £1,800. All other direct costs of the contract would arise in cash during the coming year. The general overhead expenditure will be the same whether the contract is accepted or not, but acceptance of the contract would increase production overhead expenditure by £3,250 (for additional supervisory labour, fuel and power etc.).

Required:

Calculation showing whether acceptance of the project is worthwhile and by how much.

No. 34

Mr Planet will commence business, manufacturing Elektraps, on 1 January. His plans for the first six months are as follows:

   (i)   He will manufacture 1000 units per month.
  (ii)   He will purchase machinery costing £300,000 on 1 January: an initial payment of £210,000 is to be made on 1 January and the balance will be paid in twelve monthly instalments, the first on 31 January. This machinery has the capacity to produce up to 3000 units per month. Depreciation is to be provided at the rate of £30,000 per annum.
 (iii)   Each man employed in the factory can produce ten units per month, and will require a wage of £80 per month. The minimum number of men required for the planned output will be employed.
 (iv)   Each unit requires 1 lb of material @ £4 per lb. An initial stock of material of 250 lb will be purchased and paid for on 1 January. Subsequently material will be replaced immediately it is used and paid for in the following month.
  (v)   Factory rent will amount to £6,000 per annum and it will be payable by the firm, quarterly in advance, on 1 January, etc.
 (vi)   Other overhead expenditure will require payments of £3,000 per month.

(vii) Sales will be 600 units per month for the first three months and 1000 units per month for the second three months, at the price of £25 per unit. Customers will pay in the second month after receiving the goods.
(viii) Mr Planet has been offered a bank overdraft of £30,000.
(ix) Stocks are to be valued at direct cost (labour plus materials).

Required:

(a) Budget showing the minimum amount of cash that Mr Planet must pay into his business bank account in order just to keep within the agreed bank overdraft during the first six months of operation (assume that Mr Planet will draw no cash for his personal use).
(b) Budgeted balance sheet at 30 June, assuming that this sum is paid in as capital.

No. 35

For 19xx, the master budget of Quasar Supplies, Ltd, ran thus:

	£000
Direct costs: Materials	180
Labour (120,000 hours)	75
	255
Production overhead (all fixed)	60
Total production cost	315
General overhead (all fixed)	63
Total cost	378
Sales	410
Profit	32

Required:

(a) Statements showing the costs and results of Job 79, on the alternative assumptions that the costing system is based on:

(i) Direct costing; and instead;
(ii) Full allocation of overheads ('direct-labour hour' method, for production overhead, and 'percentage of production cost' method for general overhead).

Job 79 used £3,600 of direct material and £1,400 of direct wages (2,600 hours). The price was £7,800.

(b) A conventional break-even chart on graph paper, with sales on the *OX*-axis. From your chart, state:

(i) The break-even point; and
(ii) Profit if sales reach £500,000.

No. 36

Tertium Ltd makes one product. It has a standard costing system based on the following:

Each unit of product needs 1 lb of material (normally costing £0.15 a lb) and one hour of labour (paid £0.40 per hour). Overheads (fixed, for any likely output) are budgeted at £200 per month. Sale price is £0.80. The firm carries no stocks.

The production budget for July calls for 2000 articles. But the actual results run:

	£	£
Sales (1600 units at £0.80)		1,280
Cost of sales:		
Materials: 1,000 lb at £0.15	150	
720 lb at £0.16½ approx.	120	
	270	
Wages: 1,650 hours at £0.40	660	
Overheads	184	
		1,114
Profit		166

Required:

(a) Statement showing standard cost per unit.
(b) Budget of expected total revenue and total cost for July.
(c) Revised operating statement showing standards and variances.

Examples from Chapter 12

No. 37

I am planning to build a motel with 100 double bedrooms:

(a) The initial costs are:

	£
Land	20,000
Architect's and other fees	15,000
Construction	220,000
Furnishing	70,000

I can borrow the needed funds at 7 per cent per annum by mortgaging this and other property.

(b) Running costs (less the net contribution from bars and dining rooms, etc.) will come to some £65,000 per annum. This includes maintenance of buildings, but excludes their depreciation: it also includes renewals of furniture.

(c) I expect a room to be let for about 220 nights a year, on average with one and a half persons per room.

Required:

(a)   Calculate the minimum room charge per person per night to break even on the alternative assumptions that:

(i)   The building will have a life of thirty years with residual site value £40,000.

(ii) The building will have an indefinitely long life.

(b)   If inflation raises the net running costs, and enables me to put up charges (above the amount calculated in (ii)), by 2½ per cent per annum, what will be my profit per annum at the end of twenty years on the assumption that the building will have an indefinitely long life?

No. 38

Caucus Ltd makes several products. Six years ago, it set up a department to deal with a new contract – for 1000 units per annum of product K, for £15,000 per annum. This contract has still four more years to run, and the chief engineer now suggests that a reorganization of the department (methods, materials, and plant) will cut working costs.

The cost accountant drafts the following statement to enable the directors to decide on the proposal:

		Account for year 6 £	Annual budget years 7–10 (if proposals adopted) £	Remarks
Costs:				
1	Materials: Type X	1,000	900	Less waste
	Y	2,000		Discontinued
	Z		1,600	Substitute for Y
2	Labour	6,000	4,200	Less needed
3	Departmental expense	3,000	2,100	50% of direct labour
4	Depreciation: Machine A	450	315	Straight line (10 years)
	B		550	Straight line (4 years)
		12,450	9,665	
Gain by new plan			2,785	
		12,450	12,450	

Notes:

(i)   *Materials:* X and Z: bought as and when needed. None has so far been ordered. Y: there is a firm contract to buy this quantity each year till the end of year 10, for £2,000 per annum. If not used in this department, the material can be used in other departments as a substitute for materials costing £1,750 per annum. Or it can be sold for £2,160 per annum.

(ii) *Labour* can be varied readily.

(iii) *Departmental expense:* The total for the firm is not likely to be affected by the change.

(iv) *Depreciation:* Under the plan, A will be scrapped at once; it would still (start of year 7) fetch £540 if sold, but will fetch nothing by the end of year 10. It will be replaced by a new machine, B (cost £2,350, scrap value £150 after year 10).

(v) *Interest:* Assume, for simplicity, that interest can be ignored.

Required:

Statement to assist decision, in form of alternative budgets of net cash flow (total for years 7–10) if:

(a) Old plan is retained, and
(b) New plan is adopted.

Ignore tax.

No. 39

Five years ago, you bought machine A (with a life of ten years) for £1,000. Its scrap value will be £100 at the end of its life; it has been depreciated on the straight line basis, and so now has a book value of £550. Its scrap value now is £200. Its annual running costs are £300.

An improved machine, B, could do the same job as A for running costs of only £213 a year. Its price is £500, and it will last five years and then have a scrap value of £20, so its yearly depreciation will add a further £96 to book costs.

Required:

Show whether it is in your interest to replace A. Ignore tax, and assume that running costs arise at the year's end and the cost of capital is 5 per cent per annum.

No. 40

A firm plans to install a new machine – either of type A or of type B. The cost of purchase and installation would be £6,000 (type A) and £8,000 (type B). The output capacity of the two types is the same and will remain constant over the life of each machine. A has an effective life of ten years, and B of twelve. A's running cost at the level of use expected is £1,000 per annum and B's £900 per annum. Final scrap values of both are *nil*. Funds can be borrowed readily at 7 per cent.

Required:

(a) A calculation of annual costs, based on the given data.
(b) Justify your method of solution, writing as for a layman.

Ignore tax.

Examples from Chapters 13 and 14

No. 41

The transactions of Rebus Ltd, are:

			£
Year 1. 1 January	Capital received in cash		1,000
	1 January	Cash purchase of 100 tons stock at £9	900
Year 2. 30 June	Cash sale of above stock at £15		1,500
	30 June	Cash purchase of 90 tons of same kind of stock at £12	1,080

The general price index stood at 100 on 1 January of Year 1, rose smoothly to 110 during Year 1, and stayed at 110 thereafter.

Required:

Table comparing the income accounts and balance sheets for Year 2, drafted according to:

(a) Conventional accounting principles (stock valued by FIFO).
(b) As (a) (stock valued by LIFO).
(c) Revised principles, based on £s of constant purchasing power. (Use the £ at the close of Year 2.)

The accounting profession is still debating the accounting for inflation issue. Most questions are therefore either general or on past systems and are covered in the text and the first series exercises. Readers interested in latest developments should consult the most up-to-date sources such as journals of professional bodies.

Answers to exercises:
First series

No. 1

Balance sheet
(as at 31 December 19xx)

	£	£		£	£
Capital as at 1 January		6,000	Fixed assets:		
Add Net profit for year	1,368		Freehold premises	·3,000	
Less Drawings	702		Plant and Machinery	2,560	
					5,560
		6,666	Current assets:		
Loan from H. Glass		1,000	Stock	2,845	
			Sundry debtors	1,412	
			Cash	78	
				4,335	
			Less Current liabilities:		
			Sundry creditors	1,880	
			Bank overdraft	349	
				2,229	
					2,106
		£7,666			£7,666

No. 2

Golden Gate Landscaping Company
Balance sheet
(as at 31 December 19xx)
Assets

	£	£	£
Fixed assets:			
Lorry	2,100		
Less Accumulated depreciation	560		
		1,540	
Gardening tools		317	
Total plant assets			1,857

	£	£	£
Current assets:			
Cash		562	
Debtors		2,116	
Garden Supplies		402	
Prepaid Insurance		109	
		────	
Total current assets			3,189
Total assets			£5,046

Liabilities and owners' equity

	£	£
Current liabilities:		
Creditors	107	
Contracts payable	660	
	────	
Total liabilities		767
Wilkinson, Capital		4,279
Total liabilities and owners' equity		£5,046

Golden Gate Landscaping Company
Statement of Proprietor's Capital
(year ended 31 December 19xx)

	£	£
Capital, 1 January		3,500
Capital introduced in May		1,000
		────
		4,500
Add Profit for year	3,379	
Less Drawings during year	3,600	
	────	
		−221
Capital, 31 December		£4,279

Golden Gate Landscaping Company
Profit and loss statement
(year ended 31 December 19xx)

	£	£
Sales		7,350
Expenses:		
Gardening supplies	2,516	
Depreciation – lorry	560	
Petrol and oil	373	
Telephone	50	
Office supplies	27	
Insurance	207	
Sundry expenses	238	
	────	
Total expenses		3,971
Net profit		£3,379

No. 3

Liabilities and owners' equity

	£	£	£
Current liabilities:			
Creditors		107	
Contracts payable		660	
Total liabilities			767
Wilkinson, Capital:			
Balance, 1 January		3,500	
Cash introduced in May		1,000	
		4,500	
Add Profit for year	3,379		
Less Drawings during year	3,600		
		−221	
Capital, 31 December			4,279
Total liabilities and owners' equity			£5,046

No. 4

ESBA Bookshop

(a) (i) **Profit and loss account for year ended 31 December 19x8**

	£	£	£
Sales			10,000
Less Cost of sales			7,000
			3,000
Wages and general expenses		850	
Depreciation of fittings		150	
Rent	1,500		
Less owing 1 January 19x8	(250)		
	1,250		
Less paid in advance	(250)		
		1,000	
Net profit			£1,000

(a) (ii) **Source and application of funds statement**

	£	£	£
Sources of funds			
Profit for the year		1,000	
Add Depreciation		150	
Reduction in stock		300	
Increase in trade creditors		350	
Reduction in debtors		150	
		1,950	

	£	£	£
Application of Funds			
Rent (Arrears £250 + prepayment £250)		500	
Drawings		500	
		———	1,000
Increase in funds			950
Less Bank overdraft at 1 January			(750)
Cash at bank 31 December			£200

(b) The profit and loss account is indicative of the trading performance and size of expenses incurred during the year. Gross profit at 30 per cent of sales would appear reasonable as would the volume of other expenses relative to turnover. Drawings are reasonable and on the basis of this statement the business would appear to be in a healthy position.

The source and application of funds statement indicates more efficient control of the business with reduced stock and debtors. Creditors have increased but the bank overdraft has been repaid. Prior years' figures would be useful as lower stocks and debtors could be associated with lower turnover rather than increased efficiency.

The working capital is adequate although the acid test ratio might give cause for concern unless the bank overdraft facility is still available if required.

Examples from Chapter 2

No. 5

	£
Machine	5,000
Freight	105
Insurance in transit	75
Installation cost	200
	———
Total cost	£5,380

No. 6

	£	£
Machinery	10,600	
Deferred interest	1,000	
Cash		2,000
Contracts payable		9,600
To record purchase of machine under an instalment contract		

No. 7

$$\frac{£9,800 - £200}{8 \text{ years}} = \frac{£9,600}{8 \text{ years}} = £1,200/\text{year}$$

No. 8

Derini Products
(a)   **Computation of balance in provision for bad debts**

Age of account	Amount	Loss ratio	Estimated allowance
31–60 days	£80,000	2%	£1,600
61–90 days	40,000	5%	2,000
over 90 days	30,000	10%	3,000
			£6,600

		£	£
(b)	Bad debts	4,400	
	Provision for bad debts		4,400
	To increase provision from £2,200 to £6,600		

No. 9

	£	£
Cash	192,000	
Collection charges	8,000	
Trade debtors		200,000
To record sale of £200,000 of trade debtors for £192,000		

No. 10

		£	£
(a)	Debtors		
	Pledged	150,000	
	Sundry debtors		150,000
	To separate pledged debtors from sundry debtors		
	Cash	100,000	
	Notes payable		100,000
	To record receipt of cash from the note payable under the pledging contract		

		£	£
(b)	Cash	20,000	
	Debtors – pledged		20,000
	To record receipt of cash in February on debtors pledged		
	Notes payable	20,000	
	Interest payable		
	(£100,000 × 5% ÷ 12)	417	
	Cash		20,417
	To record payment on loan plus interest on £100,000 for February		

		£	£
(c)	Cash	50,000	
	Debtors – pledged		50,000
	To record receipt of cash in March on debtors pledged		
	Notes payable	50,000	
	Interest payable ($£80,000 \times 5\% \div 12$)	333	
	Cash		50,333
	To record payment on loan plus interest on £80,000 for March		

		£	£
(d)	Cash	30,000	
	Debtors – pledged		30,000
	To record receipt of cash in April on debtors pledged		
	Notes payable	30,000	
	Interest payable ($£30,000 \times 5\% \div 12$)	125	
	Cash		30,125
	To record payment on loan plus interest on £30,000 for April		
	Sundry debtors	50,000	
	Debtors – pledged		50,000
	To return debtors pledged to the sundry debtors now that the loan is paid		

No. 11

(a)	Merchandise purchases	£6,742.90	
	Creditors or purchases ledger control account		£6,742.90
	To record purchase of merchandise for sale		
(b)	Creditors or purchases ledger control account	£6,742,90	
	Cash		£6,608.04
	Purchase discounts		134.86
	To record payments during discount period		
(c)	Creditors or purchases ledgers control account	£6,742.90	
	Cash		£6,742.90
	To record payments after discount period		

No. 12

(a)	Merchandise purchases (or merchandise inventory	£8,200	
	Creditors or purchases ledger control account		£8,200
	To record merchandise purchased in 19x8		

No. 13

(a)
$$\frac{£15,000 - £1,000}{2,000 \text{ hours}} = \frac{£14,000}{2,000 \text{ hours}} = £7/\text{hour}$$

(b)
19x7:   175 hours × £7/hour = £1,225
19x8:   62 hours × £7/hour =   £434

No. 14

$$8 + 7 + 6 + 5 + 4 + 3 + 2 + 1 = 36$$

To determine 1/36th:

$$\frac{£40,000 - £400}{36} = \frac{£39,600}{36} = £1,100$$

		£	£
Depreciation:	1st Year 8 × 1,100 =		8,800
	2nd Year 7 × 1,100 =		7,700
	3rd Year 6 × 1,100 =		6,600
	4th Year 5 × 1,100 =		5,500
	5th Year 4 × 1,100 =		4,400
	6th Year 3 × 1,100 =		3,300
	7th Year 2 × 1,100 =		2,200
	8th Year 1 × 1,100 =		1,100
		36	£39,600

No. 15

(a)
$$\frac{£25,200 - £1,200}{10 \text{ years}} = \frac{£24,000}{10 \text{ years}} = £2,400/\text{year}$$

9 months' depreciation = 9/12 × £2,400 = £1,800

Depreciation expense – machinery	£1,800	
Accumulated depreciation – Machinery		£1,800
To record 9 months' depreciation		

(b)

Accumulated depreciation – Machinery (£18,000 + £1,800)	£19,800	
Machinery (new)	33,600	
Cash (£30,000 – £1,800)		£28,200
Machinery (old)		25,200
To record trade of old machinery for new machinery		

(c)
$$\frac{£33,600 - £1,600}{8 \text{ years}} = \frac{£32,000}{8 \text{ years}} = £4,000/\text{year}$$

3 months' depreciation = 3/12 × £4,000 = £1,000

Depreciation expense – machinery	£1,000	
Accumulated depreciation – Machinery		£1,000
To record three months' depreciation		

No. 16

Increase in asset value	£93,000	
Overstreet, capital		£93,000

To record increase in value of building
to reflect current market value:

Current value	£125,000
Book value	32,000
	£93,000

Examples from Chapter 3

No. 17

Santini & Casey, Insurance Brokers
Balance Sheet
(as at 31 December 19xx)
Assets

Fixed assets	£	£	£
Office furniture	9,315		
Less Accumulated depreciation	3,702	5,613	
Motor vehicles	7,600		
Less accumulated depreciation	3,300	4,300	
Total fixed assets			9,913
Current assets:			
Cash		4,105	
Debtors		700	
Commissions receivable		5,603	
Office supplies		1,210	
Prepaid insurance		570	
Prepaid rent		600	
Total current assets			12,698
Total assets			£22,611

Liabilities and partners' equity

Partners' capital	£	£
	M.	W.
	Santini	Casey
Balance 1/1/x8	£8,000	£10,000
Cash introduced 3/3/x8	2,000	–
	£10,000	£10,000
Add Profit for Year 19x8	4,975	4,975
	£14,975	£14,975
Less Drawings for Year 19x8	5,200	5,200

	£	£	£
Current liabilities:			
Premiums payable			2,950
Creditors			111
Total liabilities			3,061
Total capital 31 December 19x8	£9,775	£9,775	19,550
Total liabilities and partners' capital			£22,611

Santini & Casey, Insurance Brokers
Income statement
(year ended 31 December 19x8)

	£	£
Commissions Income		29,585
Expenses:		
Wages	9,050	
Rent	2,400	
Motor vehicles	2,300	
Telephone	1,100	
Office supplies	560	
Insurance	210	
Depreciation – Office equipment	955	
Depreciation – Motor vehicles	2,010	
Sundry expenses	1,050	
Total expenses		19,635
Profit for the Year 19x8		£9,950
Distribution of profit		
M. Santini		4,975
W. Casey		4,975
Total profit for the Year 19x8		£9,950

No. 18

Santini & Casey, Insurance Brokers
Statement of partners' capital
(year ended 31 December 19x8)

	M. Santini	*W. Casey*	*Total*
Balance, 1 January 19x8	£8,000	£10,000	£18,000
Cash introduced 3 March 19x8	2,000	–	2,000
	£10,000	£10,000	£20,000
Add Profit for Year 19x8	4,975	4,975	9,950
	£14,975	£14,975	£29,950
Less Withdrawals for Year 19x8	5,200	5,200	10,400
Total capital 31 December 19x8	£9,775	£9,775	£19,550

Liabilities and partners' equity

	£	£
Current liabilities:		
Premiums payable	2,950	
Creditors	111	
Total liabilities		3,061
Partners' capital:		
M. Santini	9,775	
W. Casey	9,775	
Total partners' equity		19,550
Total liabilities and partners' capital		**£22,611**

No. 19

Profit and loss appropriation account
(for the year ended 31 December 19x9)

	£	£		£
Salaries: Bat	1,000		Net profit	7,430
Rubble	900			
	——	1,900		
Interest: Brick	1,120			
Bat	840			
Rubble	700			
	——	2,660		
Profit: Brick	1,230			
Bat	820			
Rubble	820			
	——	2,870		
		£7,430		£7,430

Current account – Brick

	£		£
Drawings	2,000	Balance b/f	500
Balance c/f	850	Interest on capital	1,120
		Profit	1,230
	£2,850		£2,850
		Balance, b/f	£850

Current account – Bat

	£		£
Drawings	1,400	Balance b/f	400
Balance c/f	1,660	Salary	1,000
		Interest	840
		Profit	820
	£3,060		£3,060
		Balance b/f	£1,660

Current account – Rubble

	£		£
Drawings	1,100	Balance b/f	450
Balance c/f	1,770	Salary	900
		Interest	700
		Profit	820
	£2,870		£2,870
		Balance b/f	£1,770

No. 20

(a)

	£
Valuation of business	18,000
Net worth (assets – liabilities)	13,000
Goodwill	£5,000

Balance sheet

	£	£	£		£	£
Capital: Hit	8,000			Goodwill		5,000
	3,000			Assets	20,000	
		11,000		Target's cash	6,000	
Miss	5,000					26,000
	2,000					
		7,000				
Target		6,000				
			24,000			
Liabilities			7,000			
			£31,000			£31,000

(b)   **Balance sheet**

	£	£		£
Capital: Hit	11,000		Assets	26,000
	2,000			
		9,000		
Miss	7,000			
	1,500			
		5,500		
Target	6,000			
	1,500			
		4,500		
Liabilities		7,000		
		£26,000		£26,000

(c) Purchase of three-tenths of goodwill

$\frac{3}{10} \times £5,000 = £1,500$

Payable as premium to: Hit (three-fifths)   900
Miss (two-fifths)   600

£1,500

Balance sheet

	£	£	£		£	£
Capital				Assets	20,000	
Hit		8,000		Balance of		
Miss		5,000		Target's cash	4,500	
Target	6,000					24,500
Premium	1,500					
	——	4,500				
		——	17,500			
Liabilities			7,000			
			£24,500			£24,500

Examples from Chapter 4

No. 21

	£
Capital and Reserves of Minnow Ltd at date of acquisition	52,000
One-quarter minority interest	13,000
Three-quarter interest acquired	39,000
Cost of acquiring shares	45,000
Cost of control, or goodwill on consolidation	£6,000

Shark Ltd and subsidiary
Consolidated balance sheet
(as at 31 December 19xx)

		£	£	£
Fixed assets				
Intangible assets				
Cost of control			6,000	
Tangible assets				
Fixed assets	Shark	120,000		
	Minnow	40,000		
			160,000	
				166,000
Current assets	Shark	100,000		
	Minnow	33,000		
			133,000	
Liabilities (assumed under one year)	Shark	75,000		
	Minnow	15,000		
			90,000	
Net current assets				43,000
				209,000
Capital and reserves				
Called up share capital				150,000
Reserves			40,000	
			4,500	
				44,500
				194,500
Minority interest			13,000	
			1,500	
				14,500
				209,000

No. 22

	£
Capital and reserves of Hut Ltd at date of acquisition	55,000
One-fifth minority interest	11,000
Four-fifths interest acquired	44,000
Cost of acquisition of shares	54,000
Cost of control, or goodwill on consolidation	10,000

	£
Profit for year on Hut Ltd	7,500
One-fifth minority interest	1,500
Four-fifths interest	6,000
Less profit on goods not yet sold by the group ⅕ of (£1,000–£750)	200
Added to group reserves	£5,800

House Ltd and subsidiary
Consolidated balance sheet
(as at 31 December 19xx)

	£	£	£
Fixed assets			
Intangible assets			
Cost of control		10,000	
Tangible assets			
Fixed assets	160,000		
	50,000		
		210,000	
			220,000
Current assets	90,000		
	51,500		
	800		
		142,300	
Liabilities (assumed under one year)	60,000		
	34,000		
		94,000	
Net current assets			48,300
			268,300
Capital and reserves			
Called up share capital			200,000
Reserves		50,000	
		5,800	
			55,800
			255,800
Minority interest		11,000	
		1,500	
			12,500
			268,300

Examples from Chapter 5

No. 23

(a)   **Shaky Grounds Ltd**
                  Balance sheet as at 31 December 19xx

	£	£	£
Fixed assets			
Intangible assets			
Patents at cost less amounts w/o		5,000	
Tangible assets			
Plant – cost	26,000		
Less Depreciation	6,000		
		20,000	
			25,000
Current assets			
Stocks		17,000	
Debtors less bad debts		10,190	
		27,190	
Creditors! due within one year			
Tax due	1,200		
Bank	2,250		
Trade creditors	9,000		
Accrued charges	1,500		
		13,950	
Net current assets			13,240
Total assets *less* Current liabilities			38,240
Creditors due after one year			
5½% Debentures			12,000
			26,240
Capital and reserves			
Called up share capital			
14,000 Ordinary shares of £1		14,000	
10,000 6% Preference shares of £1		10,000	
			24,000
General Reserve			2,500
Profit and Loss Account			(260)
			26,240

(b) **Shaky Grounds statement of distribution 1 January 19xx**

Realization of assets		34,450
Less Distributions: Tax due	1,200	
Bank	2,250	
5½% Debentures	12,000	
Creditors plus accrued charges	10,500	
		25,950
Available for shareholders		8,500

Since the preference shareholders are owed £10,000 there is insufficient to pay them the total amount owing. They will therefore receive a proportion of their holding equal to $\frac{£8,500}{£10,000} = 85\text{p}$ in the pound.

The ordinary shareholders would get no capital repayment and preference shareholders no dividend.

Common errors:

(a) Lack of knowledge of priorities in event of winding up.
(b) Using balance sheet values instead of revaluation.
(c) If the expenses incurred in the liquidation are given these also have priority for payment.

Keywords: Liquidation, priority (in relation to credit ranking)

Examples from Chapter 6

No. 24 (see page 532)

No. 25

T. Jones and H. Higgins
Manufacturing, trading and profit and loss accounts
for the year ended 30 September, 19x2

Note:	£	£
Stock of raw materials at 10 October, 19x1		8,000
Add: Purchases of raw materials		80,000
		88,000
1 *Less:* Stock of raw materials at 30 September, 19x2		12,000
Raw materials consumed		76,000
2 Factory wages (£50,000 + £2,000)		52,000
Prime cost		128,000

Continued over.

		£	£
	Factory overheads		
	Manager's salary	12,000	
	Factory power	6,000	
	Rent and rates (⅔ of £15,000)	10,000	
	Heat and light (⅗ of £5,000)	3,000	
4	Depreciation of plant and equipment (10% of £50,000)	5,000	36,000
			164,000
	Add: Work in progress at 1 October, 19x1	16,000	
1	*Less:* Work in progress at 30 September, 19x2	18,000	(2,000)
	Factory cost of production transferred to trading account		£162,000
	Sales, *less* returns (£210, 500–£500)		210,000
	Stock of finished goods at 1 October, 19x1	14,000	
3	*Add:* Factory cost of production		
	(£162,000 *Less* £200 Drawings)	161,800	
		175,800	
1	*Less:* Stock of finished goods at 30 September 19x1	16,000	
	Cost of goods sold		£159,800
	Gross profit		£50,200

		£	£	£
	Gross profit			50,200
	Office and administration expenses			
2	Office salaries (£9,850 + £150)	10,000		
	Rent and rates (⅓ of £15,000)	5,000		
	Heat and light (⅖ of £8,000)	2,000		
	Postage, stationery and printing	1,800		
2	Insurance £390–£40)	350		
4	Depreciation:			
	Office furniture (5% × £5,000 = £250)			
	Office machinery (20% × £3,000 = £600)	850	20,000	
	Selling and distribution expense			
	Salesmen's commission	2,100		
	Delivery expenses	4,000		
	Advertising	500	6,600	
	Financial and other expenses			
	Bank charge and interest	800		
5	Provision for bad debts (5% of £20,800)	1,040	1,840	28,440
	Net profit for the year			21,760
	Share of profits:			
	T. Jones (½)		10,880	
	H. Higgins (½)		10,880	£21,760

T. Jones and H. Higgins
Balance sheet as at 30 September 19x2

Note:

Assets employed
Fixed assets

Tangible assets	Cost	Aggregate depreciation		
	£	£	£	
Plant and equipment	50,000	25,000	25,000	
Office furniture	5,000	3,250	1,750	
Office machinery	3,000	2,400	600	
	58,000	30,650	27,350	27,350

	Current assets			
1	Stock of raw materials		12,000	
1	Work in progress		18,000	
1	Stock of finished goods		16,000	46,000
	Debtors, less provision for bad debts (£20,800 − £1,040)			19,760
2	Insurance prepaid			40
				65,800
	Less Current liabilities (due within one year)			
	Creditors		7,600	
2	Accrued expenses (£2,000 + £150)		2,150	
	Bank overdraft		20,000	29,750
	Net current assets			36,050
	Total assets *less* Current liabilities			£63,400

Financed by partners capital	T. Jones	H. Higgins	
at 1 October 1981	£28,000	£40,640	
Add: Share of profits	10,880	10,880	
	38,880	51,520	
Less: Drawings	15,000	12,000	
	£23,880	£39,520	£63,400

No. 24

	Department 1 £	%	Department 2 £	%	Department 3 £	%	Department 4 £	%	Total £	%
Total sales	85,000	100.0	72,000	100.0	93,000	100.0	110,000	100.0	360,000	100.0
Opening stock	7,000		6,000		7,000		11,000		31,000	
Net purchases	74,000		68,000		81,000		99,000		322,000	
	81,000		74,000		88,000		110,000		353,000	
Closing stock	6,000		7,000		8,000		10,000		31,000	
Cost of sales	75,000	88.2	67,000	93.1	80,000	86.0	100,000	90.9	322,000	89.5
Gross profit on sales	10,000	11.8	5,000	6.9	13,000	14.0	10,000	9.1	38,000	10.5
Selling expenses	7,000	8.3	4,000	5.5	6,000	6.5	4,000	3.6	21,000	5.8
Departmental income	£3,000	3.5	£1,000	1.4	£7,000	7.5	£6,000	5.5	17,000	4.7
Administrative expenses									8,000	2.2
Net operating profit									£9,000	2.5

Examples from Chapter 7

No. 26

Goods sent to branches account

	£		£
Southend branch account	600	Southend branch account	6,000
Purchases or trading account	5,400		
	£6,000		£6,000

Southend branch account

	Selling price £	£		Selling price £	£
Goods sent to branches	8,000	6,000	Goods sent to branches	800	600
Gross profit transferred to profit and loss account		1,550	Cash sales	6,500	6,500
			Balance (stock)	600	450
			Shortage	100*	
	£8,000	£7,550		£8,000	£7,550
Balance (stock)	£600	£450			

* This is a memorandum entry required for assessing the efficiency of the management of the branch.

No. 27

Goods sent to branches account

	£		£
Southend branch adjustment account	2,000	Southend branch account	8,000
Southend branch account	800	Southend branch adjustment account	200
Purchases or trading account	5,400		
	£8,200		£8,200

Southend branch account

	£		£
Goods sent to branches	8,000	Goods sent to branches	800
		Cash sales	6,500
		Balance c/f (stock-on-hand)	600
		Shortage transferred to profit and loss account or branch adjustment account	100
	£8,000		£8,000
Balance b/f (stock-on-hand)	£600		

Southend branch adjustment account

	£		£
Goods sent to branches	200	Goods sent to branches	2,000
Profit and loss account	1,650*		
Balance c/f (loading on stock-on-hand)	150		
	£2,000		£2,000
		Balance b/f (loading on stock-on-hand)	£150

* This figure would be reduced by £000 if the shortage were transferred to the branch adjustment account.

No. 28

Goods on consignment account

	£		£
Purchases or trading a/c	1,000	Goods to Sellers Ltd	1,000

Consignment to Sellers Ltd account

	£		£
Goods on consignment	1,000	Sales – Sellers Ltd	1,800
Cash – expenses	180	Balance c/d	429*
Sellers Ltd – expenses	250		
Sellers Ltd – commission	180		
Profit transferred to profit and loss account	619		
	£2,229		£2,229
Balance b/d	£429		

* This represents the value of 30 units still unsold.

		£
Cost 30 @ £10 each		£300
Expenses	£180	
	250	
	—— £430	
Three-tenths of £430		£129
Total		£429

Sellers Ltd

	£		£
Sales	1,800	Expenses	250
		Commission	180
		Cash	1,000
		Balance c/d	370
	£1,800		£1,800
Balance b/d	370		

Cash account

	£		£
Sellers Ltd	1,000	Expenses	180

No. 29

Senders Ltd

	£		£
Cash – expenses	250	Cash – sales	1,800
Commission receivable	180		
Cash	1,000		
Balance c/d	370		
	£1,800		£1,800
		Balance b/d	£370

Commission receivable

			£
		Senders Ltd	180

Cash account

	£		£
Sales – Goods on consignment	1,800	Expenses – Goods on consignment	250
		Cash – Senders Ltd	1,000

Note: There will be a memorandum record to show that 30 of the 100 units received on consignment are still in stock.

No. 30

Remco Ltd
Analysis of proposed credit card plan

		Proposed			
	Present (actual)	% of sales	Total	At present basis	Credit card basis
Sales	200,000	100			
25% increase in sales			250,000		
Loss of 20% of current cash				160,000	
Sales increase +20% of old basis					90,000
Cost of goods sold	170,000	85	212,500		
Gross profit	30,000	15	37,500		
Operating expenses	12,000				
Plus 5% of new sales	2,500				
Plus 6% of credit sales	5,400		19,900		
Net profit	£18,000		£17,600		

The analysis indicates that increasing sales by £50,000 will result in a loss of profit of £400, and on that basis the proposed plan should be rejected. But since there is such a small drop in profit it might be worthwhile to re-examine some of the assumptions.

(a)   Will operating expenses increase at the rate of 5 per cent for new sales? If they increase by only 4 per cent, the proposed plan would increase profits by £100 and should be adopted.
(b)   Will 20 per cent of present customers change to credit card buying? If only 15 per cent change, the proposed plan would increase profits by £200 and should be adopted.

It seems advisable, therefore, to study the proposed plan again in order to review the fact-gathering assumptions and methods.

No. 31

(a)   Ability and willingness to repay obligation; borrower's income versus outgoings (not more than 30 per cent of net income should be necessary to amortize the loan); willingness is determined by means of a credit report; recorded deed of trust so property can be taken over if payments are not made.
(b)   Sufficient down payment (different for new and used cars); steady employment (two years); two years' residence in the area; 'good credit' (Retail Credit Association check); evidence of comprehensive insurance.
(c)   Stability in employment and home address; good credit background (calls to the stores where accounts are now open); bank references.
(d)   Length of time employed; type of job; other credit accounts; bank accounts; own or rent home; credit rating (Retail Credit Association check).

No. 32

	£	£
Instalment contracts receivable	500,000	
Instalments sales		500,000
Sales on instalment		
Cost of instalment sales	300,000	
Inventory		300,000
Cost of instalment sales		
Instalment sales	500,000	
Cost of instalment sales		300,000
Unrealized gross profit on		
Instalment sales – 19x8		200,000
Close out instalment sales and cost of instalment		
Sales accounts and set up deferred profit. (Gross		
profit is 40%)		

No. 33

	£	£
Cash	70,000	
Instalment contracts receivable		70,000
Received moneys on instalment sales		
Gross profit on instalment sales – 19x8	28,000	

	£	£
Instalment sales gross profits realized		28,000
Record gross profits realized on 19x8 instalment sales collected. (£70,000 × 40%)		

No. 34

	£	£
Cash	180,000	
Instalment contracts receivable		180,000
Received moneys on instalment sales contracts		
Gross profit on instalment sales – 19x8	72,000	
Instalment sales gross profit realized		72,000
Record gross profits realized on 19x8 instalment contract collections. (£180,000 × 40%)		

No. 35

$$19x6: \frac{£20,000}{£0.32} = £62,500$$

$$19x7: \frac{£160,000 - £30,000}{£0.37} = \frac{£130,000}{£0.37} = £351,351$$

$$19x8: \frac{£500,000 - £220,000}{£0.35} = \frac{£280,000}{£0.35} = £800,000$$

No. 36

	£	£
(a) Selling price of used machine	4,500	
Mark-up on selling price (20%)	900	
	3,600	
Less Reconditioning cost	800	
	2,800	
(b) Trade-in inventory	2,800	
Instalment contracts receivable	12,500	
Instalment sales		14,800
Unearned interest income		500
[12,500 – (15,000 – 3,000)]		
Sale on instalment		
Customer traded in used machine		
Cost of instalment sales	13,000	
Inventory		13,000
Cost of instalment sales		
Instalment sales	14,800	
Cost of instalment sales		13,000
Unrealized gross profit on instalment sales – 19x8		1,800
Close out instalment sales and cost of instalment Sales accounts, and set up deferred profit. (Gross profit ratio is 12.2%)		

No. 37

19w9   Royalties due 3000 @ 50p = £1,500
∴ short workings = £4,000 − £1,500   = £2,500

19x0   Royalties due 9000 @ 50p + 200 @ 40p   = £4,850
Minimum rent   £4,000

∴ amount of short workings recouped   £580

19x1   Royalties due 9000 @ 50p + 2000 @ 40p   = £5,300
Minimum rent   = £4,000

∴ amount of short workings recouped   = £1,300

19x2   Royalties due 9000 @ 50p + 8000 @ 40p   = £7,700
Two years have elapsed therefore any unrecouped
balance on short workings account must be written
off.
Balance of Short workings
= £2,500 − [£580 + £1,300] = £620 to be written
off

Royalties payable

	£		£
19w9		19w9	
31 March Statham (3,000 @ 50p)	1,500	31 March Manufacturing account	1,500
19x0		19x0	
31 March Statham (9,000 @ 50p		31 March Manufacturing account	4,880
200 @ 40p)	4,880		
19x1		19x1	
31 March Statham (9,000 @ 50p		31 March Manufacturing account	5,300
2,000 @ 40p)	5,300		
19x2		19x2	
31 March Statham (9,000 @ 50p		31 March Manufacturing account	7,700
8,000 @ 40p)	7,700		

Statham

	£		£
19w9		19w9	
31 March Bank	4,000	31 March Royalties payable	1,500
		31 March Short workings	2,500
	4,000		4,000

19x0	£	19x0	£
31 March Short workings recouped	580	31 March Royalties payable	4,580
31 March Bank	4,000		
	4,580		4,580

19x1	£	19x1	£
31 March Short workings recouped	1,300	31 March Royalties payable	5,300
31 March Bank	4,000		
	5,300		5,300

19x2		19x2	
31 March Bank	7,700	31 March Royalties payable	7,700

Short workings

19w9	£	19x0	£
31 March Statham	2,500	31 March Statham – Short workings recouped	580
		31 March Balance c/d	1,920
	2,500		2,500

19x0	£	19x1	£
1 April Balance b/d	1,920	31 March Statham – Short workings recouped	1,300
		31 March Profit and loss account amount irrecoverable	620
	1,920		1,920

Examples from Chapter 9

No. 38

(a) *Advantages:* 1. Inexpensive because no detailed inventory cards must be kept. 2. Cost of goods sold can be determined by formula.

(b) *Disadvantages:* 1. Lack of control because the quantity on hand cannot be determined readily. 2. Counting must be done when the plant is shut down or at night or at weekends.

No. 39

Traders Ltd
Cost of goods sold statement
Financial year ended 31 March 19x9

	£	£	£
Opening stock, 1 April 19x8			130,000
Purchases		1,600,000	
Add Carriage inward		12,000	
		1,612,000	
Less Purchase returns and allowances	30,000		
Less Purchase discounts	31,000		
		61,000	
			1,551,000
			1,681,000
Less Stock, 31 March 19x9			150,000
Cost of goods sold			£1,531,000

No. 40

Stock (10 units @ £1.25 each)	£12.50	
Stock discrepancy		£12.50
To record overage of material		

No. 41

(a)

Cash	£400	
Sales		£400
To record sale of 200 units @ £2 each.		

(b) In the periodic inventory method no Cost of Goods Sold entry is made when the goods are sold.

No. 42

Stock discrepancy	£44.80	
Stock (28 units @ £1.60 each)		£44.80
To record shortage of material.		

No. 43

(a) *Advantages:* 1. Affords greater control over inventory quantity of low-volume high-value items (e.g. diamonds and watches); in items of great personal utility (e.g. hand tools and whisky); in situations of operating complexity (e.g. motorcar manufacture); in items of changing consumer demand (e.g. women's fashions). 2. Affords an immediate costing of sales.

(b) *Disadvantages:* 1. Requires an investment in filing equipment and cards. 2. Maintaining current records is expensive.

No. 44

		£	£
(a)	Cash	1,500	
	Sales		1,500
	To record sale of 300 units @ £5 each		
(b)	Cost of sales	1,200	
	Inventory		1,200
	To record reduction in stock due to sale (300 units @ £4 each)		

No. 45

	£	LIFO £	Average £	FIFO £
Sales: 3,000 @ 7.40 each	22,200			
1,500 @ 8.00 each	12,000			
4,500		34,200	34,200	34,200
Cost of goods sold				
LIFO: 2,000 @ 6.6 each	13,200			
2,000 @ 6.4 each	12,800			
500 @ 6.2 each	3,100			
4,500		29,100		
Average: 1,000 @ 5.7 each	5,700			
2,000 @ 6.2 each	12,400			
2,000 @ 6.4 each	12,800			
2,000 @ 6.6 each	13,200			
7,000	44,100			
4,500 @ 6.3 each			28,350	
FIFO: 1,000 @ 5.7 each	5,700			
2,000 @ 6.2 each	12,400			
1,500 @ 6.4 each	9,600			
4,500				27,700
Gross profit		£5,100	£5,850	£6,500
Stock, 31 May				
LIFO: 1,500 @ 6.2 each	9,300			
1,000 @ 5.7 each	5,700			
2,500		15,000		
Average: 2,500 @ 6.3 each			15,750	
FIFO: 500 @ 6.4 each	3,200			
2,000 @ 6.6 each	13,200			
2,500				16,400

Continued over.

		LIFO	Average	FIFO
	£	£	£	£
Proof:				
Cost of goods sold	4,500	29,100	28,350	27,700
Stock	2,500	15,000	15,750	16,400
Total goods	7,000	£44,100	£44,100	£44,100

No. 46

Item	No. of units	Cost	Market	Stock value
		£	£	£
A1	100	60	67	6,000
A2	120	120	110	13,200
A3	600	210	200	120,000
A4	210	300	290	60,900
B1	430	400	410	172,000
B2	10	75	72	720
B3	25	450	430	10,750
C1	900	790	810	711,000
C2	42	575	560	23,520
C3	150	815	804	120,600
C4	200	615	627	123,000
				£1,361,690

No. 47

Selling price	£5.00
Cost	4.00
Gross profit	£1.00

Gross profit as a percentage of sales:

$$\frac{£1.00}{£5.00} = 20\%$$

Gross profit as a percentage of cost:

$$\frac{£1.00}{£4.00} = 25\%$$

Notice that as the base changes, the percentage changes.

No. 48

	Details £	Debits £	Credits £
Work in progress – Job 16	38.20		
Work in progress – Job 19	100.50		
Work in progress – Job 22	22.30	161.00	
	———		
Production overhead – Department A	53.15		
Production overhead – Department B	51.70	104.85	
	———		
Inventory			265.85

   Record use of materials
   requisitioned from storeroom

No. 49

$$Q = \sqrt{\frac{2 \times R \times P}{C \times I}}$$

$$= \sqrt{\frac{2 \times 2,000 \times £14.00}{£6.40 \times 0.30}}$$

$$= 171$$

No. 50

$$\frac{2,000}{171} = 11.8 \text{ orders/year}$$

$$\frac{250}{11.8} = 21.2 \text{ days}$$

Order must be placed every twenty and twenty-one days alternatively.

No. 51

Two calendar weeks = ten days
Thirty units per day usage × ten days = 300 units minimum stock

No. 52

		Regular hours	Overtime hours	Total hours	Rate per hour	Gross pay
(a)	Jones	40	–	40	£1.75	£70.00
	Smith	40	–	40	2.10	84.00
	Blue	39	–	39	2.05	79.95
	Green	40	2	42	1.95	83.85
	Acme	38	–	38	1.52	57.76

		Regular hours	Overtime hours	Total hours	Rate per hour	Gross pay
(b)	Jones	40	–	40	1.75	70.00
	Smith	39	1	40	2.10	85.05
	Blue	38	1	39	2.05	80.98
	Green	38	4	42	1.95	85.80
	Acme	33	5	38	1.52	61.56

No. 53

Jones:	70 × 17.5p each		£12.25
Smith:	100 × 17.5p each	£17.50	
	10 × 18.0p each	£ 1.80	£19.30
Blue:	100 × 17.5p each	£17.50	
	50 × 18.0p each	£ 9.00	
	30 × 19.0p each	£ 5.70	£32.20

No. 54

Yes, Jones would have earned £16.

No. 55

Jones:	70 × 17.5p each	£12.25
Smith:	110 × 18.0p each	£19.80
Blue:	180 × 19.0p each	£34.20

No. 56

Production overhead

	£	
Payroll summary	2,302,00	
Materials requisition	1,025,00	
Administration	1,347.80	
Insurance expense	6,510,00	
Factory supplies	4,400,00	
Depreciation	15,320.00	

No. 57

£152,310 × 1.10 = £167,541

(a) $\dfrac{£167,541}{16,750 \text{ dlh}}$ = £10/direct-labour hour

(b) $\dfrac{£10/\text{dlh}}{£0.75/\text{hr}}$ = 13.3/direct-labour pound

Examples from Chapter 10

No. 58

Work in progress – Job 20

19x8		
30 November	Labour	£9,468
	Materials	2,253
	Overhead	4,450
	Balance	16,171
31 December	Labour	2,901
	Materials	905
	Overhead	1,276
	Balance	21,253
19x9		
31 January	Labour	203
	Materials	347
	Overhead	93
	Balance	21,896

No. 59

Calculations:

Material:

3,000 lb A @ 3.00/lb	£9,000
2,000 lb B @ £15.00/lb	30,000
5,000 lb Total material	£39,000
4,000 lb completed (80%)	£31,200
1,000 lb in process (20%)	7,800
5,000 lb	£39,000

Labour:

4,000 lb (of end product) × 100%	4,000 eu	£16,000
1,000 lb (of end product) × 60%	600 eu	2,400
	4,600 eu	£18,400

Overhead:

£16,000 × 1.4	£22,400
£2,400 × 1.4	3,360
	£25,760

Answers:

	Part (a)	Part (b)	Total
Material	£31,200	£7,800	£39,000
Labour	16,000	2,400	18,400
Overhead	22,400	3,360	25,760
Total	£69,600	£13,560	£83,160

No. 60

	Cost to date	Cost to complete	Total
Direct labour	£6,000	£9,000	£15,000
Direct materials	14,000	–	14,000
Overhead	12,000	18,000	30,000
Total	£32,000	£27,000	£59,000

No. 61

Direct labour	$300 \times 50\% = 150$	
	$1,500 \times 100\% = 1,500$	
	$500 \times 60\% = 300$	1,950 eu
Direct materials	$300 \times 25\% = 75$	
	$1,500 \times 100\% = 1,500$	
	$500 \times 100\% = 500$	2,075 eu
Overhead	$300 \times 50\% = 150$	
	$1,500 \times 100\% = 1,500$	
	$500 \times 60\% = 300$	1,950 eu

No. 62

Direct labour $\dfrac{£13,845}{1,950 \text{ eu}} = £\ 7.10/\text{eu}$

Direct materials $\dfrac{£20,542}{2,075 \text{ eu}} = £\ 9.90/\text{eu}$

Overhead $\dfrac{£27,495}{1,950 \text{ eu}} = £14.10/\text{eu}$

No. 63

	Sales price	Percentages	Cost to separation
(a) Product A	£60,000	60%	£24,000
Product B	40,000	40	16,000
	£100,000	100%	£40,000

	Sales price less added conversion	Percentages	Cost to separation
(b) Product A	£50,000	83.33%	£33,333
Product B	10,000	16.67	6,667
	£60,000	100,00%	£40,000

No. 64

(a)   Total cost   = £7,399.00

$$\text{Average cost} = \frac{£7,399.00}{700} = £10.57 \text{ each}$$

(b)   £18.00 − £9.75 = £8.25 each

(c)   £8.25 each

No. 65

		£	£
(a)	Work in progress – defective goods	211.40	
	Work in progress		211.40
	Record cost of defective units @ £10.57 each		
(b)	Work in progress – defective goods	165.00	
	Work in progress		165.00
	Record cost of defective units @ £8.25 each		
(c)	Work in progress – defective goods	165.00	
	Production overhead – defective goods	46.40	
	Work in progress		211.40
	Record cost of defective units @ £8.25 each but relieve		
	Work in progress for 20 units @ £10.57 each		

Examples from Chapter 11

No. 66

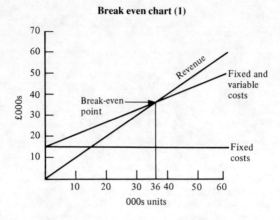

Break even chart (1)

	£	£
Revenue from 60,000 units		60,000
Variable costs		
Direct labour	13,000	
Direct material	12,000	
Factory overheads	4,000	
Selling expenses	6,000	
		35,000
Total contribution to fixed expenses and profit		25,000

Contribution per unit = 25,000 ÷ 60,000
Total contribution required for break-even point = £15,000
Break-even point = 15,000 ÷ (25,000 ÷ 60,000) units
          = 36,000 units

No. 67

	Variable £	Fixed £	Total £
Total costs as stated in Example 66	35,000	15,000	50,000
Add 10% of direct labour	1,300		1,300
2% of other variable costs	440		440
Increase in fixed costs		3,260	3,260
	£36,740	£18,260	£55,000

Revenue 60,000 units @ £1.05 £63,000

Break even chart (2)

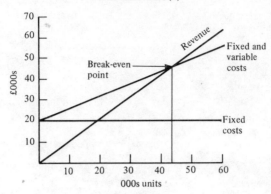

No. 68

	Actual 19x8		Budget 19x9	
	£	£	£	£
Sales		200,000		240,000
Cost of goods sold				
Labour	80,000		92,000	
Materials	46,000		55,200	
Overhead	14,000		16,800	
		140,000		164,000
Gross profit		60,000		76,000
Selling expenses	25,000		28,750	
Administrative				
expenses	20,000		22,000	
		45,000		50,750
Net profit		£15,000		£25,250

No. 69

Production overhead

Actual	£651,259	Applied (45,000 dlh × £14.612/dlh)	£657,540

Total variance: £651,259 − £657,540 = £6,281

No. 70

Budget variance: £623,950 × £651,259 = £27,309   Unfavourable
Volume variance:

$$\frac{42,700 \text{ dlh}}{80\%} = 5,337.5 \text{ dlh/1\% capacity}$$

85% × 5,337.5 = 45,368.75 dlh
(45,368.75 − 42,700) dlh × £14.612/dlh

= £38,996   Favourable

Efficiency variance:
(45,368.75 × 45,000) dlh × £14.612/dlh

= £5,388   Unfavourable

£6,299   Favourable

(The difference between the answer to Example 69 (£6,281) and this answer is due to rounding.)

No. 71

(a)	7.1 hours × £2.10/hr	= £14.91
(b)	7.0 hours × £2.00/hr	= 14.00
	Variance	= £0.91
(c)	Excess time (0.1 hr) × £2.00/hr	= £0.20
	Excess rate (£0.10) × 7.1 hr	= 0.71
		£0.91

or

Excess rate (£0.10) × 7.0 hr	=	0.70
Excess time (0.1 hr) × £2.10/hr	=	0.21
		£0.91

The first method is recommended practice.

No. 72

(a)   The level of stock would be £20,800 since this represents the same target ratio of annual sales as that operating in 19x8. The debtors will be £13,000 as this represents the same target ratio of annual sales as 19x8. The trade creditors are estimated at £10,400 as this represents the same period of credit being taken for the increased rate of supply. It is based on the previous year's relationship between creditors and cost of goods sold. The latter would be equivalent to trade purchases if the opening stock for 19x8 had been the same as closing stock.

(b) (i)

Wholesalers Ltd
Bugeted profit and loss account for
year ended 31 December 19x9

	£	£
Sales		130,000
Less Cost of goods sold		104,000
Gross profit		26,000
Less Expenses		
Rent of warehouse	1,000	
Depreciation of motor vans	1,000	
Wages and general expenses	4,000	
		6,000
Unappropriated profit for year		20,000
Add Unappropriated profit brought forward		2,500
Unappropriated profit carried forward		22,500

(b) (ii) **Balance sheet as at 31 December 19x9**

	£	£	£
Fixed assets			
Tangible assets			
Freehold buildings		15,000	
Motor vans: cost	5,000		
Less Accumulated depreciation	4,000		
		1,000	
			16,000
Current assets			
Stocks	20,800		
Debtors	13,000		
Bank	18,100		
		51,900	
Creditors due within one year			
Trade creditors		10,400	
Net current assets			41,500
Total assets *less* Current liabilities			57,500
Capital and reserves			
Share Capital			
35,000 Shares of £1 each			35,000
Profit and loss account			22,500
			57,500

Examples from Chapter 12

No. 73

Machine A:	£
Cost	75,000
Present equivalent of scrap value $5,000 \times v^8 = 5,000 \times 0.627$	3,135
	£71,865
Equivalent to an annual charge of $71,865 \div a_{\overline{8}|} = 71,865 \div 6.209$	11,570
Annual running costs	3,430
Total annual charge	£15,000
Cost per unit (£15,000 ÷ 6,000)	2.5

Machine B:	£
Cost	60,000
Present equivalent of scrap value $5,000 \times v^6 = 5,000 \times 0.704$	3,520
	£56,480
Equivalent to an annual charge of $56,480 \div a_{\overline{6}|} = 56,480 \div 4.917$	12,990
Annual running costs	8,610
Total annual charge	£21,600
Cost per unit (£21,600 ÷ 8,000)	2.7

Therefore, on the basis of the information given, four type-A machines should be purchased.

No. 74

The timing of the expenditure or proceeds of an investment are critical since money has a time value. Money received in the future is worth less than money received now as the opportunity to invest is lost. Also – for decision making purposes money which has already been spent – sunk costs are irrelevant to the decision.

Workings:

The purchase price of £5,000 is irrelevant. Choice (i) is to sell immediately for the *present* site value of £10,000. The 1,000 guineas paid to the architect is irrelevant as it is payable forthwith *in any* event.

Under Scheme (ii) £20,000 is payable immediately, £10,000 in one year's time and £10,000 in two years' time which would coincide with receipt of selling price of £40,000. The present value of £1 received or paid in one year's time is £0.9346 if the cost of capital is 7% (see page 568). Similarly the present value of £1 received or paid in two years' time is £0.8734.

Under Scheme (iii) delaying the project would result in expenditure of £500 *now*, £2,100 in one year's time, £10,500 in two years' and £10,500 in three years' which would coincide with the sale receipt of £44,000.

Solution:

(i)   If undeveloped site sold immediately present value would be equal to cash proceeds of *£10,000*.

(ii) Site developed immediately:

	Cost £	Receipt £	Net cash flow £	Discount factor	Discounted cash flow
Beginning of Year 1	2,000	–	2,000	1.0	2,000 –
End of Year 1	10,000	–	10,000	0.9346	9,346 –
End of Year 2	10,000	40,000	30,000	0.8734	26,202 +
				Net present value	£14,856 +

(iii) Site developed commencing in one year's time:

	Cost £	Receipt £	Net cash flow £	Discount factor	Discounted cash flow
Beginning of Year 1	500	–	500	1.0	500 –
End of Year 1	2,100	–	2,100	0.9346	1,963 –
End of Year 2	10,500	–	10,500	0.8734	9,171 –
End of Year 3	10,500	44,000	33,500	0.8163	27,346 +
				Net present value	£15,712

The calculation shows that the highest NPV (net present value) is £15,712, therefore construction could be delayed. There is a present gain of £856 (£15,712 − £14,856) if we do this as opposed to commencing immediately. Either of the alternatives (ii) and (iii) are substantially preferable to selling the site for a present value of £10,000.

No. 75

1   There is complete flexibility as to mix, therefore combinations of any quantity up to the maximum demand of an individual item are acceptable.

2   Selling price is constant irrespective of demand.

3   No restrictions on bought out parts.

4   *Assembly division:* Labour cost and overhead cost will be the same however the hours are deployed, therefore key factor is contribution per labour hour.

5   *Spraying division:* Labour cost and overhead cost will be the same however hours are deployed, therefore key factor is contribution per labour hour.

6   The general overhead of £51,000 will be incurred regardless of any combination.

	Mouse	*Rat*	*Beetle*	*Bee*
	£	£	£	£
Selling price	410	340	280	310
Parts and materials	220	197	172	188
Contribution/unit	190	143	108	122
Man-hours/unit				
Assembly	100	66	34	50
Spraying	32	20	36	28
Contribution per man-hour	£	£	£	£
Assembly	1.9	2.16	3.17	2.44
Spraying	5.94	7.15	3.0	4.36

The highest contribution rates are in the spraying department with the exception of the Beetle which is marginally better in assembly, therefore:

Let a = Quantity of Mouse up to 900 units
Let b = Quantity of Rat up to 1600 units
Let c = Quantity of Beetle up to 1900 units
Let d = Quantity of Bee up to 1100 units

Maximize $5.94(a) + 7.15(b) + 3.18(c) + 4.36(d)$
Subject to:
Assembly hours $100(a) + 66(b) + 34(c) + 50(d) \leq 200\ 000$
Spraying hours $32(a) + 20(b) + 36(c) + 28(d) \leq 120\ 000$
Demand $(a) \leq 900$ $(b) \leq 1600$ $(c) \leq 1900$ $(d) \leq 1100$

Examples from Chapter 13

No. 76

Each item in the profit and loss account is adjusted by the 1967 index relative to that for the year concerned e.g.:

	1944	*1951*	etc
Trading profit (£000s)	80	120	
Index	100	150	
Index 1967	290	290	

1944 profit at 1967 prices = $80 \times \dfrac{290}{100} = 232$

1951 profit at 1967 prices = $120 \times \dfrac{290}{150} = 232$

The trading profit when adjusted comes to 232 (thousand) for every year. The expenses and distribution of profit is similarly adjusted. Since the trading profit remains at 232 it is static in real terms but how have expenses fared?

	1944	*1951*	etc
Depreciation (£000)	25	10	
Index	100	150	
Index 1967	290	290	

1944 depreciation at 1967 price = $25 \times \dfrac{290}{100} = 72.5$

1951 depreciation at 1967 price $= 10 \times \dfrac{290}{150} = 19$

A summary of all these adjusted figures is as follows:

Profit and loss accounts adjusted for inflation at 1967 value equivalents

	1944	1951	1958	1966	1967
Indices	100	150	230	280	290
	£000	£000	£000	£000	£000
Trading profit	232	232	232	232	232
Depreciation	72.5	19	30	40	40
Profit before tax	159.5	213	202	192	192
Taxation	43.5	108	101	98	97
Earnings	116	105	101	94	95
Dividends	70	58	63	73	70

In each of these selected years the earnings exceed the dividends in real terms and therefore the dividends were *not* paid out of capital.

Equity capital adjusted for inflation at 1967 value equivalents

	£000	£000	£000	£000	£000
Historical values	410	434	624	832	857
Adjusted to 1967 values	1,189	839	767	862	857
Variations between dates		−350	−62	+95	−5
Variations 1944–1967					−332

This information suggests that the equity capital has not been kept intact in real value terms. This supports the contention of the financial commentator that because of the changing value of money, the company has in effect been paying dividends out of capital. However, because in the five sample years dividends are shown not to have been paid out of capital, the statement should be amended to read that dividends were paid out of capital in *some* years.

The company can be said to have prime obligations to improve the equity value of the business or at least to maintain the value. If dividends are paid, as has been so in this case, then to maintain the value would be acceptable.

Comparison of principal assets:

	1944 @ 1967 values	1967
	£000	£000
Fixed assets at cost	580	519
Less Depreciation	72.5	243
At present condition	507.5	276
Trading assets = Stock	580	580

The year 1944 appears to be the first year of operation as the depreciation charged to profit and loss account in that year is equivalent to the cumulative depreciation shown in the balance sheet.

By 1967 the cumulative depreciation is 47 per cent of cost; with the resulting lifespan of the fixed assets in existence in 1967 therefore being about half expired there must be some aged assets not yet replaced.

Although the cumulative depreciation is £243,000 in 1967 there are no liquid funds to undertake replacements – the 'quick' resources have only £1,000 of net favourable balance.

On the basis of current purchasing power interpreted by the given indices it can be said that the company has not fulfilled its obligation of maintaining the equity value of the business.

No. 77

True to a limited extent. It depends upon the length of cash cycle i.e. the time between commencing manufacture or sale and receipt of payment. The longer the cycle the greater the cash flow problem. Volatility of the particular industry, for example oil prices, are erratic irrespective of inflation. It depends upon the rate of inflation and the degree of involvement in overseas countries where inflation may be better or worse. The general impression is that if the rate is fairly low the problem is accepted but causes concern in excess of 5 per cent per annum.

No. 78

It is not true that he can ignore it. Factors of production – material, labour, capital equipment etc. suffer differing rates. Basically the arguments are those against CPP – few industries correspond to the rate produced by a mixture of consumer goods. He should attempt to incorporate particular forecast inflation rates. In a very long term if a factor was subjected to high inflation producing high cost a substitute could be generated by competitive forces. Other factors may be equally or more difficult to forecast e.g. market share, labour productivity, general economic conditions, taxational, hence the tendency to ignore inflation or regard it as only one item in the choice of proposals.

No. 79

Historical cost accounts are subjective due to the alternative accepted accounting policies, but are at least based on 'actual' figures i.e. costs paid and receipts collected. All inflation adjustments are arbitrary and there is no generally accepted system so far. Proponents for adjustment say it is ludicrous to add, say, 1948 pounds to 1988 pounds and call the result a true and fair view, yet this happens when fixed assets are aggregated 'at cost'. Main problems arise from subjectivity i.e. it is a matter of estimate and conflict between two – so far – main alternatives of CCA and CPP.

A substantial part of the profession rejects either system and such adjustments may arguably be ignored in times of low inflation. In the high rates already experienced in the past, in the UK however, it has been demonstrated convincingly how inaccurate and misleading to shareholders and other parties such data is. Pressure for some amendment will – in the UK – return if levels of inflation rise considerably. Meanwhile the problem should continue to be researched internationally to provide some reasonable alternative – or addition to – historic cost accounts.

Answers to exercises:
Second series

Examples from Chapter 1

No. 1

 (i) ROCE 8.27%; (ii) Current ratio 1.83%; (iii) Acid test 0.73:1;
(iv) Gear ratio 0.19:1; (v) Dividend ratio 11.9%.

No. 2

If we allow for drop in value of investments (£450) and outstanding mortgage of £5,500 the present value of members' interest is equal to £2,750 only – hardly security for a further loan of £5,000.

No. 3

Net loss £6,000; Total assets less liabilities £30,000.

No. 4

Net profit £726; Trading profit £1,716.

Examples from Chapter 2

No. 5
(a) Four years with cost per mile £0.10.
(b) Depreciation cost per service unit (mile) $\dfrac{£7,600}{90,000} = £0.084$

  Depreciation: Year 1 £844, Year 2 £2,533, Year 3 £1,690.

No. 6

See text sections 2.2 and 2.3.

No. 7

See text section 2.6.

No. 8

See text sections 2.1 and 2.6.

No. 9

£2,000 less consideration accepted (cash £500 + Bill £1,600) = difference of £100 representing interest and charge.

No. 10

See text sections 2.6.

Examples from Chapter 3

No. 11

(a)   £19,800; (b) £8,000.

No. 12

(a)   (i)   Before sale, Mr A £2,400, Mr B £7,200
           After sale, Mr B £7,200, Mr C £2,400
      (ii) Before sale, Mr A £1,000, Mr B £3,000
           After sale, Mr B £3,000, Mr C £1,000
(b)   (i)   Assets £9,600 financed by (B) £7,200, (c) £2,400
      (ii) Assets £4,000 financed by (B) £3,840, (c) £1,600

No. 13

(a) £1.84; (b) £1.43; (c) £1.25; (d) £95.232; (e) 0.7 : 1;
(f) Seven payments of £11,155.

No. 14

See text sections 3.3 and 3.4.

Examples from Chapter 4

No. 15

 (i)   Retained profit for year S$56,000, c/f S$154,000;
 (ii) Total assets less current liabilities S$1,182,000; Share capital plus reserves S$1,074,000; Minority interest S$108,000.

No. 16

(i) Goodwill   Norman £44,000, Oracle £52,000
   Number of shares   Norma 180,000, Oracle 90,000
   i.e.   6 for 5 and 2 for 1
(ii) Total assets less current liabilities £819,000;
   Ordinary shares £570,000; Share premium £159,000;
   Retained profit £90,000.

No. 17

Total assets less liabilities £645,000.

No. 18

(a) Ordinary share capital £42,000; Preference shares £14,000; Share premium £3,000; Reserve £9,570.
(b) Net profit for year £8,033; Appropriation goodwill £2,370.
(c) Bonus issue £10,000; Preferred dividend £980; Ordinary dividend £4,200; Unappropriated profit c/f £9,570.
(d) £405.76 per annum.
(e)   (i) £1.23.
     (ii) £2.00.

Examples from Chapter 5

No. 19

(i) Ordinary shares £220,000; Share premium £110,000; Loan stock £270,000; Capital reserve £380,000.
(ii) Total assets less liabilities £1,930,000.

No. 20

See text sections 4.2 and 4.3.

Examples from Chapter 6

No. 21

Gross profit: Total £71,200 (20%); Tobacco £57,200 (21.42%); Newspapers £14,000 (15.73%).
Net profit: £30,000; Crouch £15,000; Cook £15,000.
Total assets less current liabilities £106,600; Capital plus reserves £89,100; Loan £17,500.

No. 22

Net profit £4,252; Gross profit £6,852;
Total assets less current liabilities £15,004.

No. 23

(i)   Preincorporation profit £4,000; Post-incorporation loss £1,000.
(ii)   Profit on realization £54,000.
(iii)   Total assets less liabilities £438,000.

Examples from Chapter 7

No. 24

(a)   Branch stock £34,000 credit; Returns to head office £1,328 debit; Head office trading account £32,672 debit.
(b)   Returns to head office £1,660 credit; Branch debtors £36,780 balance c/d 3,535 credit; Branch adjustment £525 credit; Deficiency Goods from head office £42,500 debit.
(c)   Credits: Branch stock £8,500; Branch manager £425.
       Debits: Returns £332; Branch stock £525; Unrealized profit £707; Gross profit to profit and loss account £7,361.
(d)   Debit Branch stock £36,780; Credit Cash £31,240; Bad debts £1,470; Balance £4,070.

No. 25

(a)   Debits: Balance b/f £8,000; Goods sent to branch £28,000; Gross profit (balancing figure) £10,100.
       Credits: Returns to head office £100; Sales cash £31,000; Credit £5,000; Balance c/d £10,000.
(b)   Theoretical profit £8,633

No. 26

(i)   Slice   Profit £7,405;   Cash (Hook) £1,565 debit.
(ii)   Hook   Profit £6,375;   Cash (Slice) £1,565 credit.
(iii)   Net profit £13,780
        Interest   Slice £1,000, Hook £750.
        Commission   Slice £2,850, Hook £2070
        Balance   Slice £3555, Hook £3555.

No. 27

(a) £4,300 debit; (b) £1,505 credit; (c) £1,720 credit; (d) Loss on sale £580.

Example from Chapter 9

No. 28

Gross profit £38,750; Net profit £17,750;
Stock at production cost £91,250;
Intangible assets (research) £17,000; Tangible assets £477,500;
Net current assets £23,250; Net worth £517,750.

No. 29

		Physical Stock		Work in progress	
		Qty (kg)	Value £	Qty kg	Value £
	Balance given	148	6,320	158	6,598
(i)	Excess material returned	–	–	(5)	(155)
(ii)	Over addition		(30)		
(iii)	Job overlooked	–	–	2	92
(iv)	Direct cost omitted	–	68		
(v)	Direct labour charge		(18)		
(vi)	Fire loss unrecorded			(5)	(250)
(vii)	Scrap adjustment				180
	Final correction*			(2)	(125)
		148	6,340	148	6,340

* To bring WIPCA into agreement with stock sheets.

No. 30

(a) 10,400; (b) £35; Net profit £340,000.

Examples from Chapter 10

No. 31

(a) Net profit £1,000; (b) Production cost £1,060;
Cost of sale (Administration overhead 16.6% of production cost)
£1,237;
Profit 12.5% of selling price £177;
Selling price £1,414.

No. 32

(a) Net profit £16,300; (b) Net profit £4,800;
(c) Raw material £11,000; work in progress £10,400; Finished goods
£12,600.

Examples from Chapter 11

No. 33

(a) (i) £30,100; (ii) £40,133; (iii) £45,150.
(b) Opportunity cost of (b) is savings of £5,675 which is better than profit on job.

No. 34

(a) (J) £231,000 + (F) £22,500 + (M) £7,500 + (A) £9,000 + (M) £7,500 = £277,500 less o/draft £30,000 = £247,500
(b) Fixed assets £285,000 + Net current assets £(11,100) = £273,900
Capital £247,500 + profit (6 months) £26,400 = £273,900.

No. 35

(a) (i) £2,800; (ii) £240.
(b) (i) £325,000; (ii) £66,000.

No. 36

(a) £0.65, 200 units; Total revenue £1,600; Total cost £1,300; Budget profit £300.
(b) Sales volume variance £320 (A); Material price variance £12 (A); Usage variance £18 (A); Labour efficiency variance £20 (A); Overhead expenditure variance £16 (F); Capacity variance £35 (A); Efficiency variance V £5 (A).

Examples from Chapter 12

No. 37

(a) (i) £2.75; (ii) £2.66.
(b) £910 per annum.

No. 38

(a) £12,000; (b) £20,180.

No. 39

NPV A £1,220; B £1,207 therefore B better as lower *cost*.

No. 40

Equivalent annual cost A £1,302; B £1,262.

Examples from Chapter 13

No. 41

	Profit £	*Stock* £
(a)	600	1,080
(b)	330	810
(c)	510	1,080 Adjustment £90

Appendix 1
Tables of discounted values of £1

The DCF calculations in the text have normally been made with the use of four-figure tables, and tables of at least four figures are advisable for practical problems by virtue of the large sums involved. The two-figure present-value indices (Table A) minimize arithmetical calculations and enable a greater range of rates to be included. They are suitable for practice exercises and examination problems. Present value for annuity purposes can be obtained by adding the figures at the appropriate rate of interest for the years concerned.

Table B is included as indicative of the more normal format to four decimal places and for interest rates up to 16 per cent.

Table C is present value of £1 received per period for a given number of periods (n) when the interest rate is for the same period of time. If the time is in years and the interest rates per annum then the table becomes equivalent to annuity tables.

More detailed tables together with useful reference notes will be found in *Tables for Discounted Cash Flow, Annuity, Sinking Fund and Annual Capital Charge Calculations*, by G. H. Lawson and D. W. Windle, published by Oliver and Boyd.

Table A: Present value of £1

The table shows the value today of £1 to be received or paid after a given number of years

At	1%	2%	3%	4%	5%	6%	7%	8%	9%	10%
After										
1 year	0.99	0.98	0.97	0.96	0.95	0.94	0.93	0.93	0.91	0.91
2 years	0.98	0.96	0.94	0.92	0.90	0.89	0.87	0.86	0.83	0.83
3 years	0.97	0.94	0.92	0.89	0.85	0.84	0.80	0.79	0.76	0.75
4 years	0.96	0.92	0.89	0.85	0.81	0.79	0.75	0.74	0.70	0.68
5 years	0.95	0.91	0.86	0.82	0.77	0.75	0.70	0.68	0.64	0.62
6 years	0.94	0.89	0.84	0.79	0.73	0.70	0.65	0.63	0.58	0.56
7 years	0.93	0.87	0.81	0.76	0.69	0.67	0.60	0.58	0.53	0.51
8 years	0.92	0.85	0.79	0.73	0.65	0.63	0.56	0.54	0.48	0.47
9 years	0.91	0.84	0.77	0.70	0.62	0.59	0.52	0.50	0.44	0.42
10 years	0.91	0.82	0.74	0.68	0.59	0.56	0.49	0.46	0.40	0.39

	At 11%	12%	13%	14%	15%	16%	17%	18%	19%	20%
After										
1 year	0.90	0.89	0.88	0.88	0.87	0.86	0.85	0.85	0.84	0.83
2 years	0.80	0.80	0.78	0.77	0.76	0.74	0.73	0.72	0.71	0.69
3 years	0.72	0.71	0.69	0.67	0.66	0.64	0.62	0.61	0.59	0.58
4 years	0.65	0.64	0.61	0.59	0.57	0.55	0.53	0.52	0.50	0.48
5 years	0.58	0.57	0.54	0.52	0.50	0.48	0.46	0.44	0.42	0.40
6 years	0.52	0.51	0.48	0.46	0.43	0.41	0.39	0.37	0.35	0.33
7 years	0.47	0.45	0.43	0.40	0.38	0.35	0.33	0.31	0.30	0.28
8 years	0.42	0.40	0.38	0.35	0.33	0.31	0.28	0.27	0.25	0.23
9 years	0.38	0.36	0.33	0.31	0.28	0.26	0.24	0.23	0.21	0.19
10 years	0.34	0.32	0.29	0.27	0.25	0.23	0.21	0.19	0.18	0.16

Table B: Present value of £1

$(1 + r)^{-n}$

n	1%	2%	3%	4%	5%	6%	7%	8%
1	0.9901	0.9804	0.9709	0.9615	0.9524	0.9434	0.9346	0.9259
2	0.9803	0.9612	0.9426	0.9246	0.9070	0.8900	0.8734	0.8573
3	0.9706	0.9423	0.9151	0.8890	0.8638	0.8396	0.8163	0.7938
4	0.9610	0.9238	0.8885	0.8548	0.8227	0.7921	0.7629	0.7350
5	0.9515	0.9057	0.8626	0.8219	0.7835	0.7473	0.7130	0.6806
6	0.9420	0.8880	0.8375	0.7903	0.7462	0.7050	0.6663	0.6302
7	0.9327	0.8706	0.8131	0.7599	0.7107	0.6651	0.6227	0.5835
8	0.9235	0.8535	0.7894	0.7307	0.6768	0.6274	0.5820	0.5403
9	0.9143	0.8368	0.7664	0.7026	0.6446	0.5919	0.5439	0.5002
10	0.9053	0.8203	0.7441	0.6756	0.6139	0.5584	0.5083	0.4632
11	0.8963	0.8043	0.7224	0.6496	0.5847	0.5268	0.4751	0.4289
12	0.8874	0.7885	0.7014	0.6246	0.5568	0.4970	0.4440	0.3971
13	0.8787	0.7730	0.6810	0.6006	0.5303	0.4688	0.4150	0.3677
14	0.8700	0.7579	0.6611	0.5775	0.5051	0.4423	0.3878	0.3405
15	0.8613	0.7430	0.6419	0.5553	0.4810	0.4173	0.3624	0.3152
16	0.8528	0.7284	0.6232	0.5339	0.4581	0.3936	0.3387	0.2919
17	0.8444	0.7142	0.6050	0.5134	0.4363	0.3714	0.3166	0.2703
18	0.8360	0.7002	0.5874	0.4936	0.4155	0.3503	0.2959	0.2502
19	0.8277	0.6864	0.5703	0.4746	0.3957	0.3305	0.2765	0.2317
20	0.8195	0.6730	0.5537	0.4564	0.3769	0.3118	0.2584	0.2145
21	0.8114	0.6598	0.5375	0.4388	0.3589	0.2942	0.2415	0.1987
22	0.8034	0.6468	0.5219	0.4220	0.3418	0.2775	0.2257	0.1839
23	0.7954	0.6342	0.5067	0.4057	0.3256	0.2618	0.2109	0.1703
24	0.7876	0.6217	0.4919	0.3901	0.3101	0.2470	0.1971	0.1577
25	0.7798	0.6095	0.4776	0.3751	0.2953	0.2330	0.1842	0.1460
26	0.7720	0.5976	0.4637	0.3607	0.2812	0.2198	0.1722	0.1352
27	0.7644	0.5859	0.4502	0.3468	0.2678	0.2074	0.1609	0.1252
28	0.7568	0.5744	0.4371	0.3335	0.2551	0.1956	0.1504	0.1159
29	0.7493	0.5631	0.4243	0.3207	0.2429	0.1846	0.1406	0.1073
30	0.7419	0.5521	0.4120	0.3083	0.2314	0.1741	0.1314	0.0994
35	0.7059	0.5000	0.3554	0.2534	0.1813	0.1301	0.0937	0.0676
40	0.6717	0.4529	0.3066	0.2083	0.1420	0.0972	0.0668	0.0460
45	0.6391	0.4102	0.2644	0.1712	0.1113	0.0727	0.0476	0.0313
50	0.6080	0.3715	0.2281	0.1407	0.0872	0.0543	0.0339	0.0213

9%	10%	11%	12%	13%	14%	15%	16%	n
0.9174	0.9091	0.9009	0.8929	0.8850	0.8772	0.8696	0.8621	1
0.8417	0.8264	0.8116	0.7972	0.7831	0.7695	0.7561	0.7432	2
0.7722	0.7513	0.7312	0.7118	0.6931	0.6750	0.6575	0.6407	3
0.7084	0.6830	0.6587	0.6355	0.6133	0.5921	0.5718	0.5523	4
0.6499	0.6209	0.5935	0.5674	0.5428	0.5194	0.4972	0.4761	5
0.5963	0.5645	0.5346	0.5066	0.4803	0.4556	0.4323	0.4104	6
0.5470	0.5132	0.4817	0.4523	0.4251	0.3996	0.3759	0.3538	7
0.5019	0.4665	0.4339	0.4039	0.3762	0.3506	0.3269	0.3050	8
0.4604	0.4241	0.3909	0.3606	0.3329	0.3075	0.2843	0.2630	9
0.4224	0.3855	0.3522	0.3220	0.2946	0.2697	0.2472	0.2267	10
0.3875	0.3505	0.3173	0.2875	0.2607	0.2366	0.2149	0.1954	11
0.3555	0.3186	0.2858	0.2567	0.2307	0.2076	0.1869	0.1685	12
0.3262	0.2897	0.2575	0.2292	0.2042	0.1821	0.1625	0.1452	13
0.2992	0.2633	0.2320	0.2046	0.1807	0.1597	0.1413	0.1252	14
0.2745	0.2394	0.2090	0.1827	0.1599	0.1401	0.1229	0.1079	15
0.2519	0.2176	0.1883	0.1631	0.1415	0.1229	0.1069	0.0930	16
0.2311	0.1978	0.1696	0.1456	0.1252	0.1078	0.0929	0.0802	17
0.2120	0.1799	0.1528	0.1300	0.1108	0.0946	0.0808	0.0691	18
0.1945	0.1635	0.1377	0.1161	0.0981	0.0829	0.0703	0.0596	19
0.1784	0.1486	0.1240	0.1037	0.0868	0.0728	0.0611	0.0514	20
0.1637	0.1351	0.1117	0.0926	0.0768	0.0638	0.0531	0.0443	21
0.1502	0.1228	0.1007	0.0826	0.0680	0.0560	0.0462	0.0382	22
0.1378	0.1117	0.0907	0.0738	0.0601	0.0491	0.0402	0.0329	23
0.1264	0.1015	0.0817	0.0659	0.0532	0.0431	0.0349	0.0284	24
0.1160	0.0923	0.0736	0.0588	0.0471	0.0378	0.0304	0.0245	25
0.1064	0.0839	0.0663	0.0525	0.0417	0.0331	0.0264	0.0211	26
0.0976	0.0763	0.0597	0.0469	0.0369	0.0291	0.0230	0.0182	27
0.0895	0.0693	0.0538	0.0419	0.0326	0.0255	0.0200	0.0157	28
0.0822	0.0630	0.0485	0.0374	0.0289	0.0224	0.0174	0.0135	29
0.0754	0.0573	0.0437	0.0334	0.0256	0.0196	0.0151	0.0116	30
0.0490	0.0356	0.0259	0.0189	0.0139	0.0102	0.0075	0.0055	35
0.0318	0.0221	0.0154	0.0107	0.0075	0.0053	0.0037	0.0026	40
0.0207	0.0137	0.0091	0.0061	0.0041	0.0027	0.0019	0.0013	45
0.0134	0.0085	0.0054	0.0035	0.0022	0.0014	0.0009	0.0006	50

Table C: Present value of £1 received per period

$$\frac{1 - (1 + r)^{-n}}{r}$$

n	1%	2%	3%	4%	5%	6%	7%	8%
1	0.9901	0.9804	0.9709	0.9615	0.9524	0.9434	0.9346	0.9259
2	1.9704	1.9416	1.9135	1.8861	1.8594	1.8334	1.8080	1.7833
3	2.9410	2.8839	2.8286	2.7751	2.7232	2.6730	2.6243	2.5771
4	3.9020	3.8077	3.7171	3.6299	3.5460	3.4651	3.3872	3.3121
5	4.8534	4.7135	4.5797	4.4518	4.3295	4.2124	4.1002	3.9927
6	5.7955	5.6014	5.4172	5.2421	5.0757	4.9173	4.7665	4.6229
7	6.7282	6.4720	6.2303	6.0021	5.7864	5.5824	5.3893	5.2064
8	7.6517	7.3255	7.0197	6.7327	6.4632	6.2098	5.9713	5.7466
9	8.5660	8.1622	7.7861	7.4353	7.1078	6.8017	6.5152	6.2469
10	9.4713	8.9826	8.5302	8.1109	7.7217	7.3601	7.0236	6.7101
11	10.3676	9.7868	9.2526	8.7605	8.3064	7.8869	7.4987	7.1390
12	11.2551	10.5753	9.9540	9.3851	8.8633	8.3838	7.9472	7.5361
13	12.1337	11.3484	10.6350	9.9856	9.3936	8.8527	8.3577	7.9038
14	13.0037	12.1062	11.2961	10.5631	9.8986	9.2950	8.7455	8.2442
15	13.8651	12.8493	11.9379	11.1184	10.3797	9.7122	9.1079	8.5595
16	14.7179	13.5777	12.5611	11.6523	10.8378	10.1059	9.4466	8.8514
17	15.5623	14.2919	13.1661	12.1657	11.2741	10.4773	9.7632	9.1216
18	16.3983	14.9920	13.7535	12.6593	11.6896	10.8276	10.0591	9.3719
19	17.2260	15.6785	14.3238	13.1339	12.0853	11.1581	10.3356	9.6036
20	18.0456	16.3514	14.8775	13.5903	12.4622	11.4699	10.5940	9.8181
21	18.8570	17.0112	15.4150	14.0292	12.8212	11.7641	10.8355	10.0168
22	19.6604	17.6580	15.9369	14.4511	13.1630	12.0416	11.0612	10.2007
23	20.4558	18.2922	16.4436	14.8568	13.4886	12.3034	11.2722	10.3711
24	21.2434	18.9139	16.9355	15.2470	13.7986	12.5504	11.4693	10.5288
25	22.0232	19.5235	17.4131	15.6221	14.0939	12.7834	11.6536	10.6748
26	22.7952	20.1210	17.8768	15.9828	14.3752	13.0032	11.8258	10.8100
27	23.5596	20.7069	18.3270	16.3296	14.6430	13.2105	11.9867	10.9352
28	24.3164	21.2813	18.7641	16.6631	14.8981	13.4062	12.1371	11.0511
29	25.0658	21.8444	19.1885	16.9837	15.1411	13.5907	12.2777	11.1584
30	25.8077	22.3965	19.6004	17.2920	15.3725	13.7648	12.4090	11.2578
35	29.4086	24.9986	21.4872	18.6646	16.3742	14.4982	12.9477	11.6546
40	32.8347	27.3555	23.1148	19.7928	17.1591	15.0463	13.3317	11.9246
45	36.0945	29.4902	24.5187	20.7200	17.7741	15.4558	13.6055	12.1084
50	39.1961	31.4236	25.7298	21.4822	18.2559	15.7619	13.8007	12.2335

9%	10%	11%	12%	13%	14%	15%	16%	*n*
0.9174	0.9091	0.9009	0.8929	0.8850	0.8772	0.8696	0.8621	1
1.7591	1.7355	1.7125	1.6901	1.6681	1.6467	1.6257	1.6052	2
2.5313	2.4869	2.4437	2.4018	2.3612	2.3216	2.2832	2.2459	3
3.2397	3.1699	3.1024	3.0373	2.9745	2.9137	2.8550	2.7982	4
3.8897	3.7908	3.6959	3.6048	3.5172	3.4331	3.3522	3.2743	5
4.4859	4.3553	4.2305	4.1114	3.9975	3.8887	3.7845	3.6847	6
5.0330	4.8684	4.7122	4.5638	4.4226	4.2883	4.1604	4.0386	7
5.5348	5.3349	5.1461	4.9676	4.7988	4.6389	4.4873	4.3436	8
5.9952	5.7590	5.5370	5.3282	5.1317	4.9464	4.7716	4.6065	9
6.4177	6.1446	5.8892	5.6502	5.4262	5.2161	5.0188	4.8332	10
6.8051	6.4951	6.2065	5.9377	5.6869	5.4527	5.2337	5.0286	11
7.1607	6.8137	6.4924	6.1944	5.9176	5.6603	5.4206	5.1971	12
7.4869	7.1034	6.7499	6.4235	6.1218	5.8424	5.5831	5.3423	13
7.7862	7.3667	6.9819	6.6282	6.3025	6.0021	5.7245	5.4675	14
8.0607	7.6061	7.1909	6.8109	6.4624	6.1422	5.8474	5.5755	15
8.3126	7.8237	7.3792	6.9740	6.6039	6.2651	5.9542	5.6685	16
8.5436	8.0216	7.5488	7.1196	6.7291	6.3729	6.0472	5.7487	17
8.7556	8.2014	7.7016	7.2497	6.8399	6.4674	6.1280	5.8178	18
8.9501	8.3649	7.8393	7.3658	6.9380	6.5504	6.1982	5.8775	19
9.1285	8.5136	7.9633	7.4694	7.0248	6.6231	6.2593	5.9288	20
9.2922	8.6487	8.0751	7.5620	7.1015	6.6870	6.3125	5.9731	21
9.4424	8.7715	8.1757	7.6446	7.1695	6.7429	6.3587	6.0113	22
9.5802	8.8832	8.2664	7.7184	7.2297	6.7921	6.3988	6.0442	23
9.7066	8.9847	8.3481	7.7843	7.2829	6.8351	6.4338	6.0726	24
9.8226	9.0770	8.4217	7.8431	7.3300	6.8729	6.4641	6.0971	25
9.9290	9.1609	8.4881	7.8957	7.3717	6.9061	6.4906	6.1182	26
10.0266	9.2372	8.5478	7.9426	7.4086	6.9352	6.5135	6.1364	27
10.1161	9.3066	8.6016	7.9844	7.4412	6.9607	6.5335	6.1520	28
10.1983	9.3696	8.6501	8.0218	7.4701	6.9830	6.5509	6.1656	29
10.2737	9.4269	8.6938	8.0552	7.4957	7.0027	6.5660	6.1772	30
10.5668	9.6442	8.8552	8.1755	7.5856	7.0700	6.6166	6.2153	35
10.7574	9.7791	8.9511	8.2438	7.6344	7.1050	6.6418	6.2335	40
10.8812	9.8628	9.0079	8.2825	7.6609	7.1232	6.6543	6.2421	45
10.9617	9.9148	9.0417	8.3045	7.6752	7.1327	6.6605	6.2463	50

Appendix 2
Accounting and allied organizations

Association of Accounting Technicians (AAT)
154 Clerkenwell Road, London EC1R 5AD

Chartered Association of Certified Accountants (CACA)
29 Lincoln's Inn Fields, London WC2A 3EE

Chartered Institute of Management Accountants (CIMA)
63 Portland Place, London W1N 4AB

Chartered Institute of Public Finance and Accountancy (CIPFA)
3 Robert Street, London WC2N 6BH

Chartered Institute of Bankers (CIOB)
10 Lombard Street, London EC3V 9AS

Institute of Chartered Accountants in England and Wales (ICAEW)
Moorgate Place, London EC2P 2BJ

Institute of Chartered Accountants of Scotland (ICAS)
27 Queen Street, Edinburgh EH2 1LA

London Chamber of Commerce and Industry (LCCI)
69 Cannon Street, London EC4

Society of Company and Commercial Accountants
40 Tyndalls Park Road, Bristol BS8 1P

Index